CHARMING SMALL HOTEL GUIDES

ITALY

CHARMING SMALL HOTEL GUIDES

ITALY

EDITED BY

Fiona Duncan & Leonie Glass

DUNCAN PETERSEN

This new expanded and redesigned 2003 edition
conceived, designed and produced by
Duncan Petersen Publishing Ltd,
31 Ceylon Road, London W14 0PY

16th edition

Editorial Director Andrew Duncan
Editors Fiona Duncan & Leonie Glass
Contributing Editor Nicola Swallow
Production Editor Nicola Davies
Art Editor Don Macpherson
Maps Map Creation Ltd

This edition published 2003 by
Duncan Petersen Publishing Ltd,
31 Ceylon Road, London W14 0PY

Sales representation and distribution in the U.K. and Ireland by
Portfolio Books Limited
Unit 5, Perivale Industrial Park
Horsenden Lane South
Greenford, UB6 7RL
Tel: 0208 997 9000 Fax: 0208 997 9097
E-mail: sales@portfoliobooks.com

A CIP catalogue record for this book is available
from the British Library

ISBN 1-903301-25-4

DTP by Duncan Petersen Publishing Ltd
Printed by G. Canale & C., Italy

CONTENTS

INTRODUCTION

IN THIS INTRODUCTORY SECTION

Welcome to this new edition of *Charming Small Hotel Guides Italy.* We are pleased to report that the changes recently made to the guide – see below – have been well received by readers. They have found it even more accessible, and more colourful than earlier editions.

• *Every hotel now has a colour photograph and a full page of its own. No more half-page entries without a photograph.*

• *The maps have been upgraded.*

• *The layout has been changed in order to take you more quickly to essential booking information.*

We hope that you will think these real improvements, rather than change for its own sake. In all other respects, the guide remains true to the values and qualities that make it unique (see opposite), and which have won it so many devoted readers. This is its fourteenth consecutive update since it was first published in 1986. It has sold hundreds of thousands of copies in the U.K., U.S.A. and in five European languages.

WHY ARE WE UNIQUE?

This is the only independently-inspected (no hotel pays for an entry) accommodation guide that:

- has colour photographs for every entry;

- concentrates on places that have real charm and character;

- is highly selective;

- is particularly fussy about size. Most hotels have fewer than 20 bedrooms; if there are more, the hotel must have the feel of a much smaller place. We have found that a genuinely warm welcome is much more likely to be found in a small hotel;

- gives proper emphasis to the description, and doesn't use irritating symbols;

- is produced by a small, non-bureaucratic company with a dedicated team of like-minded inspectors.

See also *'So what exactly do we look for?',* page 8.

So what exactly do we look for? – Our selection criteria

• A peaceful, attractive setting. Obviously, if the entry is in an urban area, we make allowances.

• A building that is handsome, interesting or historic; or at least with real character.

• Adequate space, but on a human scale. We don't go for places that rely too much on grandeur, or with pretensions that could be intimidating.

• Good taste and imagination in the interior decoration. We reject standardized, chain hotel fixtures, fittings and decorations.

• Bedrooms that look like real bedrooms, not hotel rooms, individually decorated.

• Furnishings and other facilities that are comfortable and well maintained. We like to see interesting antique furniture that is there to be used, not simply revered.

• Proprietors and staff who are dedicated and thoughtful, offering a personal welcome, but who aren't intrusive or overly effusive. *The guest needs to feel like an individual.*

• Interesting food. In Italy, it's increasingly the norm for food to be above average. There are few entries in this guide where the food is not of a high standard.

• A sympathetic atmosphere; an absence of loud people showing off their money; or the 'corporate feel'.

Hotel Pausania, Dosoduro

A FATTER GUIDE, BUT JUST AS SELECTIVE

In order to accommodate every entry with a whole-page description and colour photograph, we've had to print more pages. *But we have maintained our integrity by keeping the selection to around 300 entries.*

Over the years, the number of charming small hotels in Italy has increased steadily – not dramatically. We don't believe that there are presently many more than about 350 truly charming small hotels in Italy, and that, if we included more, we would undermine what we're trying to do: produce a guide which is all about places that are more than just a bed for the night. Every time we consider a new hotel, we ask ourselves whether it has that extra special something, regardless of category and facilities, that makes it worth seeking out.

TYPES OF ACCOMMODATION IN THIS GUIDE

Despite its title, the guide does not confine itself to places called hotels or places that behave like hotels. On the contrary, we actively look for places that offer a home-from-home (see page 10). We include small- and medium-sized hotels; plenty of traditional Italian guesthouses (*pensioni*) – some offering just bed and breakfast, some offering food at other times of day, too; restaurants with rooms; *agriturismos*, which are usually bed-and-breakfasts on farms or working rural estates; and some self-catering apartments, in town and country houses, provided they offer something special.

NO FEAR OR FAVOUR

To us, taking a payment for appearing in a guide seems to defeat the object of producing a guide. If money has changed hands, you can't write the whole truth about a hotel, and the selection cannot be nearly so interesting. This self-evident truth seems to us to be proved at least in part by the fact that pay guides are so keen to present the illusion of independence: few admit on the cover that they take payments for an entry, only doing so in small print on the inside.

Not many people realize that on the shelves of British bookshops there are many more hotel guides that accept payments for entries than there are independent guides. This guide is one of the few that do not accept any money for an entry.

Albergo Pietrasanta, Pietrasanta, Lucca

HOME FROM HOME

Perhaps the most beguiling characteristic of the best places to stay in this guide is the feeling they give of being in a private home – but without the everyday cares and chores of running one. To get this formula right requires a special sort of professionalism: the proprietor has to strike the balance between being relaxed and giving attentive service. Those who experience this 'feel' often turn their backs on all other forms of accommodation – however luxurious.

THE ITALIAN HOTEL SCENE

Our latest survey of Italian hotels for this new, expanded edition of the guide has left us in little doubt about just how much we like them, and how much we enjoy to stay in them. Quite apart from the fact that many of them are in wonderful buildings and beautiful locations, their standards of welcome, ambience, cleanliness, attention to detail and food are – on the whole – above average. Perhaps the main quality that sets them apart from other European hotels is the genuinely relaxed, informal yet sophisticated, atmosphere that you find in even the smartest places. It's easy to feel at ease; there's much less talking in hushed tones in sepulchral public rooms than elsewhere, and staff are, by and large, warm and friendly. They won't snigger (as the French might) at a guest's attempt to speak their language, however botched, although many Italian hoteliers and their staff have several languages. Standards, once set, tend to be maintained: there's much less fluctation than in, say, English hotels, since the majority remain in the family for generations, even these days. Yet despite this reassuringly old-fashioned characteristic, Italian hoteliers have been quick to take up new technology and many, even very simple ones, have e-mail and their own websites.

The food is another bonus of Italian hotels. While you won't find many dining rooms presenting culinary fireworks, you will find it hard not to eat at least adequately and at best extremely well in all the hotels included in this guide. You will come across little international food on the menu: the emphasis is on regional, seasonal dishes using fresh local ingredients.

Impressed though we remain with the warmth of welcome of most hotels in this guide (especially in the south), we can't pretend that there isn't a marked fall in temperature, as in most other European countries, in the cities. Florence isn't too bad, Venice is not great, but Rome is the worst; indeed two strong canditates for inclusion in this edition had to be discounted purely because the receptionists were so rude. But these are quibbles; by and large, we are delighted with this selection of Italian hotels. When we have finished an inspection trip, all we want to do is return.

CHECK THE PRICE FIRST

In this guide we have adopted the system of price bands, rather than giving actual prices as we did in previous editions. This is because prices were often subject to change after we went to press. The price bands refer to the approximate price of a standard double room (high season rates) with breakfast for two people. They are as follows:

€	under 100 Euros
€€	100-200 Euros
€€€	200-300 Euros
€€€€	more than 300 Euros

To avoid unpleasant surprises, always check what is included in the price (for example, VAT and service, breakfast, afternoon tea) when making the booking.

HOW TO FIND AN ENTRY

In this guide, the entries are arranged in geographical groups. First, the whole of Italy is divided into three major sections; the book starts with Northern Italy, then proceeds to Central Italy and lastly Southern Italy. Within these sections, the entries are grouped by regions. Some of these regions correspond to the administrative regions of the country (Tuscany and Emilia Romana, for example). Some are combinations of these regions (Lazio and Abruzzo, for example). Some are broader – the North-West or the North-East, for example.

Within each regional section the entries follow a set sequence: first comes an

Area Introduction – an overview of the accommodation scene in that region, together with a few extra addresses of places which didn't quite deserve a full entry, but which might be useful if our main choices are booked up. Next come the full entries themselves, arranged alphabetically by city, town or nearest village. If several occur in or near one town, entries are arranged in alpha order by name of hotel.

To find a hotel in a particular area, use the maps following this introduction to locate the appropriate pages.

To locate a specific hotel, whose name you know, or a hotel in a place you know, use the indexes at the back, which list entries both by name and by nearest place name.

**HOW TO READ
AN ENTRY**

Name of hotel

Type of
establishment

Description – never
vetted by the hotel

Places of interest within
reach of the hotel

This sets the hotel
in its geographical
context and
should not be
taken as precise
instructions as to
how to get there;
always ask the
hotel for
directions.

Rooms described as
having a bath usually
also have a shower;
rooms described as
having a shower only
have a shower.

NORTHERN ITALY

THE NORTH-EAST

VENICE

SALUTE DA CICI

TOWN BED-AND-BREAKFAST

Fondamenta di Ca' Balla , Dorsoduro 222, 30123 Venezia
TEL 041 5235404 **FAX** 041 5222271

A LONG-TIME FAVOURITE OF OURS, this calm, civilized hotel inhabits a *palaz-zo* on a small canal in an interesting area between the Accademia and Salute. If you've had your fill of baroque churches, it's also perfectly placed for a visit to the Guggenheim Collection and a blast of abstract expressionism.

The façade is charming and typically Venetian: peeling stucco and rose-coloured brick, Gothic windows and stone balconies decked with flowers. And the interior doesn't disappoint. It has a classically elegant lobby of columns and marble floors beneath exposed rafters. A little bar is reserved for guests, and a tiny, sheltered garden offers a few sunny tables for a drink. Interconnecting basement rooms provide breakfast areas. Corridors lead off a beautifully furnished first-floor landing to simple white-painted bedrooms with high ceilings, Venetian marble floors and furniture that ranges from antique to utility. There's no difference in price, so request a room on the canal or, if you're willing to sacrifice char-acter for comfort, go for one of the nine modern rooms in the annexe.

NEARBY Guggenheim Collection; Santa Maria della Salute.
LOCATION just S of Rio Calle Terra Nuovo, 5 mins' walk E of Salute; vaporetto Salute or water taxi
FOOD breakfast
PRICE ©–©©
ROOMS 50 double and twin, single, triple and family, all with bath or shower; all rooms have phones
FACILITIES bar, sitting area, breakfast room, garden
CREDIT CARDS not accepted
DISABLED not suitable
PETS not accepted
CLOSED mid-Nov to Christmas, Jan to Mar (or Carnival if earlier)
PROPRIETOR Sebastiano Cagnin

Essential booking information.

This information is only
an indication for
wheelchair users and the
infirm. Always check on
suitability with the hotel.

City, town or village, and region, in which the hotel is located.

Some or all the public rooms and bedrooms in an increasing number of hotels are now non-smoking. Smokers should check the hotel's policy when booking.

Telephoning Italy from abroad
To call Italy from the U.K., dial 00, then the international dialling code 39, then dial the number, including the initial 0. From the U.S., dial 001 39.

Postal address and other key information.

Children are almost always accepted, usually welcomed, in Italian hotels. There are often special facilities, such as cots, high chairs, baby listening and early supper. Check first if they may join parents in the dining room.

Breakfast, is normally included in the price of the room. We have not quoted prices for lunch and dinner. Other meals, such as afternoon tea, may also be available. 'Room service' refers to food and drink, either snacks or full meals, which can be served in the room.

We list the following credit cards:
AE American Express
DC Diners Club
MC Mastercard
V   Visa

Always let the hotel know in advance if you want to bring a pet. Even where pets are accepted, certain restrictions may apply, and a small charge may be levied.

In this guide we have used price bands rather than quoting actual prices. They refer to a standard double room (high season rates, if applicable) with breakfast for two people. Other rates – for other room categories, times of the year, weekend breaks, long stays and so on – may well be available. In some hotels, usually out-of-the-way places or restaurants-with-rooms – half-board is obligatory. Always check when booking. The price bands are as follows:

€   under 100 Euros
€€   100-200 Euros
€€€   200-300 Euros
€€€€   more than 300 Eu

Tipping
Italian waiters do not rely on tips in the same way as in some other European countries (if lucky, they will get a share of the profits). However, Italians usually round up the bill if pleased with service.

REPORTING TO THE GUIDE

Please write and tell us about your experiences of small hotels, guest houses and inns, whether good or bad, whether listed in this edition or not. As well as hotels in Italy, we are interested in hotels in France, Spain, Austria, Germany, Switzerland, Greece and the U.S.A. We assume that reporters have no objections to our publishing their views unpaid.

Readers whose reports prove particularly helpful may be invited to join our Travellers' Panel. Members give us notice of their own travel plans; we suggest hotels that they might inspect, and help with the cost of accommodation.

The address to write to us is:

Editor, *Charming Small Hotel Guides*,
Duncan Petersen Publishing Limited,
31 Ceylon Road,
London W14 0PY.

Checklist
Please use a separate sheet of paper for each report; include your name, address and telephone number on each report.

Your reports will be received with particular pleasure if they are typed, and if they are organized under the following headings:

Name of establishment
Town or village it is in, or nearest
Full address, including postcode
Telephone number
Time and duration of visit
The building and setting
The public rooms
The bedrooms and bathrooms
Physical comfort (chairs, beds, heat, light, hot water)
Standards of maintenance and housekeeping
Atmosphere, welcome and service
Food
Value for money

We assume that in writing you have no objections to your views being published unpaid, either verbatim or in an edited version. Names of major outside contributors are acknowledged, at the editor's discretion, in the guide.

HOTEL LOCATION MAPS

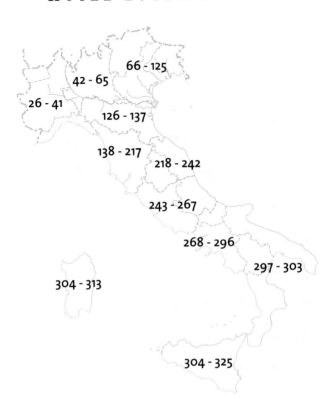

66 - 125

42 - 65

26 - 41

126 - 137

138 - 217

218 - 242

243 - 267

268 - 296

297 - 303

304 - 313

304 - 325

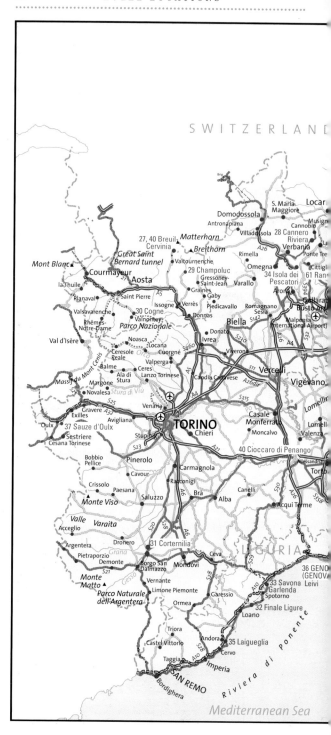

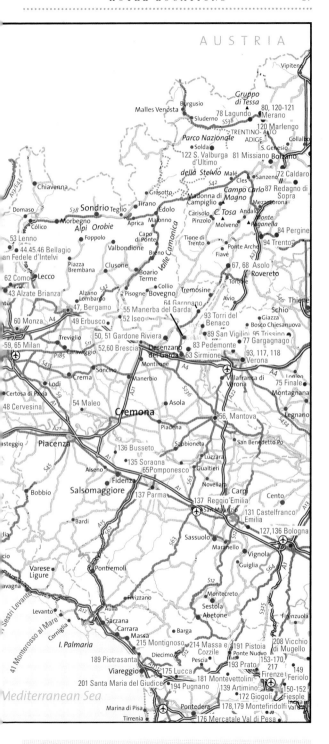

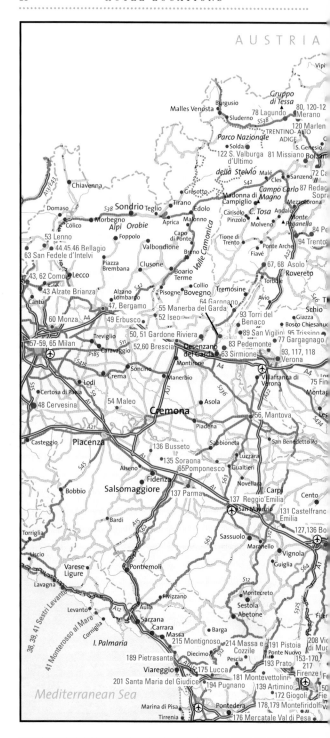

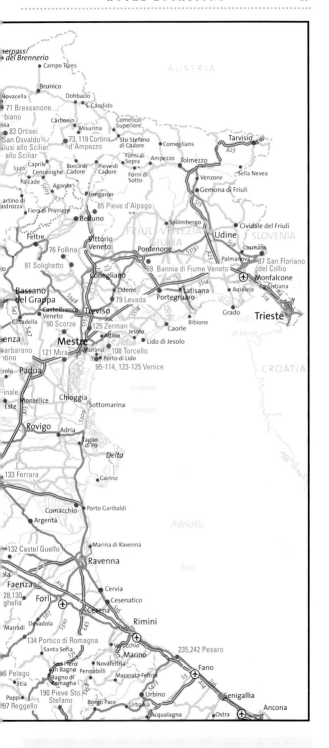

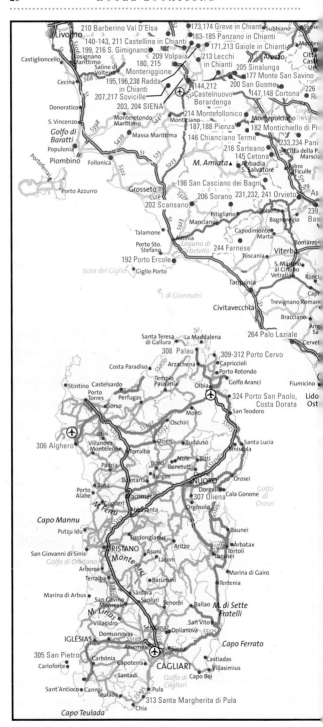

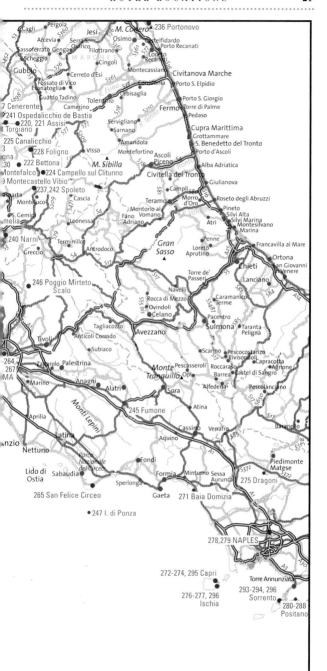

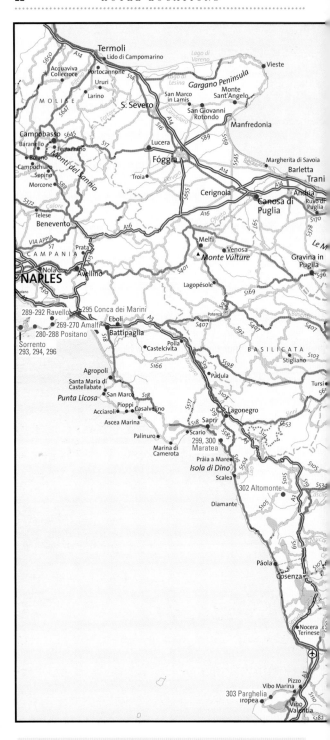

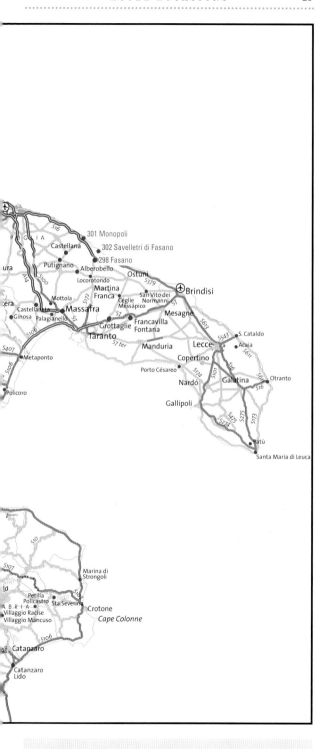

I. Strómboli

I. Panarea

Filicudi   I. Salina

Aeolian Islands

Páola
Cosenza

Villaggio Racise

Villaggio Mancuso

Nocera Terinese

Maida

Palmi

Milazzo   Scilla
Messina   Villa S. Giovanni   Gerace   Locri
                                            Gambarie
                 REGGIO DI
                 CALABRIA

Roccella Iónica

Golfo di Patti

Naso   S. Biagio
Oliveri   Barcellona
                 Giampilieri

ina di
onia
Acquedolci
S. Fratello

Floresta   Francavilla
                 di Sicilia   Roccalumera
                                     Sta. Teresa di Riva
Castiglione di Sicilia
                 Randazzo   320-323 Taormina
                 Piedimonte   317 Giardini-Naxos
                 Etneo   Fiumefreddo di Sicilia
Bronte
Monte   Giarre
Etna
Troina   Adrano
osia
                 Nicolosi   Acireale
Agira   Biancavilla   Aci Catena
Catenanuova
          Paternò   Aci Castello
          Misterbianco   CATANIA

Golfo
di
Catania

one
zza
nerina
          Palagonia   Lentini
                              Carlentini   Augusta
Grammichele
          Vizzini   Golfo
          Buccheri   di
          Buscemi   Augusta
          Palazzolo   319, 325 SIRACUSA
          Acréide   Canicattini
oria   Lido Aranella
glitti   317 Ragusa   Ognina
                 Noto   Fontane Bianche
Camarina   Módica   Calabernardo
                 Rosolini   Lido di Noto   Golfo
ta Secca   Marzamemi   di
Marina di   Scicli   Noto
Ragusa   Donnalucata   Ispica   Pachino
          Sampieri   Pozzallo

THE NORTH-WEST

HOTELS IN THE NORTH-WEST

NORTH-WEST ITALY OFFERS three contrasting regions: the land 'at the foot of the mountains', Piedmont; the mountainous Valle d'Aosta; and the coastal Liguria.

Piedmont does, no doubt, have its attractions, but they do not impress themselves on many foreign visitors, who tend to hurry across this large region on their way to the recognized glories of Italy to the east and south.

To the traveller, as to the resident, the region is dominated by the city lying at its heart – Turin. We have not found hotels in the middle of the city which deserve to be picked out in these pages but this does not mean that the city lacks comfortable hotels: there is certainly no shortage of swish, large impersonal places right in the heart of things. Of these, the most attractive (and not quite the most expensive) is the Jolly Hotel Ligure (tel 011 55641). Of the more modest places, the Genio (tel 011 6505771) and the stylish Victoria (tel 011 5611909) are smartly modern, of moderate size and central, the former particularly handy for the station. Only a little further away from the middle is the cheaper Piedmontese (tel 011 6698101) – ideal for travellers on a tight budget who do not wish to be confined to the suburbs. Within easy reach of Turin, we can recommend the Salzea (tel 011 6497809) at Trofarello, the Panoramica (tel 0125 8549) at Loranze, and the Locanda del Sant' Uffizio at Cioccaro di Penango, which is featured in the following pages.

To the north of Turin is the mainly French-speaking Valle d'Aosta, a steep-sided valley surrounded by some of the highest peaks in the Alps, and best known for its mountain scenery and winter sports facilities. It borders France to the west, where Monte Bianco (Mont Blanc) is the highest peak in Europe, and Switzerland to the north, where the Cervino (the Matterhorn) and Monte Rosa also tower well above 4,000 m. In this area we have chalet-style hotels to recommend in Champoluc and Breuil-Cervinia. To the south is Italy's highest mountain, Gran Paradiso, surrounded by a stunning national park named after it. In the middle of the park, in Cogne, we have another recommendation.

The third region is Liguria, a thin strip of mountainous coastline dominated by the Italian Riviera, for which we offer several recommendations. On the Riviera di Levante, south-east of Genoa, we include three hotels in Sestri Levante, the Porto Roca in the Cinque Terre village of Monterosso al Mare and Ca' Peo at Leivi in the hills. More hotels are featured on the Riviera di Ponente, west of Genoa, specifically at Finale Ligure and Laiguéglia, with another just inland at Garlenda. If you want to visit Genoa, you would do best to do so from a base on the coast.

THE NORTH-WEST

BREUIL-CERVINIA

HERMITAGE

⟿ MOUNTAIN CHALET ⟿

11021 Breuil-Cervinia, Aosta
TEL 0166 948998 **FAX** 0166 949032 **E-MAIL** info@hotelhermitage.com
WEBSITE www.hotelhermitage.com

WAKE UP TO A SPECTACULAR view of Monte Cervino (better known as the Matterhorn) through your bedroom window, then relax after a hard day's skiing with a massage, a mud bath or a book in front of a crackling log fire. This glossy Relais et Château hotel comes with all the trimmings: a health and beauty centre, small indoor pool, a sitting room furnished with vast deep sofas and chairs, and an elegant dining room, candlelit by night. It even boasts liveried porters and a heated garage. A low modern chalet built in traditional style, it has been done up with country-house furnishings and an appropriately Alpine flavour. Wood floors and walls, antique furniture and oak beams abound. There are as many suites as bedrooms, and all succeed in being cosy as well as luxurious, with pretty wallpaper, well-placed lamps, knick-knacks, mirrors and prints and some particularly handsome pieces of furniture. Our favourite rooms are the ones in the attic, which have sloping beamed ceilings and the most character.

The dining room, whose picture windows frame a blue larch forest, prides itself on a menu of simple local dishes accompanied by excellent regional wines. The hotel only accepts children over eight.

⟿

NEARBY golf (500 m); Aosta (50 km).
LOCATION just NE of Breuil-Cervinia; garage
FOOD breakfast, lunch, dinner
PRICE ⓔⓔⓔⓔ
ROOMS 36; 18 double and twin, 18 suites, all with bath; all rooms have phone, TV, air conditioning, minibar, hairdrier, safe
FACILITIES sitting room, dining room, meeting room, health and beauty centre, swimming-pool, lift, terrace **CREDIT CARDS** AE, DC, MC, V
DISABLED access difficult
PETS not accepted **CLOSED** May-July, Sept-Dec
PROPRIETORS Neyroz family

THE NORTH-WEST

CANNERO RIVIERA

CANNERO

~ LAKESIDE HOTEL ~

Lungo Lago 2, 28051 Cannero Riviera, Verbania
TEL 0323 788046 **FAX** 0323 788048
E-MAIL info@cannero.com **WEBSITE** www.hotelcannero.com

CANNERO IS ONE OF THE quietest resorts on Lake Maggiore and its most desirable hotels lie right on the shore. Only the ferry landing-stage and a dead-end road separate the Cannero from the waters of Maggiore.

The building was once a monastery, though only an old stone column, a couple of vaulted passageways, a quiet courtyard and a beautifully preserved 17thC well suggest it is anything other than a modern hotel. The emphasis is on comfort and relaxation, and the atmosphere is very friendly, thanks largely to the attention of Signora Gallinotto and her family. Downstairs, big windows and terraces make the most of the setting. The restaurant focuses on the lake, with an outdoor terrace running alongside. Choose the *à la carte* menu, advises a reader. Bedrooms are light and well cared for with adequate bathrooms, and the recent restoration of a next-door house provides an additional 15 rooms plus some new apartments. There are gorgeous views of lake and mountains from front rooms, all with balconies, though many guests are happy overlooking the pool at the back – which, if anything, is quieter. By day this provides a delightful spot to take a dip or hang out under the yellow parasols.

~

NEARBY Borromean Islands; Ascona (21 km), Locarno (25 km).
LOCATION in resort, overlooking lake; car parking
FOOD breakfast, lunch, dinner; poolside snacks
PRICE €
ROOMS 55 double and twin and single, all with bath or shower; all rooms have phone; 10 self-catering apartments
FACILITIES sitting room, piano bar, dining room, library, lift, 2 lakeside terraces, garden, swimming pool, tennis
CREDIT CARDS AE, DC, MC, V
DISABLED 10 rooms accessible **PETS** accepted by arrangement
CLOSED Nov to mid-Mar
PROPRIETORS Signora Gallinotto and sons

THE NORTH-WEST

CHAMPOLUC

VILLA ANNA MARIA

～ MOUNTAIN CHALET ～

Via Croues 5, 11020 Champoluc, Monte Rosa, Aosta
TEL 0125 307128 **FAX** 0125 307984
E-MAIL hotel.annamaria@flashnet.it **WEBSITE** www.hotelvillaannamaria.com

IN A QUIET WOODED HILLSIDE setting close to the village of Champoluc, the main community in a steep-sided valley beneath the mighty Monte Rosa, this traditional shuttered chalet is as charming in summer, surrounded by mountain flowers as it is deep in winter snow. Its charm lies in the fact that hardly anything seems to have changed since the house was built in 1940 by the eponymous mother and grandmother of the present owners. In the rustic dining room, for example, polished wood covers the floor, ceiling and walls, bright copper pots gleam from shelves, and red-and-white gingham curtains frame the windows. Guests sit at tables with crisp white cloths, and are served simple but delicious country fare including *fonduta* with *fontina*, the local cheese fondue.

The cosy bedrooms also have panelled walls and, whether they look up at the mountain or down the valley, benefit from utter peace and quiet, spared from traffic noise as cars are not allowed up to the hotel. Guests must park in the private car park 50 metres or so down the hill, and then walk up to the chalet through romantic pine woods, while kind staff collect their luggage. The father and son owners extend a warm welcome.

～

NEARBY Verrès (27 km); Valtournenche and Gressoney valleys.
LOCATION off lane to right at end of village, signposted to hotel; car parking
FOOD breakfast, lunch, dinner
PRICE ⓔⓔ (half board required)
ROOMS 20 double and twin, family, 14 with bath or shower; all rooms have phone, TV
FACILITIES sitting room, dining room, terrace, garden
CREDIT CARDS MC, V
DISABLED access difficult
PETS not accepted **CLOSED** never
PROPRIETORS Miki and Jean Noël Origone

THE NORTH-WEST

BELLEVUE

~ MOUNTAIN CHALET ~

Rue Grand Paradis 22, 11012 Cogne, Aosta
TEL 0165 74825 **FAX** 0165 749192 **E-MAIL** hotelbellevuecogne@notvalloo.it
WEBSITE www.hotelbellevuecogne.it

THIS HOTEL IS APTLY NAMED, nestled in the heart of a national park on the flat grassy floor of a valley dominated by Gran Paradiso and other peaks. Its 'beautiful view' stretches across meadows filled with wildflowers to the snow-capped peaks and most of the public rooms and balconied bedrooms reap the benefit. The Bellevue has been owned and run by the same family, with tradition as the keynote, since it was built in the 1920s. The simple decoration combines pale colours with the glow of wood, local artworks and antiques, lace and fresh alpine flowers. Open fires blaze in every grate. Home-baked bread is served with the imaginative regional meals by a cheerful staff, who speak French and wear national costume. In addition to the hotel dining room and small *à la carte* restaurant, you can eat at the Jeantet-Roullets' village brasserie. Start the day with the generous buffet breakfast to set you up for ski-ing or hiking.

The neat comfortable bedrooms and suites, with cosy sitting rooms and fireplaces, have ultra-modern bathrooms, some with Jacuzzis. The three chalets – sadly minus the view – are ideal for families.

~

NEARBY Valnontey Alpine Garden; Saint Pierre (20 km).
LOCATION on edge of village, 27 km W of Aosta; car parking
FOOD breakfast, lunch, dinner
PRICE €€-€€€
ROOMS 35; 16 double and twin, 16 suites, 3 chalets, all with bath or shower; all rooms have phone, TV, minibar, hairdrier
FACILITIES sitting room, TV room, playroom, dining rooms, bars, indoor swimming-pool, health centre, lift, terrace, garden
CREDIT CARDS AE, DC, MC, V
DISABLED 2 specially adapted rooms
PETS accepted by arrangement
LOSED late Sept to late Dec
PROPRIETORS Jeantet-Roullet family

THE NORTH-WEST

CORTEMILIA

VILLA SAN CARLO

~ VILLAGE HOTEL ~

Corso Divisioni Alpine 41, 12074 Cortemilia, Cuneo
TEL 0173 81546 **FAX** 0173 81235
E-MAIL info@hotelsancarlo.it **WEBSITE** www.hotelsancarlo.it

THIS HOTEL LIES in the heart of the Langhe, noted for its superb wine, hazelnuts, wild mushrooms, cheese and – above all – truffles. Truffles are naturally on the menu, and truffle-hunting trips are arranged during the season, as well as cookery and wine courses.

The charm of this hotel lies in its family atmosphere and its accomplished Piedmontese cuisine. Don't expect a charming building – it's not much better than a motel; or a pleasant setting (it's in a commercial area); or anything but standardised bedrooms, some small, with cramped showers. Despit this, it's a useful stopover if you're interested in a good dinner. The modern villa incorporates cellars from the original farmhouse, and is decorated in traditional, low-key Piedmontese style, with a cosy dining room. Bedrooms are comfortable but modest, the best of them over-looking the well-stocked garden. The hotel has been in the same family for four generations, and the homely feeling is sustained by countless small touches– the owner's young son even keeps his favourite toys in a chest in the hotel lobby.

The restaurant at Villa San Carlo is renowned for its traditional regional recipes with a creative twist, as well as for its extremely impressive wine list which reflects the family's passion for Piedmontese wines (a visit to the cellars should not be missed). As well as the main menu, there are gourmet menus and a special perfumed white truffle menu.

~

NEARBY Alba, (25 km); Asti (55 km).
LOCATION 25 km SE of Alba, on edge of village; ample car parking
FOOD breakfast, lunch, dinner
PRICE €ⓔ **ROOMS** 23; double, single and 2 suites, all with bath; all rooms have phone, TV, minibar, hairdrier **FACILITIES** sitting area, restaurant, bar, terrace, garden, swimming pool, mountain bikes **CREDIT CARDS** AE, DC, MC, V
DISABLED access possible **PETS** accepted **CLOSED** mid-Jan to mid-Feb
PROPRIETORS Carlo and Paola Zarri

THE NORTH-WEST

FINALE LIGURE

PUNTA EST

⟪ SEASIDE VILLA ⟫

Via Aurelia 1, 17024 Finale Ligure, Savona
TEL 019 600612 **FAX** 019 600611
E-MAIL puntaest@libero.it **WEBSITE** www.puntaest.com

THE ITALIAN RIVIERA west of Genoa is for the most part disappointing: most of its resorts are dreary, and most of its hotels mediocre. Happily, both the Punta Est and Finale Ligure are exceptions. The hotel is converted from a splendid 18thC villa which stands high and proudly pink above the buzz of the main coastal road, overlooking the sea. Signor Podesta, who used to be a sculptor, has acted as resident architect since the hotel was first created in the late 1960s, and with great success. By preserving the original features of the house and adding to it in a sympathetic style, he has managed to preserve the atmosphere of a private villa. The interior is cool and elegant – all dark-wood antiques, fine stone arches, fireplaces and tiled floors. But with such an impressive setting, for most months of the year the focus is on the outdoor terraces, pool and gardens, with their pines, potted plants and lovely views.

Breakfast is taken (off Staffordshire china) in a sort of canopied greenhouse – a lovely sunny spot, surrounded by greenery. Other meals are served in a dining room in the annexe, where stone arches and beams create a vaguely medieval setting. You can choose between international and Ligurian dishes, including bass cooked with strong aromatic local herbs. The beach is only a couple of minutes' walk down the hillside. A regular visitor reports that it gets 'better and better'.

NEARBY Finale Borgo (3 km); Alássio (26 km).
LOCATION E of the historic town; car parking
FOOD breakfast, lunch, dinner
PRICE €€-€€€
ROOMS 40; 30 double, 4 single, 6 suites, all with bath; all rooms have phone, minibar; some rooms have TV, air conditioning
FACILITIES sitting room, bar, TV room, meeting room, piano bar, terrace, garden, swimming pool **CREDIT CARDS** AE, DC, MC, V **DISABLED** access difficult
PETS not accepted **CLOSED** Oct to Easter **PROPRIETORS** Podesta family

THE NORTH-WEST

GARLENDA

LA MERIDIANA

~ COUNTRY HOUSE HOTEL ~

Via ai Castelli 11, 17033 Garlenda, Savona
TEL 0182 580271 **FAX** 0182 580150
E-MAIL meridiana@relaischateaux.fr **WEBSITE** www.relaischateaux.fr/meridiana

IF YOU'RE A SERIOUS GOLFER or keen to improve your handicap, La Meridiana might be the place for you – it has an 18-hole course in the grounds. Not that this gorgeous place appeals to golfers alone. Set in the Garlenda valley, but with acres of vineyards and lush gardens shielding it from the outside world, it is a rare breed: a chic Relais et Châteaux hotel without a whiff of formality. The owners and staff are caring and courteous. The rooms are in a rambling mixture of old buildings and new extensions, tastefully furnished with antiques, downy sofas, bright chintzes and checks. All the bedrooms and suites are fresh-looking and light with balconies on to the gardens.

Gourmets and gourmands alike queue up to sample the exquisite seafood and contemporary versions of traditional Ligurian dishes from the hotel's renowned kitchen, where only fresh, natural ingredients are used. The restaurant prides itself on a well-stocked and wide-ranging cellar.

For the energetic, there is riding and tennis at a nearby country club, and with a car you are in striking distance of the Italian Riviera.

~

NEARBY Albenga (10 km); Alássio (17 km).
LOCATION 10 km SW of Albegna, off A10; car parking
FOOD breakfast, dinner; lunch at pool Jun-Sept
PRICE €€€
ROOMS 30; 14 double and twin, 16 suites, all with bath; all rooms have phone, TV, air conditioning, minibar, hairdrier, safe
FACILITIES sitting room, TV room, dining room, bars, meeting room, sauna, lift, terrace, garden, swimming pool, golf, helipad
CREDIT CARDS AE, DC, MC, V
DISABLED access possible
PETS accepted by arrangement
CLOSED Nov to early Mar
PROPRIETORS Segre family

THE NORTH-WEST

VERBANO

~ LAKESIDE GUESTHOUSE ~

Via Ugo Ara 2, Isola dei Pescatori, 28049 Stresa, Novara
TEL 0323 30408/32534 **FAX** 0323 33129
E-MAIL hotelverbano@tin.it **WEBSITE** www.hotelverbano.it

THE ISOLA DEI PESCATORI may not have the *palazzo* or gardens of neigh-bouring Isola Bella (unlike the other islands, it has never belonged to the wealthy Borromeo family), but it is just as charming in its own way. The cafés and the slightly shabby, painted fishermen's houses along the front are, perhaps, reminiscent of a Greek island – though not an undis-covered one.

The Verbano is a large russet-coloured villa occupying one end of the island, its garden and terraces looking across Lake Maggiore to Isola Bella. It does not pretend to be luxurious, but it does offer plenty of char-acter and local colour. There are beautiful views from the bedrooms, and 11 of the 12 have balconies. Each room is named after a flower; most are prettily and appropriately furnished in old-fashioned style, with painted furniture; those which were a little tired-looking have apparently been refurbished, and more refurbishment is planned since a recent change of ownership.

But the emphasis is really on the restaurant, with home-made pastas a speciality. If weather prevents eating on the terrace, you can still enjoy the views through the big windows of the dining room. 'Excellent food, friendly staff,' says a visitor. Reports welcome.

~

NEARBY Isola Bella; Stresa; Pallanza; Baveno
LOCATION on tiny island in Lake Maggiore; regular boats from Stresa, where there is ample car parking space
FOOD breakfast, lunch, dinner
PRICE ©©
ROOMS 12 double and twin, 8 with bath, 4 with shower; all rooms have phone, hairdrier
FACILITIES sitting room, dining room, bar, terrace **CREDIT CARDS** AE, DC, MC, V
DISABLED no special facilities **PETS** accepted **CLOSED** never
MANAGER Signor Gafforini

THE NORTH-WEST

LAIGUÉGLIA

SPLENDID

~ SEASIDE HOTEL ~

Piazza Badaro 3, 17020 Laiguéglia, Savona
TEL 0182 690325 **FAX** 0182 690894
E-MAIL splendid@ags.sv.it **WEBSITE** www.ags.sv.it/laigueglia/splendid.htm

THE VAULTED CEILINGS and the well in the dining room testify to the monastic origins of this neat hotel in a palm-fringed *piazza* in the middle of Laiguéglia. Built in the 14th and 15th centuries, the monastery has been sympathetically converted and updated, keeping its original architecture intact while equipping the hotel with 21st-century comforts. The decoration is a happy blend of antique and modern, and incorporates ancient objects found during the restoration work.

Laiguéglia is a spruce little town on the Riviera di Ponente, a coast that faces south-east and enjoys a particularly mild climate, even in winter. On the seafront outside the hotel, immaculate rows of deckchairs and loungers are lined up on a pontoon, tempting passers-by to while away an hour or two in the sun. The sea here is noted for being sparklingly clean and has received the official 'blue flag' for cleanliness. So swimming off the Splendid's private beach is a pleasure. The hotel's other great assets are its small but pretty garden and inviting pool, where drinks are served. In the dining room, not surprisingly, fish features prominently on a mainly traditional regional menu.

~

NEARBY Alássio (3 km); Albenga (10 km).
LOCATION in centre of Laiguéglia, off riviera coast road, near seafront; car parking
FOOD breakfast, lunch, dinner
PRICE €€€
ROOMS 45; 33 double and twin, 10 single, 2 suites, all with bath or shower; all rooms have phone, TV, hairdrier
FACILITIES sitting room, dining room, lift, terrace, garden, swimming pool
CREDIT CARDS AE, DC, MC, V
DISABLED access difficult
PETS not accepted **CLOSED** Oct-Apr
PROPRIETOR Angelo Marchiano

THE NORTH-WEST

LEIVI

CA' PEO

~ RESTAURANT WITH ROOMS ~

Via dei Caduti 80, 16040 Leivi, Genova
TEL 0185 319696 **FAX** 0185 319671
E-MAIL nicosol@libero.it

THIS RAMBLING FARMHOUSE in the hills east of Portofino has been
in the Solari family for four generations. Franco and Melly Solari
opened their attractive, bay-windowed dining room, with its magnificent
views over the bay and hills, to guests in 1973. Melly produces the generous seasonal menus, while Franco provides the wine chosen from the 350
different vintages in his cellar. Both now enjoy a high reputation, and
booking for the restaurant is essential.

In addition to its home-like atmosphere, the house has many delightful
features, including black slate fixtures of varying antiquity (a local speciality – slate is mined in the hills around here). Accommodation is in
apartments with a kitchen and dining area, all modern, in an annexe set
into olive terraces below the main building; they are comfortable and airy,
with new pine furniture and bright sofas.

This makes a quiet, attractive base for exploring the Gulf de Tigullio,
between Portofino and Sestri Levante – provided you don't mind negotiating the winding access road. A recent reader's letter tells us that the food
was brilliant, the view outstanding, but that the housekeeping was not up
to scratch.

~

NEARBY Portofino (22 km); Cinque Terre villages.
LOCATION in hills 6 km N of Chiavari; car parking
FOOD breakfast, lunch, dinner
PRICE €€€
ROOMS 5 apartments; all apartments have phone, TV, kitchen facilities
FACILITIES sitting room, dining room, bar, garden
CREDIT CARDS AE, DC, MC, V
DISABLED access difficult
PETS accepted
CLOSED Nov; restaurant Mon, Tue lunch
PROPRIETORS Franco and Melly Solari

THE NORTH-WEST

IL CAPRICORNO
~ MOUNTAIN CHALET ~

Case Sparse 21, Le Clotes, 10050 Sauze d'Oulx, Torino
TEL 0122 850273 **FAX** 0122 850055

THIS TYPICAL WOODEN CHALET has a fairytale setting surrounded by pine trees on the slopes above the busy ski resort of Sauze d'Oulx and can only be reached by a steep, winding dirt track. In summer you can drive right up to the hotel, but in winter, you must park in town and be collected by snowmobile. Inside, it is as spick-and-span and cosy as a chalet should be: the snug rooms, brightened by fresh flowers, log fires and traditional wooden furniture, mostly handmade by Carlo himself. The dining room, beyond a tiny bar, is especially cheerful with its burnished copper pots and kettles, neat pile of logs beside the hearth and pretty blue-and-white tablecloths. The seven spotless bedrooms and bathrooms have recently been updated, and there are balconies for a select few.

In winter you can ski down the hill from the front door; in summer there are mountain hikes that beckon in all directions. Because they have so few guests (there are only seven rooms), the Sacchis go to great lengths to indulge them, not least with the delicious meals that Mariarosa produces every day.

After a long day's skiing or walking, this is the perfect place to return to. And as more people are beginning to realize this, you must book early.

~

NEARBY Susa (28 km); Briançon, France (28 km).
LOCATION above and 2 km E of town; car parking in summer
FOOD breakfast, lunch, dinner
PRICE €€
ROOMS 7 double and twin with bath; all rooms have phone, TV, hairdrier
FACILITIES bar, dining room, terrace
CREDIT CARDS MC, V
DISABLED access difficult **PETS** not accepted
CLOSED May to mid-Jun, mid-Sept to Dec
PROPRIETORS Carlo and Mariarosa Sacchi

THE NORTH-WEST

SESTRI LEVANTE

HELVETIA

~ SEASIDE HOTEL ~

Via Cappuccini 43, 16039 Sestri Levante, Genova
TEL 0185 43048 **FAX** 0185 457216
E-MAIL helvetia@rainbownet.it **WEBSITE** www.hotelhelvetia.it

THE HELVETIA'S CLAIM that it has 'the quietest and most enchanting position of Sestri Levante' is no exaggeration: it stands at one end of the appropriately named Baia del Silenzio. The hotel is distinguished by its spotless white façade, and the yellow and white canopies that shade its balconies and terrace.

Lorenzo Pernigotti devotes himself wholeheartedly to his guests and provides the sort of extras – including 15 gleaming yellow bikes – that you might expect to find in a four-star hotel; but the Helvetia remains small and personal; one satisfied guest says he 'felt just like part of the family'. Another was delighted by the sophisticated key system which controls the lights and music in the bedrooms. The sitting room/bar has the air of a private home – antiques, coffee-table books, newspapers, potted plants – and the breakfast room is lovely, with views of the bay. Bedrooms are light and airy, overlooking either the bay or the gardens. The day starts on the terrace, with an unusually liberal help-yourself breakfast. Luxuriant gardens climb up the hillside, with tables in the shade of palm trees. Serious sunbathers can take to sunbeds. And there is a tiny pebble beach just across the road.

~

NEARBY Portofino (28 km); Genoa (50 km).
LOCATION at end of small 'Bay of Silence' beach; limited car parking and garage
FOOD breakfast
PRICE €€
ROOMS 24 double and twin with shower; all rooms have phone, TV, video, minibar, hairdrier, safe
FACILITIES sitting room, TV/video room, dining room, bar, lift, terrace, garden, table tennis
CREDIT CARDS MC, V
DISABLED no special facilities **PETS** dogs accepted **CLOSED** Nov-Feb
PROPRIETOR Lorenzo Pernigotti

THE NORTH-WEST

SESTRI LEVANTE

MIRAMARE

~ SEASIDE HOTEL ~

Via Cappellini 9, 16039 Sestri Levante, Genova
TEL 0185 480855 **FAX** 0185 41055
E-MAIL hrm.miramare@rainbow.it

THE EXTERIOR OF THE SUBSTANTIAL pink, shuttered house in a prime spot on the Baia del Silenzio does not prepare you for the cool, contemporary style that greets you when you step inside. Extensive renovation has given the Miramare a sophisticated, luxurious new look. At its core, the lobby is usually a hub of activity, a meeting place with the other public areas – sitting, dining and conference rooms and shops – radiating off it. Huge arched windows make the best of the sea views.

Just as airy, modern and comfortable as the ground-floor spaces, the bedrooms can be cleverly combined to form apartments that sleep as many as six, ideal for families or friends. Try for one of the sought-after rooms overlooking the sea.

You won't be short of places to sit and relax out-of-doors. There's a delightful garden at the front and a spacious terrace, an idyllic spot for breakfast. We hear that food is now a serious venture here, and the *carte* features a range of delicious regional specialities.

Sestri Levante makes a useful starting point for exploring the Cinque Terre villages, or if you're impatient to get out on the links, Rapallo, some 25 km up the coast, has an 18-hole golf course.

~

NEARBY Cinque Terre villages; Portofino (28 km); Genoa (50 km).
LOCATION on small 'Bay of Silence' beach; car parking
FOOD breakfast, lunch, dinner
PRICE ©©·©©©
ROOMS 43 double and twin, single and suites, all with bath or shower; all rooms have phone, TV, air conditioning, minibar, hairdrier, safe
FACILITIES sitting rooms, meeting rooms, restaurant, lift, terrace, garden
CREDIT CARDS AE, MC, V
DISABLED not suitable **PETS** not accepted **CLOSED** Dec-Jan
PROPRIETOR Signor Carmagnini Armando

THE NORTH-WEST

BREUIL-CERVINIA

NEIGES D'ANTAN
MOUNTAIN CHALET

Frazione Cret-Perrères, 11021
Breuil-Cervinia, Aosta

TEL 0166 948775 FAX 0166 948852
E-MAIL info@lesneigesdantan.it
WEBSITE www.lesneigesdantan.it
FOOD breakfast, lunch, dinner
PRICE €€ CLOSED early May to
late Jun, Oct-Nov or mid-Sept to
early Dec   Bich family

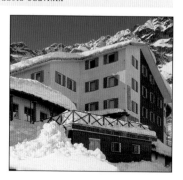

IT IS THE WARMTH and generosity of the hands-on owners, the Bich family, that make this simple hotel in the shadow of Monte Cervino (the Matterhorn) a great place for a holiday. From the outside, you couldn't call the large chalet, with its pebbled-dash and timber façade, beautiful. But the simple rustic interior is welcoming. Signora Bich is the chef, expert at reviving old family recipes and robust traditional Mediterranean dishes. Her son is the *sommelier*: in addition to a carefully-chosen cellar, he oversees an impressive range of *grappa* on offer in the snug wood-panelled and rough-stone bar. Ideal for families, and excellent value for money.

CIOCCARO DI PENANGO

LOCANDA DEL SANT' UFFIZIO
CONVERTED MONASTERY

14030 Cioccaro di Penango, Asti

TEL 0141 916292 FAX 0141 916068
E-MAIL santuffizio@thi.it
WEBSITE www.thi.it
FOOD breakfast, lunch, dinner
PRICE €€€
CLOSED 2 weeks Jan, 10 days Aug
Firato family

READERS APPROVE OF THE FINE FOOD and Firato family's hospitality at this alluring Michelin-starred restaurant-with-rooms in a converted 16thC Benedictine monastery. Set in a glorious landscape of vineyards and hills, the *locanda* impresses from the moment you catch sight of its mellow-brick exterior and, when you step through the door, the interior does the same. Original features have been preserved, and furnishings are a blend of antique and chic modern. Try to secure one of the bedrooms in the old cloisters. These have a small terrace or balcony overlooking the inviting pool and mature garden.

THE NORTH-WEST

PORTO ROCA
SEASIDE HOTEL

*Via Corone 1, 19016 Monterosso
al Mare, La Spezia*

TEL 0187 817502 **FAX** 0187 817692
E-MAIL portoroca@cinqueterre.it
WEBSITE www.portoroca.it
FOOD breakfast, lunch, dinner
PRICE €€€
CLOSED Nov-Mar
Jacazzi family

PERCHED ABOVE A SPECTACULAR, almost inaccessible stretch of coastline, Monterrosso is the largest of the charming, relatively undiscovered Cinque Terre villages. This, their best hotel clings precariously to a rocky headland. It's a steep climb up from the beach, but the location is all-important here, with sweeping views of the rugged coast and clear sea. When you book, be sure to ask for a room with a sea view. The ones at the back are desperately disappointing. Inside, the furnishings are dated but comforting. The bedrooms (at least the ones at the front) are fresher and brighter, most with balconies.

GRAND HOTEL DEI CASTELLI
CONVERTED CASTLE

*Via Penisola 26, 16039 Sestri
Levante, Genova*

TEL 0185 487220 **FAX** 0185 44767
E-MAIL htl.castelli@rainbownet.it
WEBSITE
www.rainbownet.it/htl.castelli
FOOD breakfast, lunch, dinner
PRICE €€€ **CLOSED** mid-Oct to
late Apr **MANAGER** Lino Zenotto

WITH A SPLENDID LOCATION high up on Sestri Levante's wooded peninsula, this castle hotel has been highly recommended to us by a recent visitor. 'From arrival at the gate onwards, there were no disappointments. The whole complex has been beautifully restored to a very high standard. The gardens and wooded areas are most attractive and beautifully kept with extensive views of the town and coastline. The staff were welcoming and helpful, especially in the restaurant... The food was excellent and good value, and the breakfast terrace had superb views.' Two lifts take guests down to the private beach.

LOMBARDIA

HOTELS IN LOMBARDIA

LOMBARDY IS AN ENORMOUS REGION, stretching from the high Alps bordering Switzerland almost as far as the Adriatic and Ligurian seas. It contains Lake Como, with Lakes Maggiore and Garda forming its boundary in the west and east respectively, and has at its heart the economic and industrial centre of Italy: Milan.

Of all big, glossy Italian cities, none is glossier than Milan and only Rome is bigger. Despite its considerable heritage – notably a marvellous cathedral, important art collections and the world's most famous opera house – its role as Italy's economic capital dominates the visitor's view, and most steer clear. The result is that Milan's hotels are business-oriented – and as big and glossy as the city itself.

Surprisingly though, we have been able to find a clutch of excellent small hotels in Milan, including two Antica Locandas, the Leonardo, and dei Mercanti.

Our main lakeside recommendations concentrate on Lake Como and Lake Garda. Bellagio is the main resort on Lake Como and the location of most of our hotels, with Menaggio a close second. As we don't have any recommendations here, try the Bellavista (tel 0344 32136) in Menaggio itself, or the Loveno (tel 0344 32110) in the village of Loveno 2 km away – a 13-room hotel with a garden and views of the lakes and mountains.

On Lake Garda, the main resort for the southern end is Sirmione, beautifully situated on the lake, and with the massive Castle of the Scaligers, Roman remains and lovely gardens to visit, but also very conveniently placed for the main Milan-Venice motorway and therefore very busy during the day with trippers trying to 'see' Lake Garda, Verona and Venice in a day. In Sirmione, you'll find the Grifone, a modestly-priced stalwart of the guide. Further north, on the lakes's western shore, there are more recommendations at Gargnano and Gardone Riviera, and one, I Due Roccoli, on the smaller neighbouring Lake Iseo.

LOMBARDIA

ALZATE BRIANZA

VILLA ODESCALCHI

~ COUNTRY VILLA ~

Via Anzani 12, 22040 Alzate Brianza, Como
TEL 031 630822 **FAX** 031 632079
E-MAIL info@villaodescalchi.it **WEBSITE** www.villaodescalchi.it

THE ODESCALCHI FAMILY built the splendid villa at the heart of this complex in Brianza at the beginning of the 17th century. Later Pope Innocent XI took such a fancy to its relaxing atmosphere – or perhaps to its private chapel – that he settled in himself. Set in 35 hectares of grounds, the fine formal gardens are now shared (like all the hotel's facilities) with 32 apartments. The villa, complete with a mezzanine gallery in its immense hall, has kept its period presence but has been extended to add all the usual features of a modern hotel: floodlit tennis courts, swimming pools indoors and out, gym, Jacuzzi and Turkish bath, a 9-hole golf course, conference rooms and most of the fairly standard bedrooms.

The attractive barrel-vaulted restaurant is housed in the original villa where it offers a competent mixture of international and local dishes. Highest marks here go to the presentation, excellent service and wine list. Breakfast includes a splendid assortment of cheeses and cold cuts, fruit and yoghurt. Como and Lecco are each 20 minutes away and it's a 40-minute drive to Milan.

~

NEARBY Lakes Como and Lecco; Milan (50 km)
LOCATION 10 km SE of Como; garage
FOOD breakfast, lunch, dinner
PRICE €€
ROOMS 63; 50 double and twin, 40 with bath, 10 with shower, 13 single with shower; all rooms have phone, TV, minibar, hairdrier; some rooms have air-conditioning, safe
FACILITIES restaurant, bar, conference rooms, gym, health centre, indoor and outdoor swimming pools, terrace, garden, tennis, golf
CREDIT CARDS AE, DC, MC, V
DISABLED 2 specially adapted rooms **PETS** small dogs accepted
CLOSED early Dec to mid-Jan **MANAGER** Pierre Taillandier

LOMBARDIA

BELLAGIO

FLORENCE
~ LAKESIDE HOTEL ~

Piazza Mazzini, 22021 Bellagio, Como
TEL 031 950342 **FAX** 031 951722 **E-MAIL** hotflore@tin.it
WEBSITE www.bellagio.co.nz

Bellagio is the pearl of Lake Como. It stands on a promontory at the
point where the lake divides into two branches, and the views from its
houses, villas and gardens are superb. The Florence is a handsome 18thC
building occupying a prime position at one end of the main *piazza*, overlooking the lake. A terrace under arcades, where drinks and snacks are
served, provides a welcoming entry to the hotel and the interior is no less
appealing. Whitewashed walls, high vaulted ceilings and beams create a
cool, attractive foyer; to one side, elegant and slightly faded seats cluster
round an old stone fireplace.

Bedrooms have the same old-fashioned charm as the public rooms, furnished with cherry-wood antiques and attractive fabrics; the most sought
after, naturally, are those with balconies and views over the lake. Meals
(including breakfast, with home-made pastries) can be taken on a delightful terrace under shady trees across the street from the hotel, watching
the various craft ply across the lake. In the evening there is jazz in the
cocktail bar – one of Lake Como's smarter nightspots. The hotel has been
in the same family for 150 years, and is now in the hands of brother and
sister, Ronald and Roberta Ketzlar; they both speak good English, and
have created a gourmet restaurant and two new suites. A recent visitor
was thoroughly enchanted.

~

NEARBY Villa Serbelloni; Madonna del Ghisallo (37 km).
LOCATION on main *piazza* overlooking lake; garage
FOOD breakfast, lunch, dinner
PRICE €€€-€€€€
ROOMS 34; 32 double and twin, 2 suites, all with bath; all rooms have phone, TV,
minibar, hairdrier, safe
FACILITIES dining room, bar, reading/TV room, terrace **CREDIT CARDS** AE, MC, V
DISABLED not suitable **PETS** accepted **CLOSED** late Oct to mid-Apr
PROPRIETORS Ketzlar family

LOMBARDIA

BELLAGIO

HOTEL DU LAC

Lakeside hotel

Piazza Mazzini 32, 22021 Bellagio, Como
Tel 031 950320 **Fax** 031 951624
E-MAIL dulac@tin.it **WEBSITE** www.fromitaly.net/bellagio/113/dulac

SMACK IN THE MIDDLE of Bellagio's waterfront, the Hotel du Lac's stunning view of Como is matched by the Leoni family's pretty faultless performance in all departments. If you want to be picky you might say that one or two of the rooms are on the small side, or that the decoration in some of the bathrooms is a little dated, but there your list would have to stop. The smart marble-floored reception hall runs off an arcade where the café's wicker chairs offer a comfy spot from which to keep an eye on Bellagio's pavement society. The bright and inviting bar is also on the ground floor but the staff will bring you a drink (they have an impressive selection of cocktails) anywhere in the hotel.

On the first floor the windows in the unfussy restaurant run the width of the building to make the most of the panoramic view and the inventive menu offers a broad choice of excellent dishes – with cheeses and wines to match. The impeccably maintained bedrooms are simply decorated, the beds comfortable and, it ought to go without saying, the best have views of the lake. The rooftop terrace offers another vantage point, with deckchairs for sunbathing and awnings for those who prefer some shade. Staff are friendly, professional and helpful.

NEARBY Villa Serbelloni; Madonna del Ghisallo (37 km).
LOCATION on main piazza overlooking lake; car parking
FOOD breakfast, lunch, dinner
PRICE €€
ROOMS 48; 41 double and twin, 7 single, all with bath or shower; all rooms have phone, TV, air conditioning, minibar, hairdrier
FACILITIES restaurant, bar, terrace
CREDIT CARDS MC, V
DISABLED not suitable
PETS accepted **CLOSED** Nov to mid-Mar; restaurant Tue
PROPRIETORS Leoni family

LOMBARDIA

BELLAGIO

LA PERGOLA
~ LAKESIDE HOTEL ~

Piazza del Porto 4, Pescallo, 22021 Bellagio, Como
TEL 031 950263 **FAX** 031 950253

LA PERGOLA IS RELAXED and informal, and very much a family affair. Don't come here looking for up-to-the-minute decor, or even for clues on how they did it many years ago. But, set as it is on a little bay to the south-west of Bellagio, this hotel is away from the tourist bustle and there is a fishing village feel to the area. The hotel takes its name from the pergola that shelters diners at its enchanting lakeside restaurant, the focal point of the entire establishment. Really only a matter of centimetres from the water, this proximity is not just romantic: it is also reflected in the restaurant's enticing menu which features dishes based on fish from the lake, alongside a selection of non-fishy regional alternatives with wines to match.

A long passage, attractively flagged with black stone and housing a love-seat and a few pieces of furniture, connects the small reception with the restaurant's terrace. The bedrooms are reached by a large staircase which rises from the passage. The good sized rooms are simple and clean, and most have large windows with glorious views of the lake. There's no air-conditioning but each room has a serious-looking ceiling-mounted fan.

NEARBY Villa Serbelloni; Madonna del Ghisallo (37 km).
LOCATION in village of Pescallo just SW of Bellagio, overlooking lake; public car parking
FOOD breakfast, lunch, dinner
PRICE ©
ROOMS 11; 5 double, 4 twin, 2 with bath, 7 with shower, 2 single with shower; all rooms have phone, TV, safe
FACILITIES restaurant, terrace
CREDIT CARDS AE, DC, MC, V
DISABLED no special facilities
PETS small ones accepted **CLOSED** Nov-Mar
PROPRIETORS Mazzoni family

LOMBARDIA

BERGAMO

GOURMET

~ RESTAURANT WITH ROOMS ~

Via San Vigilio 1, 24100 Bergamo
TEL and **FAX** 035 4373004

BERGAMO IS QUITE A FAVOURITE with the foodies and, given the pretty stiff competition downtown, it must have taken a certain amount of confidence to hang out a shingle in the High Town with 'gourmet' on it. Although the emphasis here is obviously on food, the rooms are not to be sniffed at. They are all of a good size, extremely well maintained and, although modern in decoration, there are plenty of wood fittings and pieces of furniture to soften them.

The entrance to Ristorante Gourmet is airy and spacious, with a pale tiled floor and a small seating area. It is immediately obvious that this is not a seasonal business: there is as much dining space indoors as there is outside on the large (covered) but uncrowded terrace. The atmosphere is gently civilized and unforced, with pleasant staff taking their cue from the charming owner. The menu is quite a refined document, wide-ranging and creative with a broad selection of regional specialities and is complemented by the extensive wine list. The whole place is dotted with lush, well-cared-for plants, and guests have the use of a lovely private garden when they feel the need for some real peace and quiet.

~

NEARBY Brescia (48 km); Milan (50 km); Lakes Como, Lecco and Iseo.
LOCATION in Città Alta (High Town); car parking
FOOD breakfast, lunch, dinner; room service
PRICE €
ROOMS 11; 2 double, 7 twin, 3 with bath, 6 with shower, 1 single with shower, 1 suite with bath; all rooms have phone, TV, air conditioning, minibar, hairdrier
FACILITIES restaurant, bar, garden
CREDIT CARDS AE, DC, MC, V
DISABLED no special facilities
PETS not accepted
CLOSED late Dec to early Jan
PROPRIETOR Aldo Battista Beretta

LOMBARDIA

CERVESINA

CASTELLO DI SAN GAUDENZIO
~ CONVERTED CASTLE ~

Loc. San Gaudenzio, 27050 Cervesina, Pavia
TEL 0383 3331 **FAX** 0383 333409
E-MAIL info@castellosangaudenzio.com **WEBSITE** www.castellosangaudenzio.com

SET IN FORMAL GARDENS less than 60 km from Milan, this spacious and elegant 15thC *castello* has been owned over the years by a succession of smart Italian families and has the ivy, walls, towers, gateways, statuary and other embellishments to prove it. Times have changed: the horses are now gone from the stables and have been replaced by an indoor swimming pool and solarium, and a spectacular barrel vault has been turned into a conference room. Period furniture is watched over by ancestral portraits, and red and black marble fireplaces remind you that wood-burning can be done in considerable style.

Most of the bedrooms are brand new, with handsome bathrooms to match, but their pale striped wallpapers and hangings, polished parquet or stone floors, panelled and frescoed ceilings and light, elegant furniture have successfully integrated them with the well-restored older portions of the castle. Almost all look out over the garden. There are three suites, the most baronial (and expensive) of which occupies two stories of a tower.

The restaurant offers Italian and international dishes and the wines on their list include some specially bottled for the *castello*. The staff are professional and helpful.

~

NEARBY Voghera (6 km); Pavia (25 km); Milan (56 km).
LOCATION 6 km NW of Voghera, exit Casei Gerola from the 'Autostrada dei Fiori'; car parking
FOOD breakfast, lunch, dinner
PRICE €€
ROOMS 45; 35 double and twin, 7 single, 3 suites, all with bath or shower; all rooms have phone, TV, minibar, safe, hairdrier; some rooms have air conditioning
FACILITIES sitting rooms, dining room, conference rooms, bar, indoor swimming pool, solarium, lift, garden
CREDIT CARDS AE, MC, V **DISABLED** 2 specially adapted rooms **PETS** not accepted
CLOSED restaurant Tue
MANAGER Pierangelo Bergaglio

LOMBARDIA

ERBUSCO

L'ALBERETA

·~ COUNTRY VILLA ·~

Via Vittorio Emanuele 11, 25030 Erbusco, Brescia
TEL 030 7760550 **FAX** 030 7760573
E-MAIL albereta@terramoretti.it **WEBSITE** www.terramoretti.it

IN THE MIDDLE OF THE famous vineyards of Francioforta, L'Albereta is an ancient manor which has had some very elegant and upmarket new life breathed into it. Home of the Moretti family, who still own it, this villa is so smart that, unless they have met you at the station or airport, you might just consider nipping through a car-wash before driving up to the front door. But you needn't bother, because the staff here are very professional though not in the least precious. You will also find muted marble, arches, parquet, wrought iron, chintz, beams, flowers and vineyards as far as the eye can see. Virtually everything has been put here to please you and this includes Gualtiero Marchesi's double-starred restaurant which is as much of a draw as the stunning modern bedrooms. His kitchen is a symphony of stainless steel, copper and starched white chefs' uniforms.

If you feel an urgent need to work off the effects of a particularly good dinner, you can either play tennis or get your exercise flitting between the Jacuzzi, the sauna and the solarium. Last but not least, just in case you are thinking of arriving by helicopter, L'Albereta helpfully publishes its GPS co-ordinates so that your navigation system can deliver you with pin-point precision.

~

NEARBY Brescia (20 km); Bergamo (30 km).
LOCATION 3 km N of A4 Milan-Venice motorway (Rovato exit); car parking
FOOD breakfast, lunch, dinner
PRICE €€€
ROOMS 41; 25 double, 10 twin, 32 with bath, 3 with shower, 3 single with shower, 3 suites with bath; all rooms have phone, TV, air conditioning, minibar, hairdrier, safe
FACILITIES sitting rooms, billiard room, restaurant, bars, meeting rooms, health and fitness centre, indoor swimming pool, garden, tennis, helipad
CREDIT CARDS AE, DC, MC, V **DISABLED** not suitable **PETS** not accepted **CLOSED** never
PROPRIETORS Moretti family

LOMBARDIA

GARDONE RIVIERA

VILLA FIORDALISO
~ LAKESIDE RESTAURANTS WITH ROOMS ~

Corso Zanardelli 132, 25083 Gardone Riviera, Brescia
TEL 0365 20158 **FAX** 0365 290011
E-MAIL fiordaliso@relaischateaux.fr **WEBSITE** www.relaischateaux.fr

MICHELIN-STARRED VILLA FIORDALISO has been well known as one of the best restaurants in Northern Italy for some years, but it is also a chic and romantic small hotel. Built in 1902, the pale pink and white lakeside villa was home to Gabriele d'Annunzio, and later to Claretta Petacci, Mussolini's mistress. Inside, the intricately carved wood and marble work on walls, floors and doorways and the splendid gold and frescoed ceilings are the perfectly preserved remnants of another age. A magnificent Venetian-style marble staircase, with columns and delicate wrought iron-work leads from the reception hall at garden level to the intimate first-floor restaurant and up to the seven luxurious bedrooms. Three of these have been left with their original furniture and decoration. The Claretta suite, a room of impressive dimensions with terrace and lake view, has a stunning marble bathroom. Other rooms are lighter in style with fresh wallpapers and fabrics.

The shady garden, bordering the lake (and, unfortunately, the main road), is a wonderful setting for the elegant summer restaurant, immaculately decked out in a terracotta and white colour scheme.

~

NEARBY Brescia (40 km); Sirmione (35 km).
LOCATION on SS572, 3 km NE of Salò; ample car parking
FOOD breakfast, lunch, dinner
PRICE €€€
ROOMS 7; 5 double and twin, 2 suites, all with bath or shower; all rooms have phone, TV, air conditioning, minibar
FACILITIES sitting room, dining room, tower with bar, terraces, garden
CREDIT CARDS AE, DC, MC, V
DISABLED access possible
PETS not accepted
CLOSED mid-Nov to Feb; restaurant Mon, Tues lunch
PROPRIETORS Tosetti family

LOMBARDIA

GARDONE RIVIERA

VILLA DEL SOGNO
~ LAKESIDE VILLA ~

Via Zanardelli 107, 25083 Gardone Riviera, Brescia
TEL 0365 290181 **FAX** 0365 290230
E-MAIL villadelsogno@gardalake.it **WEBSITE** www.gardalake.it/villadelsogno

BUILT IN 1904 AS THE HOLIDAY HOME of an Austrian silk industrialist, this imposing villa became a hotel in 1938. Like so many of the hotels around Lake Garda, it has an amazing position, above the lake but near enough to feel part of the lakeside scene. It is approached by a long winding drive and cradled in exotic gardens, where we stumbled upon two little neoclassical temples. An extension added in the 1980s contains some rather ordinary rooms, including the reception (disappointing when you first arrive). But go through to the wood-panelled hall and staircase and you'll find much more character. The huge wooden fireplace and painted ceramic tiles reveal the villa's Austrian heritage, only slightly at odds with the stone arches, Grecian urns, and other neoclassical flourishes.

Armchairs in cheerful floral prints and a bar at one end make the sitting room especially congenial. There is also a refined restaurant in two rooms, where the parquet floor gleams almost as much as the silver candlesticks. Upstairs, there are several enormous suites, furnished traditionally. Rooms in the new wing are lighter with their own terraces.

NEARBY beach (300 m); Brescia (50 km).
LOCATION 2 km N of Gardone, off SS45; car parking
FOOD breakfast, lunch, dinner
PRICE €€€
ROOMS 32; 25 double and twin, 20 with bath, 5 with shower, 7 suites with bath; all rooms have phone, TV, hairdrier; 9 have air conditioning
FACILITIES sitting room/bar, dining room, health centre, lift, terrace, garden, swimming pool, tennis
CREDIT CARDS AE, DC, MC, V
DISABLED no special facilities
PETS accepted **CLOSED** mid-Oct to end Mar (or Easter if earlier)
PROPRIETORS Caldaran family

LOMBARDIA

ISEO

I DUE ROCCOLI
~ MOUNTAIN INN ~

Via Silvio Bonomelli, 25049 Iseo, Brescia
TEL 030 9822977 **FAX** 030 9822980
E-MAIL relais@idueroccoli.com **WEBSITE** www.idueroccoli.com

L AKE ISEO IS IN THE MISTY, southernmost foothills of the Alps. Sixty miles one way would take you into Switzerland and it is not much further in another to reach Austria. The lake's principal island, Monteisola, is the largest on any European lake and home to about 2,000 people. Between the southern tip of the lake and the *autostrada* connecting Milan with Venice lies the Franciacorta, a region highly respected for the quality of its wines. Up a winding mountain road to the south-east of the lake, elegant and tranquil in its carefully tended park, lies I Due Roccoli. Built of stone, and beautifully decorated inside, here is a place to rest and recharge batteries. Simply to praise the views is selling the place short because even the swimming pool has one, and from the moment you spot the vases of fresh roses on each of the tables on the fabulous terrace you just know that you have come to the right place.

Fish from the lake, organically-grown produce from their own gardens and home-cured ham all feature on the short but well-balanced menu and you will dine by candlelight. The spacious and spotless rooms are decorated in modern style with fine prints hanging on the walls. The staff are every bit as charming as their hotel.

~

NEARBY Brescia (20 km); Lakes Idro and Garda.
LOCATION 4 km SE of Iseo up a mountain road; car parking
FOOD breakfast, lunch, dinner
PRICE €€
ROOMS 13; 10 double and twin, 1 single, 2 suites, all with bath; all rooms have phone, TV, minibar, hairdrier, safe
FACILITIES sitting room, reading room, bar, dining room, garden, swimming pool, tennis
CREDIT CARDS AE, DC, MC, V
DISABLED not suitable **PETS** accepted **CLOSED** Nov to mid-Mar
PROPRIETOR Guido Anessi

LOMBARDIA

LENNO

SAN GIORGIO
～ LAKESIDE HOTEL ～

Via Regina 81, Lenno, 22019 Tremezzo Como
TEL 0344 40415 **FAX** 0344 41591

THIS LARGE WHITE 1920S VILLA on the shores of Lake Como stands out against a backdrop of wooded hills and immaculate gardens running right down to the shore. A path lined with potted plants leads down through neatly tended lawns to the lakeside terrace and the low-lying stone wall which is all that divides the gardens from the pebble beach and the lake. There are palm trees, arbours and stone urns where geraniums flourish. For a trip on the lake the ferry landing-stage lies close by.

The interior is no disappointment. The public rooms are large and spacious, leading off handsome halls. There are antiques wherever you go, and attractive touches such as pretty ceramic pots and copper pots brimming with flowers. The restaurant is a lovely light room with breathtaking views and the salon is equally inviting, with its ornate mirrors, fireplace and slightly faded antiques. Even the ping-pong room has some interesting antique pieces. Bedrooms are large and pleasantly old-fashioned. Antiques and beautiful views are the main features, but there is nothing grand or luxurious about them – hence the reasonable prices. One of our reporters rates this his favourite hotel – 'sensational view, friendly reception, firm bed, great towels'.

～

NEARBY Tremezzo, Cadenabbia, Villa Carlotta (2-4 km); Bellagio.
LOCATION on lakefront; car parking and garage
FOOD breakfast, lunch, dinner
PRICE €€
ROOMS 29; 26 double, 20 with bath, 6 with shower, 3 single; all rooms have phone, hairdrier, safe
FACILITIES dining room, reading room, table tennis, terrace, tennis
CREDIT CARDS MC, V
DISABLED access difficult
PETS not accepted **CLOSED** Oct-Apr
PROPRIETOR Margherita Cappelletti

LOMBARDIA

MALEO

SOLE

~ RESTAURANT WITH ROOMS ~

Via Trabattoni 22, 26847 Maleo, Milano
Tel 0377 58142 **Fax** 0377 458058

THE EXTERIOR OF THIS 15THC coaching inn is marked solely by a gilt wrought-iron sun. Inside, the walls are whitewashed, the ceilings timbered and the arched chambers carefully scattered with antique furniture, copper pots and ceramics. There are three dining areas: the old kitchen, with its long table, open fire and old gas hobs where on occasion dishes are finished in front of the guests; a smaller dining room, with individual tables; and the stone-arched portico which looks out on to the idyllic garden.

The late Franco Colombani had brought his own distinctive personality to the regional cuisine – dark, tasty stews, roast meats and fish, accompanied by vegetables from the kitchen garden and fine wines from the unfathomable cellars. Now his son and daughter are continuing with the tradition that has helped rate the Sole as among Italy's finest restaurants.

The newly air-conditioned bedrooms all have individual high points, and good bathrooms. Those above the dining room are traditional, while those overlooking the garden have a less impressive mix of old and new furnishings.

~

NEARBY Piacenza; Cremona (22 km).
LOCATION behind church, off main piazza in village, 20 km NE of Piacenza; car parking
FOOD breakfast, lunch, dinner
PRICE €€
ROOMS 8 double and twin with bath; all rooms have phone, TV, air conditioning, minibar; one apartment
FACILITIES sitting room, 3 dining rooms, garden
CREDIT CARDS AE, MC, V **DISABLED** no special facilities **PETS** accepted
CLOSED Jan, Aug, restaurant Sun eve, Mon
PROPRIETORS Mario and Francesca Colombani

LOMBARDIA

MANERBA DEL GARDA

VILLA SCHINDLER

〜 COUNTRY HOTEL 〜

Via Bresciani 68, 25080 Manerba del Garda, Brescia
TEL 0365 651046 **FAX** 0365 554877
E-MAIL villaschindler@gsnet.it **WEBSITE** www.gsnet.it/villaschindler

PINES, CYPRESSES AND OLIVE TREES frame Villa Schindler as it perches up on its bench looking out at the southern end of Lake Garda. Low key, modest in price and long on looks and charm, this hotel is the perfect anti-dote to trilling mobiles and fast-track check-ins. What better use could there be for a cellar than for the storing of your own wine and olive oil and for convivial tastings of both for friends and guests? The antique desk which serves as 'reception' at the tiled entrance sets the tone of the place. Beyond the entrance a comfortable living room (with honesty bar) and a breakfast room lead on to the superb terrace. The place is stiff with art, much of it the work of Anna Brotto, the owner.

Although there is no restaurant, each room has its own fridge and cook-er. There is also a kitchen for guests' use and right outside it there are some picnic tables with a view of the lake. Otherwise you can order up generous platefuls of local cold cuts, bread and cheeses or head off to one of the recommended local restaurants. The light, spacious bedrooms have glorious wood floors, a handsome complement of antiques and are perfect-ly maintained.

〜

NEARBY Desenzano (15 km); Brescia (40 km).
LOCATION at southern end of Lake Garda, off Desenzano-Salo road; car parking
FOOD breakfast; snacks
PRICE €
ROOMS 9 double and twin, 1 with bath, 8 with shower; all rooms have phone, TV, hairdrier; one apartment
FACILITIES kitchen, wine cellar, terrace, garden, swimming pool
CREDIT CARDS not accepted
DISABLED not suitable
PETS small pets accepted
CLOSED mid-Oct to Easter
PROPRIETOR Anna Brotto

LOMBARDIA

MANTUA

SAN LORENZO

~ TOWN HOTEL ~

Piazza Concordia 14, 46100 Mantova
TEL 0376 220500 **FAX** 0376 327194
E-MAIL hotel@hotelsanlorenzo.it **WEBSITE** www.hotelsanlorenzo.it

SAN LORENZO IS SMART, CONSERVATIVE, technologically up-to-date and as central as it could possibly be. It is literally surrounded by pearls of Mantua's historic architecture. Even if you are only there for a satellite-connected conference, skip past the registration desk, go straight up to the roof terrace, look around you, and marvel at how easy it is to slip back a few centuries.

Inside is a hotel where all the 'i's have been dotted and the 't's crossed. It is the sort of place where you just know, as you step across the threshold, that there are no spiders lurking behind the plentiful antiques. The public rooms are quiet and well dressed with fresh flowers, elegant furnishings and furniture, some fine paintings, porcelain and a fascinating collection of 16thC brass offertory plates.

The staff are friendly and professional and can provide you with a potted history of Mantua and a suggested walking tour with some very helpful notes on the places and buildings you will see along the way. The bedrooms are spacious and bright, each with its own complement of things ancient and modern, and their individual bathrooms are immaculate.

~

NEARBY Piazza dell'Erbe; Basilica di Sant'Andrea; Palazzo Ducale.
LOCATION in city centre; garage
FOOD breakfast
PRICE €€€-€€€€
ROOMS 32; 23 double and twin, 9 suites, 25 with bath, 7 with shower; all rooms have phone, TV, air conditioning, minibar, hairdrier
FACILITIES sitting room, meeting rooms, bar, terrace
CREDIT CARDS AE, DC, MC, V
DISABLED 2 specially adapted rooms
PETS not accepted
CLOSED never
PROPRIETORS Giuseppe and Ottorino Tosi

LOMBARDIA

MILAN

ANTICA LOCANDA LEONARDO
~ TOWN HOTEL ~

Corso Magenta 78, 20123 Milano
Tel 02 463317 **Fax** 02 48019012
E-MAIL Leo's.Loc@cnn.it **WEBSITE** www.leoloc.com

A SCANT 30 SECONDS AWAY FROM the tourist-powered mayhem that radiates outwards from Santa Maria delle Grazie, home of Leonardo's Cenacolo, Antica Locanda Leonardo presents a rather drab and faintly inauspicious exterior to the outside world. But don't be dismayed: as you cross the threshold of the front door on the courtyard, you enter a different world. The light, bright entrance hall has a cool pale grey mosaic floor with an attractive stone staircase rising gently to the first floor. Beyond the hall is a pale yellow living room which in turn gives on to a small, peaceful and tree-shaded private terrace with a white-painted wrought-iron table, chairs and a love seat.

Upstairs are the small reception, the breakfast room and all the bedrooms. With the sensible exception of the corridor passing the bedrooms, all the floors are polished wood and the furniture and beds made of rose or cherry wood. The breakfast room manages to be cheerful and elegant at the same time, its two large windows flooding it with light. Breakfast itself is continental – including cereals, fruit and yoghurt – all very fresh and of high quality. The spotless bedrooms are of modest size, but not cramped. Some have little terraces looking over the internal courtyard. Bathrooms are modern, functional, immaculate and graced with good towels.

~

NEARBY Palazzo delle Stelline; Teatro alla Scala; duomo.
LOCATION in city centre, W of duomo; car parking outside
FOOD breakfast
PRICE €€
ROOMS 23 double and twin, 11 with bath, 12 with shower; all rooms have phone, TV, air conditioning, hairdrier, safe
FACILITIES sitting room, breakfast room, garden **CREDIT CARDS** AE, DC, MC, V
DISABLED not suitable **PETS** not accepted
CLOSED 3 weeks in Aug, late Dec to early Jan **PROPRIETOR** Mario Frefel

LOMBARDIA

MILAN

ANTICA LOCANDA DEI MERCANTI
~ TOWN HOTEL ~

Via San Tomaso 6, 20123 Milano
TEL 02 8054080 **FAX** 02 8054090
E-MAIL locanda@locanda.it **WEBSITE** www.locanda.it

IN A SMALL SIDE STREET OFF the Via Dante this is something of a 17thC treasure. No public rooms, no restaurant, no breakfast room; just three elegant floors of light, charming, meticulously decorated and maintained bedrooms of different shapes, sizes, types and, of course, prices. Those at the top end of the price scale have wonderful terraces equipped with chairs and tables and surrounded with lush plant life, but all the rooms have their own complement of fresh flowers.

Each room is decorated and furnished in a unique style, some with four-posters and some wrought-iron bedsteads and all with beautiful bedspreads and curtains set off by the (generally) pale pastels on the walls. Some of the walls are relieved by stencilled borders and others have details (like climbing roses) painted over the base colour. All are hung with good prints and watercolours. The bathrooms are small (showers only) but well appointed and, like everything else, immaculate. Everything possible is done to maintain peace and quiet: a television can come to your room if you really must have one, but not pets or small babies. Four of the rooms are air conditioned against the summer heat (the rest have fans) but if you come back here in winter you'll find feather duvets.

~

NEARBY Palazzo Clerici; Teatro alla Scala; *duomo*.
LOCATION in city centre, NW of *duomo*, between Piazzas Cordusio and Castello; public garage nearby
FOOD breakfast; snacks
PRICE €€
ROOMS 16 double and twin with shower; all rooms have phone, hairdrier; 4 rooms have air conditioning; TV on request
FACILITIES none **CREDIT CARDS** MC, V
DISABLED not suitable **PETS** not accepted **CLOSED** never
MANAGER Paola Ora

LOMBARDIA

MILAN

SPADARI AL DUOMO

~ TOWN HOTEL ~

Via Spadari 11, 20123 Milano
TEL 02 72002371 **FAX** 02 861184
E-MAIL reservation@spadarihotel.com **WEBSITE** www.spadarihotel.com

'HOTEL' MAY BE A SLIGHT MISNOMER for this chic, unusual establishment, just steps away from the Duomo. While it's true that you can stay here (very comfortably, too), you also share the space with the owners' family passion: contemporary art and design. This is not mere decoration but a substantial collection of works by both known and up-and-coming artists and sculptors. The blue-themed decoration has been chosen to show the pieces to their best advantage and even the design of the striking furniture was specially commissioned from Ugo La Pietra.

Downstairs the reception and sitting room, with the American Bar beyond it, introduce the collection. The focal point is the fireplace with a sculpture by Gio Pomodoro above it. Yet in the midst of all this elegant form there is also excellent function. Although the bedrooms are not large they are well laid out, fresh looking and in tip-top condition; each is recharged daily with fresh fruit and flowers. The top-quality carpets, curtains and bedspreads complement the pictures and eye-catching furniture, and the beautiful bathrooms, all done in blue and white, are immaculate. There is no restaurant but the friendly staff will whip you up a snack if your feet won't carry you another step that day.

~

NEARBY Galleria Vittorio Emanuele; *duomo.*
LOCATION in city centre, just SW of *duomo*; private garage
FOOD breakfast; snacks
PRICE €€€
ROOMS 39; 25 double, 10 twin, 3 single, 1 suite, 27 with bath, 12 with shower; all rooms have phone, TV, air conditioning, minibar, hairdrier, safe
FACILITIES sitting room, bar
CREDIT CARDS AE, DC, MC, V
DISABLED not suitable **PETS** not accepted
CLOSED Christmas **PROPRIETOR** Marida Martegani

LOMBARDIA

MONZA

HOTEL DE LA VILLE
~ TOWN HOTEL ~

Viale Regina Margherita 15, 20052 Monza, Milano
TEL 039 382581 **FAX** 039 367647
E-MAIL reservation@hoteldelaville.com **WEBSITE** www.hoteldelaville.com

WHEN YOU ARRIVE AT THE SLIGHTLY dreary exterior of this hotel, the former summer house of Savoy's royal family, your first thought may be that you have made a ghastly mistake. Actually you have done the opposite, because you are in for a delightful surprise. The atmosphere inside is one of opulent but understated elegance: vases of fresh flowers highlight the superb decoration, and throughout the hotel there is a never-ending succession of rare objects collected by Tany Nardi, the owner, for whom perfection is obviously a passion. The corridors are dotted with things like silver trays of little crystal glasses or pieces of perfectly preserved antique luggage. Good Persian rugs, antique furniture, pots, plants, gilt-framed pictures and polished marble are lit subtly and gently to persuade you to leave the cares of the world at the front door.

The bedrooms are beautifully furnished, decorated and appointed, the bathrooms perfect, and they are maintained by flawless housekeeping. Less than a minute away from the main hotel is a new annexe, opened on the first Valentine's day of the new century.

~

NEARBY Villa Reale; *duomo*; Milan (15 km).
LOCATION in city centre, in front of Villa Reale; car parking
FOOD breakfast, lunch, dinner
PRICE €€€
ROOMS 62; 21 double and twin, 8 with bath, 13 with shower, 39 single, 2 suites, all with shower; all rooms have phone, TV, air conditioning, minibar, hairdrier, safe
FACILITIES restaurant, bar, meeting rooms, sauna (for annexe only)
CREDIT CARDS AE, DC, MC, V
DISABLED 1 specially adapted room
PETS not accepted
CLOSED Aug, Christmas
PROPRIETORS Nardi family

LOMBARDIA

RANCO

SOLE

～ RESTAURANT WITH ROOMS ～

Piazza Venezia 5, 21020 Ranco, Varese
TEL 0331 976507 **FAX** 0331 976620
E-MAIL ivanett@tin.it **WEBSITE** www.relaischateaux.fr

TWO MICHELIN STARS EXERT quite an attraction over foodies as they offer a substantial degree of certainty. But, as you enter the Sole's light and airy foyer, you can't be sure whether you'll be met by the fifth or the sixth generation of the Brovelli family as Davide has joined his father Carlo in this long-lived family business overlooking Lake Maggiore. Either way you will instantly realize that they have avoided the demon of self-importance which so often follows in the trail of culinary honours. This is an inviting, friendly place where they have combined a superb restaurant, a splendid view of the lake and truly delightful rooms to stay in, and a pool is in the pipeline for 2002.

To add to the expectations aroused by two stars you should know that ,despite the sophistication of their menu, the Brovellis are loyal to their region and feature many local delicacies. Except in poor weather, when they retreat into what is normally the breakfast room, the dining tables are set on the lovely terrace beneath a pergola. The bedrooms are a treat, decorated in sophisticated country style with ankle-deep pile carpets and colour co-ordinated curtains, bedspreads and paintwork. The bathrooms are worthy of stars of their own, sparkling white with big tubs, bigger towels and stacked with high-quality 'freebies'.

～

NEARBY Lakes Lugano and Como; Milan (67 km).
LOCATION on E side of Lake Maggiore, N of Angera; car parking
FOOD breakfast, lunch, dinner
PRICE €€-€€€€
ROOMS 16; 3 double, 1 twin, 3 single, 9 suites, all with bath; all rooms have phone, TV, air-conditioning, minibar, hairdrier, safe
FACILITIES restaurant, breakfast room, garden
CREDIT CARDS AE, DC, MC, V
DISABLED 1 specially adapted room **PETS** small dogs accepted
CLOSED Jan to mid-Feb **PROPRIETORS** Brovelli family

LOMBARDIA

SAN FEDELE D'INTELVI

VILLA SIMPLICITAS
~ COUNTRY VILLA ~

22010 San Fedele d'Intelvi, Como
TEL 031 831132/02 4989158 **FAX** 031 830455/02 460407

As you get further from the A9 two things happen: the roads get smaller, and your blood pressure starts a delicious slide down towards normality. The final 2 km to Simplicitas are up a roughish mountain road, but when you finally reach this utterly unpretentious 19thC villa, just switch off your engine, open the door and listen to the glorious sound of absolutely nothing at all. This is a much-loved, lived-in house, filled with 19thC bits and pieces (including a magnificent billiards table) and with an air of rustic gentility. Meals, taken on the terrace in fine weather, usually feature produce from the surrounding 80-hectare farm amongst their two or three choices per course, and there is a good selection of wines.

The bedrooms (some small), most with lovely views, are like comfortable guest bedrooms in a private house: the dressing tables have bowls of pot pourri on them, one has a rocking chair in a corner and there is a liberal scattering of knick-knacks everywhere. With the exception of electric light, the 20thC hasn't made much of an impression. There is a television, but it isn't always working. Once your energy levels are restored you can walk, ride, play tennis or go for a round of golf nearby.

~

NEARBY Lakes Como, Lugano and Maggiore; Como (20 km).
LOCATION 2 km up mountain from San Fedele d'Intelvi; car parking
FOOD breakfast, lunch, dinner
PRICE €
ROOMS 10; 8 double, 2 twin, all with shower; all rooms have phone
FACILITIES restaurant, sitting room, billiards room, garden, table tennis
CREDIT CARDS AE, DC, MC, V
DISABLED not suitable
PETS accepted
CLOSED mid-Oct to Mar
PROPRIETOR Ulla Wagner Hohenlobbasa

LOMBARDIA

SIRMIONE

GRIFONE

~ LAKESIDE RESTAURANT WITH ROOMS ~

Vicolo Bisse (Via Bocchio) 5, 25019 Sirmione, Brescia
TEL 030 916014 **FAX** 030 916548

ALTHOUGH THE GRIFONE IS ONE of the cheapest and simplest hotels in this guide, it also has one of the loveliest locations, and makes a great place to stay for a night or two. Essentially it is a restaurant specializing in fish, with a mouth-watering selection of *antipasto* to start. It has an enticing tree-filled terrace overlooking both Lake Garda and the ramparts of Sirmione's castle; also a tiny sandy beach.

The entrance to the hotel is found off a narrow street just inside the city walls. A small sitting room equipped with television and cheerful bamboo furniture leads to a little patio where breakfast is served, and, if the water beckons, on to the scrap of beach. Upstairs, rooms are simple, furniture is basic, but everything is spotless. Some rooms look right over the castle walls, and the five balconies are full of flowers. Those on the top floor enjoy the best views: rooftops, mountains, and of course the lake. There is no traffic noise in this pedestrian zone, but you may be woken by church bells. The younger generation of the Marcolini family – brother and sister – who now run the Grifone are friendly and helpful.

~

NEARBY Lake Garda; Brescia (39 km); Verona (35 km).
LOCATION just inside city walls, next to castle, on lake; car parking (50 m)
FOOD breakfast, lunch, dinner
PRICE €
ROOMS 16; 12 double, twin and triple, 4 with bath, 8 with shower, 4 single with shower
FACILITIES sitting room, dining room, lift, terraces, tiny beach
CREDIT CARDS not accepted
DISABLED access difficult except to restaurant
PETS not accepted
CLOSED Nov to Easter
PROPRIETORS Marcolini family

LOMBARDIA

GARGNANO

BAIA D'ORO
LAKESIDE HOTEL

Via Gamberera 13, 25084
Gargnano, Brescia

TEL 0365 71171/72078 **FAX** 0365
72568
FOOD breakfast, lunch, dinner
PRICE €€
CLOSED mid-Nov to mid-Mar
Terzi family

GIAMBATTISTA TERZI WAS BORN in one of a pair of neighbouring fishermen's cottages built on the edge of the lake in 1780, and his wife was the moving force behind turning them into a hotel in the 1960s. Since then the facilities have slowly been updated. To appreciate the fabulous setting, you should arrive by boat. You can almost dip your hand in the lake from the romantic dining terrace, a splendid vantage point from which to watch night succeed day. The Terzis have gradually redecorated the bedrooms in slightly dubious shades of pink and blue, with painted wooden furniture, shiny fabrics and mirrored glass bedheads. Not to everyone's taste, but they are comfortable.

GARGNANO

VILLA GIULIA
LAKESIDE VILLA

Via Rimembranza 20, 25084
Gargnano, Brescia

TEL 0365 71022/71289 **FAX** 0365
72774
E-MAIL hvgiulia@gardanet.it
WEBSITE www.villagiulia.it
FOOD breakfast, lunch, dinner
PRICE €€
CLOSED mid-Oct to one week
before Easter
Bombardelli family

FROM A *PENSIONE* WITH NO private bathrooms, the Giulia has been upgraded over the years to a three-star hotel, with the renovation of existing rooms and the creation of new suites. It is a beautiful late-19thC Victorian villa with Gothic touches, which is still family run: Rina Bombardelli has been here for almost five decades. It has a glorious location, with gardens of lawns, palm trees and oleanders, running down to a low wall at the water's edge. Inside, airy rooms lead off handsome corridors: a beautiful dining room with Murano chandeliers, gold walls and elegant seats; a civilized sitting room; and refurbished bedrooms in a variety of styles: some light and modern, others large, with rafters, antiques and balconies.

LOMBARDIA

MILAN

PIERRE MILANO

TOWN HOTEL

Via de Amicis 32, 20123 Milano

TEL 02 72000581 **FAX** 02 8052157
E-MAIL info@hotelpierremilano.it
WEBSITE www.hotelpierremilano.it
FOOD breakfast, dinner
PRICE €€€
CLOSED 3 weeks Aug, late Dec to
early Jan
MANAGER Paola Piccina

REMEMBER THE OLD HOTEL TORINO? Well you wouldn't recognize it now. The Pierre Milano might be in Milan but you wouldn't be surprised to find a twin brother in central Manhattan. Marble, steel and wood, all polished to a high sheen, greet you and show you the way past the plush carpeted lounge area with sofas, coffee tables and muted lighting, to the reception desk and then onwards into the sparkling glass-roofed piano bar and beyond to the restaurant.

The well-appointed bedrooms are similar in style, quite modest in size (as are their bathrooms), and have succumbed to fitted rather than free-standing furniture. If you need more space, there are seven suites.

POMPONESCO

IL LEONE

RESTAURANT-WITH-ROOMS

*Piazza IV Mortiri, 46030
Pomponesco, Mantova*

TEL 0375 86077/86145 **FAX** 0375
86770 **FOOD** breakfast, dinner
PRICE € **CLOSED** Jan. restaurant
Sun eve and Mon **PROPRIETOR**
Signor Pasolini

POMPONESCO WAS ONCE a flourishing town under the Gonzaga family, and the old part still has faded charm. The Leone lies just off the main *piazza* - a peeling old building once the home of a 16thC nobleman. It is primarily an eating place. There are only seven bedrooms, and by far the most attractive features are the dining areas - the main restaurant has a coffered 16thC ceiling and frieze. Elsewhere, decoration is suitably elegant. The food is among the best in the region, with some unusual combinations of flavour. Beyond the restaurant a courtyard leads to the bedrooms, built around an inviting pool and garden area. They are starkly modern, but comfortable and well maintained.

The North-East

Hotels in the North-East

T HE REMARKABLE CITY OF VENICE, famed throughout the world for its incomparable beauty, artistic wealth and sheer originality is the focal point of this region. A feast of small hotels are described in the following pages, distilled from our in-depth regional guide, *The Charming Small Hotel Guide to Venice and North-East Italy*. Room prices in Venice are undeniably steep, but if you choose carefully, and secure a canal or lagoon view, you will discover some memorable places in which to stay.

An alternative to staying in Venice itself is to base yourself somewhere on the vast Veneto Plain that fans out from Venice to the foothills of the Dolomites. Here are the great cities of Padua, Treviso, Vicenza and Verona, the villas of Palladio and other attractions, such as the charming little hill towns of Asolo and Follina. You will find some excellent bases from which to explore Venice and the Veneto in these pages. We have recomended two hotels in Verona; in Treviso you could try the Alle Beccherie/Campeol (tel 0422 540871), a traditional restaurant with rooms across the street, and in Padua the Leon Bianco (tel 049 8750814). We cannot find a suitable hotel in Vicenza, but you could try the Villa Michelangelo 7 km away (tel 0444 550300).

The province of Veneto takes in the eastern shores of Lake Garda, where we also have some recommendations. Other hotels on Lake Garda can be found in the Lombardia section of this book. To the east, the Venetian Plain edges into the province of Friuli-Venezia Giulia, where we recommend a couple of places in the south. The north of the province, where it rises to the Carnic Alps with meadows and pine forests, is empty of hotels of our sort, and indeed short on any hotels at all, being little visited by tourists.

Far more popular as a mountainous destination is the province of Trentino-Alto Adige, only a couple of hours' drive but a world away from Venice and its great plain. It feels like Austria, has a special autonomous statute and is largely German-speaking. Owners and staff of the Alpine hotels you will find in its mountains may not even speak Italian... you are more likely to be greeted in German. Place names are extremely confusing, as each town and village, mountain and valley has both an Italian and German name. We have given the Italian translation. Hotels are often Tyrolean chalets, with wooden furniture, ceramic stoves, traditional fabrics; the food too, is mainly Austrian, at least on the simpler menus, while the more sophisticated hotels serve creative variations on the theme. The scenery amongst the Dolomites is beautiful, and there are plenty of activities to pursue both in winter and summer.

THE NORTH-EAST

ASOLO

AL SOLE

~ TOWN HOTEL ~

Via Collegio 33, 31011 Asolo, Treviso
TEL 0423 528111 **FAX** 0423 528399
E-MAIL albergoalsole@sevenonline.it **WEBSITE** www.albergoalsole.com

FROM A GLORIOUS POSITION, perched above the Piazza Maggiore on the steep hill up to the massive fortress, the Rocca, this albergo has a splendid view of the medieval town with its higgledy-piggledy streets. Its deep pink façade is original and appealing, while the trendy interior – hallmark of the dynamic young owner Silvia de Checchi – affords a dramatic contrast.

Almost every room has white rough-cast walls and mellow wood floors, enlivened by daring colour combinations for fabrics and furniture. Although the look is mainly cool and modern, a few antiques and the occasional bowl and pitcher hark back to the past. Recalling former stars in Asolo's firmament, such as 'Eleanor Duse' and 'Gabriele d'Annunzio', the bedrooms are all different; the former has light painted furniture, the latter, ornate church-style pieces. Some rooms have huge claw-foot baths; some have massage showers, just one of the many four-star comforts. Perhaps the ultimate of these is the state-of-the-art downstairs lavatory, which electronically flushes, lifts and then replaces the seat, complete with hygenic paper cover, at the appropriate times. A small fitness centre has recently been added.

~

NEARBY Palladian villas; Possagno (10 km).
LOCATION at the top of Piazza Maggiore; private car park
FOOD breakfast
PRICE €€-€€€€
ROOMS 23; 14 double and twin, 2 with bath, 12 with shower, 8 single, 2 with bath, 6 with shower, 1 suite with bath; all rooms have phone, TV, air conditioning, minibar, hairdrier, safe
FACILITIES breakfast room, sitting room, sitting area, bar, fitness centre, lift, terrace
CREDIT CARDS AE, MC, V
DISABLED 2 specially adapted rooms **PETS** accepted **CLOSED** never
PROPRIETOR Silvia de Checchi

THE NORTH-EAST

VILLA CIPRIANI
~ COUNTRY VILLA ~

Via Canova 298, 31011 Asolo, Treviso
TEL 0423 952166 **FAX** 0423 952095
E-MAIL res032.villacipriani@sheraton.com **WEBSITE** www.sheraton.com/villacipriani

A SOLO IS A BEAUTIFUL MEDIEVAL hilltop village commanding panoramic views, a jewel of the Veneto. The Villa Cipriani, a jewel of the huge ITT Sheraton Group, is a mellow ochre-washed house on the fringes of the village, its deceptively plain entrance leading into a warm reception area which immediately imparts the feeling of a hotel with a heart (and a house with a past: it was once the home of Robert Browning). Today it is graced by the prettiest of rose-and flower-filled gardens, and meals are served on the terrace or in the restaurant overhanging the valley. As for the gracious and comfortable bedrooms, make sure you ask for one with a view, and try for an 'exclusive' rather than a 'superior' double. The latter are not particularly spacious, while the former include a sitting area; two rooms have terraces.

Villa Cipriani is a relaxing country hotel, whose views, comfort, peaceful garden and good food make it particularly alluring. However, some reports complain of prices that were hard to justify, also mentioning intrusive wedding parties and brash clientele. Others have been full of praise.

NEARBY Palladian villas; Possagno (10 km).
LOCATION on NW side of village; with garage parking
FOOD breakfast, lunch, dinner; room service
PRICE €€€-€€€€
ROOMS 31; 29 double and twin, 2 single, all with bath; all rooms have phone, TV, air conditioning, minibar, hairdrier
FACILITIES sitting room, dining rooms, bar, meeting room, lift, terrace, garden
CREDIT CARDS AE, DC, MC, V
DISABLED access difficult
PETS accepted **CLOSED** never
MANAGER Gianpaolo Burattin

THE NORTH-EAST

BANNIA DI FIUME VENETO

L'ULTIMO MULINO

<small>~ CONVERTED MILL ~</small>

Via Mulino 45, 33080 Bannia di Fiume Veneto, Pordenone
TEL 0434 957911 **FAX** 0434 958483
E-MAIL fllonder@tin.it **WEBSITE** www.centroweb.com/hotel

AS THE NAME SUGGESTS, this 17thC building is one of the very last function-ing mills in the area. In use until the 1970s, the three old wooden wheels are still in working condition; indeed, they are set in motion in the evenings for the benefit of guests. The lovely stone house and garden are set in gentle farmland and surrounded by three rivers; the soothing sounds of water are everywhere.

Opened as a hotel in 1994, restoration work has been carried out with great taste and flair, preserving as much as possible of the original charac-ter of the house. The long, open-plan sitting room and bar area have even incorporated the hefty innards of the mill machinery. Throughout, attrac-tive Laura Ashley fabrics are teamed with handsome antique furniture, rustic stone and woodwork, and soft, elegant lighting. The comfortable and stylish bedrooms, while different in layout, are all along similar lines with wooden fittings and pale green and cream country fabrics. Those on the second floor have attic ceilings and some have squashy sofas. The sparkling, well-equipped bathrooms are in pale grey marble.

~

NEARBY Pordenone (10 km); Venice (80 km); Trieste (80 km).
LOCATION 10 km SE of Pordenone, exit from A28 at Azzano Decimo; in own garden with parking
FOOD breakfast, dinner
PRICE €€
ROOMS 8 double and twin, 4 with bath, 4 with shower; all rooms have phone, TV, air conditioning, minibar, hairdrier
FACILITIES breakfast room, sitting rooms, dining rooms, bar, music/conference room, garden, terrace
CREDIT CARDS AE, DC, MC, V
DISABLED no special facilities **PETS** accepted **CLOSED** 10 days Jan, Aug
PROPRIETORS Balestrieri family

THE NORTH-EAST

BARBIANO

BAD DREIKIRCHEN
～ MOUNTAIN HOTEL ～

San Giacomo 6, 39040 Barbiano, Bolzano
TEL 0471 650055 **FAX** 0471 650044
E-MAIL wodenegg.matthias@rolmail.ne

THE NAME OF THIS IDYLLICALLY situated hotel derives from its vicinity to the cluster of three small churches which date back to the Middle Ages. The fact that you can only reach the hotel by four-wheel-drive taxi, makes for a perfect escape.

The large old building, with its shingled roof and dark wood balconies, has wonderful views and is surrounded by meadows, woods, mountains and quantities of fresh air. There's plenty of space for guests, both inside and out, and the atmosphere is comfortably rustic with an abundance of aromatic pine panelling and carved furniture. A cosy library provides a quiet corner for reading, and simple but satisfying meals are served in the pleasant dining room or on the adjacent veranda, from which the views are superb. Bedrooms in the original part of the house are particularly charming, being entirely wood-panelled.

To sum up, the words of a guest at Bad Dreikirchen in 1908 are still appropriate: 'I stayed for some days ... the weather was continually fine, the position magnificent, and the food good.' A recent guest warmly concurs. 'I fell in love with the place. Delightfully relaxed atmosphere, charming young owners.'

NEARBY Bressanone (17 km); Val Gardena (10 km).
LOCATION 21 km NE of Bolzano, exit from Brennero Autostrada at Chiusa, head S through Barbiano (6 km); hotel car park on right (call and the hotel will send a jeep to collect you from car park)
FOOD breakfast, lunch, dinner
PRICE ⓔ (half board obligatory)
ROOMS 30; 12 double and twin, 15 single, 3 family, most with shower
FACILITIES sitting rooms, bar, restaurant, games room, library, garden, terraces, swimming pool, table tennis, tennis court (1 km)
CREDIT CARDS MC, V **DISABLED** access difficult **PETS** accepted
CLOSED Nov to mid-May
PROPRIETORS Wodenegg family

THE NORTH-EAST

BRESSANONE

ELEPHANT

～ TOWN HOTEL ～

Via Rio Bianco 4, 39042 Bressanone, Bolzano
TEL 0472 832750 **FAX** 0472 836579
E-MAIL elephant.brixen@acs.it **WEBSITE** www.acs.it/elephant

BRESSANONE IS A PRETTY TOWN at the foot of the Brenner Pass, more Austrian than Italian in character. The same is true of the charming Elephant, named after a beast which was led over the Alps for Emperor Ferdinand of Austria's amusement. The only stable big enough for the exhausted animal was next to the inn, so the innkeeper promptly changed its name to celebrate the event.

There is an air of solid, old-fashioned comfort throughout. Corridors decorated in sumptuous colours are lined with heavily carved and beautifully inlaid antiques. The public rooms are all on the first floor: an elegant 18thC-style sitting room, a large light breakfast room, and three dining rooms. The main one is panelled in dark wood with a vast green ceramic stove and stags' heads on the walls. The food is one of the highlights of a stay here. A reporter commented: 'We had a fabulous dinner; the cooking is imaginative but unfussy with lots of fresh herbs and local ingredients, beautifully presented and bountiful.' Bedrooms are large and comfortable, but disappointing compared with the more characterful public areas. Some have antiques, others have none.

～

NEARBY cathedral; Novacella monastery (3 km).
LOCATION at N end of town; in gardens with car parking and garages
FOOD breakfast, lunch, dinner
PRICE €€
ROOMS 44; 28 double and twin, all with bath, 16 single, 15 with bath, 1 with shower; all rooms have phone, TV, hairdrier
FACILITIES breakfast room, sitting room, bar, dining rooms, garden, swimming pool, tennis courts
CREDIT CARDS AE, DC, MC, V
DISABLED 2 ground-floor rooms in annexe
PETS accepted **CLOSED** Nov to Christmas, Jan to Mar
PROPRIETOR Elizabeth Falk

THE NORTH-EAST

CALDARO

LEUCHTENBURG
~ COUNTRY GUESTHOUSE ~

Campo di Lago 100, 39052 Caldaro, Bolzano
TEL 0471 960093/960048 **FAX** 0471 960155 **E-MAIL** pensionleuchtenburg@
kalterersee.com **WEBSITE** alterersee.com/pensionleuchtenburg

THIS SOLID STONE-BUILT 16thC hostel once housed the servants of
Leuchtenburg castle, an arduous hour's trek up the steep wooded
mountain behind. Today, guests in the *pension* are well cared for by the
friendly young owners, while the castle lies in ruins. The setting is envi-
ably tranquil, right on Lago di Caldaro, better known (at least to wine
buffs) as Kalterer See. Cross a road and you are at the water's edge, where
a little private beach is dotted with umbrellas and sunloungers.

Back in the *pension*, the Sparers provide solid breakfasts and three-
course dinners of regional cuisine in an unpretentious, homely atmosphere. White-painted low-arched dining rooms occupy the ground floor;
above is the reception, with a large table littered with magazines and surrounded by armchairs. There is another sitting area on the first floor, leading to the bedrooms. These have pretty painted furniture and tiled floors
(second-floor rooms are plainer). Each one tells a story: for example, the
'old smoke room' was where food was smoked. All are large, and some
share the views enjoyed from the terrace across vineyards to the lake.

~

NEARBY swimming and fishing in lake.
LOCATION 5 km SE of Caldaro, on the edge of the lake; in courtyard with car parking
FOOD breakfast, dinner
PRICE €
ROOMS 19; 15 double and twin, 3 with bath, 12 with shower, 2 single, 2 triple, all
with shower; rooms have TV (on request)
FACILITIES sitting area, dining area, bar, terrace, beach **CREDIT CARDS** MC, V
DISABLED not suitable **PETS** accepted
CLOSED Nov to Easter
PROPRIETOR Markus Sparer

THE NORTH-EAST

CORTINA D'AMPEZZO

MONTANA

~ TOWN HOTEL ~

Corso Italia 94, 32043 Cortina d'Ampezzo, Belluno
TEL 0436 862126 **FAX** 0436 868211
WEBSITE www.venere.it/veneto/cortina/montana/

THIS SMALL, FRIENDLY HOTEL is situated in a pedestrian precinct in the centre of Cortina d'Ampezzo, 1,224 metres above sea level and surrounded by mountain scenery. It is just a few minutes' walk from the Faloria cable car, which makes it a popular choice with skiiers between December and the end of April, so booking in advance is essential.

The Montana is owned and run with great enthusiasm by Adriano Lorenzi, whose passion for art manifests itself in the numerous original paintings he has collected and which decorate the hotel. The bedrooms are rustic in style, with pine floors and ceilings, some with flower-bedecked balconies overlooking the village and mountains. All have immaculate en suite bathrooms. A buffet breakfast with home-made jam is served in a dining area with pretty, red, flower-print tablecloths, or in the bedrooms at a small extra charge.

Cortina is a popular upmarket resort – as well as skiing there is also a bobsleigh run, a ski jump, skating and curling. In summer the mild climate makes it an ideal location for walking, fishing, rock climbing and tennis.

~

NEARBY Faloria lift station; ice stadium; the Dolomites.
LOCATION in pedestrian precinct in centre of Cortina d'Ampezzo; private car park
FOOD breakfast
PRICE €€
ROOMS 30; 15 double, 15 single; all with bath or shower; all rooms have phone, TV, safe
FACILITIES breakfast room, TV room
CREDIT CARDS AE, DC, MC, V
DISABLED not suitable
PETS accepted
CLOSED Jun and Nov
PROPRIETOR Adriano Lorenzi

THE NORTH-EAST

TURM

~ MOUNTAIN VILLAGE HOTEL ~

Piazza della Chiesa 9, 39050 Fié allo Sciliar, Bolzano
TEL 0471 725014 **FAX** 0471 725474
E-MAIL turmwirt@cenida.it **WEBSITE** www.romantikhotels.com/rhvoels

A SOLID FORMER COURTHOUSE dating from the 12th century, with views across pastures and mountains, Hotel Turm offers typical Tyrolean hospitality with style and warmth. Bedrooms are all different and vary considerably in size, but even the smallest has everything you could want for a comfortable stay, including traditional furniture and somewhere cosy to sit. Our inspector's little room was enlivened by a charming group of naive paintings; another has a working ceramic stove, another a huge pine four-poster. The mini-apartments in particular are excellent value: one, in a little stone tower, is done as a wood-panelled *stübe*, with spiral staircase to a double room and a children's room. The Pramstrahler family's fine collection of contemporary art is displayed in every room and spills out along the whitewashed corridor walls.

The main dining room is light and spacious, with low wood ceiling and windows overlooking the valley; or you can dine in a romantic little room with heavy cast-iron door at the base of the 11thC tower. Either way, the elegantly presented food, cooked by Stefan Pramstrahler, who trained in France, is superb.

~

NEARBY Val Gardena; Bolzano (16 km); Castelrotto (10 km).
LOCATION in village, 16 km E of Bolzano; with garden and limited car parking
FOOD breakfast, lunch, dinner; room service
PRICE ⓔⓔ
ROOMS 25 double and twin, 1 single; all with bath or shower; 5 apartments with kitchen, all rooms have phone, TV, minibar, hairdrier, safe
FACILITIES sitting room, dining rooms, bar, lift, garden, sauna, indoor and outdoor swimming pools
CREDIT CARDS MC, V **DISABLED** access possible
PETS accepted **CLOSED** Nov to mid-Dec
PROPRIETOR Karl Pramstrahler

THE NORTH-EAST

FINALE

VILLA SARACENO

~ SELF-CATERING VILLA ~

For all information and booking contact: *The Landmark Trust, Shottesbrooke, Maidenhead, Berkshire SL6 3SW, England* **TEL** 01626 825 925 **FAX** 01628 825417
E-MAIL booking@landmarktrust.co.uk **WEBSITE** www.landmarktrust.co.uk

Highlights of the Veneto are the villas built by the great Renaissance architect Andrea Palladio. If you would like to stay in one, here is your chance. Villa Saraceno, on a plain to the west of the Euganean Hills, is owned by the Landmark Trust, a British organization which acquires and restores buildings of historic interest and then lets them to holidaymakers.

Designed in the mid-16thC as a country retreat as well as a working farm for a well-to-do Vicenzan, Biagio Saraceno, the complex consists of the airy, beautifully proportioned main house as well as other earlier buildings, including the simple Casa Vecchia, in which most of the bedrooms are located. The interior of the Palladian house has been restored to recreate iits original arrangement - a grand sala with two-room apartments opening off it, and huge granaries above. Dim frescoed friezes have been cleaned to reveal scenes of high drama, probably painted for Biagio's son. Saraceno can accommodate up to 16 people. One recent tenant wrote to the Landmark Trust: 'a perfect balance between the elegant understatement of the Palladian building and modern-day comforts ...'.

~

NEARBY Montagnana (14 km); Vicenza (32 km).
LOCATION in village 32 km S of Vicenza, 12 km N of SS10 between Este and Montagnana
FOOD none
PRICE on application; weekly lets only in high season, shorter stays available at other times
ROOMS accommodates up to 16 in 2 double, 3 twin, 2 single, one family room; 5 bathrooms
FACILITIES kitchen with dishwasher and washing machine, sitting room, dining room, garden, swimming pool **CREDIT CARDS** MC, V
DISABLED access difficult **PETS** accepted
CLOSED never
PROPRIETORS Landmark Trust

THE NORTH-EAST

FOLLINA

ABBAZIA
~ TOWN HOTEL ~

Via Martiri della Libertà, 31051 Follina, Treviso
TEL 0438 971277 **FAX** 0438 970001
E-MAIL info@hotelabbazia.it **WEBSITE** www.hotelabbazia.it

THE HOTEL CONSISTS of two buildings: a 17thC *palazzo* and, adjacent, an enchanting little art nouveau villa. Standards of decoration and comfort in both are exceptionally high – rarely have we met hoteliers (brother and sister) more keen to please their guests. If you find the lobby and balconied breakfast area a bit much – a sugary pink confection of candy-striped walls strewn with roses, draped tables and floral china – you will not be disappointed by the bedrooms. Each one is individually decorated, and all are delightful: sophisticated and very feminine in English style, full of thoughtful touches. Three rooms have private balconies, at no extra cost. Best of all is the villa with its pillared portico, carved flourishes on its four façades and sweeping staircase. The hotel now has its own restaurant, beautifully decorated with stone walls and pillars and an enchanting mural depicting the highlights of the region as seen from a balcony.

The owners have prepared a helpful list of local information, including routes you can follow on the hotel's bicycles. There are two good restaurants nearby: Da Lino in Solighetto and Da Gigetto in Miane (be sure to visit the wine cellars).

~

NEARBY 11thC abbey; Palladian villas; Asolo (20 km).
LOCATION in town centre, facing the abbey; car parking
FOOD breakfast, lunch, dinner; room service
PRICE €€€
ROOMS 24; 16 double and twin, 1 single, 7 suites, all with shower, bath or Jacuzzi; all rooms have phone, TV, hairdrier; 12 have air conditioning and safe
FACILITIES breakfast room, sitting room, dining room, tea room, terrace, garden
CREDIT CARDS AE, DC, MC, V
DISABLED not suitable
PETS not accepted **CLOSED** never
PROPRIETORS Giovanni and Ivana Zanon

THE NORTH-EAST

GARGAGNAGO

FORESTERIA SEREGO ALIGHIERI

~ COUNTRY VILLA APARTMENTS ~

37020 Gargagnago di Valpolicella, Verona
TEL 045 7703622 **FAX** 045 7703523
E-MAIL serego@easynet.it **WEBSITE** www.seregoalighieri.it

IN 1353, THE SON OF DANTE, who had been exiled in Verona, bought Casal dei Ronchi, and there his direct descendants have lived ever since. Today, overseen by Count Pieralvise Serègo Alighieri, the estate is a prosperous producer of Valpolicella wines (much improved in recent years and shaking off their 'cheap and nasty' reputation) as well as olive oil, balsamic vinegar, honey, jams and rice. The family home is a lovely yellow ochre building fronted by formal gardens which overlook the vineyards. Beyond are the former stables, now beautifully converted to make eight apartments, simple yet sophisticated, sleeping two to four people. In each one you find a gleaming chrome kitchen, country furniture, soothing green cotton fabrics, white walls, marble bathrooms. No. 8 spirals up a slim tower: minute sitting room, stairs to a minute kitchen, more stairs to the bedroom. Open a door in the bedhead and there's a tiny window behind. No. 1 is the most spacious, with dining table and elegant chairs. Breakfast is served in a room decorated with old family photographs on the ground floor. Dinner can be arranged for eight people or more. There are some good restaurants nearby.

~

NEARBY Verona (18 km); Lake Garda (14 km).
LOCATION signposted off the road from Pedemonte to San Ambrogio, 18 km NE of Verona; in own extensive grounds with ample car parking
FOOD breakfast
PRICE apartment sleeping 2-4 people €€ per night; weekly rates available
ROOMS 8 apartments for 2, 3 or 4 people, each with kitchen, bathroom with shower, phone, TV, air conditioning
FACILITIES reception, breakfast room, terrace meeting room, estate produce shop
CREDIT CARDS AE, MC, V
DISABLED not suitable
PETS accepted **CLOSED** Jan
PROPRIETOR Conte Pieralvise Serègo Alighieri

THE NORTH-EAST

DER PÜNTHOF
~ COUNTRY HOTEL ~

Via Steinach 25, 39022 Lagundo, Bolzano
TEL 0473 448553 **FAX** 0473 449919

VIA CLAUDIO AUGUSTO, a Roman road to Germany, passed what is now the entrance to Der Pünthof, and the watchtower built to guard the road forms an integral part of the hotel. The main building was a medieval farmhouse and has been in the Wolf family since the 17th century. They opened it as a hotel 40 years ago, housing guests in the barn, but over the decades other buildings have been added. Although Lagundo is a rather dreary suburb of Merano, once inside the hotel's electronic barrier you could be miles from anywhere with only orchards, vineyards and stunning scenery in view.

The public rooms are in the old building: breakfast is served in a pale green *stübe* with wooden floor, low ceiling, ceramic stove and traces of the original decoration on the panelled walls. Bedrooms in the barn are modern and comfortable, but uniform, though some have private terraces on to the garden. The most appealing are the rooms in the square tower. One has polished floorboards, a wood ceiling and antique bed. There are five well-equipped self-catering chalets, and six simpler cheaper rooms in another annexe.

~

NEARBY Bolzano (28 km); Brennero (70 km); the Dolomites.
LOCATION 3 km NW of Merano, outside village; in own grounds with ample car parking
FOOD breakfast, dinner
PRICE €
ROOMS 12 double and twin, 2 with bath, 10 with shower; all rooms have phone, TV, minibar, safe
FACILITIES 2 breakfast rooms, sitting room, bar, restaurant, sauna, solarium, garden, tennis courts, swimming pool **CREDIT CARDS** AE, DC, MC, V
DISABLED 1 room on ground floor
PETS accepted **CLOSED** Nov to mid-Mar
PROPRIETORS Wolf family

THE NORTH-EAST

LEVADA

GARGAN

~ COUNTRY GUESTHOUSE ~

Via Marco Polo 2, Levada di Piombino Dese, Padova
TEL 049 9350308 **FAX** 049 9350016
E-MAIL agargan@tin.it **WEBSITE** www.gargan.it

THE SETTING IS RURAL, on a working farm, and the farmhouse is typical – attractive enough, but not especially prepossessing. A donkey brays in the garden. We walked in quite unprepared for the level of sophistication of this *agriturismo;* it's in a league of its own. The ground floor comprises a hallway with cool white walls and beams painted pale green, plus five interconnecting dining rooms. Furnished only with antiques, these rooms have delicate lace curtains, timbered ceilings, and an array of pictures on their white walls. Our visit coincided with Sunday lunch, and every table was immaculately laid with a white cloth, fine china and gleaming silver; an open fire crackled in the hearth.

The ingredients used in the delicious dinners are mainly produced on the farm. Signora Calzavara is in charge of the cooking and provides a full American breakfast and other meals when required.

The six bedrooms are enchanting. Floors are strewn with rugs; most have wrought-iron bedheads and fine walnut furniture. It's best to book by fax unless you speak Italian.

~

NEARBY Palladian villas; Venice (20 km); Padua (26 km).
LOCATION 20 km N of Venice, in Levada take Via G. Carducci opposite the church and turn left into Via Marco Polo; in own garden with car parking
FOOD breakfast, lunch, dinner
PRICE €
ROOMS 6; 4 double and twin, 2 family rooms, all with shower; all rooms have TV
FACILITIES dining rooms, sitting area, garden
CREDIT CARDS not accepted
DISABLED access difficult
PETS not accepted
CLOSED Jan, Aug
PROPRIETORS Calzavara family

THE NORTH-EAST

MERANO

VILLA TIVOLI

~ EDGE-OF-TOWN HOTEL ~

Via Verde 72, 39012 Merano, Bolzano
TEL 0473 446282 **FAX** 0473 446849
E-MAIL info@villativoli.it **WEBSITE** www.villativoli.it

ALMOST IN COUNTRYSIDE, standing in apple orchards, the pale yellow villa is surrounded by an 'exquisite' terraced garden filled with over 2,000 different plants. Inside all is cool and chic, spacious and light, yet not intimidating. The ground floor is open-plan, with a glass-walled dining room; over the bar an extraordinary contemporary fresco of many-breasted Artemis, a recurring theme in the hotel. Another corner holds a sitting area, elegantly furnished with antiques and there is a traditional wood-panelled Tyrolean *stübe*. Outside, a terrace with tables shaded by yellow umbrellas, and in the basement, a pool room with gaily painted walls. Bedrooms are all different, all comfortable, with south-facing balconies. Some are huge, with separate sitting areas; some are furnished with antiques, others are very contemporary. Bathrooms are large, with double basins. Our reporter was hooked: 'Smart but relaxed; staff warm and welcoming, owners genuinely friendly and aiming to please; mountainous breakfast buffet, designed to see you through till evening, and a delicious dinner (half board includes five courses) with excellent local wines.'

~

NEARBY Passirio river promenades; Passirio valley; the Dolomites.
LOCATION on edge of town; in own grounds with ample car parking
FOOD breakfast, lunch, dinner
PRICE €€
ROOMS 21; 16 double and twin, all with bath or shower, 5 suites with bath; all rooms have phone, TV, hairdrier
FACILITIES sitting room, dining room, bar, library, indoor swimming pool, sauna, lift, terrace, garden
CREDIT CARDS AE, DC, MC, V
DISABLED access difficult
PETS accepted **CLOSED** mid-Dec to mid-Mar
PROPRIETORS Defranceschi family

THE NORTH-EAST

MISSIANO

SCHLOSS KORB

~ CONVERTED CASTLE ~

Missiano, 39050 San Paolo, Bolzano
TEL 0471 636000 **FAX** 0471 636033
E-MAIL hotel-schloss-korb@dnet.it **WEBSITE** www.highlight-hotels.com/korb

RISING UP ABOVE THE FERTILE vineyards and orchards that surround the outskirts of Bolzano is the 11thC tower which forms the centrepiece of Schloss Korb.

The entrance to the hotel is a riot of colour – flowering shrubs and plants set against walls of golden stone and whitewash. Inside, furnishings and decorations are in traditional style, and antiques and fresh flowers abound. Reception is a cool, dark, tiled hall set about with a most eccentric collection of objects including carvings, golden angels on the walls, huge plants, busts, heavy mirrors, brass ornaments and armoury – the oldest part of the hotel. Surrounding the main restaurant is a terrace, hanging out over the valley and awash with plants, where breakfast and drinks can be enjoyed. The feel of the place is relaxed, though not intimate.

The bedrooms in the castle are generous in size, with separate sitting areas and lovely views out over the vineyards. Best are those in the tower, or the traditional apartment with its carved furniture. Rooms in the annexe all have balconies, and here there is a lift and an indoor heated swimming pool.

~

NEARBY Bolzano (8 km); Merano (36 km); the Dolomites.
LOCATION 8 km W of Bolzano, in gardens; ample car parking
FOOD breakfast, lunch, dinner
PRICE €€
ROOMS 62; 54 double and twin, 2 single, all with bath; 6 suites, 5 with bath, 1 with shower; all rooms have phone, TV; half the rooms have safe
FACILITIES sitting rooms, dining room, bar, sauna, beauty salon, terraces, garden, tennis courts, indoor and outdoor swimming pools
CREDIT CARDS not accepted
DISABLED access difficult
PETS accepted **CLOSED** Nov to Mar
PROPRIETORS Dellago family

THE NORTH-EAST

ORTISEI

UHRERHOF DEUR

∼ MOUNTAIN CHALET ∼

Bulla, 39046 Ortisei, Bolzano
TEL 0471 797335 **FAX** 0471 797457
E-MAIL uhrerhof@val-gardena.com **WEBSITE** www.val-gardena.com/hotel/uhrerhof

THE NAME MEANS 'HOUSE OF THE CLOCKS', and their ticking and chiming, along with birdsong, are very often the only sounds which break the silence at this traditional chalet set in a tucked-away hamlet 1,600 metres above sea level. Indeed, noise levels hardly rise above a whisper, and Signora Zemmer is at pains to point out that this is a place only for those seeking total peace and quiet. Outside, there is a grassy garden from which to enjoy the wide and wonderful view. Inside, all the rooms, including the balconied bedrooms, are bright, simple and beautifully kept, with plenty of homely details. The core of the chalet is 400 years old, and includes the all-wood *stübe* with working stove. The three adjoining dining rooms have wooden benches round the walls, Tyrolean fabrics for curtains and cushions, bright rugs on terracotta floors and pewter plates displayed in wall racks. Signor Zemmer is the chef, and his simple yet delicious food is elegantly presented on pewter plates.

Underneath the house is a surprisingly smart health complex, with huge picture windows so that you can relax in the open-plan Turkish bath and soak up the view.

∼

NEARBY Val Gardena; Castelrotto (13 km); Bolzano (26 km).
LOCATION in mountainside hamlet, 13 km E of Castelrotto, off Castelrotto-Ortisei road; garage parking
FOOD breakfast, dinner
PRICE €-€€
ROOMS 11; 5 double and twin, 4 with bath, 1 with shower, 2 single with shower; 4 apartments for 2 to 5 people with kitchen, living room; all rooms have phone, TV, hairdrier, safe
FACILITIES dining room, bar, sitting room, garden, health centre
CREDIT CARDS MC, V
DISABLED not suitable
PETS not accepted **CLOSED** Nov, 2 weeks after Easter
PROPRIETORS Zemmer family

THE NORTH-EAST

PEDEMONTE

VILLA DEL QUAR

～ COUNTRY VILLA ～

Via Quar 12, 37020 Pedemonte, Verona
TEL 045 6800681 **FAX** 045 6800604
E-MAIL villadelquar@c-point.it **WEBSITE** www.integra.Fr/relaischateaux/delquar

SITUATED IN THE FERTILE VALPOLICELLA valley, this 'typical patrician dwelling' has for the past ten years been a luxury hotel, a member of Relais et Châteaux. The ebullient owner and her family live in the fine main villa, while her hotel occupies the east wing. Public rooms in particular make a great impression. The galleried sitting room, an enclosed arcade with beamed roof, is delightfully light, airy and sophisticated. The two dining rooms – resplendent with mirrors, Venetian torches, vast Murano glass chandelier, cream silk tablecloths and elegant dining chairs – are also extremely attractive and make delightful rooms in which to eat. A new reception room, doubling as a library and tea room, has recently been added by the swimming pool. Bedrooms are restrained, masculine even, many with lovely old cupboard doors. Bathrooms feel luxurious, swathed in prettily coloured marble. If you take a suite, ask for the one with its own terrace, which is no more expensive.

In summer a white awning covers the terrace and the immaculate pool sparkles invitingly. The villa's setting, though quiet, is not so idyllic; though it is surrounded by a sea of vines, the road is close by and there is a modern housing development on the nearest hillside.

～

NEARBY Verona (11 km); Lake Garda (20 km).
LOCATION in Pedemonte follow signs for Verona and hotel at traffic lights; after about 1,500 m turn right for hotel; in own grounds with ample car parking
FOOD breakfast, lunch, dinner; room service
PRICE ⓔⓔⓔ
ROOMS 22; 19 double and twin, 3 suites, all with bath; all rooms have phone, TV, air conditioning, minibar, hairdrier, safe **FACILITIES** sitting room, 2 dining rooms, breakfast room, bar, terrace, swimming pool, small gym
CREDIT CARDS AE, DC, MC, V
DISABLED rooms on ground floor **PETS** accepted
CLOSED 15th Nov to 15th Mar
PROPRIETORS Evelina Acampora and Leopoldo Montresor

THE NORTH-EAST

CASTEL PERGINE
~ CONVERTED CASTLE ~

38057 Pergine, Valsugana, Trento
TEL 0461 531158 **FAX** 0461 531329
E-MAIL castelpergine@valsugana.com

THIS MEDIEVAL HILLTOP FORTRESS is managed with love and enthusiasm by an energetic and cultured Swiss couple, Verena and Theo. Past and present coexist happily in a rather alternative atmosphere, and the castle has a truly lived-in feel despite its grand dimensions and impressive history. A recent visit confirmed that this is one of the most affordable and distinctive hotels in the entire region.

The route from the car park to the hotel leads you under stone arches, up age-worn steps and through vaulted chambers to the airy, round reception hall where breakfast is also served. The two spacious dining rooms afford wonderful views, and the cooking, based on the regional cuisine, is light and innovative. The bedrooms are by no means luxurious, and some are very small, but all are furnished in simple good taste; the best have splendid, heavy, carved wooden furniture and wall panelling.

One of the most enchanting features of the castle is the walled garden. Spend an hour reading a book, or simply watching the mountains through the crumbling ramparts, and you may never want to leave.

~

NEARBY Trento (11 km); Lake Caldonazzo (3 km); Segonzano.
LOCATION off the SS47 Padua road, 2 km SE of Pergine; in own grounds with ample car parking
FOOD breakfast, dinner
PRICE €
ROOMS 21; 13 double and twin, 8 with shower, 4 single, 3 with shower, 4 triple, 3 with shower; all rooms have phone
FACILITIES sitting room, dining rooms, bar, garden
CREDIT CARDS AE, MC, V
DISABLED access difficult
PETS accepted
CLOSED Nov to Easter
PROPRIETORS Verena and Theo Schneider-Neff

THE NORTH-EAST

PIEVE D'ALPAGO

DOLADA
~ RESTAURANT-WITH-ROOMS ~

Via Dolada 21, Plois, 32010 Pieve d'Alpago, Belluno
TEL 0437 479141 **FAX** 0437 478068
E-MAIL dolada@tin.it **WEBSITE** www.dolada.it

A twisting road leads from the Alpago valley to Pieve, and then corkscrews on up to the little hamlet of Plois. Dolada turns out to be a handsome turn-of-the-century building with faded apricot walls and green-shuttered windows with a little garden which looks out over snow-capped mountains and the Santa Croce lake and valley far below. Our inspector reports that although the food was well worth the trip from Belluno, he was glad to be staying the night and not negotiating the hair-pin bends afterwards 'although the bright pink of our modern bedroom was a bit of a shock after our delicious food in the more sophisticated and mellow surroundings of the dining room'. Each room is themed in a different colour, which can cause a mild feeling of panic if the colour grates.

The point of Dolada is its restaurant, Michelin-starred, which deftly mixes traditional Italian dishes with inventive new ones, and offers a very good wine list. In a series of rooms, lace-clothed tables set with silver cutlery, with ribbed aluminium lamps suspended over each. Chef/patron Enzo De Pra and his wife, Rossana, are friendly.
~

NEARBY Belluno (20 km); Nevegàl ski area (18 km).
LOCATION in the hamlet of Plois, signposted from Pieve d'Alpago; ample parking
FOOD breakfast, lunch, dinner
PRICE ⓔ
ROOMS 7 double and twin, all with shower; all rooms have phone, TV,
FACILITIES restaurant, terrace, garden **CREDIT CARDS** AE, DC, MC, V
DISABLED no special facilities **PETS** accepted
CLOSED Jan to Feb; restaurant closed Mon and Tues lunch except Jul and Aug
PROPRIETORS Enzo and Rossana De Pra

THE NORTH-EAST

REDAGNO DI SOPRA

ZIRMERHOF
∼ MOUNTAIN HOTEL ∼

39040 Redagno, Bolzano
TEL 0471 887215 **FAX** 0471 887225
E-MAIL info@zirmerhof.com **WEBSITE** www.zirmerhof.com

SITUATED JUST OUTSIDE the tiny hamlet of Redagno di Sopra, this 12thC *mas* has been in the Perwanger family since 1890. Views are of mountains, green pastures and forests with few signs of civilization to mar the landscape. 'Idyllic', a recent guest tells us. The interior has been carefully restored. The dim, low-ceilinged hall with its intricate wood carving, ticking grandfather clock and old fireplace, immediately plunges you into the atmosphere of an old family home. There is a tiny cosy library, a sitting-cum-breakfast room with an open fire for winter days, and a rustic bar with a grassy terrace, from which to enjoy the superb views. The large wood-panelled dining room houses two elaborate ceramic stoves, and makes a fine setting in which to enjoy the local dishes and sophisticated wines on offer.

The comfortable bedrooms vary enormously in size, but all are attractive with traditional carved furniture (much of it made on the premises) and pretty fabrics; the largest rooms are on the top floor. For the energetic, there's plenty to do, particularly in winter, from skating and curling on the lake to cross-country and downhill skiing. A sauna has recently been added.

∼

NEARBY Cavalese (15 km).
LOCATION 5 km N of Fontanefredde, off the SS48; in garden with ample car parking
FOOD breakfast, lunch, dinner
PRICE €-€€
ROOMS 31; 23 double and twin, 2 with bath, 21 with shower, 7 single, 2 with bath, 5 with shower, 1 suite with shower; rooms have TV on request
FACILITIES dining room, sitting room, bar, library, garden
CREDIT CARDS AE, DC, MC, V
DISABLED ground-floor bedrooms available
PETS accepted **CLOSED** early Nov to day after Christmas, after Easter to mid-May
PROPRIETOR Sepp Perwanger

THE NORTH-EAST

SAN FLORIANO DEL COLLIO

GOLF HOTEL

~ CONVERTED CASTLE ~

Via Oslavia 2, 34070 San Floriano del Collio, Gorizia
TEL 0481 884051 **FAX** 0481 884052

UNFORTUNATELY, THIS IS ONE OF only a handful of hotels which we have been unable to inspect recently, although it has long been included in our guide. Judging by past reports, however, we are still happy to recommend it, but we would welcome some more recent feedback.

The hotel's name, referring to its nine-hole golf course (closed Mon; green fee L45,000), gives the impression of something modern, but it is in fact two ancient renovated houses just outside the walls of Castello Formentini, which has belonged to the Formentini family since the 16th century. The present owner, Contessa Isabella Formentini, has filled the rooms of the tiny hotel with family furniture and pictures. Each beautifully decorated and spacious bedroom is named after a prestigious wine, emphasizing the vinous interest of the Formentini family. Three of them are within the castle walls, but all guests are at liberty to use the castle grounds and its swimming pool. The family also run an excellent restaurant called Castello Formentini (closed Mon, Tues lunch). This is a charming spot, with gentle, wooded countryside spread out around the hilltop castle.

~

NEARBY Gorizia (4 km); Trieste (47 km).
LOCATION in town, just outside castle walls; private grounds; car parking
FOOD breakfast
PRICE €€€
ROOMS 15; 12 double and twin, 2 single, 1 suite in tower, all with bath or shower; all rooms have TV, minibar; 12 rooms have phone; 3 rooms have no phone but air conditioning
FACILITIES sitting room, breakfast room, garden, swimming pool, tennis court, nine-hole golf course
CREDIT CARDS AE, DC, MC, V
DISABLED not suitable
PETS accepted **CLOSED** Dec to Mar
PROPRIETOR Contessa Isabella Formentini

THE NORTH-EAST

GASTHOF TSCHOTSCHERHOF

~ COUNTRY GUESTHOUSE ~

San Osvaldo 19, 39040 Siusi, Bolzano
TEL 0471 706013 **FAX** 0471 704801
E-MAIL tschoetscherhof@rolmail.net

DON'T BE PUT OFF by the unpronounceable name; for lovers of simple, farmhouse accommodation in an unspoiled rural setting, this hostelry could be ideal. The narrow road from Siusi winds through apple orchards, vineyards and open meadows, eventually arriving at the tiny hamlet of San Osvaldo and this typical 500-year-old farmhouse with its adjacent dark wood barn. The name, painted on the outside of the building, is almost hidden by the clambering vines, and the old wooden balconies are a colourful riot of cascading geraniums. The sun-drenched terrace is a perfect spot for relaxing and eating.

Inside, we were beguiled by smells from the kitchen at the end of the hall, and were drawn to the warmth of the low-ceilinged old *stübe* with gently ticking clock, rough wood floor and simple white ceramic stove.

A rustic stone stairway leads up to the modest but tidy bedrooms, some of which have balconies. They have no frills, but after a long day in glorious countryside, we were too tired to notice.

~

NEARBY Castelrotto (5 km); Bolzano (17 km); Sciliar Natural Park (10 km).
LOCATION in hamlet, 5 km W of Castelrotto; with parking
FOOD breakfast, lunch, dinner
PRICE €
ROOMS 8; 7 double and twin, 1 single, all with shower
FACILITIES dining rooms, terrace
CREDIT CARDS not accepted
DISABLED access difficult
PETS accepted **CLOSED** Dec to Mar
PROPRIETORS Jaider family

THE NORTH-EAST

SAN VIGILIO

LOCANDA SAN VIGILIO

⟨∼ LAKESIDE HOTEL ∼⟩

San Vigilio, 37016 Garda, Verona
TEL 045 7256688 FAX 045 7256551
E-MAIL sanvigilio@gardanews.it WEBSITE www.gardanews.it/sanvigilio

IN GENERAL THE EAST SIDE of Lake Garda is less upmarket than the west but this hotel's idyllic setting, on a lush peninsula dotted with olive trees and cypresses, is a conspicuous exception. The property is owned by Conte Agostino Guarienti, who lives in the 16thC villa that dominates the headland. An air of discreet exclusivity pervades the *locanda* (royalty are among regular guests) yet the atmosphere is far from stuffy. Of the public rooms, our favourite is the elegant dining room, right on the lake, with a comfortingly creaky wooden floor. A ceramic stove occupies one corner and sideboards display plates and bottles. You can eat in here, on a little arched veranda or under huge white umbrellas on the terrace where terracotta pots overflow with flowers. Next door is a cosy sitting room.

The seven bedrooms in the main house are all different, though they have beautiful antiques and fabrics in common. Only one has no view. Other bedrooms are in separate buildings and more rustic in style. In the evening the place comes into its own: with the day trippers gone, guests can wander the peninsula or sit with a drink at one of the Taverna's vine-shaded tables.

⟨∼⟩

NEARBY Garda (2 km); Verona (45 km); ferry services (4 km).
LOCATION 2 km W of Garda, on promontory; parking available 150 m away
FOOD breakfast, lunch, dinner
PRICE €€€€-€€€€
ROOMS 14; 11 double and twin, 3 suites, all with bath or shower; all rooms have phone, TV, air conditioning, minibar, hairdrier; most rooms have safe
FACILITIES sitting room, dining room, bar, terrace, walled garden
CREDIT CARDS AE, DC, MC, V
DISABLED not suitable
PETS accepted
CLOSED Nov to just before Easter
PROPRIETOR Conte Agostino Guarienti

THE NORTH-EAST

SCORZE

VILLA SORANZO CONESTABILE

~ TOWN VILLA ~

Via Roma 1, 30037 Scorzè, Venezia
TEL 041 445027 **FAX** 041 5840088
E-MAIL vsoranzo@tin.it

STANDING AT THE CENTRE of the hard-working town of Scorzè, this aristo-cratic villa dates back to the 16th century, but was remodelled in the 18th century in elegant neoclassical style. Visible from its earliest period (especially if you take room No. 1) are fragments of gorgeous School of Veronese frescoes. There are also fine ceilings and floors, an impressive double staircase and a park modelled in the early 19th century in Romantic English style. The spacious first-floor rooms are somewhat staid but full of character, recalling the last century when they were the bed-rooms of the noble Conestabile family, retaining their lofty proportions, and, in some cases, original *faux* marble walls. Rooms on the second floor, formerly the household quarters, are plainer but spacious and furnished in different styles.

On a recent spring visit our inspector reports that she ate alone in the dining room, but was comforted by the familial ambience, with copper pans hanging from the ceiling and old dressers laden with wine bottles, and by a simple but well-prepared set menu. She also notes that her visit was marred by one of the coolest welcomes in reception that she can remember. However, other satisfied guests have encountered much friendlier staff.

NEARBY Riviera del Brenta; Venice (24 km); Padua (30 km).
LOCATION in Scorzè, 24 km NW of Venice; in own grounds with ample car parking
FOOD breakfast, lunch, dinner
PRICE €-€€
ROOMS 20; 14 double and twin, 3 single, all with bath or shower, 3 suites; all rooms have phone, TV
FACILITIES sitting room, dining room, bar, breakfast room, terrace, garden
CREDIT CARDS AE, DC, MC, V
DISABLED not suitable
PETS accepted **CLOSED** restaurant only, Nov to Mar
PROPRIETORS Martinelli family

THE NORTH-EAST

SOLIGHETTO

LOCANDA DA LINO

Restaurant-with-rooms

Via Brandolini 31, 31050 Solighetto, Treviso
TEL 0438 82150/842377 **FAX** 0438 980577
E-MAIL dalino@trun.it **WEBSITE** www.seven.it/locanda-da-lino

THE CREATION of an inspired chef, Lino Toffolin, this country restaurant became an institution. Championed by the diva Toti Dal Monte, the young Lino was soon cooking for the *glitterati* and being patronized by stars such as Marcello Mastrioni. Although Lino has now died, the place is still run by his family and continues to attract a faithful following. One long room, with smaller rooms leading off it, can seat 400 for dinner at full stretch. The ceilings are hung idiosyncratically with hundreds of copper pots. A table in the 'inner sanctum' enables you to glimpse food being grilled over a blazing furnace. From a menu of local delicacies, we particularly enjoyed *antipasto misto della Locanda, braciole di vetello ai ferri and polpettine in umido con polenta*, and there's an impressive wine list from the beautifully laid-out cellar.

The bedrooms are in annexes and range from comfortable doubles to the extravagantly rococo Elsa Vazzoler suite with its bright blue walls, enormous glilt lamps, and cherubs above the bed. The L-shaped entrance/bar/breakfast area is also furnished with rococo pieces, mixed eclectically but successfully with modern art. A one off.

NEARBY Palladian villas; Asolo (20 km).
LOCATION in Solighetto on the Follina road; ample car parking
FOOD breakfast, lunch, dinner
PRICE €
ROOMS 17; 10 double and twin, 7 suites, all with bath; all rooms have phone, TV, minibar, hairdrier
FACILITIES breakfast area/bar, restaurant, terrace **CREDIT CARDS** AE, DC, MC, V
DISABLED several rooms on ground floor **PETS** accepted
CLOSED restaurant Mon, Christmas Day, July
PROPRIETORS 'Lino' family

THE NORTH-EAST

SIUSI ALLO SCILIAR

BAD RATZES

～ MOUNTAIN HOTEL ～

Bagnidi Razzes, 39040 Siusi allo Sciliar, Bolzano
TEL and **FAX** 0471 706131
E-MAIL info@badratzes.it **WEBSITE** www.badratzes.it

LEAVING THE SMALL TOWN OF SIUSI in search of Bad Ratzes, the road winds uphill past green meadows and into a dense forest where Hansel and Gretel would have felt at home. When at last you reach it in a clearing, the hotel, large and modern, looks disconcertingly grim, but the warmth and enthusiasm of the Scherlin sisters will put you immediately at ease. Inside, the decoration is dull 1960s and 1970s, but comfortable. Public areas – including a formal sitting room with open fireplace, a children's playroom and two dining rooms – are extensive. All but four of the spotless bedrooms have balconies.

Food is important at Bad Ratzes: local dishes are carefully prepared and pasta is home made. One of the sisters bakes regularly, and her recipes are recorded in a little booklet. This is one of a group of family hotels in the area and there are many thoughtful child-orientated extras: pots of crayons and paper on the dining tables, a booklet of local bedtime stories, walks for children, a special menu and so on. Adults are not neglected; there is wonderful and varied walking in the neighbourhood and a free ski bus runs to the slopes in winter.

NEARBY Bolzano (22 km); Siusi National Park; skiing (10 km).
LOCATION 22 km NE of Bolzano, 3 km SE of Siusi; in own grounds with ample car parking
FOOD breakfast, lunch, dinner
PRICE €
ROOMS 52; 36 double, 9 single, 7 family rooms, all with bath; all rooms have phone, hairdrier; 18 rooms have TV and safe
FACILITIES dining rooms, sitting rooms, bar, playroom, indoor swimming pool, sauna, garden, garage
CREDIT CARDS not accepted
DISABLED not suitable **PETS** accepted
CLOSED Sunday after Easter to mid-May
PROPRIETORS Scherlin family

THE NORTH-EAST

TORRI DEL BENACO

GARDESANA
~ LAKESIDE HOTEL ~

Piazza Calderini 20, 37010 Torri del Benaco, Verona
TEL 045 7225411 **FAX** 045 7225771
E-MAIL gardesana@easynet.it **WEBSITE** www.hotel-gardesana.com

TORRI DEL BENACO IS ONE of the showpiece fishing villages which are dotted along the shore of Lake Garda, and Gardesana is in a plum position. It is a treat to tuck into the chef's speciality fish soup on the delightful first-floor dining terrace which overlooks the central *piazza*, 14thC castle and bustling port. The wrought-iron balustrade is decked with cascading geraniums, the tables are elegant, the waiters smartly uniformed, and the food, particularly the fish, fresh and delicious. It makes a perfect vantage point for watching the boats come and go, and the changing colours of the lake. Drinks can also be taken on the ground-floor terrace, which extends out on to the *piazza*.

The building has a long history, as its exterior would suggest, with its stone arches and mellow stucco walls; but the entire interior has been smartly modernized in recent years to produce an essentially modern and very comfortable hotel. The green and white bedrooms are almost all identical: wooden furnishings, soft fabrics, plenty of little extras. If you can, try to book one of the corner rooms; these have the advantage of facing both the lake and the *piazza*.

NEARBY Bardolino (11 km); Malcesine (21 km); Gardaland.
LOCATION in town centre, on waterfront, in pedestrian zone; unload at hotel, private parking 150 m away
FOOD breakfast, dinner
PRICE €
ROOMS 34; 31 double, 3 single, all with shower; all rooms have phone, TV, air conditioning (Jul and Aug)
FACILITIES dining room, bar, lift, terrace
CREDIT CARDS AE, DC, MC, V
DISABLED no special facilities
PETS not accepted **CLOSED** Nov and Dec
PROPRIETOR Giuseppe Lorenzini

THE NORTH-EAST

TRENTO

ACCADEMIA

~ TOWN HOTEL ~

Vicolo Colico 4-6, 38100 Trento
TEL 0461 233600 **FAX** 0461 230174
E-MAIL info@accademiahotel.it **WEBSITE** www.accademiahotel.it

FAVOURED BY SHOWBIZ TYPES, this upmarket hotel is run by two lively sisters and their efficient staff, and occupies an attractive medieval house on a tiny street in the old centre of Trento. Quaint wooden shutters and geranium-filled window boxes break up the four storeys of elegant cream stucco façade. Inside, elements of the original architecture are also visible: a stone stairway leading up from reception, doorways and vaulted ceilings. The building's clean white lines are enlivened by vibrant rugs, parquet floors and strategically placed antiques.

The atmosphere is carried through to the bright, airy bedrooms, decorated predominantly in blue and white. Some have a rustic air, varnished wood floors and attic ceilings. The wood-panelled suite at the top is particularly appealing, furnished with smart modern sofas, colourful kilims and modern prints.

The restaurant – a white vaulted room, with crisp tablecloths – serves interesting, creative food. There is also a homely *enoteca*, where you can taste a wide range of local wines or have a snack. Breakfast is a particular pleasure when taken on the walled terrace, shaded by a giant horsechestnut tree.

~

NEARBY Santa Maria; Piazza del Duomo.
LOCATION in old part of town between Duomo and Piazza Dante; with free car parking nearby
FOOD breakfast, lunch, dinner
PRICE €-€€
ROOMS 43; 32 double and twin, 16 with bath, 16 with shower, 9 single with shower, 2 suites with bath; all rooms have phone, TV, air-conditioning, minibar, hairdrier **FACILITIES** sitting rooms, restaurant, *enoteca*, terrace
CREDIT CARDS AE, DC, MC, V **DISABLED** no special facilities
PETS accepted
CLOSED Christmas to early Jan, restaurant Monday
PROPRIETORS Fambri family

THE NORTH-EAST

TRISSINO

RELAIS CA'MASIERI
∽ RESTAURANT-WITH-ROOMS ∽

Località Masieri, Via Masieri, 36070 Trissino, Vicenza
TEL 0445 490122 **FAX** 0445 490455
E-MAIL info@camasieri.com **WEBSITE** www.camasieri.com

THE COUNTRYSIDE AROUND industrial Arzignano is uninspiring, but things improve as you wind your way to Masieri through willow-fringed meadows. Through wrought-iron gates and at the end of a long drive, the sight of Ca' Masieri itself, a fine old shuttered mansion with swimming pool and shady terrace further lifts the spirits. In our case, they were immediately cast down, because we were late and the chef had just gone home: we had been dreaming of the much-vaunted food all morning. The sight of the charming little restaurant, its walls decorated with delicate 18thC frescoes, only made our disappointment worse. Had we been in time, we might have had the salad of crayfish tails followed by risotto with herbs, and then the casserole of pigeon.

The bedrooms are in an adjacent building which retains its old wooden beamed ceilings, but is otherwise furnished in contemporary style. Two rooms have spiral metal staircases from a sitting area up to the mezzanine beds. No. 201 is huge, with a terrace overlooking the hills and Trissino. There are pretty bedspreads in William Morris leaf-print, curvy modern tables, and stylish bathrooms with walls painted the colour of aluminium.

NEARBY Vicenza (21 km); Verona (49 km).
LOCATION from Trissino, follow signs to Masieri, and in Via Masieri to Ca' Masieri up a private drive; ample car parking
FOOD breakfast, lunch, dinner
PRICE €
ROOMS 12; 5 double, 2 single, 5 apartments, all with shower; all rooms have phone, TV, minibar; 9 have air conditioning
FACILITIES sitting room, bar, breakfast room, dining room, terrace, swimming pool
CREDIT CARDS AE, MC, V
DISABLED not suitable
PETS accepted **CLOSED** never; restaurant closed Sun, Mon lunch
PROPRIETOR Angelo Vassena

THE NORTH-EAST

ACCADEMIA
~ TOWN HOTEL ~

Fondamenta Bollani, Dorsoduro 1058, 30123 Venezia
TEL 041 5210188/5237846 **FAX** 041 5239152
E-MAIL pensione.accademia@flashnet.it

THOUGH IT'S NOT THE BARGAIN it used to be, the Accademia still has afford-able prices and a convenient but calm location. What really distin-guishes the *pensione* is its gardens – the large canal-side patio, where tables are scattered among plants in classical urns, and the grassy rear garden where roses and fruit trees flourish.

Built in the 17th century as a private mansion, it retains touches of grandeur. Most of the furnishings are classically Venetian (the Murano chandeliers for once tasteful and harmonious), although the ground floor has recently been redecorated in a disappointingly bland style with the addition – to our inspector's horror – of automatic glass doors. Perfect for sitting and relaxing is the thankfully unchanged and finely furnished first-floor landing. The airy breakfast room has crisp white tablecloths and a beamed ceiling; but, weather permitting, guests will inevitably opt to start their day in the garden. The bedrooms, renovated a few years ago to a high standard, have inlaid wooden floors and antiqued mirrors. Our inspector found some members of staff 'charming', but others 'churlish', though the latter don't seem to deter a loyal clientele from returning here year after year.

~

NEARBY Accademia gallery; Scuola Grande dei Carmini.
LOCATION where the Toletta and Trovaso canals meet the Grand Canal; vaporetto Accademia or water taxi
FOOD breakfast
PRICE ⓔⓔ
ROOMS 29; 22 double and twin, 9 with bath, 13 with shower, 7 single, 6 with shower; all rooms have phone, TV; most have air conditioning, hairdrier, safe
FACILITIES breakfast room, bar, sitting room, garden
CREDIT CARDS AE, DC, MC, V
DISABLED no special facilities
PETS accepted **CLOSED** never
PROPRIETOR Stefania Salmaso

THE NORTH-EAST

VENICE

AGLI ALBORETTI

~ TOWN GUESTHOUSE ~

Rio Terrà Foscarini, Dorsoduro 884, 30123 Venezia
TEL 041 5230058 **FAX** 041 5210158
E-MAIL alboretti@gpnet.it

THE ALBORETTI IS DISTINGUISHED by its warm welcome, and genuine family atmosphere. Reception is a cosy wood-panelled room with paintings of Venice on the walls and a model of a 17thC galleon in its window; the ground-floor sitting room is small, but a second sitting room on the first-floor makes a comfortable retreat (the TV is rarely used); the terrace behind the hotel, entirely covered by a pergola and set simply with tables and chairs, is a delight, especially for a leisurely breakfast in summer.

The style of the bedrooms is predominantly simple and modern, though a few rooms have an antique or two (such as No. 5). Like the rest of the hotel, they are well cared for and spotlessly clean, but the bathrooms, though totally renovated, are tiny, as are some of the rooms. None are large, but Nos 15, 18 and 22 are recommended for their garden view, and the former for its balcony on which you can breakfast.

Signora Linguerri runs a sophisticated restaurant next door, where you can eat in the pretty dining room or outside under the pergola; she is an expert on wine and her list offers an interesting selection.

~

NEARBY Accademia gallery; Zattere; Gesuati.
LOCATION alongside the Accademia gallery; vaporetto Accademia
FOOD breakfast, lunch, dinner
PRICE €€
ROOMS 20; 13 double and twin, 6 single, 1 family room, all with bath or shower; all rooms have phone, TV, air conditioning, hairdrier
FACILITIES sitting rooms, dining room, TV room, bar, terrace
CREDIT CARDS AE, MC, V
DISABLED no special facilities
PETS accepted
CLOSED Jan occasionally; restaurant Wed, Thurs lunch
PROPRIETOR Anna Linguerri

THE NORTH-EAST

AI SANTI APOSTOLI
~ TOWN HOTEL ~

Strada Nova, Cannaregio 4391, 30131 Venezia
TEL 041 5212612 **FAX** 041 5212611

BE ON THE LOOKOUT FOR A PAIR of handsome dark green doors which herald the discreet entrance of this converted *palazzo*. Beyond is a scruffy courtyard and a quirky lift that takes you up to the third floor. What lies in store for you here is totally unexpected: a lovely apartment that has been transformed by the Bianchi Michiel family into an elegant, if pricey, B&B. The sitting room is the epitome of style: oil paintings hang on glossy apricot walls; heavy lamps rest on antique tables; sofas and chairs are covered in quiet chintz or swathed in calico. At the far end, a triptych of wood-framed windows overlooks the Grand Canal. Ornaments and books left casually around make it feel more like a home than a hotel.

Large and individually decorated, the bedrooms have been done out recently in glazed chintzes and stunning strong colours. Like the sitting room, they are dotted with antiques and pretty china knick-knacks. The two on the Grand Canal are considerably dearer than the rest. Stefano also owns a one-bedroom apartment on the second floor, with a vibrant green colour scheme, no view of the canal, but a sunny roof terrace.

~

NEARBY Ca' d'Oro; Santi Apostoli; Miracoli.
LOCATION just E of Campo Santi Apostoli; vaporetto Ca' d'Oro
FOOD breakfast
PRICE €€€€; apartment prices on request
ROOMS 11 double and twin, 6 with bath, 4 with shower; all rooms have phone, TV, air conditioning, minibar, hairdrier
FACILITIES breakfast room, sitting room, lift
CREDIT CARDS AE, DC, MC, V
DISABLED not suitable
PETS accepted
CLOSED Jan to mid-Feb, 2-3 weeks in Aug, sometimes 2 weeks in Dec
PROPRIETOR Stefano Bianchi Michiel

THE NORTH-EAST

VENICE

AMERICAN

~ TOWN HOTEL ~

Rio di San Vio, Dorsoduro 628, 30123 Venezia
TEL 041 5204733 **FAX** 041 5204048
E-MAIL reception@hotelamerican.com **WEBSITE** www.hotelamerican.com

SET IN A PEACEFUL BACKWATER of Dorsoduro, yet close to the Accademia and the Grand Canal, this is a quiet, dignified hotel with spacious reception rooms and a tiny terrace where you can take breakfast under a pergola in summer. The public areas have a sombre Edwardian air, with wood panelling and silk damask on the walls, tapestry or velvet upholstered chairs, oriental rugs on Venetian mosaic floors, frilly white curtains and potted plants. Corridors are also panelled in wood, with little tables and chairs placed here and there. Bedrooms – some newly renovated – vary in size, as do the bathrooms, and though unexceptional they have pretty Venetian painted furniture (with minibars mercifully disguised as free-standing cupboards), ornate gilt mirrors and pretty Paisley-print bedspreads. Our reporter's bathroom had a black-and-white shower curtain covered in comical cats.

If you choose the American, you should do what you can to secure one of the nine bedrooms that overlook the canal. Nos 14 and 23 are particularly recommended, with three canal-facing French windows on two sides, and narrow balconies from where you can watch the water traffic drift by.

~

NEARBY Accademia gallery; Zattere; Santa Maria della Salute.
LOCATION midway along canal, which runs between Grand Canal and Giudecca Canal; vaporetto Accademia or water taxi
FOOD breakfast
PRICE €€€
ROOMS 28; double and twin and single, all with bath or shower; all rooms have phone, TV, air conditioning, minibar, hairdrier, safe
FACILITIES sitting area, breakfast room, terrace
CREDIT CARDS AE, MC, V
DISABLED no special facilities
CLOSED never
PROPRIETOR Salvatore Sutera Sardo

THE NORTH-EAST

BUCINTORO

~ TOWN GUESTHOUSE ~

Riva San Biagio, Castello 2135, 30122 Venezia
TEL 041 5223240 **FAX** 041 5235224

WE MET A COUPLE AT VENICE airport who had splashed out on the Londra
Palace (which they liked very much) for the first few days of their
stay and then sharply downgraded to the Bucintoro – which they almost
preferred. Apart from the wonderful views across St Mark's Basin, which
the two hotels share, the contrast could not be greater. Rooms at this
basic *pensione*, little changed since the family bought it 30 years ago, are
as plain as a pikestaff; breakfast is frugal; and the sitting room, despite its
newly upholstered armchairs, remains unappealing.

The secret of its success is its position: every clean and simple room has
a lagoon view and is flooded with Venetian light. Corner rooms, beloved
by artists, are the best, with windows on to both the lagoon and San Marco
(try for Nos 1, 7, 9, 11). Room No. 4 is one of the pleasantest, with large
bed, pretty bedspread, airy curtains and the waters of the lagoon gently
lapping below. No. 26 can fit up to four people and has a fair-sized bathroom. The modest cement-rendered building with tables outside in summer is conveniently close to the Arsenale vaporetto stop.

NEARBY Arsenale; Naval Museum; Piazza San Marco.
LOCATION on the waterfront, at the far end of Riva degli Schiavoni; vaporetto
Arsenale, Tana or water taxi
FOOD breakfast, dinner (Apr-Oct)
PRICE ©©
ROOMS 28; 22 double, twin and triple, 17 with bath, 5 with shower, 6 single, 5 with
shower, 1 with basin; all rooms have phone, fan on request, hairdrier
FACILITIES breakfast room, sitting room, terrace
CREDIT CARDS not accepted
DISABLED not suitable
PETS not accepted **CLOSED** Dec, Jan
PROPRIETORS Bianchi family

THE NORTH-EAST

VENICE

CA' FOSCARI
~ TOWN GUESTHOUSE ~

Calle della Frescada, Dorsoduro 3888-3887/b, 30123 Venezia
TEL 041 710401/710817 **FAX** 041 710817

YOU WILL NEED HELP FINDING Calle Frescada, a little lane tucked almost out of sight and unmarked on most maps: take Calle Larga Foscari towards the Frari, and at the junction with Crosera, turn right. Calle Frescada runs across the end, and the hotel faces down Crosera. Happily our inspector's maddening search for this little one-star hotel was worth the effort – Ca' Foscari is a cut above. Somehow its charming, modest exterior – smart front door and bell pull, little lantern displaying its name – tells the story, and the interior does not disappoint, nor the welcome from Valter and Giuliana Scarpa.

On the ground floor is a little breakfast room. A couple of flights of stairs, and you are in a fresh, white corridor with white-painted doors leading to the bedrooms. These are modest, as you would expect, but pristine, with lacy curtains and pretty bedspreads and white-tiled minute bathrooms, or, in rooms without bathrooms, decent basins. Note that the communal bathroom only has a shower, not a bath. The metal-framed beds are much more comfortable than they look. An excellent budget hotel in a bustling residential neighbourhood.

~

NEARBY Scuola Grande di San Rocco; Frari; Accademia gallery.
LOCATION between Campo San Tomà and Palazzi Foscari; vaporetto San Tomà
FOOD breakfast
PRICE €
ROOMS 11; 6 double and twin, 3 with shower, 3 with basin only; 1 single with shower, 2 triples without shower, 2 family rooms without shower; communal bathroom with shower
FACILITIES breakfast room **CREDIT CARDS** MC, V
DISABLED not suitable
PETS accepted **CLOSED** 15 Nov to Feb
PROPRIETOR Valter Scarpa

THE NORTH-EAST

LA CALCINA
~ TOWN HOTEL ~

Fondamenta Zattere ai Gesuati, Dorsoduro 780, 30123 Venezia
TEL 041 5206466 **FAX** 041 5227045
E-MAIL la.calcina@libero.it **WEBSITE** www.italyhotel.com/venezia/calcina/

THE HOUSE WHERE RUSKIN LIVED is hard to resist, both for its historical connection and for its location facing the sunny straits of the Giudecca canal. The simple *pensione*, inherited by a go-ahead young couple, has recently been given a facelift, and transformed into a stylish small hotel whose calm uncluttered rooms provide a welcome antidote to an excess of Venetian rococo. Attention to detail includes fresh flowers and classical music in the lobby, and incense in the bedrooms to clear stuffy smells.

Unlike many hotels in the city there is a marked difference in price between the rooms at the front, with views across the glittering water, and the darkish back rooms, which have no view, but are equally comfortable. Most expensive are the corner rooms, where the sun streams in from two directions. None of the rooms is large, but all compensate with cool cream walls, warm parquet floors, antiques and gleaming bathrooms with heated towel rails. Breakfast is served in summer on the blue-and-white terrace (or you can book the romantic roof garden for two), and in winter in a marble-floored bar with a picture window, so that even if you opt for a bedroom at the back you can still enjoy the vista.

~

NEARBY Gesuati church; Accademia gallery.
LOCATION on W side of San Vio canal; vaporetto Zattere or water taxi
FOOD breakfast
PRICE ©©©
ROOMS 29; 22 double and twin, 2 with bath, 20 with shower, 7 single, 1 with bath, 3 with shower, 3 with washbasin; all rooms have phone, air conditioning, hairdrier, safe; apartments also available with space for 2
FACILITIES breakfast room/bar, sitting area, terrace, roof terrace
CREDIT CARDS AE, DC, MC, V
DISABLED not suitable
PETS not accepted **CLOSED** never
PROPRIETORS Alessandro and Debora Szemere

THE NORTH-EAST

VENICE

CA' PISANI
~ TOWN HOTEL ~

Dorsoduro 979/a, 30123 Venezia
TEL 041 2771478 **FAX** 041 2771061
E-MAIL info@capisanihotel.it **WEBSITE** www.capisanihotel.it

BLATANTLY FLYING IN THE FACE of Venetian hotel tradition, the brand new Ca' Pisani, built in the shell of a deep-pink 16thC *palazzo*, is cool, hip and undeniably chic.

Inside, the overall style is designer minimalist, but the odd original feature (brick arches, roof beams, painted coffered ceilings, marble floors), and the collection of fine '30s and '40s beds, mirrors and wardrobes softens this to a certain extent. Decorative themes are consistent throughout both public areas and bedrooms. Silver (above the reception area, in bedroom furniture, in mirror frames, on light fittings, in steel chair frames) is a staple and lightens dark ebony, pale acid-green and pale violet paintwork, and black and orange leather chairs. Warm, hardwood floors and wood doors are all given a contemporary twist. Bathrooms, in either deep mauve or palest grey marble specked with silver, are straight from the pages of a design magazine. The bedrooms have Bang&Olufsen phones and TVs and electrically-operated window blinds. Biscuit-coloured bedcovers and cushions look smart against crisp white linen sheets. Breakfast is served in the basement wine bar where you can also enjoy a light meal. The hotel has opened quite recently; reports would be welcome.
~

NEARBY Accademia gallery; Guggenheim museum.
LOCATION between the Accademia and Zattere; vaporetto Accademia, Zattere
FOOD breakfast, lunch, dinner
PRICE €€€
ROOMS 29; 25 double and twin, 4 suites, all with bath; all rooms have phone, TV, air conditioning, minibar, hairdrier
FACILITIES sitting room, internet point, restaurant, bar, Turkish bath, terrace
CREDIT CARDS AE, DC, MC, V
DISABLED 2 specially adapted rooms
PETS accepted **CLOSED** never
PROPRIETORS Serandei family

THE NORTH-EAST

CLUB CRISTAL
~ TOWN BED-AND-BREAKFAST ~

For further information all nationalities should contact: Liz Heavenstone,
188 Regent's Park Road, London NW1 8XP, England
TEL (London) 020 7722 5060 **FAX** 020 7586 3004 **E-MAIL** susan.venice@iol.it

THE SETTING COULD HARDLY BE more ideal, at least for those seeking a peaceful backwater: an airy, palatial townhouse overlooking a tree-lined courtyard and a little canal in a quiet residential corner of Cannaregio, yet only five minutes' walk from the Ca' d'Oro. It is the family home of Susan Schiavon, an Englishwoman ('not pure English; lots of other nationalities come into it besides') who has lived in Venice for many years and lets five of its bedrooms to discerning visitors for whom she is a fund of knowledge about the city.

An elegant white marble staircase leads to the *piano nobile* and a high-ceilinged sitting room filled with books and squashy sofas and armchairs. A perfect breakfast is served on the plant-filled terrace beyond. The bedrooms, entered through original doors painted with birds and flowers, vary in size, some large; all are full of character, with family furniture, comfortable beds, and crisp linen. Susan serves dinner by arrangement, and you should take advantage of her accomplished home cooking at least once. Take note that Club Cristal is emphatically a home, not a hotel; couples often return, and lone women feel particularly at ease. Susan also has apartments to rent, for example the charming Sant' Andrea; for information, tel. (London) 020 7348 3800.

~

NEARBY Gesuiti; Ca' d'Oro; Rialto.
LOCATION on a small canal, between Ca' d'Oro and Gesuiti; vaporetto Ca' d'Oro, Fondamente Nuove
FOOD breakfast, dinner by arrangement
PRICES (payable to London office in sterling only) €€
ROOMS 4 double, 1 single, all with bath or shower; all rooms have hairdrier
FACILITIES sitting room, dining room, terrace
CREDIT CARDS AE, DC, MC, V
DISABLED not suitable **PETS** not accepted **CLOSED** never
PROPRIETOR Susan Schiavon

THE NORTH-EAST

VENICE

FIRENZE

~ TOWN HOTEL ~

Salizzada San Moisè, San Marco 1490, 30124 Venezia
TEL 041 5222858 **FAX** 041 5202668
E-MAIL hotelfirenze@flashnet.it **WEBSITE** www.hotel-firenze.com

THE DISTINGUISHING FEATURES of the Firenze are its rooftop terrace – reached from the top floor by an external staircase – where you can breakfast in summer while picking out the landmarks, and the three bedrooms with private terrace which cost no more than ones without.

The building, just along from the florid, blackened façade of San Moisè, has a fine marble-and-iron art nouveau front (in need of restoration – the owner has plans); at the turn of the century it was an Austrian hat factory, as the splendid first floor windows announce. Inside, a recent total renovation has left the bedrooms uniform: unadorned Venetian marble floors (not cosy), peach-coloured walls, pale green headboards and matching cupboards, pretty Murano glass wall lights and white ruched net curtains. The first-floor breakfast room was designed to echo the famous café Florian in Piazza San Marco, with polished wood benches and tables lining the walls, but it doesn't quite come off and feels merely awkward. Choose the Firenze – managed with good humour by its owner, Signor Fabris – during the summer when you can make use of the terrace.

~

NEARBY Piazza San Marco.
LOCATION 30 m from Piazza San Marco, alongside San Moisè; vaporetto San Marco
FOOD breakfast
PRICE €€€
ROOMS 25; 22 double, 3 single, all with bath; all rooms have phone, TV, air conditioning, minibar, hairdrier, safe
FACILITIES breakfast room, rooftop terrace, lift
CREDIT CARDS AE, MC, V
DISABLED not suitable
PETS accepted
CLOSED never
PROPRIETOR Paolo Fabris

THE NORTH-EAST

FLORA
～ TOWN HOTEL ～

Calle Larga XXII Marzo, San Marco 2283/a, 30124 Venezia
TEL 041 5205844 **FAX** 041 5228217
E-MAIL info@hotelflora.it **WEBSITE** www.hotelflora.it

SUCH IS THE POPULARITY of this small hotel, tucked away down a cul-de-sac close to San Marco, that to get a room here you have to book weeks, even months in advance. You only need to glimpse the garden to know why it is sought after. Creepers, fountains and flowering shrubs cascading from stone urns create an enchanting setting for breakfast, tea or an evening drink in summer.

The lobby is small and inviting, enhanced by the views of the garden through a glass arch; the atmosphere is one of friendly efficiency. There are some charming double bedrooms with painted carved antiques and other typically Venetian furnishings, but beware of other comparatively spartan rooms, some of which are barely big enough for one, let alone two. Coveted rooms include two on the ground floor facing the garden and the three spacious corner rooms, the topmost of which has a marvellous view of Santa Maria della Salute. The venerable Flora has been run by the charming Romanelli family, father, son and grandson, for the past 38 years. Fire doors have recently been installed throughout, and rooms re-wallpapered. A new nine-room sister hotel, the Novicento, has sprung up off nearby Campo San Maurizio. Enquire at the Flora for details.

～

NEARBY Piazza San Marco.
LOCATION 300 m from Piazza San Marco in cul-de-sac off Calle Larga XXII Marzo; vaporetto San Marco
FOOD breakfast
PRICE €€€
ROOMS 44; 32 double and twin, 6 single, 6 family, all with bath or shower; all rooms have phone, TV, air conditioning, hairdrier, safe
FACILITIES reading room, breakfast room, bar, lift, garden
CREDIT CARDS AE, DC, MC, V
DISABLED 2 rooms on ground floor **PETS** accepted **CLOSED** never
PROPRIETORS Roger and Joel Romanelli

THE NORTH-EAST

VENICE

LEON BIANCO
~ TOWN GUESTHOUSE ~

Corte Leon Bianco, Cannaregio 5629, 30131 Venezia
TEL 041 5233572 **FAX** 041 2416392
E-MAIL info@leonbianco.it **WEBSITE** www.leonbianco.it

HIDDEN AWAY IN AN ENCLOSED COURTYARD, behind a sturdy door in the wall, and approached by stone steps rising up a cavernous brick-walled stairwell, we recently discovered this gem. Opened a couple of years ago by three friends, the *locanda* occupies one floor of an old *palazzo* and has a reception area and seven large, attractive bedrooms with small, modern bathrooms. Once upstairs, the only signs of the building's age are undulating floors – some marble, some parquet – and immense tilted wooden doors. There is a kitchen but no breakfast room, so breakfast is served in the bedrooms.

Three of the bedrooms boast that most sought-after of Venetian views: over the Grand Canal. They are furnished simply but tastefully with a mix of antiques and pretty painted furniture, and freshly decorated in pale colours with cherubs frescoed on the ceilings. A more dramatic fresco is emblazoned across one wall of a huge bedroom on the street side. Although the Leon Bianco doesn't offer the services or address of the ritzy San Marco hotels, the modest prices are irresistible by comparison.

~

NEARBY Santi Apostoli; Miracoli; Rialto.
LOCATION in courtyard between Santi Apostoli and Santa Giovanni Crisostomo canals; vaporetto Ca' d'Oro, Rialto
FOOD breakfast
PRICE €€
ROOMS 7; 6 double and twin with shower, one family with bath; all rooms have phone
FACILITIES none
CREDIT CARDS AE, DC, MC, V
DISABLED not suitable
PETS not accepted
CLOSED never
PROPRIETORS Spellanzon family

THE NORTH-EAST

LOCANDA CIPRIANI
~ RESTAURANT-WITH-ROOMS ~

Torcello, 30012 Burano, Venezia
TEL 041 730150 **FAX** 041 735433 **E-MAIL** info@locandacipriani.com
WEBSITE www.locandacipriani.com

THE GREAT NEWS IS THAT, after several years of enforced closure (due to a planning dispute), this very special inn has reopened its six charming bedrooms to guests. We can think of nowhere more romantic to stay in all of northern Italy.

The tiny lagoon island of Torcello is the cradle of the Venetian civilization, yet all that remains are two serenely beautiful churches, Santa Fosca and the ancient cathedral, the last with its haunting Byzantine mosaic of the Madonna. When the crowds drift home, Torcello's magic begins to work, and only a handful of residents and the Locanda's guests are privileged to witness it. These have included Hemingway, Chaplin and Paul Newman, while the entire British royal family has lunched here. The rooms are simple and homely, yet sophisticated, with polished wood floors, attractive pictures on white walls, writing desks, *objets d'art*, comfortable sofas and armchairs. Air conditioning has now been installed, but mercifully not televisions, and bathrooms have been upgraded.

The Locanda's *raison d'être*, its restaurant, has always remained open, and continues to do so. Though it is a memorable experience to eat here, either in the rustic dining room or on the lovely terrace overlooking the cathedral, prices are steep, reflecting not so much the quality of the food, but its long-standing fame.

~

NEARBY Venice (40 mins); lagoon islands.
LOCATION in centre of island, overlooking the cathedral; vaporetto Torcello
FOOD breakfast, lunch, dinner
PRICE ©©©
ROOMS 6; 3 double with sitting rooms, 3 single, all with bath; all rooms have phone, air conditioning
FACILITIES sitting room, dining room, bar, terrace, garden **CREDIT CARDS** AE, MC, V
DISABLED not suitable **PETS** accepted **CLOSED** Jan
PROPRIETOR Bonifacio Brass

THE NORTH-EAST

VENICE

PALAZETTO SAN LIO
∼ TOWNHOUSE APARTMENTS ∼

Contact Venetian Apartments, 413 Parkway House, Sheen Lane, London SW14 8LS
TEL (London)020 8878 1130 **FAX** 020 878 0982
E-MAIL enquiries@venice-rentals.com **WEBSITE**: www.venice-rentals.com

IN THIS ENIGMATIC, CRUMBLY OLD HOUSE, skirted by canals, you can live out a Venetian fantasy amongst frescoed ceilings, silk covered walls, Murano glass chandeliers, rococo beds and antique painted Venetian furniture. The gaps are filled with unlovely sofas and lampstands and the eight apartments all have a genteel, slightly shabby air, which only adds to their romantic appeal. Perhaps the most charming is 'Affresco' on the *piano nobile*. In the reception room is the bed, screened off behind curtains. As depicted in paintings by Longhi, this was the custom, so that the lady of the house could receive guests in her boudoir, yet retire when she wished. The room is old fashioned and very Venetian, with an original frescoed ceiling. There is a tiny room with bunks, suitable for children, a simple kitchenette and an even simpler bathroom.

The house has a fine long entrance hall with original watergate. Here the family's gondola was kept. There is a marble staircase, antique mosaic on the landings, and, on the first floor, a tiny stuccoed chapel. We include only a handful of self-catering options in our guides: this is a peach; contact Venetian Apartments for other options.

∼

NEARBY Campo Santa Maria Formosa; Rialto.
LOCATION at the end of an alley off Salizzada San Lio between Rialto and Campo Santa Maria Formosa; vaporetto Rialto
PRICE apartments from £499 to £995 per week (minimum rental one week); 'Affresco' £725 per week
ROOMS apartments range from studios to 2 bedrooms; all with kitchenette and bathroom; phone, heating
DISABLED not suitable
PETS not accepted
CLOSED never

THE NORTH-EAST

PALAZZETTO DA SCHIO
～ APARTMENTS IN PRIVATE HOUSE ～

Fondamenta Soranzo, Dorsoduro 316/b, 30123 Venezia
TEL and **FAX** 041 5237937
E-MAIL avenezia@tin.it **WEBSITE** web.tin.it/sangregorio

FONDAMENTA SORANZO IS A TRANQUIL backwater lined with attractive houses, including this red-painted *palazzetto*, home of the da Schio family for the past 300 years. The present incumbent, Contessa da Schio, lives on the ground floor and *piano nobile* while other parts of the house have been converted into three charming and comfortable apartments, available from any period of time from two days to six months. Note, though, that the apartments are considerably less expensive when taken per week or per month, rather than per night. They are largely furnished with family antiques, including pictures and mirrors, with modern bits and pieces to fill the gaps. The topmost apartment (not for those who don't like stairs) has wide views and a large sitting room, while the rooms in the mezzanine apartment all face the canal. It has a cosy, antique-filled living room.

The entrance hall of the *palazzetto*, lit by precious Venetian torch lamps and opening on to the garden, is splendid. This, and the fine three-bedroom *piano nobile* apartment, can be hired for parties at any time of the year and is available to stay in for one month in the summer.

～

NEARBY Santa Maria della Salute; Accademia; Zattere.
LOCATION on canal between Grand and Guidecca Canals; vaporetto Salute or water taxi
FOOD none
PRICE rates per night €€€; rates per week €-€€
ROOMS 3 apartments, 1 with 1 bedroom, 2 with 2 bedrooms; all with kitchen and bathroom; phone; maid service
CREDIT CARDS AE, MC, V
DISABLED not suitable
PETS not accepted **CLOSED** never
PROPRIETOR Contessa Anna da Schio

THE NORTH-EAST

VENICE

QUATTRO FONTANE
~ SEASIDE HOTEL ~

Via Quattro Fontane 16, 30126 Lido, Venezia
TEL 041 5260227 **FAX** 041 5260726
E-MAIL quattrofontane@ila.chateau.com **WEBSITE** www.ilachateau.com/quattrof/

THE LONGER WE LINGER at the Quattro Fontane, the more it grows on us. At first the 150-year-old mock Tyrolean building struck us as rather gloomy and suburban, but we soon warmed to the charmingly decorated reception rooms, particularly the *salone* and the little writing room. Mementos of the owners' travels are dotted around the hotel on walls and shelves – carved wooden figures, painted shells, model ships, porcelain, stamps. In the baronial dining room, with its cavernous hearth and bold red chairs, service was directed with courtesy by the long-serving head waiter. In warm weather you can eat on the wide tree-filled terrace that encircles the hotel.

The bedrooms in the main building have plenty of character and are individually decorated with an assortment of furniture, pictures and fabrics, comfortable if not luxurious. Those in the 1960s annexe are more streamlined, but here too each is different, attractive and cosy, with gaily tiled bathrooms. A dignified hotel, elderly now, but still spruce, and in our opinion the best on the Lido. Only giggling, secretly smoking chambermaids let the side down on our last visit.

~

NEARBY Venice; lagoon islands.
LOCATION set back from seafront on S side of Lido, near Casino; vaporetto Santa Maria Elisabetta
FOOD breakfast, lunch, dinner
PRICE €€€
ROOMS 58; 54 double, 4 single, 35 with bath, 23 with shower; all rooms have phone, TV, air conditioning, hairdrier, safe
FACILITIES sitting room, writing room, dining room, bar; tennis court and beach cabins available
CREDIT CARDS AE, DC, MC, V
DISABLED access difficult
PETS accepted **CLOSED** Nov to April
PROPRIETORS Friborg-Bevilacqua family

THE NORTH-EAST

LA RESIDENZA
~ TOWN HOTEL ~

Campo Bandiera e Moro, Castello 3608, 30122 Venezia
TEL 041 5285315 **FAX** 041 5238859

LA RESIDENZA APPEALS to true lovers of Venice who appreciate the chance to stay in the grand Gothic *palazzo* which dominates this dusty and enigmatic square, whose little church, San Giovanni in Bragora is one of the city's most appealing.

Just to enter is an experience: huge doors swing open to reveal an ancient covered courtyard and stone steps leading up to a vast baroque hall with beautifully coloured, lavishly carved plaster walls. Taking breakfast here in the early morning light is a rare treat, though the hushed atmosphere can be a little oppressive. This, however, is not a grand hotel, but a modest two star in immodest surroundings. Those who appreciate the combination of grotty, kitsch and antique in the bedrooms will mourn the fact that half of them have been renovated (calm and pretty, but standard), and the rest are due for the same treatment. Perhaps Signor Ballestra will heed the pleas of his regulars and leave them alone. Then you can choose: old on the right or new on the left, the perfect solution.

By the way, the famous smell – of cats? or is it boiled cabbage? – seems to have retreated to the hallway; some say it's gone altogether.

~

NEARBY San Giorgio degli Schiavoni; Arsenale.
LOCATION on small square 100 m behind Riva degli Schiavoni; vaporetto Arsenale, San Zaccaria
FOOD breakfast
PRICE €€
ROOMS 14; 11 double and twin, 3 single, all with bath or shower; all rooms have phone, TV, air conditioning, minibar
FACILITIES sitting room, breakfast area
CREDIT CARDS AE, MC, V
DISABLED not suitable **PETS** accepted **CLOSED** never
PROPRIETOR Giovanni Ballestra

THE NORTH-EAST

VENICE

SALUTE DA CICI

~ TOWN BED-AND-BREAKFAST ~

Fondamenta di Ca' Balla , Dorsoduro 222, 30123 Venezia
TEL 041 5235404 **FAX** 041 5222271

A LONG-TIME FAVOURITE OF OURS, this calm, civilized hotel inhabits a *palazzo* on a small canal in an interesting area between the Accademia and Salute. If you've had your fill of baroque churches, it's also perfectly placed for a visit to the Guggenheim Collection and a blast of abstract expressionism.

The façade is charming and typically Venetian: peeling stucco and rose-coloured brick, Gothic windows and stone balconies decked with flowers. And the interior doesn't disappoint. It has a classically elegant lobby of columns and marble floors beneath exposed rafters. A little bar is reserved for guests, and a tiny, sheltered garden offers a few sunny tables for a drink. Interconnecting basement rooms provide breakfast areas. Corridors lead off a beautifully furnished first-floor landing to simple white-painted bedrooms with high ceilings, Venetian marble floors and furniture that ranges from antique to utility. There's no difference in price, so request a room on the canal or, if you're willing to sacrifice character for comfort, go for one of the nine modern rooms in the annexe.

~

NEARBY Guggenheim Collection; Santa Maria della Salute.
LOCATION just S of Rio Calle Terra Nuovo, 5 mins' walk E of Salute; vaporetto Salute or water taxi
FOOD breakfast
PRICE €-€€
ROOMS 50 double and twin, single, triple and family, all with bath or shower; all rooms have phones
FACILITIES bar, sitting area, breakfast room, garden
CREDIT CARDS not accepted
DISABLED not suitable
PETS not accepted
CLOSED mid-Nov to Christmas, Jan to Mar (or Carnival if earlier)
PROPRIETOR Sebastiano Cagnin

THE NORTH-EAST

SAN CASSIANO

~ TOWN HOTEL ~

Calle della Rosa, Santa Croce 2232, 30135 Venezia
TEL 041 5241768 **FAX** 041 721033
E-MAIL sancassiano@sancassiano.it **WEBSITE** www.sancassiano.it

ARRIVING BY BOAT AT SAN CASSIANO's private jetty on the Grand Canal is considerably easier than finding your way by foot through a maze of tortuous, narrow alleyways from the nearest *vaporetto* or *traghetto* point (ask for a brochure to be sent so that you can follow its map). It also means that you can appreciate the 14thC *palazzo's* best feature: its deep red Gothic façade which faces the Grand Canal's greatest glory, the Ca' d'Oro. Inside, the hotel has a rather fusty feel to it, with heavy Venetian furnishings and a fairly lackadaisical staff – characteristics we also found in its sister hotel, the Marconi (page 122).What it does have, however, is some endearingly grandiose rooms, and the six facing the canal are splendid, with capacious reproduction antique wardrobes, matching desks and carved bedheads, floating white curtains bordered by velvet or brocade pelmets, and oriental carpets. They are the same price as rooms without a view, and you should be tempted to look elsewhere if you can't secure one. The light, elegant breakfast room with huge windows and waterfront views is a delight.

~

NEARBY Ca' d'Oro; Rialto markets; Rialto Bridge.
LOCATION on Grand Canal, opposite Ca' d'Oro; vaporetto San Stae or water taxi
FOOD breakfast
PRICE €€€
ROOMS 36; 20 double and twin, 12 triple and family, 4 single, all with bath or shower; all rooms have phone, TV, air conditioning, minibar, hairdrier, safe
FACILITIES sitting room, breakfast room, bar
CREDIT CARDS AE, MC, V
DISABLED 2 rooms specially adapted
PETS accepted **CLOSED** never
PROPRIETOR Franco Maschietto

THE NORTH-EAST

VENICE

SEGUSO

~ TOWN GUESTHOUSE ~

Zattere ai Gesuati, Dorsoduro 779, 30123 Venezia
TEL 041 5222340/5286858 **FAX** 041 5222340

SITTING ON THE SUNNY PROMENADE of the Zattere, lapped by the choppy waters of the wide Giudecca canal, gives you the distinct feeling of being by the seaside. This open setting, with a grand panorama across the lagoon, is just one of the charms of the Seguso. A *pensione* in the old tradition, it is family-run, friendly and solidly old-fashioned. And (unlike most hotels in Venice) prices are modest; the Seguso is not noted for its food, but half board here costs no more than bed-and-breakfast alone in hotels of similar comfort closer to San Marco.

The best bedrooms are the large ones at the front of the house, overlooking the canal – though for the privilege of the views and space you may have to forfeit the luxury of a private bathroom (only half the rooms have their own facilities). The main public rooms are the dining room, prettily furnished in traditional style, and the modest sitting room where you can sink into large leather chairs and peruse ancient editions of travel writing and guidebooks. Breakfast is taken on the front terrace – delightful. Fellow guests are often friendly, interesting and great Venice enthusiasts.

~

NEARBY Accademia gallery; Gesuati church.
LOCATION 5 mins' walk S of Accademia, overlooking Giudecca canal; vaporetto Zattere or water taxi
FOOD breakfast, lunch, dinner
PRICE ©©
ROOMS 36; 31 double and twin, 5 single, 9 with bath, 9 with shower; all rooms have phone
FACILITIES dining room, sitting room, lift, terrace
CREDIT CARDS AE, MC, V
DISABLED access possible **PETS** accepted
CLOSED Dec to Feb
PROPRIETORS Seguso family

THE NORTH-EAST

STURION
~ TOWN HOTEL ~

Calle del Storione, San Polo 679, 30125 Venezia
TEL 041 5236243 **FAX** 041 5228378
E-MAIL sturion@tin.it **WEBSITE** www.locandasturion.com

FIRST YOU HAVE TO CONQUER THE STAIRS, a seemingly endless flight which rises like a ladder from the ground floor to the hotel on the third floor. The friendly receptionist must be used to her guests collapsing in front of her desk, for she refrained from smirking when this inspector presented herself gulping for air. There is no porter, but receptionists will help with luggage.

Once you have recovered sufficiently to take in your surroundings, you will find them plush. Deep-red silk fabric adorns the walls in several of the bedrooms (these are non-smoking), with pale silk damask in others. Furniture throughout is walnut and mahogany, with floors of Venetian marble or covered in deep-red carpet. Two rooms look on to the Grand Canal. They are spacious for two people, and can sleep two extra, one on a bed cleverly hidden during the day in a wooden box masquerading as a cupboard. A little library of guidebooks, many in English, adds a homely touch. An internet facility has recently been added.

Locanda Sturion, found in a dark street hung with washing, has long been a hostelry. It stands on the site of a 13thC house built for foreign merchants taking their wares to the market.

NEARBY Rialto; Rialto markets; Ca' d'Oro.
LOCATION off Riva del Vin, close to Rialto Bridge; vaporetto Rialto, San Silvestro
FOOD breakfast
PRICE €€
ROOMS 11; 8 double, twin and triple, 3 family, 10 with bath, 1 with shower; all rooms have phone, TV, air conditioning, minibar, hairdrier, safe
FACILITIES breakfast room; internet point
CREDIT CARDS AE, MC, V
DISABLED not suitable
PETS accepted **CLOSED** never
PROPRIETOR Signor Fragiacomo

THE NORTH-EAST

VERONA

GABBIA D'ORO
~ TOWN HOTEL ~

Corso Portoni Borsari 4a, 37121 Verona
TEL 045 8003060 **FAX** 045 590293
E-MAIL gabbiadoro@easynet.it **WEBSITE** www.hotelgabbiadoro.it

THIS STYLISH HOTEL in a 17thC *palazzo*, luxurious but never ostentatious, boasts an attention to detail rarely encountered nowadays. A small, beautifully wrapped gift awaits your arrival, and the staff are as charming and polished as the hotel itself. The public rooms, entered through massive wood doors with gilt decoration, are comfortable as well as elegant: there are plenty of places in which to sit and relax, and sofas are large and deep. Wooden floors, beams and brickwork are much in evidence; the sitting room shares one wall with the Gardello Tower. Furnishings, chandeliers, silver-framed photographs, ornaments and antiques are always in keeping. Little lamps lend a glow to the panelled bar, and the new orangery is restful, with its green-and-white colour scheme and view to the terrace.

Frescoes, restored or reproduced from the originals, recur as friezes both downstairs and in the bedrooms. Suites outnumber doubles. In almost all, beds are shrouded in a canopy of antique lace. No. 404, dark red with sloping walls, rafters, and nooks and crannies, is so romantic that it's normally chosen for honeymooners. Prices are high, but we felt justifiably so.

~

NEARBY Piazza delle Erbe; Loggia del Consiglio; Arena.
LOCATION in medieval centre of the city, S of Porta Borsari; garage parking available
FOOD breakfast
PRICE €€€€
ROOMS 27; 8 double and twin, 19 suites, all with bath or shower; all rooms have phone, TV, air conditioning, minibar, hairdrier, safe
FACILITIES breakfast room, sitting room, orangery, bar, meeting room, lift, terrace
CREDIT CARDS AE, DC, MC, V
DISABLED access difficult **PETS** accepted **CLOSED** never
PROPRIETOR Camilla Balzarro

THE NORTH-EAST

TORCOLO
~ TOWN HOTEL ~

Vicolo Listone 3, 37121 Verona
TEL 045 8007512 **FAX** 045 8004058

THE TORCOLO IS AN INEXPENSIVE hotel in an excellent location at the heart of lively Verona. 'Its most outstanding quality,' writes one recent guest, 'was the warmth and friendliness of our welcome and the consistent helpfulness of the staff.' Every room is individually decorated in varying styles – Italian 18thC, art nouveau, modern – and all are fresher and have more charm than one normally finds at this price. Ours contained a complete set of Liberty-style bedroom furniture which had belonged to owner Silvia Pommari's parents when they first married. It was set off by white linen curtains and a colourful patchwork bedspread. Ceramic tiled bathrooms are somewhat cramped; the best have separate shower cubicles. Rooms are double-glazed against the considerable street sounds (people, not cars) but, despite air conditioning, they can get fuggy, especially in warm weather. Breakfast, including a jug of fresh orange juice, a good assortment of bread and croissants and yoghurt, can be taken in your room, which might be preferable to the rather cramped little breakfast room. In summer, it is served buffet-style in the small off-street courtyard.

~

NEARBY Arena; Via Mazzini, Piazza delle Erbe.
LOCATION just off Piazza Brà; garage parking
FOOD breakfast
PRICE €-€€
ROOMS 19; 13 double and twin, 4 single, 2 family, one with bath and 18 with shower; all rooms have phone, TV, air conditioning, hairdrier; 10 rooms have minibar and safe
FACILITIES sitting area, breakfast room, courtyard, lift
CREDIT CARDS AE, MC, V
DISABLED access difficult
PETS accepted **CLOSED** Jan
PROPRIETORS Silvia Pommari and Diana Castellani

THE NORTH-EAST

BARBARANO VICENTINO

IL CASTELLO
COUNTRY VILLA APARTMENTS

Via Castello 6, 36021 Barbarano,
Vicenza

TEL and FAX 0444 886055
E-MAIL ilcastello@tin.it
FOOD none
PRICE €
CLOSED never
Elda Marinoni

I L CASTELLO REFERS TO A HANDSOME villa built in the 17thC on the ruins of an ancient castle which looks down over the medieval village of Barbarano Vicentino. Occupied for the last 100 years by the Marinoni family, it retains the original perimeter walls of the castle, and its cellars. There is a formal Renaissance garden. you can choose from three separate apartments, for which reservations must be made on a weekly basis, each with one or two bedrooms, and fully equipped kitchens and bathrooms; or you can take the whole house. Rooms, white-painted and airy, with Venetian marble floors, are somewhat spartan in feel, despite the use of old family furniture throughout.

CORTINA D'AMPEZZO

MENARDI
TOWN HOTEL

Via Majon 110, 32043 Cortina
d'Ampezzo, Belluno

TEL 0436 2400 **FAX** 0436 862183
E-MAIL hmenardi@sunrise.it
WEBSITE www.sunrise.it/cortina/
alberghi/menardi
FOOD breakfast, lunch, dinner
PRICE €€ **CLOSED** Oct to mid-
Dec, mid-Apr to mid-Jun
Menardi family

T his family-run hotel evolved from a coaching inn when its owners, the Menardi family, began hiring out horses. During the First World War, Luigi Menardi began to transform the rustic inn into a proper hotel. Today the long white building has proliferated carved green wood balconies and tumbling geraniums, plus extra rooms and a separate annexe behind, but the Menardi family can still justifiably proclaim: 'same house, same family, same relaxed atmosphere'. Inside, antique pieces, painted religious statues and old work tools are mixed with local custom-made furnishings which look somewhat dated, but which are nonetheless comfortable. The atmosphere is one of traditional warmth and service is polished.

THE NORTH-EAST

MARLENGO

OBERWIRT
MOUNTAIN RESORT HOTEL

Vicolo San Felice 2, Marlengo,
39020 Merano, Bolzano

TEL 0473 222020 FAX 0473 447130
E-MAIL OBERWIRT@dnet.it
WEBSITE www.highlight-
hotels.com/oberwirt
FOOD breakfast, lunch, dinner
PRICE €€
CLOSED mid-Nov to mid-Mar the
Waldner family

Originally a simple inn, Oberwirt has been run by the Waldner family since 1749. Today, three generations currently work in the hotel: Signor Waldner's beaming mother, dressed in a *dirndl*, is at reception, while his daughter runs the restaurant. The hotel is often full, and, though it has plenty to recommend it, character and intimacy are not strong features.

The highlight is the food, which features local produce – highlights include fried duck liver, lamb cutlets in a herb crust and *marscapone* and compote of bitter cherries between layers of strudel pastry. The new kitchen is shown off to guests every Monday before dinner.

MERANO

CASTEL FRAGSBURG
CONVERTED CASTLE

Via Fragsburg 3, 39012 Merano,
Bolzano

TEL 0473 244071 FAX 0473 244493
E-MAIL info@fragsburg.com
WEBSITE www.fragsburg.com
FOOD breakfast, lunch, dinner
PRICE €€ CLOSED Nov to Easter
Ortner family

A LONG DRIVE ALONG A NARROW, twisting country lane, through mixed wood-land and past Alpine pastures, brings you to the east of Merano where Castel Fragsburg – 300 years old and a hotel for more than 100 years – commands splendid views of the Texel massif.

Externally, Fragsburg still looks very much the hunting lodge, with carved wooden shutters and balconies. A terrace along the entire front of the house, covered in wistaria, is a wonderful place to eat or drink. The adjoining dining room offers Italian, Tyrolean and vegetarian menus. The bedrooms all have balconies, carved pine furniture and colourful country fabrics.

THE NORTH-EAST

MERANO

CASTEL LABERS
CONVERTED CASTLE

Via Labers 25, 39012 Merano, Bolzano

TEL 0473 234484
FAX 0473 234146
FOOD breakfast, lunch, dinner
PRICE €€
CLOSED Nov to April
Stapf-Neubert family

O N A HILLSIDE TO THE EAST of Merano, Castel (or Schloss) Labers is immersed in its own lush orchards and vineyards, with direct access to mountain walks through Alpine pastures. The hotel has been in the Neubert family since 1885.

On a bad day, the Castel wouldn't look out of place in an Addams family film, but it has its charm, and the interior is welcoming. These vary enormously in size and standard: some elegantly proportioned with antique furniture, others rather too drab and basically furnished.

The ambience? 'Elderly', writes a guest. 'Very pleasant, very quiet, but elderly.'

MIRA PORTE

VILLA MARGHERITA
COUNTRY VILLA

Via Nazionale 416, 30030 Mira, Venezia

TEL 041 4265800 **FAX** 041 4265838
E-MAIL hvillam@tin.it **WEBSITE**
www.romantikhotels.com/rhmira
FOOD breakfast, lunch, dinner; room service PRICE €€ CLOSED never
Dal Corso family

A NOTHER COUNTRY VILLA in the Venetian hinterland, this time on the Brenta Riviera, overlooking a flat, industrial landscape but offering peace, seclusion while being well placed for excursions into Venice, which is just 10 kilometres away. Villa Margherita was built in the 17th century as a nobleman's country retreat, and has been open as a hotel since 1987. It is less imposing outside than some of its rival villa-hotels, but attractively furnished. Bedrooms, refurbished recently, are thoroughly comfortable; the best lead to the breakfast terrace. The Dal Corso family is the driving force behind the hotel and its highly regarded restaurant, 200 metres away across a terrifying road.

THE NORTH-EAST

SAN VALBURGA D'ULTIMO

EGGWIRT
MOUNTAIN GUESTHOUSE

39016 San Valburga d'Ultimo, Bolzano

TEL 0473 795319 **FAX** 0473 795471
E-MAIL eggwirt@rolmail.net
FOOD breakfast, lunch, dinner
PRICE €
CLOSED 10 Nov to 24 Dec
Schwienbacher family

THE QUIET AND UNSPOILED Val d'Ultima lies 30 kilometres south-west of Merano. In this ideal setting for both summer and winter sports, the Gasthof Eggwirt has existed as a hostelry since the 14th century, and today the Schwienbacher family welcome guests as if to their own home. The hotel is on the edge of the village with a large terrace at the front and superb views all around.

The bright bedrooms have lots of wood and cheerful duvet covers. An inexpensive, relaxed and friendly family hotel offering some excellent ski deals for children.

VENICE

CA' DEL BORGO
VILLAGE HOTEL

Piazza delle Erbe, Malamocco, Lido, 30126 Venezia
TEL 041 770749 **FAX** 041 770799
E-MAIL mabapa@venicehotel.com
WEBSITE
www.venicehotel.com/mabapa
FOOD breakfast **PRICE** €€
CLOSED Dec, Jan
Signor Vianello

IF YOU ARE LOOKING FOR SOMEWHERE calm and refined in which to install a group of friends, Ca' del Borgo could be an answer; as well as operating as an ordinary hotel, it is particularly well suited to private parties. Ca' del Borgo stands in a wide, quiet street in Malamocco. It retains the air of a gracious and civilized home, with eight spacious, comfortable and smartly decorated bedrooms with a large terrace and a little garden. Bedrooms have parquet floors, oriental rugs, excellent beds. Service is discreet.

A car would be useful. The hotel is out of the way, and it could transport guests to the Ca' del Moro sports and health club, which they are entitled to use; similarly the Hotel Excelsior's beach. Free bikes.

THE NORTH-EAST

VENICE

MARCONI
TOWN HOTEL

Riva del Vin, San Polo 729, 30125
Venezia

TEL 041 5222068 **FAX** 041 5229700
E-MAIL marconi@marconi.it
WEBSITE www.marconi.it
FOOD breakfast
PRICE €€€
CLOSED never
Franco Maschietto

THE MARCONI IS A TYPICAL VENICE HOTEL, encapsulating both what is right and what is wrong about many of them. As so often, the location is enviable (right by Rialto Bridge). The building is a 16thC *palazzo* with a 19thC entrance hall, marbled pillars, velvet hangings, and green and gold embossed ceiling. Best of all, the two rooms with balconies which overlook the Grand Canal cost no more than the rest. Bedrooms are fairly simple, but mahogany furniture and damask curtains make them seem old-fashioned. The hotel was renovated only a few years ago, but its dark wood fittings and rather dated fabrics give it a gloomy air. One senses that the staff are not as interested in their guests as they might be.

VENICE

PAUSANIA
TOWN HOTEL

Fondamenta Gherardini,
Dorsoduro 2824, 30123 Venezia

TEL 041 5222083
FAX 041 5222989
FOOD breakfast
PRICE €€€
CLOSED never
Guido Gatto

THE SAN BARNABA AREA, traditionally the home of impecunious Venetian nobility, is quiet and picturesque, and now highly desirable as the better-known San Marco district becomes increasingly overpriced. The Pausania is a small hotel lying close to the last surviving floating vegetable shop in Venice – a colourful barge on the San Barnaba canal.
The building is a weathered Gothic *palazzo*. A battered but beautiful stone staircase is a feature of the original building. Bedrooms are all in the same tasteful style. Cautions: a visitor reports being asked for cash on arrival – unacceptable, surely. And don't be pressurized into using the hotel's airport taxi service – unless other transport really is 'not working'.

THE NORTH-EAST

PICCOLA FENICE
TOWN HOTEL

Calle della Madonna, San Marco 3614, 30124 Venezia

TEL and FAX 041 5204909
FOOD breakfast (at adjacent Hotel Fenice et des Artistes)
PRICE €€-€€€; weekly rates available CLOSED Jan
Michele Facchini

THE TEATRO LA FENICE still waits to rise again from the ashes after the disastrous fire which rendered it a stark shell. The famous adjacent hotel, Fenice et des Artistes, where performers used to put up, was looking too gloomy and faded for us to include, but we were impressed by its sister hotel, the Piccola Fenice. It consists of seven suites sleeping between two and six people. On the wide first-floor landing there is a sitting area with desk and armchairs. The topmost apartment would be perfect for a family.

SAN SAMUELE
TOWN BED-AND-BREAKFAST

Salizzada San Samuele, San Marco 3358, 30124 Venezia
TEL and FAX 041 5205165
FOOD breakfast
PRICE €
CLOSED never
San Samuele Association

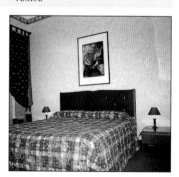

A BUDGET ESTABLISHMENT with new young managers, a fresh lick of paint, 300-year old Venetian marble floors and a pleasant, airy feel to the bedrooms. The *pensione* is installed on the upper floors of a pretty house in a wide street leading to the San Samuele *vaporetto* and *traghetto* landing stage. Ring the bell for admission, enter a pleasant little courtyard and climb the stairs – there are quite a few.

All the bedrooms have been redecorated, their main feature being a square of pink colour on the wall behind each low, skimpy-looking bed (an inspector informs us that they are adequately comfortable). Bathrooms are new. Breakfast is served in the rooms.

THE NORTH-EAST

VENICE

SERENISSIMA
TOWN HOTEL

*Calle Goldoni, San Marco 4486,
30124 Venezia*

TEL 041 5200011 **FAX** 041 5223292
FOOD breakfast
PRICE €€
CLOSED after Carnival to mid-Mar
Roberto dal Borgo

READERS' REPORTS CONFIRM that this is one of the most endearing and best-kept two-star hotels in town. Our inspector told us that she found it much pleasanter to stay here than in many a more expensive three star, and, given its central location just a few paces from the Doge's Palace, she deemed it value for money – a rare experience in Venice. Bedrooms are admittedly small (a triple will give two people more room), but neat and pretty, some with purpose-made wooden fittings, others – the ones that have been most recently redecorated – with more attractive Venetian painted headboards, cupboards and bedside tables.

ZERMAN DI MOGLIANO VENETO

VILLA CONDULMER
COUNTRY VILLA

*Via Zermanese 1, 31020 Zerman
di Mogliano Veneto, Treviso*

TEL 041 457100 **FAX** 041 457134
E-MAIL condulme@tin.it
FOOD breakfast, lunch, dinner
PRICE €€-€€€
FSED never
Davide Zuin

FOR THE PRICE OF A THREE STAR in San Marco you can stay in this impressive 18thC villa a 20-minute drive away. It stands four-square in a miniature park landscaped by Sebatoni. The vast central hall is decorated with baroque stucco in different hues, inset with murals. The menu in the restful, pale green-and-white dining room verges on the pretentious, but don't pass up the chance of a drink in the intimate stuccoed bar. The most exotic bedrooms are the upstairs suites (Ronald Reagan slept in No. 4). The double rooms in the main villa have been redecorated, but we preferred the more restrained annexe rooms.

EMILIA-ROMAGNA

HOTELS IN EMILIA-ROMAGNA

THE VIA EMILIA, THE ROMAN ROAD (now a motorway) stretching along the foothills of the Apeninne mountains from Piacenza to Rimini, gives this region its name. Bounded by the River Po to the north and the wooded slopes of the Apennines to the south, Emilia-Romagna is fertile and prosperous, its countryside a patchwork of fields, hills and plains, with most of its cities strung out along the Via Emilia, with Bologna in the centre.

Bologna, the regional capital, famed for its food, is primarily a business centre with business-style hotels to match; but it is also a city of learning (it has the oldest university in Europe) and of art (including beautiful Renaissance buildings) so there is much to attract the tourist, and we can recommend two of the three hotels owned by the Orsi family (see pages 139, 140). In Modena, Bologna's long-time rival with a stunning Romanesque cathedral, we recommend the Canalgrande (tel 059 217160). With 78 bedrooms, it is somewhat large for a full entry in this guide, but it is nevertheless a stylish, peaceful and comfortable villa set in beautiful gardens in the middle of the city.

Finding a satisfactory hotel in Parma is also tricky; we hope that our one modest recommendation, the very central Torino (page 147) will remain much the same after a recent change of ownership. In Ferrara we have found a homely B&B right in the centre of the historic walled town. For something grander, try the Ripagrande (tel 0532 675250), a Renaissance *palazzo* converted in 1980, or the luxurious Duchessa Isabella (tel 0532 202121). In Reggio Emilia, noted for its Parmigiano Reggiano and its balsamic vinegar, we can recommend the Hotel Posta (page 149).

The Adriatic coast of this region is not notable for small hotels, and we have still drawn a blank in Ravenna. You could try the Bisanzio (tel 0544 217111) or the simple but central Centrale Byron (tel 0544 212225).

Dotted about the region, in small towns or villages and in the countryside, we can recommend a clutch of other hotels, some of which are old favourites, others new discoveries.

EMILIA-ROMAGNA

BOLOGNA

CORONA D'ORO
∼ TOWN HOTEL ∼

Via Oberdan 12, 40126 Bologna
TEL 051 236456 **FAX** 051 262679
E-MAIL hotcoro@tin.it **WEBSITE** www.cnc.it/bologna

THE CORONA D'ORO lies in the historic old city, close to the two famous leaning towers, in a cobbled street which for most of the time is closed to traffic. Enticing food shops (including a wonderful delicatessen) give you some idea of why the city is nicknamed Bologna La Grassa (the Fat).

The Corona d'Oro became a hotel in 1890, though the original building dates back to 1300. It is here that Italy's first printing press was established and there are still a few features surviving from the original *palazzo*. In the early 1980s the hotel was bought by a packaging magnate, who elevated it from a simple hotel to four-star status, successfully combining the old features with the stylish new. The 14thC portico and Renaissance ceilings were preserved, while the plush bedrooms were provided with all modern conveniences. The showpiece was the hallway, with its fine art nouveau frieze supported on columns. Light streaming from above, fresh flowers and lush feathery plants create a cheerful, inviting entrance.

If arriving by car, be sure to get the hotel's route-map; without it, you will never find your way through the Bologna maze.

∼

NEARBY Piazza Maggiore; Piazza del Nettuno.
LOCATION in city centre, close to the two leaning towers in Piazza di Porta Ravegnan; with garage parking
FOOD breakfast
PRICE ©©©
ROOMS 35; 27 double, 8 single, all with shower; all rooms have phone, TV, air conditioning, minibar, safe
FACILITIES breakfast room, sitting area, bar, TV room
CREDIT CARDS AE, DC, MC, V
DISABLED not suitable
PETS accepted **CLOSED** Aug
PROPRIETOR Mauro Orsi

EMILIA-ROMAGNA

BRISIGHELLA

GIGIOLE

~ RESTAURANT-WITH-ROOMS ~

Piazza Carducci 5, 48013 Brisighella, Ravenna
TEL 0546 81209 **FAX** 0546 81275
E-MAIL gigiole.gigiole@tin.it **WEBSITE** www.charmerelax.it/gigiole

BRISIGHELLA IS A PICTURESQUE small town and thermal spa 13 km south-west of Faenza in an area famous for its production of clay and ceramics. The town is also known for its excellent olive oil. The Gigiolè stands across from the main church, a vaguely French-looking shuttered building with a shaded terrace in front.

The French style extends to the food: Tarcisio Raccagni, the chef, has been put on a par with the famous Paul Bocuse. Like Bocuse, he places great stress on using local seasonal ingredients of top quality and the results are superb: succulent meats, delicious soups and imaginative use of vegetables and herbs – all that is best in contemporary Italian cooking, and at affordable prices. The restaurant is a mixture of rustic and elegant; stone arches and walls are hung with copper pots and local ceramics while tables are laid with crisp, white linen and glasses gleam. Our inspectors' only complaint was the loud piped music.

The once sub-standard bedrooms and bathrooms have been recently upgraded to four-star standard. Spacious rooms now incorporate a sitting area (one suite has a kitchen). Floors are parquet and the furniture is modern.

~

NEARBY Bologna (50 km); Ravenna (42 km); Faenza (17 km).
LOCATION in centre of town; with public car parking in front
FOOD breakfast, lunch, dinner
PRICE €-€€
ROOMS 10; 7 double, 2 single, 1 suite, all with shower; all rooms have phone, TV, air conditioning, minibar, hairdrier
FACILITIES restaurant, bar, sitting room, lift, terrace
CREDIT CARDS AE, DC, MC, V
DISABLED no special facilities
PETS accepted
CLOSED hotel closed one month Jan-Feb, restaurant closed Mon
PROPRIETOR Tarcision Raccagni

EMILIA-ROMAGNA

BRISIGHELLA

RELAIS VARNELLO
~ COUNTRY GUESTHOUSE ~

Borgo Rontana 34, 148013 Brisighella, Ravenna
TEL 0546 85493 FAX 0546 83124 E-MAIL info@varnello.it
WEBSITE www.varnello.it

A NEWLY CONVERTED FARMHOUSE, undiscovered (yet) by most other guides, in the extraordinary, barren-but-beautiful Rontana hills, where you will get (even by the best Italian standards) a great welcome and personal attention. Some Dutch readers discovered it for us and were 'deeply impressed' by the hospitality of the Liverzanis. Of course, when you have a new enterprise, you try hard to please, but it really seems that the Liverzanis are natural hosts with a love for their locality, which is full of historical interest.

Everything is in superb new condition and artfully restored. A pleasantly home-like sitting-room is furnished with antiques, some from Liverzani family homes. The same private-house feel continues in the four bedrooms, each decorated and equipped differently, with attractive, unobtrusive fabrics, handsome iron bedsteads; one suite has a four-poster with hangings. Two apartments are available in an annexe. The grounds are extensive, and it's good walking country. By the way, the Liverzani family have lived in this corner of Italy for 1,000 years and Giovanni was an Olympic rapid-fire pistol shooter.

NEARBY Ravenna, Faenza (14 km).
LOCATION about 14 km W of Faenza, in own grounds with private car parking; ask for directions
FOOD breakfast; lunch and dinner by arrangement
PRICE €€
ROOMS 4, 3 double and one single; 2 apartments sleeping up to 5 but best for a couple; all rooms have bath, shower, phone, TV, air-conditioning, hairdryer, fridge
CREDIT CARDS AE, DC, MC, V
DISABLED no specially adapted rooms
PETS by arrangement
CLOSED Jan and Feb
PROPRIETORS Giovanni and Liana Liverzani

EMILIA-ROMAGNA

BRISIGHELLA

TORRE PRATESI
~ COUNTRY HOTEL ~

Via Cavina 11, 48013 Brisighella, Ravenna
TEL 0546 84545 **FAX** 0546 84558
E-MAIL torrep@tin.it **WEBSITE** www.torrepratesi.it

THE SOLID, SQUARE TOWER that forms part of this unusual hotel dates from 1510, while the adjacent farmhouse was added much later. Lovingly restored in 1993, it enjoys a remote and spectacular position on a hill with superb views over vineyards, olive groves and woods. As many of the original features of the building as possible have been preserved, and modernization has been carried out using traditional materials; wood, stone, wrought iron and marble. Modern equipment in the bedrooms is discreetly hidden in drawers and cupboards. Furnishings and colour schemes have been kept simple throughout – terracotta floors, warm, honey-coloured walls, leather armchairs and imaginative contemporary lighting. Bedrooms and bathrooms are surprisingly stylish; those housed in the tower itself enjoy 360° views as each occupies an entire floor.

The Raccagni's encourage a house party atmosphere and are warm and charming hosts. Guests can help themselves from the complimentary bar before a delicious dinner made largely with produce from the estate. There are plenty of spots for relaxing: by a huge stone fireplace, in the library/ music room or outside in the lovely grounds.

~

NEARBY Faenza (25 km); Ravenna (50 km).
LOCATION 8 km SW of Brisighella: take the SS302 for Florence, turn off to Valetta just after Fognano and follow signs; car parking
FOOD breakfast, dinner; light lunch on request
PRICE €€
ROOMS 9; 3 doubles and 6 suites, 8 with bath, 1 with shower; all rooms have phone, TV, air conditioning, complimentary minibar, hairdrier
FACILITIES sitting rooms, dining room, garden, swimming pool
CREDIT CARDS AE, DC, MC, V
DISABLED 2 adapted suites
PETS accepted **CLOSED** never
PROPRIETORS Nerio and Letizia Raccagni

EMILIA-ROMAGNA

CASTELFRANCO EMILIA

VILLA GAIDELLO CLUB

~ COUNTRY HOTEL ~

Via Gaidello 18, 41013 Castelfranco Emilia , Roma
TEL 059 926806 **FAX** 059 926620
E-MAIL gaidello@tin.it **WEBSITE** http://members.aol.com/gaidello

VILLA GAIDELLO CLUB is the creation of three sisters, one an architect, who took on the long neglected land and farm buildings of the old family home, situated in green, peaceful surroundings with a lake full of wildfowl. Today it is still run by one sister, Paola Giovanna Bini (another went to live in the United States, where she runs a similar operation in Middleburg, Virginia). Recent renovation and restoration has resulted in a total of eight apartments, each with kitchen and bathroom, of varying sizes, as well as two double bedrooms. Three of the apartments are in the *casa padronale*, one, for example, occupies the old beamed stable, using the manger for a bedroom. Other apartments are elsewhere on the estate, a couple of minutes' drive away. All display a simple, rustic elegance.

Emphasis at Il Gaidello is on the rural, the simple and the fresh. The restaurant is in another converted stable, where the food is prepared by *rezdore* (skilled country women) and overseen by Paola, who personally cuts the *prosciutto* and adds the finishing touches to each dish. The regional speciality, *tortellini in brodo*, is always on the menu, as well as wonderful *antipasto* and excellent dishes of chicken, rabbit and guinea hen. The food is usually served family-style at long wooden tables. Don't miss Paola's walnut liqueur.

~

NEARBY Modena (10 km); Bologna (25 km).
LOCATION on outskirts of Castelfranco Emilia on the Via Emilia (State Highway 9), between Modena and Bologna; ample car parking
FOOD breakfast, lunch, dinner
PRICE €-€€
ROOMS 8 apartments sleeping 2-6 people, 2 double rooms with bath; all rooms have TV, hairdrier
FACILITIES sitting room, dining room, terrace, garden, lake, solarium **CREDIT CARDS** AE, DC, MC, V **PETS** not accepted **DISABLED** access difficult **CLOSED** Aug; restaurant closed Sun eve, Mon **PROPRIETOR** Paola Giovanna Bini

EMILIA-ROMAGNA

CASTEL GUELFO

LOCANDA SOLAROLA

~ COUNTRY RESTAURANT-WITH-ROOMS ~

Via Santa Croce 5, 40023 Castel Guelfo, Bologna
TEL 0542 670102 **FAX** 0542 670222
E-MAIL solarola@imola.queen.it

THE LOCANDA SOLAROLA (situated in the middle of very flat nowhere in rural Emilia Romagna) started life as a modest *'agriturismo'* with a few rooms above a rustic eatery, but in 1995 the owners met Bruno Barbieri, the talented young chef who was to transform the restaurant into the establishment that it is today, one of only 19 in Italy to hold two Michelin stars.

The hotel has now expanded into another building in the farm complex. The decoration might be too 'pretty-pretty' for some tastes; flowers dominate throughout, starting with the reception area. Each bedroom is named after a different flower and has the appropriate floral wallpaper, quantities of lace, painted bedheads, embroidered linens and framed floral prints. Antonella's passion for collecting results in each room being very individual and full of her personally chosen *'objets'*. The comfortable public rooms are crammed with prints and old photos, tiffany lamps, lace cloths, pot plants, books and magazines. Jazz plays softly in the relaxed and cosy restaurant with its sloping, beamed ceilings and low lighting; a fire crackles in the grate in winter. Food is served under a pergola looking on to open fields in summer. The food is, of course, superb and the service impeccable.

~

NEARBY Bologna (25 km); Ravenna (45 km); Faenza (30 km).
LOCATION 4 km SE of Medicina; A14 motorway exit Castel San Pietro Terme; ample car parking
FOOD breakfast, lunch, dinner
PRICE €€€
ROOMS 15; 14 double and twin, 1 suite, 2 with bath, 13 with shower; all rooms have phone, TV, minibar, hairdrier; 10 have air conditioning
FACILITIES breakfast room, restaurant, bar, sitting rooms, billiard room, library, garden, swimming pool **CREDIT CARDS** AE, DC, MC, V
DISABLED ground floor rooms **PETS** accepted **CLOSED** restaurant closed Mon, Tues lunch, hotel never **PROPRIETORS** Valentino Parmiani and Antonella Scardovi

EMILIA-ROMAGNA

FERRARA

LOCANDA BORGONUOVO

~ TOWN BED-AND-BREAKFAST ~

Via Cairoli 29, 44100 Ferrara
TEL 0532 211100 **FAX** 0532 248000
E-MAIL info@borgonuovo.com **WEBSITE** www.borgonuovo.com

A SURPRISING FIND RIGHT IN THE HEART of this old walled city, on which the
noble d'Este family (which held sway from the late 13th century until
1598) has left a lasting impression, this is a most welcome place to stay,
and makes a pleasant change from normally characterless city-centre
accommodation. It's a genuine, family-run private bed-and-breakfast, with
four simple rooms available in the house – built inside the walls of a 15thC
monastery – of its courteous and friendly owners, the Orlandini's (who
speak fluent English and French).

The four bedrooms are soberly furnished with antiques; they are
thoughtfully equipped, and one has a kitchenette. In fine weather generous, home-made breakfasts are served on the outdoor patio; in cooler
weather you eat at a table in the Orlandini's own living room. Advice is on
hand about how to spend your time in Ferrara, and bicycles are provided
free of charge to get you about. The Locanda Borgonuovo has a superb
location, a few yards from the Castello Estense and the cathedral. Your
hosts can also recommend the best places to eat – restaurants, *trattorie*
and *osterie*, and they have discount agreements with some restaurants
and shops, as well as the local golf course.

~

NEARBY Castello d'Estense; Palazzo del Comune; cathedral.
LOCATION in pedestrian zone in the centre of Ferrara; with car parking (cars may be
brought to the hotel)
FOOD breakfast
PRICE €-€€
ROOMS 4 single, double and twin, all with bath, one with kitchenette; all rooms
have phone, TV, air conditioning, minibar, safe, hairdrier
FACILITIES sitting room, breakfast room, patio garden **CREDIT CARDS** AE, MC, V
DISABLED not suitable
PETS accepted
CLOSED never
PROPRIETOR Filippo Orlandini

EMILIA-ROMAGNA

PORTICO DI ROMAGNA

AL VECCHIO CONVENTO

~ CONVERTED MONASTERY ~

Via Roma 7, 47010 Portico di Romagna, Forlì
TEL 0543 967053 **FAX** 0543 967157
E-MAIL info@vecchioconvento.it **WEBSITE** www.vecchioconvento.it

PORTICO DI ROMAGNA is a sleepy medieval village centred on a single paved street – the location of the Vecchio Convento. The house was built in 1840 and converted in the mid-1980s into a hotel – with panache that comes as a surprise in this backwater.

The dining room, at the back of the house, is the main focus. With its beamed, pitched ceiling, tiled floor and open fireplace, it has a stylishly rustic air. There is also a stone-flagged family sitting room, with piano, card table, books and games, but in practice your sitting is more likely to be done on the small terrace outside the front door; the bar, just inside the door, offers standing room only.

A severe stone staircase leads up to the bedrooms. Here, the decoration is again plain and classy – but set against that is some glorious antique furniture. The beds are particularly notable – we've rarely seen such a collection of elaborate pieces. (The bases and mattresses, we're pleased to report, modern and firm.) Most rooms are adequately spacious, though some bathrooms at the top of the house have outrageously low ceilings. Signor Cameli cooks traditional dishes with flair – even his chips are a herby delight – while Marisa leads diners through the day's choices with great good humour (and passable English). Sumptuous breakfasts, with home-made preserves.

~

NEARBY Faenza (46 km); Ravenna (70 km); Florence (80 km).
LOCATION 30 km SE of Forli, in village; with limited garage parking
FOOD breakfast, lunch, dinner
PRICE €€
ROOMS 15; 12 double and twin, 9 with shower, 3 single, 2 with shower; all rooms have phone
FACILITIES sitting room, dining room, breakfast room, bar, terrace
CREDIT CARDS AE, DC, V **DISABLED** access difficult **PETS** accepted
CLOSED never **PROPRIETORS** Marisa Raggi and Giovanni Cameli

EMILIA-ROMAGNA

SORAGNA

LOCANDA DEL LUPO
~ RESTAURANT-WITH-ROOMS ~

Via Garibaldi 64, 43019 Soragna, Parma
TEL 0524 597100 **FAX** 0524 597066
E-MAIL info@locandadellupo.com **WEBSITE** www.locandadellupo.com

SORAGNA IS A QUIET LITTLE TOWN in the fertile lowlands of the Po Valley. It is dominated by its fortress-castle, which is still inhabited by the princely Meli Lupi family. The Locanda del Lupo, in the centre of town, was built by the family in the 18th century, and retains a timeless air, especially in the series of dining rooms which make up its noted restaurant. Like the rest of the hotel, they are simply decorated yet remain rather grand, with beamed ceilings, terracotta floors, antiques and old fireplaces and copper pans hanging on whitewashed walls. Tables are set with fine white linen, silverware, china and glass. The food is highly rated.

The air of quiet refinement is continued through the formal sitting room (there's also a small bar) and into the handsome bedrooms, reached by a flight of stairs. These are mostly spacious, with heavily beamed ceilings and cool tiled floors, and furnished with antiques (wooden chests, wrought-iron and mahogany beds). Modern conveniences such as TV and minibar did not detract from the feeling of being in another age.

Staff at the Locanda del Lupo were courteous and helpful.

NEARBY Soragna castle; Busseto (6 km); Roncole (6 km); Fontanellato (8 km); Parma (30 km).
LOCATION just off main square, 33 km NW of Parma; with car parking
FOOD breakfast, lunch, dinner
PRICE €€
ROOMS 46 single, double and twin, all with bath or shower; all rooms have phone, TV, air-conditioning, minibar, hairdrier
FACILITIES lift
CREDIT CARDS AE, DC, MC, V
DISABLED access dicfficult
PETS accepted
CLOSED 5 days over Christmas
PROPRIETOR Signor Dioni

EMILIA-ROMAGNA

BOLOGNA

COMMERCIANTI
TOWN HOTEL

Via Pignattari 11, 40124 Bologna

TEL 051 233052 **FAX** 051 224733
E-MAIL hotcom@tin.it
WEBSITE www.cnc.it/bologna
FOOD breakfast
PRICE €€€
CLOSED never
Paolo Orsi

A S ITS NAME SUGGESTS, the Commercianti caters primarily for the business market, but in a city with few tourist hotels it is a useful place to know about, and several recent visitors have been impressed. It has an excellent position – right in the heart of things, just off Bologna's main square, next to a smart pedestrian shopping street. The hotel exudes an air of efficiency rather than notable character ('rooms aren't particularly memorable but they are very comfortable', says one reporter). The hotel makes a good central base. There is no restaurant – just a café-like breakfast room. Although the Commercianti is situated in a traffic-free zone, guests can gain access by car in order to park in the hotel's garage.

BUSSETO

I DUE FOSCARI
TOWN HOTEL

*Piazza Carlo Rossi 15, 43011
Busseto, Parma*

TEL 0524 930031 **FAX** 0524 91625
WEBSITE
www.italiaabc.it/az/duefoscari
FOOD breakfast, lunch, dinner
PRICE €-€€ **CLOSED** Aug, Jan;
restaurant closed Mon
Marco Bergonza and Roberto
Morsia

I T IS HARD TO BELIEVE that this Gothic building is in fact only a few decades old, so convincing are its beamed ceilings, heavy antiques and iron candelabras. The hotel is situated on a fine *piazza* in the gentle city of Busseto, home town of Guiseppe Verdi, and also of the illustrious tenor, Carlo Bergonzi, who opened the hotel in 1965. Today it is run by his son, Marco, along with Roberto Morsia, with chef Enrico Piazzi in charge of the kitchen. The *raison d' être* of the place is its traditional restaurant (with terrace). As for wine, the restaurant boasts one of those amazing cellars which you can visit, stocked with more than 750 wines, from humble country bottles to the finest vintages. Bedrooms have been refurbished.

EMILIA-ROMAGNA

PARMA

TORINO
TOWN HOTEL

*Via Angelo Mazza 7, 43100
Parma*

TEL 0521 281046
FAX 0521 230725
FOOD breakfast
PRICE €€
CLOSED never
Signor Zecchino

THE ADVANTAGES OF THIS little hotel, perfect for a night or two in the urbane and prosperous city of Parma, are its location, its reasonable prices and its 'well organized' private parking – a great bonus. Situated right in the heart of the city, within a stone's throw from the principal sights of interest, the Torino is the perfect base for 'doing' Parma in a short time. We recommend bedrooms over the pleasant internal courtyard decorated with flowers. These are quieter than the front rooms. Bedrooms and bathrooms are fairly spartan, but vey clean and well cared for, with air conditioning. The hotel stands on the site of a convent, but its smart lobby recalls the art nouveau era.

REGGIO'EMILIA

POSTA
TOWN HOTEL

*Piazza del Monte 2, 42100 Reggio
Emilia*

TEL 0522 432944
FAX 0522 452602
E-MAIL info@hotelposta.re.it
WEBSITE www.hotelposta.re.it
FOOD breakfast
PRICE €€€
CLOSED never
MANAGER Caroline Salomon

ALTHOUGH ON THE LARGE SIDE for this guide, we draw attention to this city centre hotel for two reasons: firstly, we have no other recommendations here, and secondly, we like its rococo interior. Built in 1280, the *palazzo* has an austere façade decorated with frescoed coats of arms, but the interior is altogether a diffent story. The best bit is the bar, whose fittings and furniture were transferred here from a famous 19thC *pasticceria* in nearby Via Emilia some 30 years ago. Surprisingly for the hotel's size, there is no restaurant; breakfast is taken in a little stucco-decorated hall under a skylight on the first floor. Bedrooms, all different, are prettily decorated, and are well equipped, with comfortable bathrooms.

TUSCANY

HOTELS IN TUSCANY

NO OTHER REGION OF ITALY is as rich in good small hotels as Tuscany. The greatest concentration are naturally around the tourist highlights of Florence. In Florence itself we have four new entries (the Aprile, Casci, Palazzo Castiglione and Villa Poggio San Felice; but on recent visits we have been struck by the momentum that tourism is gaining in the rolling countryside of vineyards, cypresses and medieval hilltowns between Florence and Siena – the Chianti wine region and cradle of Renaissance art. There have been fine hotels in this area for many years, many of them in former monasteries and noblemen's villas; but alongside the old favourites there are some new discoveries to which, with the new format of the guide, we are now able to give full descriptions. We also have new finds in more far-flung places: for example, in and near Cortona and in Sorano, a remote corner of Maremma which was an ancient Etruscan stronghold.

Finding notably welcoming places to stay along the Tuscan coast is not so easy. We have recommendations in Pugnano, Pietrasanta and Porto Ercole and, although many of the better hotels in resorts such as Forte dei Marmi and Marina di Pietrasanta have attractive shady gardens, few have any other distinguishing features. In the north, at Livorno, you might consider the Villa Godilonda (tel 0586 752032): it did not quite deserve a full entry, but it is a spotless, modest seaside hotel near two sandy beaches.

Further south and just off the coast (but within easy reach of the long sandy beach at Marina de Castagneto) is an old stone villa, La Torre at Castagneto Carducci (tel 0565 775268), which, as its name suggests, stands next to a ruined tower. It has been converted into a simple hotel with 11 rooms, offering B&B and basic evening meals. Again, it didn't make a full entry, but it's a useful address.

The Tuscan island of Elba is big enough to absorb the many summer visitors it attracts without being swamped in the way that some of the smaller and more southerly islands have been, although there are few charming small hotels here. There is one hotel which we do not feature in the guide but can recommend: Capo Sud (tel 0565 964021) is a complex of little modern villas, scattered among trees in Lacona, a rather remote part of the island. There is a pool and a private beach. In general, however, Elba's small hotels are, to be honest, less attractive than many of the larger ones which cannot properly be given entries here.

TUSCANY

ARTIMINO

PAGGERIA MEDICEA

~ COUNTRY HOTEL ~

Viale Papa Giovanni XXIII, 59015 Artimino, Firenze
TEL 055 8718081 **FAX** 055 8718080
E-MAIL artimino@tin.it **WEBSITE** www.artimino.it

ARTIMINO IS A VILLAGE of some distinction, drawing visitors to see its museum and nearby Etruscan tombs. It also has a number of imposing buildings, one being a grand villa built by Ferdinand I of Medici in the 16th century, who was struck by the beauty of the surroundings. Now the outbuildings and servants' quarters of this villa have been converted into an elegant and peaceful hotel.

As befits its aristocratic pedigree, the atmosphere is classy, but unshowy. Furnishings are a stylish, unpretentious mix of new and old, and original features such as sloping rafters, chimneys and ceilings have, where possible, been retained both in bedrooms and in public areas.

A short walk across manicured lawns brings you to the restaurant Biagio Pignatta (named after a celebrated Medici chef). Its specialities are Tuscan dishes 'with a Renaissance flavour' (*pappardelle sul coniglio*, for instance – broad noodles with rabbit sauce), served on a terrace overlooking hillsides of vines and olives. The estate produces its own wine, which is reverently decanted at your table.

~

NEARBY Prato (15 km); Florence (24 km); Etruscan museum.
LOCATION 24 km NW of Florence; car parking
FOOD breakfast, lunch, dinner
PRICE €€
ROOMS 37; 36 double and twin with bath or shower, 1 single with shower; all rooms have phone, TV, air conditioning, minibar; 43 apartments in village
FACILITIES sitting room, breakfast room, TV room, restaurant, garden, swimming pool, tennis
CREDIT CARDS AE, DC, MC, V
DISABLED access possible
PETS accepted
CLOSED never
MANAGER Alessandro Gualtieri

TUSCANY

CASTELLINA IN CHIANTI

IL COLOMBAIO
∼ COUNTRY HOTEL ∼

Via Chiantigiana 29, 53011 Castellina in Chianti, Siena
TEL 0577 740444 **FAX** 0577 740402

A NEW ADDITION TO the typically Tuscan farmhouse hotels that cluster around Castellina in Chianti, Il Colombaio is a successful example of a proven formula, and at a very reasonable price. As you come from Greve in Chianti on the busy Chiantigiana road (SS 222), you will notice Il Colombaio on the right surrounded by lawns, shrubs and trees. Stone-built and capped with the tiled roofs at odd angles to one another so characteristic of Tuscany, the house has a pleasing aspect. It is, however, close to the road.

The restoration has been carried out with attention to detail, using country furniture to complement the rustic style of the building. The sitting room, which used to be the farm kitchen, is spacious and light with beamed ceilings, a traditional open fireplace and, in the corner, the old stone sink now filled with house plants. Breakfast is served in a small stone-vaulted room on the terrace.

Fifteen of the bedrooms are in the main house (the other six are in an annexe across the road) and have been furnished with wrought-iron beds and old-fashioned dressing tables; all have modern bathrooms.

∼

NEARBY Siena (20 km); Florence (40 km); San Gimignano (30 km).
LOCATION just N of Castellina in Chianti; car parking
FOOD breakfast
PRICE €-€€
ROOMS 21 double with bath or shower
FACILITIES sitting room, breakfast room, garden, swimming pool
CREDIT CARDS AE, DC, MC, V
DISABLED access possible
PETS accepted by arrangement
CLOSED never
MANAGER Roberta Baldini

Tuscany

Castellina in Chianti

Le Piazze
~ Country hotel ~

Loc. Le Piazze, 53011 Castellina in Chianti, Siena
Tel 0577 743190 **Fax** 0577 743191

A WELCOME ADDITION TO the booming hotel scene in the area around Castellina in Chianti which, we feel, has the edge on many of its competitors. Although only 6 km from the bustling town, the hotel is in completely secluded countryside reached by a long unsurfaced road which seems to go on forever.

The hotel is, needless to say, a converted 17thC farmhouse, but in this case the owners have deployed more imagination and a greater sense of elegance than usual. The buffet breakfast, for instance, is served on tiled sideboards in a room adjacent to the kitchen and separated from it by a glass partition. Or you can remove yourself to any of the numerous terraces that surround the house for uninterrupted views of classical Chianti countryside.

Rustic antiques have, of course, been used in the furnishing with the usual terracotta, exposed beams and white plaster, but here and there the pattern is broken by pieces from Indonesia. Bedrooms are individually furnished with lavish use of striped fabrics (avoid those in the roof space – they can become unbearably hot); bathrooms are large, with Jacuzzis or walk-in showers big enough for a party. No children under 12.

~

NEARBY Siena (27 km); Florence (50 km).
LOCATION 6 km W of Castellina in Chianti; car parking
FOOD breakfast; lunch and dinner on request
PRICE €€-€€€
ROOMS 15 double and twin with bath or shower; all rooms have phone
FACILITIES sitting room, breakfast room, bar, terraces, garden, swimming pool
CREDIT CARDS AE, DC, MC, V
DISABLED 1 specially adapted room
PETS quiet dogs accepted by arrangement
CLOSED never
PROPRIETOR Maureen Skelly Bonini

TUSCANY

CASTELLINA IN CHIANTI

SALIVOLPI

~ COUNTRY GUESTHOUSE ~

Via Fiorentina, 53011 Castellina in Chianti, Siena
TEL 0577 740484 **FAX** 0577 740998
E-MAIL info@hotelsalivolpi.com **WEBSITE** www.hotelsalivolpi.com

FOR NO IMMEDIATELY OBVIOUS REASON, the unremarkable Chianti village of Castellina contains a cluster of Tuscany's most appealing hotels. This welcome addition to the catalogue, open since 1983, offers a much cheaper alternative to its two illustrious neighbours – Tenuta de Ricavo (page 159) and Villa Casalecchi (page 160). It occupies two well-restored farm buildings and one new bungalow in a peaceful open position on the edge of the village – supposedly the location of the ancient Etruscan Castellina – affording broad views across the countryside.

There is a Spanish feel to the older of the houses – iron fittings, exposed beams, white walls, ochre tiles – and the spacious rooms are both neat and stylish, with some splendid old beds and other antiques. The whole place is well cared for, and has a calm, relaxed atmosphere.

The garden is impeccably tended, with plenty of space, some furniture and a fair-sized swimming pool. Breakfast ('*molto abbondante*', claims the boss) is served in a crisp little room in the smaller of the houses, and although it is the only meal provided, there is no shortage of restaurants nearby.

~

NEARBY Siena (21 km); San Gimignano (31 km); Florence (45 km).
LOCATION 500 m outside town, on road to San Donato in Poggio; car parking
FOOD breakfast
PRICE €-€€
ROOMS 19 double and twin with bath or shower; all rooms have phone
FACILITIES sitting room, breakfast room, garden, swimming pool
CREDIT CARDS MC, V
DISABLED 1 specially adapted room
PETS not accepted
CLOSED never
PROPRIETOR Angela Orlandi

TUSCANY

CASTELLINA IN CHIANTI

TENUTA DI RICAVO

~ COUNTRY HOTEL ~

Loc. Ricavo 4, 53011 Castellina in Chianti, Siena
TEL 0577 740221 **FAX** 0577 741014
E-MAIL ricavo@chiantinet.it **WEBSITE** www.ricavo.com

IF AWAY FROM IT ALL IS where you want to get – while retaining the possibility of doing some serious sightseeing – Ricavo is hard to beat. The hotel occupies an entire hamlet, which was deserted in the 1950s when people left the land for the cities in search of work.

The grouping of houses along a wooded ridge in the depth of the countryside might have been conceived as a film-set replica of a medieval hamlet. The main house, facing a little square of other mellow stone cottages, contains some of the bedrooms, and the several sitting rooms, which are comfortably furnished with a pleasant jumble of antique chairs and sofas (one of them with a small library of English, Italian, French and German books). The hotel's restaurant, La Pecora Nera ('The Black Sheep'), is open to non-residents so advance booking is essential.

Breakfast can be taken out-of-doors, in the shade of linden trees. At the right time of the year the gardens are bright with flowers, and there are plenty of secluded corners, which make the place seem calm and quiet even when the hotel is full. The small garden pool is ideal for quiet cooling off, the larger one is more out of the way.

A visitor pronounces the hotel 'expensive, but professional and worth it', and the food 'very satisfactory'. ~

NEARBY Siena (22 km); Florence (45 km).
LOCATION 1 km N of Castellina in Chianti; car parking
FOOD breakfast, lunch, dinner
PRICES ⒠⒠⒠
ROOMS 23; 13 double and twin, 2 single, 8 suites, all with bath or shower; all rooms have phone, TV, minibar, safe (3-day minimum stay in high season)
FACILITIES sitting rooms, bar, restaurant, terrace, gym, garden, 2 swimming pools, table tennis **CREDIT CARDS** MC, V
DISABLED ground-floor rooms available **PETS** not accepted **CLOSED** Nov to Easter; restaurant Tue, Wed; lunch (summer) Mon,Thur
PROPRIETOR Christina Lobrano-Scotoni

TUSCANY

RELAIS BORGO SAN FELICE
~ HILLTOP HOTEL ~

Loc. Borgo San Felice, 53019 Castelnuovo Berardenga, Siena
TEL 0577 359260/396561 **FAX** 0577 359089
E-MAIL borgosfelice@flashnet.it **WEBSITE** www.relaischateaux.fr/borgofelice

BORGO SAN FELICE IS LARGER THAN MOST of the entries in this guide, but we include it in the guide without hesitation. It is a carefully renovated hilltop hamlet – like a collection of charming small hotels. Surrounded by cypresses and the vineyards of the renowned San Felice estate, the peaceful village feels as if it has been suspended in time: no intrusive neon signs, no lines of cars, just the original Tuscan qualities of perfectly proportioned space setting off simple buildings of brick and stone, and topped by a jumble of terracotta roofs. Even the swimming pool (which in these parts all too often resembles a gaping, blue gunshot wound) has been discreetly tucked away. Gravel paths, carved well heads, pergolas, lemon trees in gigantic terracotta pots, a church, a bell tower and a chapel – this is the real Tuscany.

All the original features of the various buildings have been retained: vaulted brick ceilings, imposing fireplaces, old tiled floors. The furniture is a stylish mixture of old and modern and the sitting rooms are full of intimate alcoves. An elegant restaurant completes the picture. Top of the range – with prices to match.

~

NEARBY Siena (21 km).
LOCATION 21 km NE of Siena in former estate village; car parking
FOOD breakfast, lunch, dinner
PRICES €€€
ROOMS 45; 27 double and twin, 6 single, 12 suites, all with bath or shower; all rooms have phone, TV, minibar
FACILITIES sitting rooms, conference rooms, billiards room, restaurant, beauty centre, gym, swimming pool, tennis, bowls
CREDIT CARDS AE, DC, MC, V
DISABLED access difficult
PETS not accepted
CLOSED Nov-Apr
MANAGER Birgit Fleg

TUSCANY
CETONA

LA FRATERIA
~ CONVERTED CONVENT ~

Convento di San Francesco, 53040 Cetona, Siena
TEL 0578 238015 **FAX** 0578 239220
E-MAIL frateria@ftbcc.it **WEBSITE** www.mondox.it

O NE OF THE MORE UNUSUAL entries in this guide and not a hotel in the strict sense but a place of hospitality run by a community that has withdrawn from the world. The buildings, grouped around a hillside church founded in 1212 by St Francis, built of light, golden stone, form a rambling complex. Only seven rooms and suites are available, so, even when it is fully booked, one never has the sensation of being in a busy hotel. There is no swimming pool and none of the rooms has a television.

This may sound monastic, but the setting and furnishings are of the same standard as a top-class hotel: antiques, paintings and colourful wooden carvings (generally religious in theme) and spacious rooms with stone and beige stucco walls. The restaurant is unexpectedly sophisticated (and expensive), serving a mixture of refined and hearty food using fresh produce from the gardens.

A stroll around the monastery with its church and chapel, cloisters and courtyards, and hushed, peaceful atmosphere will help you realize why the young people of this community want to share their peace.

NEARBY Pienza (40 km); Montepulciano (26 km); Montalcino (64 km).
LOCATION 26 km S of Montepulciano; car parking
FOOD breakfast, lunch, dinner
PRICE €€€
ROOMS 7; 5 double, 2 suites, all with bath or shower
FACILITIES sitting rooms, restaurant, terrace, garden
CREDIT CARDS AE, MC, V
DISABLED no special facilities
PETS not accepted
CLOSED Jan; restaurant Tue in winter
MANAGER Maria Grazia Daolio

TUSCANY

CHIANCIANO TERME

LA FOCE

~ COUNTRY APARTMENTS ~

Strada della Vittoria 63, 53042 Chianciano Terme, Siena
TEL and **FAX** 0578 69101
E-MAIL lafoce@ftbcc.it

ANYONE WHO IS FAMILIAR WITH the writing of Iris Origo will be particularly interested in La Foce, the estate whose history during the Second World War is so vividly described in her book, *War in the Val d'Orcia*. Iris died in 1988, but her family still lives on the property in this remote but strangely beautiful corner of Tuscany, running it as a working farm.

Several of the buildings on the large estate have been converted into superior self-catering accommodation, ranging from the delightful two-person Bersagliere to superb and quite grand Montauto which sleeps ten; the latter stands in its own extensive garden with lavender borders and a small pool.

Furnishings throughout the comfortable apartments are in sophisticated and tasteful country style, predominantly antique, but with a few well-chosen modern pieces. There is plenty of colour, provided by bright rugs, cushions and cheerful fabrics. Each has its own piece of private garden and the use of a pool. Music lovers will appreciate the excellent chamber music festival which takes place on the estate each July.

~

NEARBY Pienza (20 km); Montepulciano (10 km).
LOCATION 5 km SW of Chianciano Terme (follow signs for Monte Amiata and Cassia); car parking.
FOOD dinner on request
PRICE €
ROOMS 9 self-catering apartments/houses sleeping 2-10, all with bath and shower; all apartments/houses have phone, TV on request
FACILITIES terraces, garden, swimming pools, tennis, children's playground
CREDIT CARDS not accepted
DISABLED 2 specially adapted rooms
PETS not accepted
CLOSED never
PROPRIETORS Benedetta and Donata Origo

TUSCANY

CORTONA

IL FALCONIERE

~ COUNTRY VILLA ~

Loc. San Martino, 52044 Cortona, Arezzo
TEL 0575 612 679 **FAX** 0575 612 927
E-MAIL rfalco@ats.it **WEBSITE** www.ilfalconiere.com

T HE PLAIN SURROUNDING Lake Trasimeno, over which Il Falconiere looks, was once the scene of some of Hannibal's fiercest battles against the Romans, and many of the place names hereabouts refer to bones and blood. Nowadays, the only carnage takes place on the A1 *autostrada* (the 'Sunny Motorway') but Il Falconiere is such a haven of civilized living that you will never realize that you are only 20 minutes away from one of Italy's riskiest tourist experiences.

Reached through quiet country lanes, bordered by vineyards, just outside Cortona, the main villa (built in the 17th century around an earlier fortified tower) is set in landscaped grounds of olives, rosemary hedges, fruit trees and roses, which also contain the old lemon house (now a top-class restaurant) and the still-functioning chapel with an adjoining suite. Meticulous attention has been given to every aspect of decoration and furnishing, from *trompe-l'oeil* number scrolls outside each room to the hand-embroidered window-hangings and finest bed linen. Persian rugs rest easily on uneven, antique terracotta floors. In the pigeon-loft of the old tower, reached by a narrow, stone spiral staircase, is a small bedroom with an unsurpassed view of the Valdichiana. A villa nearby has recently been converted to create eight new bedrooms with their own breakfast room. A recent report praises the hotel unequivocally: 'Everything combines to make this one of the most stylish hotels in Italy.'

~

NEARBY Cortona (3 km); Arezzo (29 km); Lake Trasimeno (10 km).
LOCATION just outside Cortona overlooking Valdichiana; car parking
FOOD breakfast, lunch, dinner
PRICE ©©© **ROOMS** 20; 17 double, 3 suites, all with bath or shower; all rooms have phone, TV, air conditioning, minibar, hairdrier, safe **FACILITIES** restaurant, garden, swimming pool (May-Sep) **CREDIT CARDS** AE, DC, V
DISABLED no special facilities **PETS** accepted **CLOSED** early Jan to mid-Feb
PROPRIETORS Riccardo Baracchi and Silvia Regi

TUSCANY

CORTONA

SAN MICHELE
~ TOWN HOTEL ~

Via Guelfa 15, 52044 Cortona, Arezzo
TEL 0575 604348 **FAX** 0575 630147
E-MAIL sanmichele@ats.it **WEBSITE** www.cortona.net/sanmichele

IT MIGHT SOUND LIKE an easy matter to turn a fine 16thC Renaissance palace into a hotel of character, but we have seen too many examples of good buildings that have brutalized by excessive and unwanted luxury, over-modernization and an almost wilful blindness to the original style, not to be delighted when the job has been properly done.

The Hotel San Michele has not fluffed the opportunities offered by the former seat of the Etruscan Academy, but has steered a precise course between the twin dangers of unwarranted adventurousness and lame timidity. White plaster and stark beams are complemented with rich modern fabrics; sofas of the finest leather stand on terracotta floors that seem glazed with a rich wax. Carefully-placed lights emphasize the gracefully interlocking curves of the cortile. The common rooms are full of such stylish features as frescoed friezes and immense carved stone fireplaces.

The bedrooms are more modest in style, with wrought-iron beds and rustic antiques, and in need of refurbishment according to our most recent report. Some of the more spacious ones have an extra mezzanine to provide separate sleeping and sitting areas.

NEARBY Diocesan Museum, Arezzo (29 km); Perugia (51 km).
LOCATION in middle of town; garage nearby
FOOD breakfast
PRICE €€
ROOMS 40 double and twin with bath or shower; all rooms have phone, TV, minibar
FACILITIES sitting room, breakfast room, conference room
CREDIT CARDS AE, DC, MC, V
DISABLED access possible
PETS small dogs accepted
CLOSED mid-Jan to early Mar
PROPRIETOR Paolo Alunno

TUSCANY

FERIOLO

CASA PALMIRA

~ COUNTRY GUESTHOUSE ~

Via Faentina – Loc. Feriolo, 50030 Borgo San Lorenzo, Firenze
TEL and **FAX** 055 8409749
E-MAIL palmira@cosmos.it **WEBSITE** www.casapalmira.it

L EAVING FLORENCE, THE OLD Faenza road winds through olive groves and
cypresses before reaching the beautiful and relatively unknown area of
the Mugello, and continuing up and over the Apennines. Casa Palmira is
set just off this road in an oasis of green, a converted barn attached to a
stone farmhouse with medieval origins. It takes its name from Palmira,
the nonagenarian *contadina*, or farmer, who lives next door.

Stefano and Assunta, the warm and charming hosts, have done a beautiful job on converting the barn into a relaxed and comfortable guesthouse. The ground-floor sitting room is spacious and welcoming, with a
huge fireplace, squashy sofas and chairs, an open kitchen area where
breakfast is prepared, and a dining area. Upstairs, the bedrooms all lead
off a lovely sunny landing, and while the public areas have terracotta flagstones, the bedrooms all have beautiful chestnut wood floors made by
Stefano (who also made the doors and some of the furniture). Pretty fabrics and patchwork quilts complement cream walls and dusty green paintwork. There are mountain bikes and a Smart for guests to hire and wonderful walking nearby. Who needs Florence?

~

NEARBY Florence (16 km); Fiesole (9 km).
LOCATION halfway between Florence and Borgo San Lorenzo just off the SS302, Via
Faentina (from Florence turn right to Feriolo just past Olmo); car parking
FOOD breakfast, dinner on request
PRICE €
ROOMS 7; 5 double and twins, 1 single, 1 triple, 1 with bath, 6 with shower
(although not all are en suite); rooms have hairdrier on request
FACILITIES sitting room, breakfast/dining room, terraces, garden with barbecue
CREDIT CARDS not accepted
DISABLED access difficult
PETS not accepted **CLOSED** Jan-Mar
PROPRIETORS Assunta Fiorini and Stefano Mattioli

TUSCANY

FIESOLE

BENCISTÀ

~ COUNTRY GUESTHOUSE ~

Via B. da Maìano 4, 50014 Fiesole, Firenze
TEL and **FAX** 055 59163
E-MAIL bencista@uol.it

'DON'T SEND US TOO MANY TOURISTS,' the smooth Simone Simoni begged our inspector – and he genuinely meant it. It is easy to see why the Bencistà is so popular. The *pensione* stands on a hillside overlooking Florence and the Tuscan hills; views from the terrace and many of the bedrooms are unforgettable. Added to this are the charms of the building, once a monastery: a handsome hall, three salons almost entirely furnished with antiques (including a little reading room with shelves of books and a cosy fire), plus plenty of fascinating nooks and crannies.

No two bedrooms are alike, and each one has some captivating feature – perhaps a beautiful view, a fine piece of furniture, a huge bathroom or, in some, a private terrace. They are nearly all old-fashioned, with plain whitewashed walls and solid antiques, and the accent is more on character than luxury. Not all the rooms have en suite bathrooms, although they are gradually being added.

The dining room is simple, light and spacious, overlooking gardens where olives, roses and magnolias flourish. Breakfast is taken on the terrace – a glorious spot to start (and end) the day. Dinner is on the dot at 7.30 pm and no choice is offered (except soup as an alternative to pasta). The house wine is excellent.

~

NEARBY Roman theatre; cathedral; monastery.
LOCATION 2.5 km S of Fiesole on Florence road; garage and car park
FOOD breakfast, lunch, dinner
PRICE €€
ROOMS 42; 29 double, 13 single, 32 with bath or shower; all rooms have phone
FACILITIES 3 sitting rooms, dining room
CREDIT CARDS not accepted
DISABLED no special facilities
PETS accepted
CLOSED sometimes Dec-Jan
PROPRIETOR Simone Simoni

Tuscany

Fiesole

Le Cannelle

〜 Town bed-and-breakfast 〜

Via Gramsci 52-56, 50014 Fiesole, Firenze
Tel 055 5978336 **Fax** 055 5978292
E-mail info@lecannelle.com **Website** www.lecannelle.com

HERE IS THAT RARITY, a new discovery, not featured in other guides (or not yet). The proprietors, Sara and Simona Corsi, have a father with a building business, so who better to restore these two old townhouses on Fiesole's main street, a little way north of the main square. Once finished, he handed over the management of the little bed-and-breakfast to his two daughters who have enthusiastically set about their new activity since opening in November 1999.

The cool hills surrounding Fiesole are studded with spectacular villas, and many of the hotels in the area are correspondingly expensive. We are therefore pleased to include Le Cannelle as a low-cost, but charming, alternative. It has been carefully decorated in simple, yet comfortable style. Bedrooms are quite spacious and one even has a duplex with two single beds at the top. Two offer lovely views of the hills to the north. Those on the somewhat noisy street have double glazing. The blue-and-white bathrooms are spotless. The pretty room where Sara and Simona prepare breakfast is, unfortunately, right on the street.

〜

Nearby Roman Amphitheatre; Florence (8 km).
Location on main street N of the main square; public car parking
Food breakfast
Price €€
Rooms 2 double, 1 single, 1 triple, 1 family, all with bath or shower; all rooms have phone, TV, air conditioning
Facilities breakfast room
Credit cards AE, MC, V
Disabled not suitable
Pets not accepted
Closed 2 months in winter
Proprietors Sara and Simona Corsi

TUSCANY

FIESOLE

VILLA SAN MICHELE
~ COUNTRY VILLA ~

Via Doccia 4, 50014 Fiesole, Firenze
TEL 055 59451 **FAX** 055 598734
E-MAIL villasanmichele@firenze.net **WEBSITE** www.orient/expresshotels.com

ACCORDING TO ITS BROCHURE, the villa was designed by Michelangelo – which perhaps accounts in part for the high prices. The rooms are among the most expensive in Italy – only a fraction less than those at the hotel's more swanky sister, the Cipriani in Venice – and beyond the reach of most of our readers. But the guide would be incomplete without this little gem on the peaceful hillside of Fiesole – originally a monastery, built in the early part of the 15thC century, enlarged towards the end of it, and much expanded recently with the creation of 13 extra suites.

What you get for your money is not extravagant decoration or ostentatious luxury, but restrained good taste and an expertly preserved aura of the past. The rooms are furnished mostly with solid antiques including 17thC masterpieces (religiously maintained every winter, we are told); many of the bedrooms have tiled floors of notable antiquity. Bathrooms, on the other hand, are impressively contemporary. Views from the villa are exceptional. One of the great delights of the place is to dine in the *loggia*, gazing down slopes of olives and cypresses to the city below. The pool terraces share this glorious view. Breakfast is an American buffet feast; half board includes an *à la carte* meal, lunch or dinner.

~

NEARBY Roman theatre; cathedral; monastery of San Francesco.
LOCATION on Florence-Fiesole road, just below Fiesole; car parking
FOOD breakfast, lunch, dinner
PRICE €€€€
ROOMS 40; 25 double and twin, 15 suites, all with bath; all rooms have phone, air conditioning; TV and minibar on request
FACILITIES reading room/bar, piano bar, dining room with *loggia*/terrace, garden, swimming pool (open Jun-Sep)
CREDIT CARDS AE, DC, MC, V
DISABLED access possible **PETS** small dogs accepted
CLOSED late Nov to mid-Mar **MANAGER** Maurizio Saccani

TUSCANY

FLORENCE

ANNALENA
~ TOWN BED-AND-BREAKFAST ~

Via Romana 34, 50125 Firenze
TEL and **FAX** 055 222402/3
E-MAIL annalena@hotelannalena.it **WEBSITE** www.annalena.it

One of Florence's traditional *pensioni*, still very much in the old style, with a regular clientele. The Annalena is located opposite the Boboli gardens (the famous park laid out by Medici dukes) and many of the rooms look out on to a horticultural centre next door. Luckily, none of them has windows on the busy Via Romana.

The *palazzo* is said to be 15th century, belonging at one point to a young noblewoman, Annalena, whose tragic love story and early widowhood led her to withdraw from the world and give over her property as a place of retirement for other young widows. Since then, the *palazzo* has been offering hospitality of one sort or another, and during the war gave refuge to many foreigners in flight from Mussolini's police.

The tradition of hospitality continues to this day, and while the Annalena is no luxury hotel, it offers solid comforts not without hints of style at reasonable prices, with an owner attentive to his guests' needs. A huge salon now serves as reception, sitting room, breakfast room and bar. Bedrooms vary in size and bathrooms are acceptable.

~

NEARBY Pitti Palace; Ponte Vecchio; Palazzo Vecchio; Uffizi.
LOCATION 3 minutes' walk from Pitti Palace on S side of river; public car parking nearby
FOOD breakfast
PRICES €€-€€€
ROOMS 20; 16 double and twin, 4 single, all with bath or shower; all rooms have phone, TV
FACILITIES sitting room/bar/breakfast room, terrace
CREDIT CARDS AE, DC, MC, V
DISABLED no special facilities
PETS accepted
CLOSED never
PROPRIETOR Claudio Salvestrini

TUSCANY

FLORENCE

APRILE
~ TOWN HOTEL ~

Via della Scala 6, 50123 Firenze
TEL 055 216237 **FAX** 055 280947
E-MAIL relais.uffizi@flashnet.it **WEBSITE** www.venere.it/firenze/aprile

The bust of Cosimo I de' Medici over the door gives a clue to the origins of the 15thC *palazzo* which houses this attractive hotel: it once belonged to the city's most famous family. More stylish use could possibly have been made of its architectural inheritance, but it has a charming, old-fashioned feel to it and the decoration is highly individual.

Public rooms are at the back of the building. The elegant breakfast room has a frescoed ceiling, the bar doubles as sitting room and there is a delightful little garden and conservatory. Bedrooms vary enormously in shape and size. Although they are all gradually being upgraded, a few are still very traditional. Others have vaulted ceilings, frescoes or fragments of graffiti. The owners have just bought the next-door *palazzo* where sponged paintwork in pale pastels, thick carpets and soft lighting in the bedrooms make for a more modern feel.

Bathrooms in smart grey marble have all been upgraded. Many rooms have a spectacular and unusual view over the rooftops of nearby Santa Maria Novella and its cloister. A free lecture on some aspect of Florence and its history is given each evening for guests.

~

NEARBY Santa Maria Novella; *duomo*; San Lorenzo.
LOCATION just S of Santa Maria Novella station and 10 minutes' walk from the *duomo*; paid car parking nearby
FOOD breakfast
PRICE €€
ROOMS 40; 30 double and twin, 6 single, 4 family, all with bath or shower; all rooms have phone, TV, air conditioning, minibar, hairdrier
FACILITIES sitting room, breakfast room, bar, conservatory, lift, garden
CREDIT CARDS AE, DC, MC, V
DISABLED 2 specially adapted rooms **PETS** accepted
CLOSED never
PROPRIETOR Riccardo Zucconi

TUSCANY

FLORENCE

CASCI
∼ TOWN HOTEL ∼

Via Cavour 13, 50129 Firenze
TEL 055 211686 **FAX** 055 2396461
E-MAIL casci@italyhotel.com **WEBSITE** www.hotelcasci.com

Music LOVERS MAY GET A THRILL from the fact that the 15thC *palazzo* which now houses this hotel once belonged to Giacomo Rossini. Located on a busy main road just north of San Lorenzo, the Casci is an unpretentious family-run hotel where you can be assured of the warmest of welcomes from the helpful Lombardis.

The decoration is modern and functional, but painted ceilings in some of the public areas give a clue to the age of the building. The open-plan reception area is bright, cheerful and always busy. The first thing our inspector noticed were two bookcases overflowing with guidebooks and leaflets for guests' use. To the right is the breakfast room, and to the left a bar/sitting area both of which have painted ceilings. The rooms vary in size and shape (some sleep five), and are fairly spartan, but quite attractive with pale yellow walls and modern green wooden furniture.

Many of the bathrooms are new; some have tubs and all have heated towel rails, an unexpected bonus in a two-star hotel. The most peaceful rooms look over a garden at the back of the building; others have double glazing.

∼

NEARBY San Lorenzo; Magi chapel; Medici chapels; *duomo*.
LOCATION on busy street N of *duomo*; paid car parking nearby
FOOD breakfast
PRICE €€
ROOMS 26; 14 double and twin, 4 single, 8 family, 7 with bath, 19 with shower; all rooms have phone, TV, air conditioning, hairdrier
FACILITIES breakfast room, bar, lift
CREDIT CARDS AE, DC, MC, V
DISABLED 1 specially adapted room
PETS small ones accepted
CLOSED Jan
PROPRIETORS Lombardi family

TUSCANY

FLORENCE

CLASSIC
〜 TOWN HOTEL 〜

Viale Machiavelli 25, 50125 Firenze
TEL 055 229351/229352 **FAX** 055 229353

STANDING IN ITS OWN LUSH GARDEN and rubbing shoulders with some of the most impressive residences in Florence, this pink-washed villa is on a leafy avenue just five minutes from Porta Romana, the old gate into the south of the city. A private residence until 1991, the house was rescued from decay and turned into a comfortable and friendly hotel which maintains admirably reasonable prices.

Bedrooms vary in size, but all are fairly spacious, with parquet floors, original plasterwork, antique furniture and pretty bedspreads. Two have frescoes, and another hosts an impressive fireplace. The high ceilings on the first floor allow for a duplex arrangement with extra space for beds or sitting areas on a higher level, while top-floor rooms have sloping, beamed attic ceilings and air conditioning. A romantic annexe suite tucked away in the garden, complete with tiny kitchen area, offers extra privacy for the same price as a standard double.

In warmer weather, breakfast is served outside under a pergola, but even in winter the conservatory allows for a sunny – possibly even a warm – start to the day.

〜

NEARBY Pitti Palace; Piazzale Michelangelo; Museo La Specola.
LOCATION in residential area 5 minutes' walk from Porta Romana; car parking
FOOD breakfast
PRICE €€
ROOMS 10 double and twin, 1 single, 3 suites, all with bath or shower; all rooms have phone, TV; top-floor rooms have air conditioning
FACILITIES breakfast room, conservatory, garden
CREDIT CARDS AE, DC, MC, V
DISABLED access difficult
PETS accepted
CLOSED 2 weeks Aug
PROPRIETOR Corinne Kraft

TUSCANY

FLORENCE

GALLERY, ART HOTEL

~ TOWN HOTEL ~

Vicolo del' Oro 5, 50120 Firenze
TEL 055 27263 **FAX** 055 268557
E-MAIL galleryhotel@lungarnohotels.com **WEBSITE** www.lungarnohotels.it

IT WAS NO PROBLEM TO STRETCH our normal size limit to include Florence's newest hotel: first because it is unique, and second because it feels like a much smaller place. In a quiet *piazzetta* just a few steps from the Ponte Vecchio, the Gallery is a temple of contemporary design, a combination of east and west which provides endless curiosities to look at and to touch. While the style is minimalist, it avoids being cold. Colours are muted and restful. Greys, creams, taupes and white dominate, while dark African wood is used throughout to add warmth and contrast. Contemporary art hangs on the walls. There is an impressive feeling of space in the public rooms.

A smart bar with squashy sofas houses a large video screen, while the reading room is dominated by a huge bookcase filled with interesting tomes to be browsed through at leisure. Inviting knee rugs are draped over the pale sofas almost begging the guest to curl up with a book.

Bedrooms vary in size but are all along the same stylish, sober lines. The bathrooms, with their classic chrome fittings, are splendid.

~

NEARBY Ponte Vecchio; Pitti Palace; Uffizi.
LOCATION in centre of town next to Ponte Vecchio; valet car parking nearby
FOOD breakfast, light lunch, dinner
PRICE €€€
ROOMS 65; 60 double and twin, 5 suites, all with bath or shower; all rooms have phone, TV, air conditioning, safe, hairdrier
FACILITIES sitting room, library, bar, breakfast room, terrace
CREDIT CARDS AE, DC, MC, V
DISABLED 2 specially adapted rooms
PETS small dogs accepted
CLOSED never
MANAGER Nedo Naldini

TUSCANY

FLORENCE

HELVETIA AND BRISTOL

~ TOWN HOTEL ~

Via dei Pescioni 2, 50123 Firenze
TEL 055 287814 **FAX** 055 288353 **E-MAIL** information–hbf@charminghotels.it
WEBSITE www.charminghotels.it/helvetia

THE HELVETIA WAS ORIGINALLY a Swiss-owned hotel right in the centre of Florence which added the name Bristol to attract 19thC British travellers. After 1945, it gradually fell into decay until new management took it over and began restoration in 1987, sparing no expense in their imaginative recreation of a 19thC luxury hotel.

Those with classical tastes, used to the stark simplicity of the Tuscan style, may find the results cloying and indigestible, but others will enjoy the rich colour schemes and heavy, dark antiques. The restaurant is undeniably elegant and hung with two amazing art nouveau lamps shaped like shells and rocks. The least overwhelming room is a 1920s winter garden, full of handsome cane furniture and potted palms, with a green-tinted glass ceiling. The bedrooms are, if anything, even more ornate than the public rooms. Antiques, Venetian mirrors and chandeliers add to the opulence. One of the finest features of the hotel is its extensive collection of prints and pictures. Staff and service are smooth and professional. In 2000 the hotel extended into the next-door building, adding 18 new doubles and three suites.

~

NEARBY Ponte Vecchio; Uffizi; Vecchio and Pitti Palaces.
LOCATION in the centre of town, opposite Palazzo Strozzi, W of Piazza Repubblica; public car parking nearby
FOOD breakfast, lunch, dinner
PRICES €€€€
ROOMS 67 double and twin, single and suites, all with bath or shower; all rooms have phone, TV, minibar, air conditioning
FACILITIES sitting rooms, restaurant, bar, winter garden
CREDIT CARDS AE, DC, MC, V
DISABLED some facilities
PETS small dogs **CLOSED** never
MANAGER Pietro Panelli

TUSCANY

FLORENCE

HERMITAGE

～ TOWN HOTEL ～

Vicolo Marzio 1, Piazza del Pesce, 50122 Firenze
TEL 055 287216 **FAX** 055 212208
E-MAIL florence@hermitagehotel.com **WEBSITE** www.hermitagehotel.com

THE LOCATION, JUST NORTH OF the Ponte Vecchio, is highly central, and highly favoured: few hotels this close to Florence's main drag could be described as peaceful, but this Lilliputian-scale retreat is not inappropriately named. There is an air of tranquillity about it – helped by a judicious, although not always sufficient, amount of double glazing on the busier riverside aspect.

Everything about the Hermitage is small, like a doll's house – only upside down, with neat, graceful bedrooms on the lower floors, while the reception desk and public rooms are on the fifth floor, overlooking the Arno. It's worth the climb: both bar-sitting room and breakfast room are delightfully domestic, in cool lemony yellows made intimate and welcoming with flowers and pictures.

The Hermitage was once no more than one of the typical, older-style *pension* that are becoming rare in Florence. But it has had a marked facelift and, as a recent inspection revealed, is now more tasteful and well-kept than average. A flower-filled roof terrace offers views across the pantiles of old Florence to the Duomo – an appealing place for breakfast.

～

NEARBY Uffizi; Ponte Vecchio.
LOCATION in heart of city, facing river; garage
FOOD breakfast, snacks
PRICES €€€
ROOMS 28 double and twin, 21 with bath, 7 with shower; all rooms have phone, TV, air conditioning
FACILITIES breakfast room, bar/sitting room, roof terrace
CREDIT CARDS MC, V
DISABLED access difficult
PETS small dogs accepted **CLOSED** never
PROPRIETOR Vincenzo Scarcelli

TUSCANY

J AND J
~ TOWN HOTEL ~

Via di Mezzo 20, 50121 Firenze
TEL 055 2345005 **FAX** 055 240282
E-MAIL jandj@dada.it **WEBSITE** www.hoteljandj.com

A CONVERTED MONASTERY provides the setting for this cool, chic hotel some distance east of the Duomo, on the way to the Sant' Ambroggio market. The street is comparatively quiet, and inside, the hotel feels a haven from heat and dust, so effective is its air conditioning and so peaceful is its ambience.

Many original features of the building are still intact – columns, vaulted ceilings, frescoes and wooden beams – and furnishings, though stylishly modern in places, are sympathetic to the spirit of the antique setting, and certainly not lacking personality. A small, pretty patio garden at the rear of the hotel, with elegant white parasols and plants in tubs, tempts breakfast-eaters to venture out through the plate-glass doors, though the interior option is equally charming in shades of yellow and green with wicker seating.

Bedrooms vary. All are of high standard; some exceptionally spacious, with split-level floors and seating areas, and high ceilings with exposed beams. A recent visitor felt that their eclectic style made them more like private rooms than hotel ones.

We found the reception knowledgeable and efficient.

~

NEARBY *duomo*; church of Santa Croce.
LOCATION E of *duomo*, N of Santa Croce; garage parking nearby
FOOD breakfast
PRICES €€€
ROOMS 20; 18 double, 2 family, all with bath; all rooms have phone, TV, air conditioning, minibar, hairdrier
FACILITIES sitting room, bar
CREDIT CARDS AE, DC, MC, V
DISABLED no special facilities
PETS not accepted
CLOSED never
PROPRIETORS Cavagnari family

TUSCANY

FLORENCE

LOGGIATO DEI SERVITI

~ TOWN HOTEL ~

Piazza SS Annunziata 3, 50122 Firenze
TEL 055 289592 **FAX** 055 289595 **E-MAIL** loggiato_serviti@italyhotel.com
WEBSITE www.venere.it/firenze/loggiato_serviti

ONE OF FLORENCE'S NEWEST charming hotels is in one of its loveliest
Renaissance buildings, designed (around 1527) by Sangallo the Elder
to match Brunelleschi's famous Hospital of the Innocenti, opposite. Until
a few years ago the building housed a modest *pensione* and the beautiful
square was a giant car park. But the Loggiato is now elegantly restored
and, thanks to the city council's change of heart, much more peaceful.

The decoration is a skilful blend of old and new, all designed to complement the original vaulting and other features with a minimum of frill and
fuss. Floors are terracotta-tiled, walls rag-painted in pastel colours.
Bedrooms are individually decorated with sympathy and flair. There is a
small, bright breakfast room in which to start the day (with fruit juice,
cheese and ham, *brioches*, fruit and coffee) and a little bar where you can
recover from it, browsing glossy magazines and sipping a Campari.

A recent reporter praised the 'admirable' comfort and standards, 'individual' welcome and service, and 'calm, comfortable and quiet' atmosphere. They provided 'the best breakfast we have had in Italy' and 'excellent' value for money. His sole quibble was 'slightly gloomy lighting'.

~

NEARBY church of Santissima Annunziata; Foundlings' Hospital.
LOCATION a few minutes' walk N of *duomo*, on W side of Piazza SS Annunziata;
garage service on request
FOOD breakfast
PRICES €€€
ROOMS 29; 19 double and twin, 6 single, 4 suites, all with bath or shower; all
rooms have phone, TV, air conditioning, minibar, hairdrier, safe
FACILITIES breakfast room, bar
CREDIT CARDS AE, DC, MC, V
DISABLED not suitable
PETS accepted **CLOSED** never
PROPRIETOR Rodolfo Budini-Gattai

TUSCANY

MORANDI ALLA CROCETTA
~ TOWN HOTEL ~

Via Laura 50, 50121 Firenze
TEL 055 2344747 **FAX** 055 2480954
E-MAIL welcome@hotelmorandi.it **WEBSITE** www.hotelmorandi.it

THIS LOVELY OLD HOUSE, formerly a convent, is the family home of Mrs Kathleen Doyle Antuono, an Englishwoman who has lived here since the 1920s. Now widowed, Mrs Doyle Antuono and her son and daughter share their house with visitors, and have made a great success of it.

The house is decorated throughout with taste and care. Antique Tuscan furnishings, patterned rugs, interesting pictures and fresh flowers abound. You may spot corbels carved with coats of arms in the reception hall, ancient painted tiles or fragments of fresco in the bedrooms, or a portrait of Mrs Doyle as an 18-year-old beauty. Our most recent inspector was impressed not only by her lovely frescoed room, but by the attention to detail, such as the thoughtful lighting, heated towel rail and even a telephone in the bathroom. Other visitors, though, found the walk up two flights of stairs to the lobby, unaided with luggage, a struggle. The house, which is close to the Piazza Santissima Annunziata with is famous Spedale Innocente, is convenient for exploring the historic centre of the city.

~

NEARBY *duomo*; archaeological museum; Academy of Fine Art.
LOCATION in quiet street NW of Piazza del Duomo; public car parking
FOOD breakfast
PRICE ©©
ROOMS 4 double, 2 single, 4 family, all with shower; all rooms have phone, TV, airconditioning, minibar, hairdrier, safe
FACILITIES sitting room, breakfast room
CREDIT CARDS AE, DC, MC, V
DISABLED no special facilities
PETS small well-behaved dogs accepted
CLOSED never
PROPRIETORS Kathleen Doyle Antuono and family

TUSCANY

FLORENCE

PALAZZO CASTIGLIONE

~ TOWN BED-AND-BREAKFAST ~

Via del Giglio 8, 50123 Firenze
TEL 055 214886 **FAX** 055 2740521
E-MAIL torre.guelfa@flashnet.it

THE ONLY SIGN BETRAYING the existence of this smart little B&B is a tiny, discreet brass plaque next to the bell. The solid 16thC *palazzo* is situated on one of the side streets which runs into the San Lorenzo market area, and was owned by the Castiglione family until some 20 years ago.

The hotel is on the second floor where a warmly-lit reception area doubles as sitting and breakfast room. The colour scheme is elegant pale green and cream. Sofas and chairs are upholstered in a smart brocade with co-ordinating curtains and paintwork. Several of the six bedrooms are frescoed. One particularly pretty room is entirely covered in pastoral scenes, while another is a *trompe l'oeil* of a castle courtyard complete with coats of arms, suits of armour in niches and birds circling in the sky above. All the rooms are furnished with a mixture of antiques and reproduction pieces and have armchairs, padded bedheads and curtains in handsome fabrics.

Bathrooms are a refreshing step away from the white-tiled hotel norm, with yellow and pale blue sponged paintwork, deep blue ceramic-tiled floors, and prints and painted mirrors on the walls.

~

NEARBY San Lorenzo; Medici chapels; Santa Maria Novella.
LOCATION between *duomo* and station; paid car parking next door
FOOD breakfast
PRICE €€
ROOMS 6 double, 1 with bath, 5 with shower; all rooms have phone, TV, air conditioning, minibar, hairdrier
FACILITIES sitting room, breakfast room, lift
CREDIT CARDS AE, MC, V
DISABLED no special facilities
PETS small ones accepted
CLOSED Christmas
PROPRIETOR Giancarlo Avuri

TUSCANY

FLORENCE

RESIDENCE JOHANNA CINQUE GIORNATE
~ TOWN GUESTHOUSE ~

Via delle Cinque Giornate 12, 50129 Firenze
TEL and **FAX** 055 473377

FLORENCE IS NOTORIOUS for being one of the most expensive cities in Italy for hotel rooms. We were therefore delighted to discover this new 'residence', offering great value for money.

Some way north-west of the centre of the city, but on several bus routes, the Johanna's existence is announced by a discreet brass plaque next to a solid iron gate; the pleasant building stands in its own small gravelled garden.

Inside, you find yourself in an elegant private house, with cool, cream-coloured walls, and high ceilings throughout give a sense of space. At the back of the house, a comfortable sitting room doubles as the reception.

The bedrooms are all fairly large (one particularly so), and are furnished with large beds and a mixture of antiques and modern pieces. Tasteful fabrics, of predominantly pale green-and-cream stripes, add style. The bathrooms vary in size, but even the smallest is adequate. Each room has the wherewithal for a simple DIY breakfast: electric kettle, coffee, tea, biscuits and *brioche*.

~

NEARBY Santa Maria Novella; Fortezza da Basso.
LOCATION in residential area 15 minutes' walk NW of the station; limited car parking
FOOD breakfast
PRICE €
ROOMS 9; 6 double, 3 twin, 1 with bath, 8 with shower; all rooms have TV; 3 have air conditioning
FACILITIES sitting room, small garden
CREDIT CARDS not accepted
DISABLED no special facilities, but 3 ground-floor rooms
PETS accepted **CLOSED** never
PROPRIETOR Lea Gulmanelli

TUSCANY

FLORENCE

TORNABUONI BEACCI

~ TOWN GUESTHOUSE ~

Via Tornabuoni 3, 50123 Firenze
TEL 055 212645/268377 **FAX** 055 283594
E-MAIL info@bthotel.it **WEBSITE** www.BThotel.it

ONE COULD NOT ASK FOR more in terms of location. Via Tornabuoni is one of Florence's most elegant and central shopping streets, where leading designers such as Gucci, Ferragamo and Ferré have their stores, and within easy walking distance are all the main sights of the city. Yet its position on the fourth and fifth floors of the 15thC Palazzo Minerbetti Strozzi, at one corner of Piazza Santa Trinita, makes it a haven from Florence's crowded, noisy streets.

The *pensione* has a turn-of-the-century atmosphere. Fans of E.M. Forster's *A Room with a View* will find this a close approximation of the Edwardian guesthouse described in the novel. Many of the rooms have views, but none so fine as the rooftop terrace, with its plants and pergola, which looks over the city to the towers and villas of the Bellosguardo hill. Even in the hot, still days of July and August, you may catch a refreshing breeze here.

The decoration and furnishings are old-fashioned but well maintained, like the house of a maiden aunt. Parquet floors and plain-covered sofas are much in evidence. Rooms vary – some are quite poky – but new management has been making improvements.

~

NEARBY Santa Trinita; Ponte Vecchio; Palazzo della Signoria.
LOCATION in centre of town; private garage nearby
FOOD breakfast, dinner, snacks (in summer)
PRICES €€-€€€
ROOMS 28; 20 double and twin, 8 single, all with bath or shower; all rooms have phone, TV, air conditioning, minibar, hairdrier
FACILITIES sitting room, restaurant, roof terrace
CREDIT CARDS AE, DC, MC, V
DISABLED access difficult
PETS small dogs accepted
CLOSED never
PROPRIETOR Francesco Bechi

TUSCANY

TORRE DI BELLOSGUARDO
~ HILLTOP VILLA ~

Via Roti Michelozzi 2, 50124 Firenze
TEL 055 2298145 **FAX** 055 229008
E-MAIL torredibellosguardo@dada.it

GIOVANNI FRANCHETTI BEGAN renovating his beautiful 16thC family home, on the hilly outskirts south of the Arno, in 1980. His aim to create 'a peaceful oasis where travellers can feel as comfortable as in their own homes' has certainly succeeded, though few visitors to Torre di Bellosguardo can be lucky enough to live in such delightful surroundings (Bellosguardo means 'beautiful view') and is an apt name.

There are 16 luxurious guest rooms in the house which, although grand, is not at all gaunt or dreary. Each room is a separate world, as much a sitting room as a bedroom, carefully and individually furnished with fascinating antiques; some are split-level, others have splendid inlaid panelling. The gardens of well-kept lawns and lily ponds, ancient cypress trees and shady terraces (not forgetting a secluded swimming pool), exert as much pulling power as the interior. The unassuming geniality of the owner is a refreshing contrast to many a haughty hireling in Florence's central hotels.

Energetic guests could easily walk into the city – though the gradients on the return journey may suggest a taxi-ride.

NEARBY Ponte Vecchio; Pitti Palace; Passeggiata ai Colli.
LOCATION on hill overlooking city, just S of Porta Romana; car parking
FOOD breakfast, lunch (by pool)
PRICE €€€
ROOMS 16; 8 double, 1 single, 7 suites, all with bath; all rooms have phone; 5 rooms have air conditioning
FACILITIES sitting room, breakfast rooms, bar, lift, garden, swimming pool
CREDIT CARDS AE, DC, MC, V
DISABLED access possible
PETS accepted
CLOSED never
PROPRIETOR Giovanni Franchetti

TUSCANY

FLORENCE

TORRE GUELFA
~ TOWN BED-AND-BREAKFAST ~

Borgo SS Apostoli 8, 50123 Firenze
TEL 055 2396338 **FAX** 055 2398577
E-MAIL torre.guelfa@flashnet.it **WEBSITE** www.home.venere.it/florence/torreguelfa

THERE CAN BE FEW BETTER SPOTS in Florence in which to enjoy a quiet *aperitivo* after a hard day's sightseeing: this is the tallest privately-owned tower in the city, dating from the 13th century and enjoying a 360° view over a jumble of rooftops, taking in all the most important landmarks and the countryside beyond.

The hotel is very popular, particularly with the fashion crowd during trade fair season. The Italian-German owners have created a comfortable and unstuffy atmosphere rejecting a heavy, Florentine look for a lighter touch. Bedroom walls are sponge-painted in pastel shades and curtains are mostly fresh, embroidered white cotton. Furniture is a mixture of wrought iron and prettily-painted pieces with some antiques. Bathrooms are in smart grey Carrara marble.

One room has its own spacious terrace complete with olive tree; be prepared to fight for it. A glassed-in *loggia* provides space for a sunny breakfast room and the double 'salon', with its boxed-wood ceiling and little bar, is a comfortable and quiet place in which to relax.

~

NEARBY Ponte Vecchio; Vecchio and Pitti palaces.
LOCATION in centre of town in traffic-limited area; garage nearby
FOOD breakfast
PRICE €€
ROOMS 16; 13 double and twin, 1 single, 2 family, all with bath or shower; all rooms have phone, TV, air conditioning, minibar
FACILITIES sitting room, breakfast room, bar, terraces
CREDIT CARDS AE, EC, MC, V
DISABLED 1 specially adapted room but access difficult
PETS small ones accepted
CLOSED never
PROPRIETOR Giancarlo Avuri

TUSCANY

VILLA AZALEE
～ TOWN HOTEL ～

Viale Fratelli Rosselli 44, 50123 Firenze
TEL 055 214242 **FAX** 055 268264
E-MAIL villaazalee@fi.flashnet.it **WEBSITE** www.villaazalee.it

CONVENIENT FOR THE STATION, but slightly remote from the monumental district (about 15 minutes by foot) Villa Azalee will appeal to visitors who prefer family-run hotels with some style to larger, more luxurious operations; and by the standards of most hotels in Florence, prices are very reasonable. The hotel consists of two buildings: the original 19thC villa and, across the garden, a new annexe, full of the potted azaleas that give the place its name.

A highly individual style has been used in the decoration and furniture: some will find the results delightful, others excessively whimsical. Pastel colours, frilly canopies and matching curtains and bedcovers characterize the bedrooms. They are all air conditioned, with spotless, new bathrooms. The public rooms are more restrained with an interesting collection of the family's paintings. Breakfast is served either in your room, in the garden (somewhat noisy) or in a separate breakfast room.

One of the drawbacks of the hotel is its location on the *viali* (the busy traffic artery circling Florence). Sound-proofing has been used, but rooms in the annexe, or overlooking the garden, are preferable.

～

NEARBY Santa Maria Novella; Ognissanti; San Lorenzo; *duomo*.
LOCATION a few minutes' walk W of the main station, towards Porta al Prato; garage nearby
FOOD breakfast
PRICES €€
ROOMS 24; 22 double and twin, 2 single, all with bath or shower; all rooms have phone, TV, air conditioning, minibar; some rooms have hairdrier
FACILITIES sitting room, bar, garden
CREDIT CARDS AE, DC, MC, V
DISABLED no special facilities
PETS accepted by arrangement **CLOSED** never
PROPRIETOR Ornella Brizzi

TUSCANY

FLORENCE

VILLA BELVEDERE

COUNTRY VILLA

Via Benedetto Castelli 3, 50124 Firenze
TEL 055 222501 **FAX** 055 223163
E-MAIL reception@villa_belvedere.com **WEBSITE** www.villa_belvedere.com

THIS FAMILY-RUN HOTEL lies in a pleasant hilly residential district on the southern outskirts of the city, commanding excellent views through classically Tuscan cypress trees when Florentine smog permits. The building itself is no great beauty, being practical and modern, but its well-kept gardens and small swimming pool are a great boon in hot weather, and its peaceful surroundings, away from any passing traffic, a relief from the city centre at any time of the year.

The Ceschi-Perotto family manage their business with welcoming enthusiasm and efficiency, and have embarked on an ambitious programme of refurbishment. Bedrooms and bathrooms are in excellent decorative order in a smart matching scheme of *fleur de lys* motifs, racing greens and high-quality solid wood furnishings. Bathrooms gleam, with white tiles offset by restrained geometric friezes. Public areas are light, spacious and comfortable – and the breakfast room makes the best of the garden.

A limited evening snack menu is available until 8.30 pm – particularly useful after a tiring day's sightseeing, since there are few restaurants within easy walking distance.

NEARBY Pitti Palace; Boboli gardens.
LOCATION 3 km S of city; car parking
FOOD breakfast, snacks
PRICES ©©-©©©
ROOMS 26; 21 double and twin, 2 single, 3 suites, all with bath or shower; all rooms have phone, TV, air conditioning, safe
FACILITIES 2 sitting rooms, breakfast room, bar, TV room, veranda, garden, swimming-pool, tennis
CREDIT CARDS AE, DC, MC, V
DISABLED no special facilities **PETS** not accepted
CLOSED Dec-Feb
PROPRIETORS Ceschi-Perotto family

TUSCANY

VILLA POGGIO SAN FELICE
~ HILLTOP VILLA ~

Via San Matteo in Arcetri 24, 50125 Firenze
TEL 055 220016 **FAX** 055 2335388
E-MAIL ilpoggio@tin.it **WEBSITE** www.wel.it/Sanfelice

THE HILLS IMMEDIATELY to the south of Florence are full of grand and beautiful villas, many of them erstwhile summer residences of wealthy Florentine families. The 15thC Villa Poggio San Felice is such a house; perched on a little *poggio* or hill, it could be in the heart of Chianti but is, in fact, only ten minutes from the city centre. The villa was bought by Gerardo Bernardo Kraft – a Swiss hotelier – in the early 19th century and was recently inherited and restored by his descendants.

The mellow old villa is set in a lovely garden designed by Porcinaie in the late 1800s. Inside, the feeling is very much of an elegant private house, but it is not at all stuffy. Cheerful fabrics and interesting colours give a young feel to the place while blending nicely with family antiques and pictures. The day starts in the long, high-ceilinged breakfast room where French windows open on to the garden. For relaxation, there is a pretty, partially arched *loggia*, plenty of seats dotted around the grounds or a sitting room for cooler weather. The comfortable and spacious bedrooms – each different from the next – lead off a landing on the first floor; two have working fireplaces. The suite has a little reading room and a terrace overlooking the city.

~

NEARBY San Miniato, Piazzale Michelangelo
LOCATION S of Porta Romana, follow the signs for Arcetri; car parking
FOOD breakfast
PRICE €€
ROOMS 5; 4 double, 1 twin, 4 with bath, 1 with shower; all rooms have phone; hairdrier on request
FACILITIES sitting room, breakfast room, terraces, garden, free shuttle service to and from Ponte Vecchio
CREDIT CARDS AE, DC, MC, V
DISABLED access difficult **PETS** small pets accepted **CLOSED** Jan-Mar
PROPRIETORS Livia Pulcinelli and Lorenzo Magnelli

TUSCANY

GAIOLE IN CHIANTI

CASTELLO DI TORNANO

~ COUNTRY APARTMENTS ~

Loc. Lecchi, Gaiole in Chianti, 53013 Siena
TEL and **FAX** 0577 746067/055 6580103 (bookings)
E-MAIL castellotornano@chiantinet.it **WEBSITE** www.chiantinet.it/castelloditornano

ONE OF THE COUNTLESS DEFENCE and watchtowers that dot Tuscany, solidly built of grey stone in positions with commandng views of the surrounding countryside, many of them in line of sight with their neighbours. Here, you find yourself in one of the wilder parts of Chianti with views of steep wooded hills, bleak in winter and, even in summer, with a feeling of inviolable isolation.

Most of the apartments are in a farmhouse adjoining the base of the thousand-year-old tower. Each has a living room with a kitchen area, and one or two bedrooms, furnished in a rustic style, deployed in a relatively simple manner. Some of the apartments are in the tower, and these are decorated with a more studied elegance. Each has its own entrance and a private outdoor area.

The swimming pool is in a common area and, fittingly for the location, has been fashioned from the remains of the former moat, still spanned by a wooden bridge. Nearby is a small fishing lake and, at the bottom of the hill, a typical Tuscan *trattoria*. Produce from the estate (wine, oil, vinegar, cheese, eggs and salami) can be bought on the spot.

~

NEARBY Siena (16 km); Florence (50 km).
LOCATION 5 km S of Gaiole; car parking
FOOD none (family *trattoria* nearby)
PRICE €-€€
ROOMS 9 apartments for 2-6 people; all apartments have bath or shower, kitchen
FACILITIES bar, garden, swimming pool, tennis (cleaners on request)
CREDIT CARDS AE, DC, MC, V
DISABLED 1 suitable apartment
PETS small pets accepted by arrangement
CLOSED never
MANAGER Barbara Sevolini

TUSCANY

GIOGOLI

IL MILIONE

~ FARM GUESTHOUSE ~

Loc. Galluzzo, Via di Giogoli 14, 50124 Firenze
TEL 055 2048713 **FAX** 055 2048046

IN MANY WAYS AN IDEAL LOCATION for those who like to combine city tourism with a country retreat. Il Milione is theoretically within Florence's city limits, but you could just as well be in deepest Tuscany. Convenient access to the *autostrada* brings Siena, San Gimignano, Pisa, Lucca and Arezzo all within easy driving distance. Nearby is the famous Certosa di Galluzzo. Yet Il Milione has everything that a farm should have: vines, olives and honey, fresh eggs and vegetables, and acres of countryside in which to roam. A swimming pool and a small lake are bonuses.

The eccentric name originates with Signora Husy's husband (now, alas, dead) Guscelli Brandimarte, a silversmith who, when he wanted to buy the farm, borrowed a million lire from each of his friends, repaying them with examples of his own workmanship. His irrepressible spirit lives on at Il Milione in the sculptures that are scattered throughout the gardens and in the silver place settings at the dining table. Rooms and apartments are spread throughout the farm's buildings. Booking ahead is essential for one of the best bargains in the Florence area.

~

NEARBY Florence (8 km); Siena (60 km).
LOCATION 8 km S of city centre; car parking
FOOD dinner on request (fresh farm breakfast ingredients supplied)
PRICES €-€€
ROOMS 2 apartments for 2 people, 5 apartments for 4 people, all with bath or shower; all apartments have phone, TV (3-day minimum stay)
FACILITIES sitting room, dining room, garden, swimming pool, bowls, horse riding
CREDIT CARDS not accepted
DISABLED no special facilities
PETS not accepted
CLOSED never
PROPRIETOR Jessica Husy

TUSCANY

GREVE IN CHIANTI

CASTELLO DI UZZANO

~ COUNTRY APARTMENTS ~

Via Uzzano 5, Greve in Chianti, 50022 Firenze
TEL 055 854032 **FAX** 055 854375

ORIGINALLY A 12THC CASTLE which the additions of centuries have converted to an elegant and civilized country villa, surrounded on its hilltop by stately cypresses and umbrella pines. Adjacent to the villa is a delightful ornamental garden with geometrically laid out box hedges, battered old statues and terracotta urns filled with flowers. On the other side is a formal terrace which is neatly divided by gravel paths and weathered stone balustrades.

The apartments surround a courtyard to which the graceful *loggia* of the castle forms a backdrop. A great deal of imagination and flair has been put into their restoration and decoration. Each has been individually furnished with interesting antiques and fine old prints and paintings of a higher standard than one normally finds in this type of place.

Smart kitchens have been unobtrusively incorporated, but if you prefer to eat out, there are many excellent restaurants in the area. An aristocratic, historic place, offering a civilized experience.

~

NEARBY Florence (30 km); Siena (45 km).
LOCATION 1 km N of Greve; car parking
FOOD none
PRICES €€€-€€€€€ (3-night minimum stay)
ROOMS 6 apartments with bath for 2-4 people; all apartments have phone, kitchen
FACILITIES garden
CREDIT CARDS MC, V
DISABLED no special facilities
PETS accepted by arrangement
CLOSED never
PROPRIETOR Marion de Jacobert

TUSCANY

VILLA DI VIGNAMAGGIO
~ COUNTRY VILLA ~

Greve in Chianti, 50022 Firenze
TEL 055 854661 **FAX** 055 8544468
E-MAIL agriturismo@vignamaggio.com **WEBSITE** www.vignamaggio.com

CHIANTI HAS MORE THAN ITS SHARE OF hilltop villas and castles, now posing as hotels, or, as in this case, self-catering (*agriturismo*) apartments. Vignamaggio stands out from them all: one of those rare places that made us think twice about advertising it. The villa's first owners were the Gherardini family, of which Mona Lisa, born here in 1479, was a member. This could even have been where she and Leonardo met. More recently, it was the setting for Kenneth Branagh's film of Shakespeare's *Much Ado About Nothing*.

Villa di Vignamaggio is a warm Tuscan pink. A small formal garden in front gives way to acres of vines. The pool, a short distance from the house, is among fields and trees. The interior is a perfect combination of simplicity and good taste, with the emphasis on natural materials. Beds, chairs and sofas are comfortable and attractive. Old wardrobes cleverly hide small kitchen units. The two public rooms are equally pleasing, and breakfast there or on the terrace is thoughtfully planned, with bread from the local bakery and home-made jam. The staff were charming and helpful when we visited. 'Service' is kept to a minimum ("This is not a hotel.").

NEARBY Greve (5 km); Florence (19 km); Siena (38 km).
LOCATION 5 km SE of Greve on the road to Lamole from the SS222; car parking
FOOD breakfast; dinner 3 evenings a week
PRICE ⓔⓔⓔ-ⓔⓔⓔⓔ
ROOMS 21 rooms, suites, self-catering apartments for 2-4 people, all with bath; all rooms/apartments have phone; some have air conditioning
FACILITIES sitting room, bar, gym, terrace, garden, 2 swimming pools, tennis court, children's playground
CREDIT CARDS AE, MC, V
DISABLED 1 specially adapted apartment
PETS accepted
CLOSED never
PROPRIETOR Gianni Nunziante

TUSCANY

LOCANDA L'ELISA

~ COUNTRY VILLA ~

Via Nuova per Pisa (SS 12 bis), Massa Pisana, 55050 Lucca
TEL 0583 379737 **FAX** 0583 379019
E-MAIL locanda.elisa@lunet.it

A FRENCH OFFICIAL OF THE NAPOLEONIC times who accompanied the Emperor's sister, Elisa Baciocchi, to Lucca acquired this 18thC villa for his own residence. Perhaps that accounts for the discernibly French style of the house that makes it unique among Tuscan hotels. A square building, three storeys high, painted in an arresting blue, with windows and cornices picked out in gleaming white, the villa stands just off the busy old Pisa-Lucca road.

The restorers have fortunately avoided the oppressive Empire style (which, in any case, the small rooms would not have borne) and aimed throughout at lightness and delicacy. The entrance is a symphony in wood, with geometrically patterned parquet flooring and panelled walls, and the illusion of space created with large mirrors. To the right is a small sitting room, furnished with fine antiques and Knole sofas. A round 19thC conservatory is now the restaurant. Each suite has been individually decorated using striped, floral and small-check patterns, canopied beds and yet more antiques – no expense has been spared. A glorious mature garden insulates it from the main road.

~

NEARBY Lucca (3 km); Pisa (15 km).
LOCATION 3 km S of Lucca on the old road to Pisa; car parking
FOOD breakfast, lunch, dinner
PRICE €€€€-€€€€
ROOMS 10; 1 double, 1 single, 8 suites, all with bath or shower; all rooms have phone,TV, air conditioning, minibar, safe
FACILITIES sitting rooms, restaurant, garden, swimming pool
CREDIT CARDS AE, DC, MC, V
DISABLED ground-floor rooms available
PETS small dogs accepted
CLOSED early Jan to early Feb
PROPRIETOR Giancarlo Mugnani

TUSCANY

SALVADONICA
~ COUNTRY ESTATE ~

Via Grevigiana 82, 50024 Mercatale Val di Pesa, Firenze
TEL 055 8218039 **FAX** 055 8218043
E-MAIL salvadonica@tin.it

THIS DELIGHTFUL ASSEMBLY OF RUSTIC buildings amid olive groves and vine-yards will gladden the heart of any lover of Tuscan scenery. Two entre-preneurial young sisters have energetically converted a family home, on what was until recently a feudal estate, into a thriving bed-and-breakfast and *agriturismo* business. A recent visitor was thoroughly enchanted by the place.

Now the two main buildings of the farm – one rich red stucco, the other mellow stone and brick – offer five well-equipped, comfortable guest rooms and ten apartments to let. They have clay-tiled floors and wood-beamed ceilings, and range from the merely harmonious and comfortable to the positively splendid (in the case of a brick-vaulted former cowshed).

From the paved terraces surrounding the buildings, you look over an olive grove to the neat swimming-pool area with Jacuzzi. Tennis courts and riding stables offer alternative pastimes. Breakfast, with a changing variety of cakes and breads, is served in a pleasant stone-walled dining room or on a sunny terrace overlooking unspoiled sweeps of countryside, where the local Gallo Nero Chianti and excellent olive oil are still produced.

~

NEARBY Florence (20 km).
LOCATION 20 km S of Florence, E of road to Siena; car parking
FOOD breakfast
PRICE €€
ROOMS 5 double, 10 apartments, all with shower; all rooms have phone, TV on request; apartments have fridge
FACILITIES billiards room, garden, swimming pool, tennis
CREDIT CARDS AE, DC, MC, V
DISABLED 1 specially-adapted room and 1 apartment
PETS not accepted
CLOSED Nov-Feb
PROPRIETORS Baccetti family

TUSCANY

MONTE SAN SAVINO

CASTELLO DI GARGONZA

~ CONVERTED CASTLE ~

Gargonza, 52048 Monte San Savino, Arezzo
TEL 0575 847021 **FAX** 0575 847054
E-MAIL gargonza@teta.it **WEBSITE** www.gargonza.it

GARGONZA IS NOT SO MUCH a castle as a whole hilltop village, perfectly preserved in a typically Tuscan landscape, encircled by walls and surrounded by cypresses. Its paved alleyways are car-free, except that you are allowed to drive in with your luggage.

Mostly dating from the 13th century, the houses offer good value for families or other small groups. They are, by and large, spacious, and simply furnished, and each has its own character and name ('the farmer's house', 'the guard's house', 'Lucia's house'). Bear in mind that this is meant to be self-catering accommodation, even if you don't plan to cater for yourself. There is no daily cleaning and bed-making, for example.

All the individual houses have kitchens but there is also a so-so restaurant just outside the walls – specialities include spinach and ricotta *roulade*, and wild boar; you can take breakfast in the old oil-pressing house (*il fantoio*).The houses are let on a weekly basis but there is also a guesthouse, whose rather spartan rooms can be rented nightly. In addition to the new swimming pool, the grounds have just been improved and the houses have undergone refurbishment. A report just-in confirms our positive appraisal: 'a peaceful, magical setting'; 'unable to fault maintenance'; and 'housekeeping spotless'.

~

NEARBY Arezzo (25 km); Chianti; Val di Chiana.
LOCATION 35 km E of Siena on SS73, 7 km W of Monte San Savino; car parking outside village walls
FOOD breakfast, lunch, dinner
PRICE ⓔⓔ
ROOMS 7 double in main guesthouse; 25 self-catering houses; all rooms have phone; main guesthouse rooms have minibar
FACILITIES 2 sitting rooms, 2 meeting rooms, TV room, garden, swimming pool
CREDIT CARDS AE, DC, MC, V **DISABLED** not suitable **PETS** small dogs accepted
CLOSED 3 weeks Nov, Jan **PROPRIETOR** Conte Roberto Guicciardini

TUSCANY

IL BORGHETTO
~ COUNTRY VILLA ~

Via Collina S Angelo 23, Montefiridolfi, S. Casciano Val di Pesa, 50020 Firenze
TEL 055 8244442 **FAX** 055 8244247
E-MAIL rcaval@galactica.it

DISCRETION, TASTE AND REFINEMENT are the key characteristics of this family guesthouse, recently opened but already appreciated by a discerning (and returning) clientele that enjoys civilized living in a peaceful, bucolic setting.

A manicured gravel drive leads past the lawn, with its rose beds and cypress trees, to the main buildings, which include the remains of two 15thC military towers. From a covered terrace, where breakfast is improved by views of miles of open countryside, a broad-arched entrance leads to the open-plan ground floor of the main villa. Within, the usual starkness of the Tuscan style has been softened by the use of muted tones in the wall colours and fabrics. Comfortable furniture abounds without cluttering the spacious, airy quality of the public areas. Upstairs, in the bedrooms (some of which are not particularly large), floral wallpaper and subdued lighting create a balmy, relaxed atmosphere. No intrusive phone calls or blaring televisions; a minibar would be considered vulgar.

Even the refined like a swim; but for those who consider swimming pools raucous, there is a soothing water garden. This is not a suitable hotel for young children.

Cookery courses are organized here at certain times of the year.

~

NEARBY Florence (18 km); Siena (45 km); San Gimignano (40 km).
LOCATION 18 km S of Florence, E of Siena road; on right before village; car parking
FOOD breakfast; lunch and dinner if requested by enough people
PRICE ©©© (2-day minimum stay)
ROOMS 8; 6 doubles, 2 suites all with shower
FACILITIES sitting room, dining room, terrace, garden, swimming pool
CREDIT CARDS DC, MC, V
DISABLED 1 suitable room
PETS not accepted
CLOSED Nov-Mar **MANAGER** Antonio Cavallini

TUSCANY

FATTORIA LA LOGGIA

~ COUNTRY ESTATE ~

Via Collina 40, 50020 Montefiridolfi, Firenze
TEL 055 8244288 **FAX** 055 8244283 **E-MAIL** fatlaloggia@ftbcc.it
WEBSITE www.fatlaloggia.it

MONTEFIRIDOLFI IS SET in classic Chianti countryside scattered with ancient estates producing wine and olive oil. Many of the mellow, stone farm buildings hereabouts are being turned into tourist accommodation of one sort or another, and Fattoria la Loggia is one of the most successful of its type: a range of spacious and attractive apartments agreeably housed in a hamlet-like collection of rural dwellings, in a hilltop setting with views over gloriously peaceful surroundings. The apartments are let daily or weekly. But this is not simply a self-catering complex – cooking lessons and dinners with wine tastings are sometimes organized in the cellar.

Each unit is carefully furnished with country-style pieces and many personal touches; kitchens and bathrooms, however, are efficiently modern, and are finished to a very high standard. Visitors can swim, ride, or walk on the estate, which produces its own wine and olive oil. La Loggia has recently established an artists' studio, with a permanent museum of contemporary art, as well as providing a venue for concerts and live theatre.

~

NEARBY Florence (18 km), San Gimignano (40 km), Siena (45 km).
LOCATION 18 km S of Florence, E of road to Siena; car parking
FOOD breakfast; dinner occasionally
PRICES €€
ROOMS 4 double, 11 apartments for 2-6 people, all with bath or shower; all rooms/apartments have phone, fridge, safe
FACILITIES restaurant, garden, solarium, swimming pool, table tennis, barbeque
CREDIT CARDS not accepted
DISABLED no special facilities
PETS accepted by arrangement
CLOSED never
PROPRIETOR Giulio Baruffaldi

TUSCANY

MONTERIGGIONI

MONTERIGGIONI

~ VILLAGE HOTEL ~

Via 1 Maggio 4, 53035 Monteriggioni, Siena
TEL 0577 305009/305010 **FAX** 0577 305011

VISITORS TO TUSCANY HAVE BEEN increasingly keen to drop by well-preserved, medieval Monteriggioni and spend a couple of hours relaxing in the *piazza* (where a bar serves snacks), browsing the antique shops or sampling the menu of Il Pozzo, one of the finest restaurants in the Siena area. Finally, somebody had the bright idea that a small hotel would not go amiss, especially since the town is peaceful and well placed for exploring the locality.

A couple of old stone houses were knocked together and converted with sure-handed lightness of touch to make this attractive hotel. The former stables now make a large, light and airy public area used as reception, sitting room and breakfast room.

At the back, a door leads out to a well-tended garden running down to the town walls and containing what is possibly the smallest swimming pool in Tuscany. The bedrooms are perfectly acceptable, furnished to a high rustic-antique standard with stylish hypermodern bathrooms.

~

NEARBY Siena (10 km); San Gimignano (18 km); Florence (55 km); Volterra (40 km).
LOCATION within the walls of Monteriggioni, 10 km N of Siena; car parking available outside the walls
FOOD breakfast
PRICES €€-€€€
ROOMS 12; 10 double, 2 single, all with bath or shower; all rooms have phone, TV, minibar, air conditioning
FACILITIES sitting area, breakfast room, bar, garden, swimming pool
CREDIT CARDS AE, DC, MC, V
DISABLED no special facilities
PETS accepted by arrangement
CLOSED Jan-Feb
MANAGER Michela Gozzi

TUSCANY

MONTEVETTOLINI

VILLA LUCIA

~ FARMHOUSE BED-AND-BREAKFAST ~

Via dei Bronzoli 144, 51010 Montevettolini, Pistoia
TEL 0572 617790 **FAX** 0572 628817
E-MAIL villalucia@yahoo.com **WEBSITE** www.bboftuscany.com

LUCIA VALLERA ALSO CALLS her delightful hillside farmhouse the 'B&B of Tuscany' and runs her establishment along English bed-and-breakfast lines – guests and family mingle informally, eating together in the traditional Tuscan kitchen or at the huge wooden table in the dining room if numbers require.

A strong Californian influence can be detected in the cooking and in the laid-back, elegant style of the place. (Lucia is an American of Italian extraction who has returned to Italy after living in the States.) There are plenty of up-to-date touches: CD player, satellite TV, computer. The clientele, too, is mainly American – lawyers, doctors and so on – often on return visits.

The dining room has various dressers crammed with colourful china and glass; there is a double sitting room with comfortable sofas and armchairs in traditional fabrics, plus shelves of books. Bedrooms are attractive, with working fireplaces, patchwork bedspreads, terracotta floors and antique furniture. Bathrooms, either adjoining or across the hall from the bedrooms, are decked in blue and white tiles, and spotlessly clean. The house has a lovely garden, and looks up to the old town of Montevettolini.

NEARBY Montecatini Terme (5 km); Lucca (30 km); Pisa (50 km).
LOCATION on hillside outside Montevettolini; car parking
FOOD breakfast; dinner on request
PRICE ©©-©©©
ROOMS 5 double, 2 apartments for 2, all with bath; all rooms have phone, TV, air conditioning
FACILITIES sitting room, conference room, terraces, garden, swimming pool
CREDIT CARDS AE, EC. MC, V
DISABLED no special facilities
PETS not accepted
CLOSED Nov-Apr
PROPRIETOR Lucia Vallera

TUSCANY

L'OLMO

~ COUNTRY GUESTHOUSE ~

53020 Montichiello di Pienza, Siena
TEL 0578 755133 **FAX** 0578 755124
WEBSITE www.nautilus-mp.com/olmo

THE INITIAL IMPRESSION GIVEN by this solid stone building set on a hillside overlooking the rolling hills of the Val d'Orcia towards Pienza is a little stark. A few trees would soften the lines. Once inside, however, the elegant, comfortable sitting room with its oriental rugs, low beamed ceiling, antiques and glass-topped coffee table laden with books dispels any such feeling. When we visited, there was a fire roaring in the grate and Mozart playing softly in the background.

The spacious bedrooms and suites (two of which have fireplaces) are individually and stylishly decorated in smart country style with floral fabrics, fresh white cotton bedcovers, botanical prints, soft lighting and plenty of plants and dried flowers. One room has the floor-to-ceiling brick-grilled wall (now glassed in) that is so typical of Tuscan barns. The wrought-iron fixtures throughout are by a local craftsman. Two suites have private terraces leading on to the large garden.

The pool has a wonderful view and the arched courtyard makes a pleasant spot for an aperitif.

~

NEARBY Siena (50 km); Pienza (7 km); Montepulciano (12 km).
LOCATION 7 km S of Pienza; car parking
FOOD breakfast, dinner on request
PRICE €€€€
ROOMS 6; 1 double, 5 suites, all with bath; all rooms have phone, TV, minibar, hairdrier, safe; 1 self-catering apartment
FACILITIES sitting room, breakfast/dining room, terraces, garden, swimming pool
CREDIT CARDS AE, MC, V
DISABLED 1 ground-floor room available
PETS not accepted
CLOSED mid Nov to April
PROPRIETOR Loredana Lindo

TUSCANY

PANZANO IN CHIANTI

VILLA LE BARONE
~ COUNTRY VILLA ~

Via San Leolino 19, 50020 Panzano in Chianti, Firenze
TEL 055 852621 **FAX** 055 852277
E-MAIL villalebarone@libero.it **WEBSITE** www.tuscanynet/lebarone

L E BARONE, THE ATTRACTIVE 16thC country house of the della Robbia family (of ceramics fame), became a hotel in 1976, but still feels very much like a private home.

The small scale of the rooms helps, but there are several other factors. The antique furniture is obviously a personal collection; reception amounts to little more than a visitors' book in the hall; there are plenty of books around – including English ones – and there are always fresh flower arrangements in the elegant little sitting rooms; and you help yourself to drinks, recording your consumption as you do so. In the past a minimum stay of three nights has further contributed to the low-key house-party atmosphere; but the rule has now been dropped.

Guests who are not out on sightseeing excursions have plenty of space to themselves in the peaceful woody garden or by the lovely pool, which gives a glorious panorama of the surrounding hills of Tuscany.

The restaurant and some of the rooms are in converted outbuildings. One of our most recent reports speaks of Villa le Barone as friendly and comfortable, at a fair price.

~

NEARBY Siena (31 km); Florence (31 km).
LOCATION 31 km S of Florence off SS222; covered car parking
FOOD breakfast, lunch, dinner
PRICE €€€
ROOMS 29; 28 double and twin, 22 with bath, 6 with shower, 1 single with shower; all rooms have phone, hairdrier; 5 rooms have air conditioning
FACILITIES 3 sitting rooms, TV room, self-service bar, dining room, breakfast room, garden, table tennis, swimming pool, tennis
CREDIT CARDS AE, MC, V
DISABLED not suitable
PETS not accepted
CLOSED Nov-Mar
PROPRIETOR Duchessa Franca Visconti della Robbia

TUSCANY

PANZANO IN CHIANTI

VILLA ROSA
~ COUNTRY GUESTHOUSE ~

Via S. Leolino 59, Panzano in Chianti, Firenze
TEL 055 852577 **FAX** 055 8560835
E-MAIL torre.guelfa@flashnet.it **WEBSITE** www.home.venere.it/florence/torreguelfa

A RECENT ADDITION TO the countless hotels and guesthouses in this part of Chianti, Villa Rosa is a solid structure dating from the early 1900s. Looming over the road from Panzano to Radda, its appearance makes a refreshing change from the usual rustic stone Tuscan farmhouse formula: it is painted bright pink.

Inside, a light touch is evident in the decoration. The terracotta floors and white walls downstairs are typical, but bedrooms have pastel-coloured, sponged paintwork, wrought-iron four poster beds and a mixture of wicker furniture, together with antique pieces here and there. The attractive, rather quirky, light fittings are by a local craftsman. Bathrooms also have touches of colour and heated towel rails add a hint of luxury.

The building is too near the road to be ideally situated, but at the back there is a peaceful, partially shaded terrace for open-air eating, while the garden slopes up the hillside to a pleasant pool and open, vine-striped countryside. Reasonable prices and a relaxed style of management make this hotel very popular, and we are pleased to hear that four new bedrooms have been added in the past year, raising the total from 12 to 16.

~

NEARBY Florence (34 km); Siena (28 km).
LOCATION 3 km SE of Panzano on Radda road; car parking
FOOD breakfast, dinner
PRICE €€
ROOMS 16 double and twin with bath or shower; all rooms have phone, TV, minibar
FACILITIES sitting room, restaurant, terraces, garden, swimming pool
CREDIT CARDS AE, DC, MC, V
DISABLED 1 specially adapted room, but access difficult
PETS accepted
CLOSED mid-Nov to just before Easter
PROPRIETOR Sabine Buntenbach

Tuscany

Panzano in Chianti

Villa Sangiovese

~ Country villa ~

Piazza Bucciarelli 5, 50020 Panzano in Chianti, Firenze
Tel 055 852461 **Fax** 055 852463

THE BLEULERS USED TO MANAGE the long-established Tenuta di Ricavo at Castellina (see page 159). They opened their doors in Panzano, a few miles to the north, in 1988 after completely renovating the building, and winning high praise from our readers.

The main villa is a neat stone-and-stucco house fronting directly on to a quiet back street; potted plants and a brass plate beside the doorway are the only signs of a hotel. Attached to this house is an old, rambling, stone building beside a flowery, gravelled courtyard-terrace offering splendid views. The landscaped garden below includes a fair-sized pool.

Inside, all is mellow, welcoming and stylish, with carefully chosen antique furnishings against plain, pale walls. Bedrooms, some with wood-beamed ceilings, are spacious, comfortable, and tastefully restrained in decoration. The dining room is equally simple and stylish, with subdued wall lighting and bentwood chairs on a tiled floor.

A limited but interesting *à la carte* menu is offered, which changes each night – service on the terrace in summer. A reporter praises the food and the wine.

~

Nearby Greve (5 km); Siena (31 km); Florence (31 km).
Location on edge of town, 5 km S of Greve; car parking
Food breakfast, lunch, dinner
Price €€
Rooms 19; 15 double, 1 single, 3 suites, all with bath or shower; all rooms have phone; rooms facing the *piazza* have air conditioning
Facilities 2 sitting rooms, library, dining room, bar, terrace, garden, swimming pool
Credit cards MC, V
Disabled no special facilities
Pets not accepted
Closed Jan-Feb; restaurant Wed
Proprietors Ulderico and Anna Maria Bleuler

TUSCANY

PELAGO

LA DOCCIA
~ COUNTRY GUESTHOUSE ~

19-20 Ristonchi, 50060 Pelago, Firenze
TEL 055 8361387 **FAX** 055 8361388 **E-MAIL** ladoccia@tin.it
WEBSITE www.ladocciawelcomes.com

EDWARD AND SONIA MAYHEW opened their beautifully converted stone farmhouse to guests in May 1999. Stunningly situated high up in the hills in a refreshingly undiscovered corner of Tuscany, the style is comfortable rustic with handmade terracotta flagstones, beamed ceilings, stone staircases and brick arches. Warm colours on the walls make a welcome change from the usual stark white. The furniture is a successful mix of locally made pieces and the Mayhews' own English antiques while books, pictures on the walls and knick-knacks give it the feel of a private house. This style is continued in the comfortable bedrooms and self-contained apartments, which are carefully furnished and have particularly smart bathrooms.

There are two sitting rooms, both with fireplaces (one is enormous), and an honesty bar. Breakfast and dinner (the latter prepared by Edward) are served at a long communal table. The house stands at 630 metres above sea level, so the long stone terrace, shaded by large, white umbrellas and bordered by lavender and roses, has fabulous views over the hills and down to Florence far below.

~

NEARBY Florence (27 km); Vallombrosa (8 km).
LOCATION 27 km E of Florence, 5 km S of Pelago; car parking
FOOD breakfast; lunch and dinner by arrangement
PRICE ©©
ROOMS 5 double, 4 apartments for 2-4 people, all with bath or shower
FACILITIES sitting rooms, dining room, bar, terraces, garden, swimming pool
CREDIT CARDS AE, MC, V
DISABLED no special facilities
PETS accepted
CLOSED never
PROPRIETORS Edward and Sonia Mayhew

Tuscany

PIENZA

IL CHIOSTRO DI PIENZA
~ CONVERTED MONASTERY ~

Corso Rossellino 26, 53026 Pienza, Siena
Tel 0578 748400 **Fax** 0578 748440

IN THE MODEST WAY OF Renaissance popes, Pius II renamed his home town of Corsignano after himself and made it a model of 15thC urban planning. So it is appropriate that the modern tourist-pilgrim should find lodgings in this stylishly converted monastery. The entrance is located at the back of the austere white cloister that gives the hotel its name and on to which half the rooms look; the other half face away, over the serenely magnificent hills of Val d'Orcia.

Many of the original features of the monks' cells have been retained: frescoed, vaulted ceilings and tiled floors. The furniture, however, breaks with monkish antiquity and concentrates on modern comfort without sinning against the character of the building. Bathrooms, though hardly spacious, are fully equipped.

The sitting rooms, with their old beamed ceilings, and the restaurant give on to a delightful terrace garden, where a pool has recently been built – a great bonus in a town. There could be no more agreeable place for an evening aperitif than its shady peace before strolling down Pienza's elegant Corso to the town's many restaurants.

~

Nearby Palazzo Piccolomini; *duomo*; Siena (52 km).
Location centre of town next to Palazzo Piccolomini; public car parking outside walls
Food breakfast, lunch, dinner
Price €€
Rooms 29; 25 double and twin, 2 single, 2 suites, all with bath; all rooms have phone, TV
Facilities sitting rooms, bar, restaurant, garden, swimming pool
Credit cards AE, DC, MC, V
Disabled access difficult
Pets not accepted
Closed Nov-Mar
Manager Loriana Codogno

TUSCANY

PIENZA

LA SARACINA

∼ COUNTRY GUESTHOUSE ∼

Strada Statale 146, 53026 Pienza, Siena
TEL 0578 748022 **FAX** 0578 748018
E-MAIL saracina@bccmp.com **WEBSITE** www.emmeti.it

BY THE TIME THE McCOBBS retired from La Saracina to return to the U.S.A. in 1996, they had created an extremely comfortable guesthouse. With the attention to detail that seems to be a characteristic of foreigners who go into the business, they turned an old stone farmhouse and its outbuildings, set in glorious countryside, into something special.

Refinement and good taste predominates: the bedrooms, all with their own entrance from out of doors, are spacious and elegant; suites have sitting areas. Antique furnishings mingle well with bright Ralph Lauren fabrics and there is a distinct leaning towards American country style. The luxurious bathrooms are fitted with marble sinks and Jacuzzis – several are enormous. Breakfast is served on the terrace in warm weather or in a neat breakfast room. There is an attractive swimming pool surrounded by smooth lawns.

This is an upmarket place and quite a challenge for the new, young owner. We are hoping that her fresh approach and enthusiasm will win through.

∼

NEARBY Pienza (7 km); Montepulciano (6 km).
LOCATION on quiet hillside, 7 km from Pienza on Montepulciano road; car parking
FOOD breakfast
PRICES €€-€€€
ROOMS 5; 2 double, 3 suites, all with bath or shower; all rooms have phone, TV, minibar; one self-catering apartment
FACILITIES breakfast room, garden, swimming pool, tennis
CREDIT CARDS AE, MC, V
DISABLED no special facilities, but all rooms are on ground floor
PETS not accepted
CLOSED never
PROPRIETOR Simonetta Vessichelli

TUSCANY

PIETRASANTA

ALBERGO PIETRASANTA
~ TOWN HOTEL ~

Via Garibaldi 35, 55045 Pietrasanta, Lucca
TEL 0584 793726 **FAX** 0584 793727
E-MAIL a.pietrasanta@versilia.toscana.it **WEBSITE** www.albergopietrasanta.com

PIETRASANTA (THE 'SAINTED STONE') has long been associated with the marble industry. The world-famous quarries at Carrara are nearby, and the attractive little town thrives on marble studios, bronze foundries, and a subculture of artists from all over the world. Recently, tourism here has moved upmarket, and the Albergo Pietrasanta is a response to this development. Opened in 1997, the hotel occupies elegant 17thC Palazzo Barsanti-Bonetti. The interior maintains many of the embellishments of a nobleman's house: intricate plasterwork, delicate frescoes, a couple of superbly-carved marble fireplaces, spacious rooms and antiques. However, the addition of the owners' contemporary art collection adds a totally new dimension.

The comfortable, unfussy bedrooms have warm, parquet floors, armchairs, smart fabrics and varying colour schemes. Thoughtful extras (cool linen sheets, plenty of mirrors, well-designed lighting and the tray of *vin santo* and biscuits) impressed our inspector. Downstairs, the winter garden doubles as breakfast room and bar while the pretty gravelled garden, dominated by three old palm trees, is a cool spot in summer.

~

NEARBY Pisa (25 km); Lucca (25 km); beaches (4 km)
LOCATION on pedestrian street in town centre; private garage
FOOD breakfast
PRICES ⓔⓔ-ⓔⓔⓔ
ROOMS 19; 8 double and twin, 1 single, 10 suites, all with bath or shower; all rooms have phone, TV, minibar, air conditioning, safe
FACILITIES sitting rooms, bar, breakfast room/winter garden, gym, Turkish bath, garden
CREDIT CARDS AE, DC, MC, V
DISABLED 2 specially adapted rooms
PETS accepted by arrangement **CLOSED** early Jan to Mar
MANAGER Marisa Giuliano

TUSCANY

PIEVE SANTO STEFANO

LOCANDA LA PERGOLA
~ COUNTRY INN ~

Via Tiberina, Pieve Santo Stéfano, Arezzo
TEL 0575 797053

LOCANDA LA PERGOLA IS A reincarnation of the Locanda Sari, a local inn and convenient port of call on the road over to Ravenna, which has recently changed hands. When a few years ago the traffic which once passed within feet of the front door diverted to whizz up a neo-motorway on the other side of the narrow valley, the previous owners Carmen and Pio Pierangeli seized the opportunity to turn the Locanda into a place worth seeking out. It changed hands in June 2000, and is now run by three capable women: Marida, Oriana and Valeria.

The house has been restored with real panache in classy country style. In the bedrooms, rustic antiques and painted reproduction wardrobes sit on glistening tiled floors, with creamy rugs and bedspreads woven to a special pattern. Old iron bedheads are fixed to the walls, but the beds themselves are new (and splendidly firm); the shower rooms are compact but smart. The dining room shows the same simple good taste, but the real attraction here is Marida's exquisite country cooking, of the kind that tourists rarely taste. Most guests agree that the daily batch of ravioli, made with local ricotta, for example, is superb.

Marida, Oriana and Valeria are charming and hospitable and most visitors find the proximity of the main road 'a bore but surprisingly unobjectionable'.

~

NEARBY Sansepolcro (16 km); La Verna (20 km).
LOCATION in countryside 3 km N of village, on minor road; car parking across the road
FOOD breakfast, lunch, dinner
PRICES €-€€€
ROOMS 8 double and twin, 1 with bath, 7 with shower
FACILITIES dining room, lobby, bar, terrace
CREDIT CARDS AE, DC
DISABLED access difficult **PETS** not accepted **CLOSED** never
PROPRIETORS Marida Gorini and Loreana Marini

TUSCANY

PISTOIA

VILLA VANNINI

~ COUNTRY VILLA ~

Villa di Piteccio, 51030 Pistoia
TEL 0573 42031 **FAX** 0573 42551
E-MAIL v.vannini@dada.it **WEBSITE** www.dadacasa.com/villavannini

HERE IS A REAL GEM, lying in an area which has surprisingly few small, charming places to stay – in a remote and delightfully quiet setting, high on a hill about 2 km above the small village of Piteccio and not far from the lively little city of Pistoia. To get there, you wind your way up a narrow, roughly surfaced road through unspoiled countryside. Although Signora Vannini is about the place less than she used to be – she now has help from a delightful couple, the Borderones, whose cooking is 'inspirational and exquisitely fresh' – you'll still get a warm welcome.

There are various little sitting areas with large vases of flowers, chintz-covered or chunky modern seats, prints and watercolours, and the sort of antiques that complete an elegant family home. The dining room, with its whitewashed walls, china plates, polished parquet floor and marble fireplace, makes an elegant setting for the excellent Tuscan specialities that are served here ('delicious and plentiful,' says one recent report). Bedrooms are beautifully and individually furnished – many in flowery fabrics and with fine antiques. In front of the house a simple terrace provides a haven after a day's sightseeing in Pistoia, Florence or Lucca. Although children are allowed, this is not a very suitable place for youngsters. We've had an exceptional number of warmly approving readers' letters about the place since the last edition.

~

NEARBY *duomo*; Ospedale del Ceppo and church of Sant' Andrea.
LOCATION 6 km N of Pistoia, take Abelone road from Pistoia and branch right towards Piteccio before *piazza*; car parking
FOOD breakfast, lunch, dinner
PRICE €
ROOMS 8 double and twin with bath
FACILITIES 2 sitting rooms, games room, 2 dining rooms, terrace, garden
CREDIT CARDS not accepted **DISABLED** no special facilities **PETS** not accepted
CLOSED never **PROPRIETOR** Maria-Rosa Vannini

TUSCANY

PORTO ERCOLE

IL PELLICANO
∾ SEASIDE HOTEL ∾

Cala dei Santi, 58018 Porto Ercole, Grosseto
TEL 0564 858111 **FAX** 0564 833418
E-MAIL Pr@Pellicanohotel.com **WEBSITE** www.Pellicanohotel.com

PORTO ERCOLE IS ONE OF those fashionable little harbours where wealthy Romans moor their boats at weekends. Il Pellicano is an elegant, russet-coloured vine-clad villa with gardens tumbling down to the rocky shoreline, where the flat rocks have been designated the hotel's 'private beach'. It offers the luxury and exclusivity that you might expect from a very expensive four-star seaside hotel but manages at the same time to preserve the style and informality of a private Tuscan villa – and the exposed beams, stone arches and antique features make it feel older than it really is. Antique country-house furnishings are offset by whitewashed walls, brightly coloured, stylish sofas and large vases of flowers.

Fish and seafood are the best things in the restaurant – if you can stomach the prices. Meals in summer are served on the delightful open-air terrace in the garden, or beside the pool where the spread of *antipasti* is a feast for the eyes. Service is impeccable. Peaceful bedrooms, many in two-storey cottages, combine antiques and modern fabrics. The majority are cool and spacious, and all of them have a terrace or balcony. Watch out for swarms of mosquitoes, warns our inspector.

Only children over 12 are accepted.

∾

NEARBY Orbetello (16 km).
LOCATION 4 km from middle of resort; car parking
FOOD breakfast, lunch, dinner
PRICE €€€€€
ROOMS 41; 27 double, 14 suites, all with bath; all rooms have phone, TV, air conditioning, minibar
FACILITIES sitting area, restaurants, bars, beauty centre, terraces, sea-water swimming pool, tennis, clay pigeon shooting, riding, water-skiing
CREDIT CARDS AE, DC, MC, V
DISABLED some ground-floor rooms, but access difficult **PETS** not accepted **CLOSED** Nov-Mar
MANAGER Signora Cinzia Fanciulli

TUSCANY

PRATO

VILLA RUCELLAI
~ COUNTRY VILLA ~

Via di Canneto 16, 59100 Prato, Firenze
TEL and **FAX** 0574 460392

THIS IS A QUINTESSENTIAL charming small hotel. Industrial Prato creeps almost to the doors of the mellow old villa, and the railway line skirts the property, but this should not stop you from visiting a very special place. Its origins date back to a medieval watchtower, and it has been in the venerable Rucellai family since 1740. The unsightly views from the lovely terrace – filled with lemon trees – and the *loggia*, are more than compensated for by the atmosphere of the house, the warm welcome and the modest prices. Behind the property rise the beautiful Pratese Hills, which can be explored on foot from the house.

Guests have the run of the main part of the house, with its baronial hall and comfortable sitting room, filled with pictures and books. Breakfast is self-service and is taken around a communal table in the homely dining room. The bedrooms are simply furnished and full of character; they reflect the rare attribute of the place – that of a well-run hotel which gives no hint of being anything but a cultivated family home. A recent visitor was impressed overall – but had reservations about some of the home-made food and wine; another had reservations about the condition of the swimming pool.

~

NEARBY Prato; Florence (20 km).
LOCATION down a narrow street, in Bisenzio river valley, 4 km NE of Prato (keep parallel with river and railway line on your left); car parking
FOOD breakfast
PRICE ©
ROOMS 13; 12 double and twin, 1 family, all with bath or shower
FACILITIES sitting room, TV room, dining room, gym, terrace, garden, swimming pool
CREDIT CARDS not accepted
DISABLED not suitable **PETS** not accepted
CLOSED never
PROPRIETORS Rucellai Piqué family

TUSCANY

CASETTA DELLE SELVE
~ COUNTRY BED-AND-BREAKFAST ~

56010 Pugnano, Pisa
TEL and **FAX** 050 850359

YET ANOTHER ELEVATED Tuscan farmhouse, but this one has a personality all of its own thanks to the owner, Nicla Menchi, a most unusual hostess. The approach to the white building is through a thick chestnut wood. Once at the top of the rough 2-km drive, the peaceful surroundings, the flower-filled garden and the wonderful views from the red-tiled terrace start to work their magic.

The interiors are very different from the norm. For a start, Nicla's own vivid paintings occupy much of the wall space. The house is exceptionally well maintained and the bedrooms have bold, bright colour schemes involving bedheads, rugs, bedspreads (all handmade by Nicla) and, of course, her pictures. It might be a little fussy for some tastes; even the coat hangers are colour co-ordinated. However, public areas are a little more restrained, but still full of pictures, books and ornaments. Breakfast (including fresh eggs, home-made cakes and jams) is, when possible, served on the terrace.

Nicla Menchi's enthusiasm for her home and her guests is infectious and many leave as her friend. Not suitable for children under 12.

~

NEARBY Lucca (10 km); Pisa (12 km); beaches (15 km)
LOCATION in countryside 2 km off SS12, E of Pugnano, 10 km SW of Lucca; car parking
FOOD breakfast
PRICE € (minimum 3-day stay)
ROOMS 6 double with bath or shower (2 are adjacent)
FACILITIES sitting room, terrace, garden
CREDIT CARDS not accepted
DISABLED not suitable
PETS accepted
CLOSED never
PROPRIETOR Nicla Menchi

TUSCANY

RADDA IN CHIANTI

RELAIS FATTORIA VIGNALE

~ COUNTRY HOTEL ~

Via Pianigiani 15, 53017 Radda in Chianti, Siena
TEL 0577 738300 **FAX** 0577 738592
E-MAIL vignale@vignale.it **WEBSITE** www.vignale.it

THIS HAS ALWAYS BEEN a favourite with our inspectors, and recent visits have left their enthusiasm undimmed. The house is built on a slope down from the middle of the village. On the main 'ground' floor are four interconnecting sitting rooms, each on a domestic scale, and beautifully furnished with comfy sofas, antiques, muted rugs on polished terracotta floors, walls (either white and dotted with paintings or covered by murals) and one or two grand stone fireplaces. The bedrooms above are similarly classy, with waxed wooden doors, white walls and antique beds. The sitting rooms, the back bedrooms and the pool all share a grand view across the Radda Valley.

A recent addition to the Relais Fattoria Vignale is the lovely breakfast terrace; in cool weather there is a neat breakfast room in a brick vault beneath the hotel, where an excellent buffet is set out, and coffee and extras are served by friendly waitresses. There is also a *taverna* for light dinners.

The best-known local restaurant, serving the innovative creations of its chef-patron (also called Vignale), is only 300 metres away; the hotel will make reservations for you.

Although they are tolerated, children will not be popular here unless they are as quiet as mice.

~

NEARBY Siena (31 km); Florence (52 km).
LOCATION in middle of village, 31 km N of Siena; car parking
FOOD breakfast, snacks
PRICE €€€€-€€€€
ROOMS 29; 20 double, 4 with bath, 16 with shower, 3 single with shower, 3 family with bath, 3 suites with shower; all rooms have phone, air conditioning, minibar
FACILITIES 3 sitting rooms, breakfast room, bars, conference room, terrace, garden, swimming pool
CREDIT CARDS AE, MC, V **DISABLED** access difficult **PETS** not accepted **CLOSED** 3 weeks Dec, early Jan to late Mar **MANAGER** Silvia Kummer

TUSCANY

VESCINE – IL RELAIS DEL CHIANTI

~ COUNTRY HOTEL ~

Loc. Vescine, 53017 Radda in Chianti, Siena
TEL 0577 741144 **FAX** 0577 740263

WE LIST THIS FAIRLY RECENT addition under Radda, but it is in fact miles from anywhere, and well suited to those who want peace and seclusion. When we visited, most of the guests were silently bronzing themselves by the smart pool, occasionally lifting an eye to the glorious Chianti countryside stretching away from Vescine.

Vescine is yet another little Tuscan hamlet that has been rescued from dereliction to form a hotel – in this case, opened only in 1990. Its restoration was exceptionally thorough: there is vegetation only where the architects intended vegetation – every other square centimetre of ground is neatly covered in brick and tile, while borders and terraces overflow with greenery and blooms. Bedrooms are in several separate houses, employing the formula of plain walls with occasional pictures, tiled floors, exposed beams and sparse furnishings. There is a stylish breakfast room, and above it a pleasant bar/sitting room with a spacious terrace. But dining means stirring yourself for a 700-metre expedition to the associated restaurant, La Cantoniera, or a longer drive into Radda or Castellina. 'Spartan, but divinely isolated,' according to a recent, relaxed visitor.

~

NEARBY Siena (31 km); Florence (52 km).
LOCATION in countryside midway between Radda and Castellina, 31 km N of Siena; car parking
FOOD buffet breakfast; associated restaurant 700 m away
PRICE €€€
ROOMS 25; 19 double and twin, 6 suites, all with bath or shower; all rooms have phone, TV, minibar
FACILITIES bar/sitting room, breakfast room, garden, swimming pool, tennis
CREDIT CARDS AE, MC, V
DISABLED access difficult
PETS accepted **CLOSED** Nov, Feb
MANAGER Birgit Fleig

TUSCANY

REGGELLO

VILLA RIGACCI

~ HILLTOP VILLA ~

Vággio 76, 50066 Reggello, Firenze
TEL 055 8656718/562 **FAX** 055 8656537
E-MAIL hotel@villarigacci.it **WEBSITE** www.villarigacci.it

THIS CREEPER-COVERED 15thC farmhouse, in the second decade since its
transformation from private home to charming small hotel, is in a
beautiful secluded spot – on a hilltop surrounded by olive groves, pines,
chestnut trees and meadows – yet only a few kilometres from the
Florence-Rome *autostrada*, and a short drive from Florence and Arezzo.

Many of the original features of the house have been preserved –
arched doorways, beamed bedrooms, tiled or stone-flagged floors – and it
is furnished as a cherished private house might be. The sitting room has
an open fire in chilly weather. The bedrooms – the best (though not all) of
them gloriously spacious – are full of gleaming antiques, and overlook the
gardens or swimming pool, which is of fair size, with a pleasant tile-and-
grass surround and woodland views. For relaxation, there are plenty of
quiet, shady spots in the park, which contains some magnificent trees.

An otherwise satisfied visitor who 'enjoyed a lovely holiday here' was
disappointed that the food was predominantly 'sophisticated French' in
style, but we are assured that although the cuisine is international,
Tuscan dishes are also offered. Don't plan your family holiday here – it is
not really a suitable hotel for children.

~

NEARBY Florence (30 km); Arezzo (45 km).
LOCATION 300 m N of Vággio, 30 km SE of Florence (exit Incisa from A1); car
parking
FOOD breakfast, lunch, dinner
PRICE €€
ROOMS 23; 16 double and twin, 3 single, 4 suites, all with bath or shower; all
rooms have phone, TV, minibar, air conditioning
FACILITIES sitting rooms, library, dining room, garden, swimming pool
CREDIT CARDS AE, DC, MC, V
DISABLED not suitable
PETS small ones accepted **CLOSED** never
PROPRIETORS Frederic and Florence Pierazzi

TUSCANY

SAN CASCIANO DEI BAGNI

SETTE QUERCE
~ VILLAGE GUESTHOUSE ~

53040 San Casciano dei Bagni, Siena
TEL 0578 58174 **FAX** 0578 58172
E-MAIL settequerce@krenet.it **WEBSITE** www.evols.it/settequerce

SEVERAL GENERATIONS OF Daniela Boni's family have run the local bar in this tiny spa town, located high in the hills in a remote corner of southern Tuscany. The family business expanded in 1997 to include this delightful and original hotel, and, most recently, the bar has extended into an excellent restaurant (located 100 m from the main building).

The name derives from the fact that the rambling townhouse backs on to an oak wood. The contemporary interior design is a refreshing change from the Tuscan norm. At ground level, earth tones, vivid reds and pinks prevail. Bedrooms on the second floor are in sunny yellows and greens, and, at the top, shades of blue predominate. The cheerful fabrics on chairs, curtains, cushions and duvets are by Designers Guild. The rooms are all dotted with ornaments (old irons, rustic ceramics, basket ware) while framed black-and-white photos depicting the history of the town hang on the walls. Each bedroom has a comfortable sitting area (compensating for the lack of public sitting room) and a cleverly-designed kitchenette. Bathrooms are immaculate and several have Jacuzzis.

~

NEARBY thermal baths; Orvieto (40 km); Montepulciano (40 km).
LOCATION on street just outside town; public car parking next door
FOOD breakfast
PRICE €€-€€€
ROOMS 9 suites with bath; all rooms have phone, TV, air conditioning, minibar, hairdrier
FACILITIES bar, restaurant, terraces
CREDIT CARDS AE, MC, V
DISABLED 2 specially adapted suites
PETS small ones accepted
CLOSED 2 weeks Jan
PROPRIETORS Daniela, Maurizio and Silvestro Boni

TUSCANY

SAN GIMIGNANO

L'ANTICO POZZO
~ TOWN GUESTHOUSE ~

Via San Matteo 87, 53037 San Gimignano, Siena
TEL 0577 942014 **FAX** 0577 942117
E-MAIL info@anticopozzo.com **WEBSITE** www.anticopozzo.com

THE ANCIENT BRICK WELL in question (*pozzo* means well) is in the entrance hall of this fine, 15thC townhouse situated on one of the pedestrian streets leading up to San Gimignano's central Piazza del Duomo. The building was beautifully restored in 1990, and is now, in our view, possibly the best hotel in town.

A stone staircase leads up to the large first-floor bedrooms and the breakfast room, the latter known as the *sala rosa*, thanks to its deep pink walls. The waxed and worn terracotta tiles on this floor are original, as are the high, beamed ceilings. Several rooms have delicate frescoes; in one, the walls and ceiling are entirely painted with garlands of flowers and elegant, dancing figures.

Rooms on the upper floors are smaller, but still most attractive. Those at the top have attic ceilings and views of the famous towers or countryside to compensate for their small size.

The furnishings throughout are in simple good taste; carefully-chosen antiques mix well with the wrought-iron beds; colours are muted. Bathrooms have recently been smartened up. A pretty, walled terrace is an added bonus.

~

NEARBY *duomo*; Museo Civico; Torre Grossa.
LOCATION on pedestrian street in centre of town; public car parking (300 m)
FOOD breakfast
PRICE €€
ROOMS 18; 17 double and twin, 1 single, all with bath or shower; all rooms have phone, TV, air conditioning, minibar
FACILITIES bar, breakfast room, terrace
CREDIT CARDS AE, DC, MC, V
DISABLED 2 specially adapted rooms
PETS not accepted
CLOSED 6 weeks in winter
PROPRIETOR Emanuele Marro

TUSCANY

SAN GUSME

VILLA ARCENO

~ COUNTRY VILLA ~

Loc. Arceno, San Gusme, 53010 Castelnuovo Berardenga, Siena
TEL 0577 359292 **FAX** 0577 359276

VILLA ARCENO ORIGINALLY SERVED as a hunting lodge for a Tuscan noble family, but 'lodge' is too humble a word to describe this aristocratic building. A long, private road winds through the thousand-hectare estate (which has many farmhouses converted into apartments) to the square, rigidly symmetrical villa with its overhanging eaves, surrounded by lawns, gravel paths and flower-filled terracotta urns. In front of the villa is a separate, walled park in the Romantic style, with shady paths leading down to a small lake.

Inside, a cool, elegant style prevails: off-white walls and vaulted ceilings contrast with the warmth of terracotta floors (strewn with Persian carpets), reproduction antique furniture and light yellow drapes. The atmosphere is formal, but not stiffly so: the highly professional staff make guests feel more than welcome.

Upstairs, the guest rooms, which are all light and spacious, have been individually decorated. Particularly attractive is the suite, which has a bay of three arched windows. Some rooms have their own terraces. You should also ask to see the spiral stairway of the central tower that finishes in a rooftop gazebo.

The hotel does not accept children.

~

NEARBY Siena (30 km); Florence (90 km).
LOCATION 30 km NE of Siena; car parking
FOOD breakfast, lunch, dinner
PRICE €€€-€€€€
ROOMS 16; 15 double, 1 suite, all with bath; all rooms have phone, TV, air conditioning, minibar
FACILITIES sitting rooms, restaurant, garden, tennis, swimming pool
CREDIT CARDS AE, DC, MC, V
DISABLED not suitable **PETS** small dogs accepted by arrangement
CLOSED mid-Nov to mid-Mar
PROPRIETOR Gualtiero Mancini

TUSCANY

SANTA MARIA DEL GIUDICE

VILLA RINASCIMENTO

~ COUNTRY VILLA ~

Loc. Santa Maria del Giudice, 55058 Lucca
TEL 0583 378292 **FAX** 0583 370238
E-MAIL hotelvr@mbox.lognet.it

ALMOST EXACTLY HALFWAY between Pisa and Lucca, this hillside villa presents, at first sight, something of an architectural conundrum. On the right-hand side is a rosy coloured, rustic Renaissance villa, three storeys high, constructed with a mixture of brick and stone. Its main feature is a lovely corner *loggia*, enclosed by four brick arches supported by Doric columns in stone. On the left, it is joined by a much simpler farmhouse structure. The two are united by a long, paved terrace with lemon trees in large terracotta pots. One can breakfast here, or take an *aperitivo* in the evening.

Inside, a more uniform rustic style prevails. The public rooms are all in a row, facing the terrace, and distinguished by exposed-beam or brick-vaulted ceilings, all immaculately restored and including interesting features such as the remnants of an old stone olive press. Great effort has been put into the bedroom furnishings. Some of the bathrooms are small, but adequate.

Up the hill from the villa is the annexe, with some more modern rooms and studios, and a pool designed to exploit to the full its hillside position.

~

NEARBY Lucca (9 km); Pisa (11 km).
LOCATION 9 km SW of Lucca; car parking
FOOD breakfast, dinner
PRICE ⓔⓔ
ROOMS 17 double and twin with bath or shower; all rooms have phone; some have TV; 4 simpler rooms and 6 studios (one-week minimum) in annexe
FACILITIES sitting rooms, bar, restaurant, garden, swimming pool
CREDIT CARDS MC, V
DISABLED 1 suitable room
PETS accepted by arrangement
CLOSED Nov-Mar; restaurant Wed
PROPRIETOR Carla Zaffora

TUSCANY

SCANSANO

ANTICO CASALE DI SCANSANO
~ COUNTRY HOTEL ~

Scansano, 58054 Grosseto
TEL 0564 507219 **FAX** 0564 507805
E-MAIL antico.casale@tiscalinet.it **WEBSITE** www.wel.it/Casale

TWO WIDELY-TRAVELLED readers wrote in enthusiastic terms to draw our attention to this captivating hotel in the coastal region of Tuscany known as the Maremma, south-east of Grosseto. We can scarcely improve on their verdicts: 'Rooms sweetly decorated with country antiques and a lovely restaurant with terrace overlooking a spectacular green valley with vineyards and olive groves; a truly relaxing experience.' And: 'In four months touring the country, we thought this hotel number one; we were impressed by the welcome and hospitality, the surroundings – even the beds were the best we encountered in Italy.' Other reporters, however, are critical of the food.

The Antico Casale is a beautifully restored, 200-year-old farmhouse which retains more of its origins than most such places. The Macereto estate of which it is part produces a range of *grappa,* olive oil and wines (including the Morellino di Scansano DOC); many surrounding farms produce olive oil, and the Casale's stables are in very active use: riding holidays are offered (with instruction if you need it), and the hotel even offers special 'DB&B and horse' rates. Wine-tasting courses too.

~

NEARBY thermal spa of Saturnia; Argentarian coast.
LOCATION in countryside 30 km SE of Grosseto; car parking
FOOD breakfast, lunch, dinner, snacks
PRICE €€-€€€
ROOMS 31; 21 double, 3 single, 1 family, 6 suites, all with shower; 2 apartments; all rooms have phone, TV, air conditioning, minibar, hairdrier
FACILITIES sitting room, dining room, bar, terrace, swimming pool, horse riding
CREDIT CARDS AE, DC, MC, V
DISABLED no special facilities
PETS accepted if well behaved
CLOSED mid-Jan to late Feb
PROPRIETOR Massimo Pellegrini

TUSCANY

CERTOSA DI MAGGIANO

~ CONVERTED MONASTERY ~

Via Certosa 82, 53100 Siena
TEL 0577 288180 **FAX** 0577 288189
E-MAIL certosa@relaischateaux.fr **WEBSITE** www.relaischateaux.fr/certosa

A RECENT VISIT SHOWED that all was very well here, and if you are looking for an exclusive but unostentatious hotel in Siena, this is probably it: a former Carthusian monastery – the oldest in Tuscany – secluded in a large park (yet only minutes by car from the enchanting old city). Although it is extremely expensive, this is not a swanky place: the calm good taste, the atmosphere of a delightful country house and the discreet service appeal mainly to those in search of peace and privacy.

Superb modern *haute cuisine* dishes are served in an exquisite dining room, in the peaceful 14thC cloisters or under the arcades by the swimming pool. Guests can help themselves to drinks in the book-lined library, play backgammon or chess in a little ante-room, or relax in the lovely sitting room. Flower arrangements are just about everywhere and bowls of fresh fruit in the bedrooms add a personal touch, although the decoration here does not quite live up to the ravishing public rooms. Bear in mind that exploration of Siena will have to be by taxi or bus – it's too far to walk, and parking is almost impossible in the centre.

~

NEARBY Siena sights; San Gimignano (40 km); Florence (58 km).
LOCATION 1 km SE of city centre and Porta Romana; car parking opposite entrance and garage available
FOOD breakfast, lunch, dinner
PRICE €€€€
ROOMS 17; 5 double, 12 suites, all with bath; all rooms have phone, TV, radio
FACILITIES sitting room, dining room, bar, library, garden, swimming pool, tennis, heliport
CREDIT CARDS AE, DC, MC, V
DISABLED access possible
PETS not accepted
CLOSED never
MANAGER Margherita Grossi

TUSCANY

PALAZZO RAVIZZA
~ TOWN HOTEL ~

Pian dei Mantellini 34, 53100 Siena
TEL 0577 280462 **FAX** 0577 221597
E-MAIL bureau@palazzoravizza.it **WEBSITE** www.palazzoravizza.it

SIENA IS NOTORIOUS FOR its dearth of decent hotels in the centre of town, so we were delighted to see that Palazzo Ravizza has undergone a facelift and is now a very pleasant place in which to stay. Fortunately, the old-fashioned, slightly faded charm has not been sacrificed to modernization. The bedrooms still have their heavy – at times quirky – period furniture and polished parquet or terracotta floors, but the fabrics have been smartened up and bathrooms are all shining new with heated towel rails. Some even have double Jacuzzis.

Downstairs, the public rooms (in part with smart black and white floor tiles) have pretty painted ceilings and comfortable armchairs and sofas. There is a cosy library, as well as a smart new bar and an elegantly-appointed dining room.

The slightly overgrown garden at the back is a great asset, providing a cool and shady respite from the city heat, and tables are laid outside for breakfast and dinner in the summer.

~

NEARBY *duomo*; Ospedale Santa Maria della Scala.
LOCATION just SW of town centre in residential street; car parking
FOOD breakfast, dinner
PRICE ©© (half board compulsory in high season)
ROOMS 40; 35 double and twin, 5 suites, all with bath or shower; all rooms have phone, TV, minibar
FACILITIES sitting rooms, bar, restaurant, garden
CREDIT CARDS AE, DC, MC, V
DISABLED no special facilities
PETS accepted
CLOSED never
PROPRIETOR Francesco Grotanelli de Santi

TUSCANY

SINALUNGA

LOCANDA DELL'AMOROSA

～ COUNTRY INN ～

53048 Sinalunga, Siena
TEL 0577 677211 **FAX** 0577 632001
E-MAIL mailbox@abitarelastoria.it **WEBSITE** www.abitarelastoria.it

THE LOCANDA DELL'AMOROSA is as romantic as it sounds. An elegant Renaissance villa-cum-village, within the remains of 14thC walls, has been converted into a charming country inn.

The old stables, beamed and brick-walled, have been transformed into a delightful rustic (but pricey) restaurant serving refined *nouvelle*-style versions of traditional Tuscan recipes, using ingredients from the estate, which also produces wine. The restaurant can serve up to 80 people (though it is arranged to feel more intimate) but is often full.

Only a fortunate few can actually stay here – either in apartments in the houses where peasants and farmworkers once lived, or in ordinary bedrooms in the old family residence. The bedrooms are cool, airy and pretty, with whitewashed walls, terracotta floors, antique furniture and Florentine curtains and bedspreads – and immaculate modern bathrooms.

To complete the village there is a little parish church with lovely 15thC frescoes of the Sienese school. With discreet, attentive service, the Locanda is a paradise for connoisseurs of Tuscany, for gourmets and for all romantics.

～

NEARBY Siena (45 km); Arezzo (45 km); Chianti.
LOCATION 2 km S of Sinalunga; car parking
FOOD breakfast, lunch, dinner
PRICE €€€€
ROOMS 16; 12 double, 4 suites, all with bath or shower; all rooms have phone, TV, air conditioning, minibar
FACILITIES sitting room, dining room, bar
CREDIT CARDS AE, DC, MC, V
DISABLED access difficult
PETS not accepted
CLOSED mid-Jan to late Feb; restaurant Mon, Tue
MANAGER Carlo Citterio

TUSCANY

SORANO

HOTEL DELLA FORTEZZA
~ CASTLE GUESTHOUSE ~

Piazza Cairoli, 58010 Sorano, Grosseto
TEL 0564 632010 **FAX** 0564 632012
E-MAIL fortezzahotel@tin.it **WEBSITE** www.fortezzahotel.it

FOR ENTHUSIASTS OF ARCHAEOLOGY, this remote corner of the Maremma – with its abundance of Etruscan remains – is a dream. The ancient, picturesque town of Sorano is built on a tufa outcrop and is surrounded by the hills of the Alta Maremma. The imposing 11thC Orsini fortress is dramatically situated on the edge of the town and now partially occupied by a new hotel. After dark, the place is floodlit, and the approach to the hotel across an old suspension bridge and through several courtyards is like taking a step back into the Middle Ages.

Once inside, however, the comforts are very much of this century although the tasteful and careful restoration has been carried out with full respect for the building's origins. The solid walls are pale throughout, warmed by soft lighting while beamed ceilings and terracotta floors are in tone with the surroundings. A collection of 19thC antiques blend well with fine reproduction pieces and fabrics in deep blue and gold. There are some wonderful old beds in the comfortable bedrooms which vary enormously in shape and size. All have fabulous views over the rooftops of unspoiled countryside.

~

NEARBY Pitgliano (9 km); Lake Bolsena (20 km).
LOCATION 9 km NE of Pitigliano, on edge of town; car parking
FOOD breakfast
PRICE €€
ROOMS 16; 14 double and twin, 2 suites, all with bath; all rooms have phone, TV, minibar, hairdrier
FACILITIES breakfast room, sitting room, terraces
CREDIT CARDS AE, MC, V
DISABLED 1 specially adapted room
PETS small ones accepted
CLOSED early Jan to Mar
PROPRIETOR Amparo Hurtado Perez

TUSCANY

SOVICILLE

BORGO PRETALE

∼ HILLSIDE HAMLET ∼

Loc. Pretale, 53018 Sovicille, Siena
TEL 0577 345401 **FAX** 0577 345625
E-MAIL info@borgopretale.it **WEBSITE** www.borgopretale.it

A LONG, WINDING, UNSURFACED road through wooded hills brings you to this group of grey stone houses clustered around a massive 12thC watch-tower. Local historians claim that it was part of a system of such towers, spread across the Sienese hills, all within line of sight, to communicate quickly any news of approaching invaders and to provide protection against their rampages. Nowadays, this civilized retreat offers a haven from the stresses of modern life.

Every detail has been considered in the restoration and decoration. The harshness of the medieval structure has been lessened by the use of well-chosen antiques, mellow lighting and rich, striped fabrics. A serenely beautiful 15thC carved wooden Madonna, bearing the Infant Christ, stands in a brick-framed niche.

Every bedroom contains a different blend of the same artful ingredients, each splendid in its own way, though we particularly liked those in the tower. The stylish restaurant serves a limited choice of dishes (but all well prepared) and has an extensive wine list on which a *sommelier* can offer advice. And tucked away, close to the edge of the woods, is an inviting pool.

∼

NEARBY Siena (20 km); San Gimignano (28 km).
LOCATION 20 km SE of Siena on quiet hillside; car parking
FOOD breakfast, lunch, dinner
PRICE €€€
ROOMS 35; 32 double, 3 suites, all with bath or shower; all rooms have phone, TV, air conditioning, minibar
FACILITIES sitting room, restaurant, bar, sauna, garden, swimming pool, tennis, archery
CREDIT CARDS AE, DC, MC, V
DISABLED not suitable **PETS** not accepted
CLOSED Nov to early Apr
MANAGER Daniele Rizzardini

TUSCANY

VICCHIO

VILLA CAMPESTRI
~ COUNTRY VILLA ~

Via di Campestri 19, 50039 Vicchio di Mugello, Firenze
TEL 055 8490107 **FAX** 055 8490108
E-MAIL villacampestri@villacampestri.it **WEBSITE** www.villacampestri.it

GET CLEAR DIRECTIONS before you set off for this hilltop villa: it is in an isolated location, some way south of the village of Vicchio di Mugello.

The house looks classically Renaissance, but actually dates back to the 13thC. It overlooks sloping hillsides of mown grass, and miles of unspoiled countryside – much of it part of the villa's own estate. Inside, many original features remain: an old chapel, 14thC frescoes, massive interior doors, and timbered ceilings. Furnishings blend with this venerable setting, including some valuable antiques, notably a vast and regal four-poster bed and an 18thC sofa. Plain white walls offset the dark wood of beams and furniture. Most of the bedrooms are handsomely furnished and spacious – some might find them too grand for comfort. Although one satisfied guest found them 'very comfortable indeed' and 'well worth' the high prices. Bathrooms are beautifully tiled in blue and white. The open-plan sitting room and dining room are traditionally furnished and fairly formal; the restaurant is renowned, and local dignitaries make the long trek to enjoy its food. Breakfast was a disappointment for one visitor, though. The staff are kind and welcoming, and if you're lucky the owner may entertain you with a little piano music after dinner.

~

NEARBY Florence (35 km).
LOCATION in countryside 3 km S of Vicchio, 35 km NE of Florence; car parking
FOOD breakfast, dinner; snacks
PRICE €€€-€€€€
ROOMS 21; 14 double and twin, 1 single, 6 suites, all with bath or shower; all rooms have phone, TV, minibar
FACILITIES sitting room, dining room, garden, swimming pool
CREDIT CARDS MC, V
DISABLED 4 specially adapted bedrooms
PETS accepted by arrangement
CLOSED Jan-Mar
PROPRIETOR Paolo Pasquali

TUSCANY

VOLPAIA

LA LOCANDA

~ COUNTRY GUESTHOUSE ~

Loc. Montanino, Volpaia, 53017 Radda in Chianti, Siena
Tel and **Fax** 0577 738833
E-MAIL info@lalocanda.it **WEBSITE** www.lalocanda.it

THE BEVILAQUAS (HE NEAPOLITAN, SHE MILANESE) began their search for the
ideal spot in which to set up their guesthouse four years ago. In April
1999, what was once a collection of ruined farm buildings high up in the
Chianti hills finally opened for business, and you would be hard pressed to
find a more beautiful setting. At 600 m above sea level, views from the terraces, garden, pool and some of the rooms are of layers of hills, striped
with vines and shaded with woods; in the foreground is the mellow old
fortified hamlet of Volpaia.

The restoration of the pale stone buildings has been done with unerring
good taste. Interiors, while maintaining many of the rustic features, have a
refreshingly contemporary look with an imaginative use of colour throughout to offset plenty of terracotta and wood.

The comfortable bedrooms have an uncluttered feel, and the bathrooms are spacious and gleaming. One end of the long, sunny living room
is dominated by a massive stone fireplace, and filled with colourfully-
upholstered sofas and armchairs.

~

NEARBY Florence (48 km); Siena (38 km).
LOCATION 4 km W of Volpaia (signed from *piazza* in the village) follow signs to the
hotel; car parking.
FOOD breakfast, dinner on request
PRICE €€€
ROOMS 7; 6 double and twin, 1 suite, all with bath; all rooms have phone, TV,
hairdrier, safe
FACILITIES sitting rooms, bar, dining room, terraces, garden, swimming pool
CREDIT CARDS AE, DC, MC, V
DISABLED ground-floor rooms available
PETS not accepted
CLOSED mid-Jan to mid-March
PROPRIETORS Guido and Martina Bevilaqua

TUSCANY

BARBERINO VAL D'ELSA

LA CHIARA DI PRUMIANO
FARM GUESTHOUSE

Strada di Cortine 12, 50021
Barberino Val d'Elsa, Firenze

TEL 055 8075583 **FAX** 055 8075678
E-MAIL prumiano@tin.it
FOOD breakfast; lunch and dinner
on request **PRICE** (€) **CLOSED**
Christmas to mid-Jan
Gaia Mezzadri and Antonio
Pescetti

WHEN FOUR FAMILIES BOUGHT the Chiara di Prumiano (formerly a country residence of the Corsini family) some 15 years ago with plans to make it pay for itself, they took on an enormous project. The estate runs to 40 hectares of land with a grand villa at the centre of a small hamlet. Now run by two of the original owners, the Chiara has become a successful business, but the atmosphere is laid-back and alternative. The creeper-clad villa hosts modestly furnished but spacious bedrooms, a sitting room of baronial proportions, two dining rooms and various spaces used for seminars and workshops.

BARBERINO VAL D'ELSA

IL PARETAIO
COUNTRY GUESTHOUSE

Loc. San Filippo, 50021
Barberino Val d'Elsa, Firenze

TEL 055 8059218 **FAX** 055 8059231
E-MAIL ilparetaio@tin.it
WEBSITE www.ilparetaio.it
FOOD breakfast, dinner
PRICE (€)
CLOSED never
Giovanni and Cristina de Marchi

A GREAT ADDRESS FOR THOSE interested in horse riding but not to be dismissed by any traveller in search of the country life. Strategically located between Florence and Siena, in hilly surroundings, Il Paretaio is a 17thC stone-built farmhouse on its own large estate. The accommodation is simple but attractive. The ground-floor entrance and sitting area was originally a work room, and still retains the old stone paving. A huge brick arch spans the central space and brick-vaulting contrasts with the plain white walls. Upstairs, the rustic style is continued in the exposed-beam ceilings and worn terracotta floors.

TUSCANY

CASTELLINA IN CHIANTI

PALAZZO SQUARCIALUPI
TOWN HOTEL

Via Ferruccio 26, 53011
Castellina in Chianti, Siena

TEL 0577 741186 **FAX** 0577 740386
E-MAIL squarcialupi@
italyexpo.com
FOOD buffet breakfast; snacks in
the bar **PRICE** €-€€
CLOSED mid-Jan to mid-Mar
Targioni family

PALAZZO SQUARCIALUPI IS SET in the medieval village of Castellina in Chianti, and when our reporter first came here, she was struck by the friendly, peaceful atmosphere and the lovely rooms. It is a 14thC stone building with arched doors and windows, which was formerly an imposing farmhouse. It has been renovated in a simple, stylish way, while retaining its traditional farm character. There are 17 large bedrooms and suites with plain white walls, beamed ceilings and dark wooden furniture. Downstairs there is a rustic sitting room in muted tones of white, cream and terracotta, and another elegant room with frescoes.

CASTELLINA IN CHIANTI

VILLA CASALECCHI
COUNTRY VILLA

Loc. Casalecchi, 53011 Castellina
in Chianti, Siena

TEL 0577 740240 **FAX** 0577 741111
WEBSITE www.villacasalecchi.it
FOOD breakfast, lunch, dinner
PRICE €€-€€€
CLOSED Oct-Mar
Elvira Lecchini-Giovannoni

THIS 18thC VILLA STANDS ON a series of hillside terraces between woods and vineyards, just south of Castellina. The house is no architectural gem, but its secluded position and attractive location compensate for a certain austerity. The interiors are furnished with heavy, bourgeois antiques which give a hushed character. The dining room is frescoed with elegant old light fittings, but a more pleasant place to eat is the terrace with its views of open countryside. Bedrooms are either in the villa (individually furnished), or in the extension, with access to the gardens and pool. Parquet floors and a lighter style of antique makes them more convivial than the public rooms.

TUSCANY

CASTELNUOVO BERARDENGA

PODERE SAN QUIRICO
FARM GUESTHOUSE

*Via del Paradiso 1, 53019
Castelnuovo Berardenga, Siena*

TEL 0577 355206
FAX 0577 355206
Food breakfast on request
Price €
Closed never
Maria Consiglio Picone

Guests receive a real Neapolitan welcome from Maria Consiglio Picone. The first thing she did when we arrived, on a hot July day, was rush into her kitchen and make us some some freshly squeezed peach juice. From that moment on, she could do no wrong. The house is a slightly battered relic from the 14th century, built of the local light-coloured stone. The interiors are decorated with more vivacity than is usual in this part of Tuscany: the walls are festooned with plates and paintings, and a lifetime's collection of bric-a-brac cheerfully clutters up the space. The bedrooms are less festive. A reader reports missing bedside lamps, no soap and a sense of slipping standards. Reports especially welcome.

CASTELNUOVO BERARDENGA

VILLA CURINA
COUNTRY VILLA

*Loc. Curina, 53019 Castelnuovo
Berardenga, Siena*

TEL 0577 355586
FAX 0577 355412
E-MAIL infolucy@tin.it
WEBSITE www.villacurina.it
FOOD breakfast, dinner
PRICE €€
CLOSED Nov-Mar/Apr
MANAGER Franco Sbardelati

A VIVACIOUS, CONVIVIAL ATMOSPHERE pervades this hotel-and-apartment complex set in low, rolling countryside north of Siena. When we visited, it was full of activity, with people enjoying themselves in the pool, playing tennis or setting off for bike rides. The main villa, surrounded by ornamental gardens and trees, is a large, cream-coloured, 18thC building and contains the guest bedrooms as well as the principal public rooms. Most of the apartments are in three old stone farmhouses with small, brown-shuttered windows and connected by pathways of Siena brick. An attractive restaurant, spanned by strong brick arches, serves fresh produce from the estate.

TUSCANY

GAIOLE IN CHIANTI

CASTELLO DI SPALTENNA
CASTLE HOTEL

Gaiole in Chianti, 53013 Siena

TEL 0577 749483 **FAX** 0577 749269
E-MAIL info@spaltenna.it
WEBSITE spaltenna.it
FOOD breakfast, lunch, dinner
PRICES €€€
CLOSED early Jan to late Mar
MANAGER Giancarlo Bellvonini

A DRAMATICALLY SITUATED, fortified monastery on a hilltop next to the medieval church of Santa Maria di Spaltenna. Constructed from hewn stone with towers at each corner, the castle is built around a central courtyard. It is no longer owner-managed since its former proprietor left to start up a restaurant in Brolio, and we'd welcome reports on the ambience: with the addition of some elaborate new features, some say that the place has a different feel. Meals are served either in the swish restaurant or in the courtyard. No two bedrooms are the same.

LECCHI IN CHIANTI

SAN SANO
VILLAGE HOTEL

Loc. San Sano, 53010 Lecchi in Chianti, Siena

TEL 0577 746130 **FAX** 0577 746156
E-MAIL
hotelsansano@chiantinet.it
WEBSITE
www.chiantinet.it/hotelsansano
FOOD breakfast, dinner
PRICE €€
CLOSED mid-Nov to mid-Mar
Giancarlo and Heidi Matarazzo

T HE MEDIEVAL HAMLET OF SAN SANO, has at its heart an ancient defence tower, destroyed and rebuilt many times. Now, in its latest incarnation, this imposing structure forms the core of a delightful, family-run hotel in a relatively little visited, authentic part of Chianti. The restoration has been meticulous and restrained. The decoration is in classic, rustic Tuscan style, somewhat stark for some tastes, but with individual touches. Each bedroom has its individual character. There's a hillside swimming pool.

TUSCANY

MASSA E COZZILE

VILLA PASQUINI
COUNTRY VILLA

Via Vacchereccia 56, Margine
Coperta, 51010 Massa e Cozzile,
Pistoia

TEL 0572 72205 **Fax** 0572 910888
Food breakfast, dinner
Price €€
Closed late Nov to mid-Mar
Innocenti family

Stay at Villa Pasquini and you step back into the 19th century. Little has changed here, either in furnishings, or decoration, since then. Until seven years ago, it was the autumn retreat of an aristocratic Roman family, the Pasquinis; then it was bought, fully furnished, by the present incumbents, who have lovingly preserved it, combining a family home with a most unusual hotel. The bedrooms are, of course, all different, some quite grand with canopied beds. Bathrooms are old-fashioned, but well equipped. In the attractive dining room – originally the entrance hall – the emphasis is on traditional recipes. Our reporter chose the fixed-price menu (five delicious courses) and thought the price very reasonable.

MONTEFOLLONICO

LA CHIUSA
COUNTRY GUESTHOUSE

Via della Madonnina 88, 53040
Montefollonico, Siena

TEL 0577 669668 **Fax** 0577 669593
Food breakfast, lunch, dinner
Price €€€€-€€€€€
Closed Jan-Mar; restaurant Tue
Dania Masotti and Umberto
Lucherini

Quite a few of the better small hotels in this guide started off as restaurants and over the years have converted a few rooms for overnight visitors, with such success that they have extended this side of their business. But in general it is true to say that the restaurant remains the centre of the enterprise. Not that at La Chiusa, a stone farmhouse and *frantoio* (olive press), the comfort of guests is secondary. The greatest care and attention has been given to the bedrooms and suites each has been individually furnished with antiques. Bathrooms are among the best we have seen. Dania Masotti is justifiably proud of her achievements as a cook, and meals in the elegant (and pricey) restaurant are gastronomic experiences.

TUSCANY

MONTERIGGIONI

SAN LUIGI
COUNTRY HOTEL

*Loc. Strove, Via della Cerreta 38,
53030 Monteriggioni, Siena*

TEL 0577 301055
FAX 0577 301167
FOOD breakfast, lunch, dinner
PRICE €€€
CLOSED never
Signor Michelagnoli

THERE HAS BEEN NO cutting corners in the conversion of the farm buildings of San Luigi into a country hotel with a difference, which we think will appeal to some readers, especially those travelling with a young family. A long, unpaved drive takes you through acres of grounds to the main building and reception. The park is crammed with things to do: swimming, tennis, volleyball, basketball, bowls, even a giant chessboard. It would be unfair to describe San Luigi as a holiday camp, but it would be equally misleading to recommend it to readers in search of a tranquil break. Guests, when we visited, seemed incredibly active – especially the younger generation – and copious buffets helped to fuel their energies.

MONTIGNOSO

IL BOTTACCIO
RESTAURANT WITH ROOMS

*Via Bottaccio 1, 54038
Montignoso*

TEL 0585 340031 **FAX** 0585 340103
E-MAIL
bottaccio@relaischateaux.fr
WEBSITE www.relaischateaux.fr/
bottacio
Food breakfast, lunch, dinner
Price €€€-€€€€
Closed never
Stefano and Elizabeth D'Anna

IL BOTTACCIO LIES A COUPLE of miles inland from the beaches of Forte dei Marmi, amid pale-coloured hill towns and grey-green olive groves. It is primarily a restaurant, serving 10-course meals of 'creative dishes inspired by Mediterranean tradition', which have earned high praise from the gourmet guides (and from our inspector). But it is also a fantastic place to stay: overlooked by a ruined castle, it was originally an olive oil mill and the D'Anna family have successfully blended old and new in their conversion. Sitting areas are spacious and airy with black leather seating against white walls, exposed brick and rafters.

TUSCANY

SAN GIMIGNANO

LE RENAIE
COUNTRY HOTEL

*Loc. Pancole, 53037 San
Gimignano, Siena*

TEL 0577 955044 **FAX** 0577 955126
E-MAIL lerenaie@iol.it **WEBSITE**
sangimignano.com/lerenaie
FOOD breakfast, lunch, dinner
PRICE €
CLOSED Nov
Leonetto Sabatini

A SIMPLE, WELL-RUN COUNTRY HOTEL – built up over the years by the present owners from a bar and restaurant – which makes a respectable base within a short drive of San Gimignano. The building is no architectural masterpiece, but a typical example of a modern rustic construction. Inside, modern terracotta flooring and cane furniture make for a light, fresh atmosphere. The restaurant, Da Leonetto, is popular with locals (especially for large functions) but gets mixed notices from reporters. Upstairs are the bedrooms, which have a mixture of modern, built-in furniture and reproduction rustic. Guests seem to appreciate the peaceful location, services (including a swimming pool and access a tennis court).

SARTEANO

LE ANFORE
COUNTRY GUESTHOUSE

*Via di Chiusi 30, 53047 Sarteano,
Siena*

TEL 0578 265969 **FAX** 0578 265521
E-MAIL leanfore@priminet.it
WEBSITE www.balzarini.it
FOOD breakfast, dinner
PRICE €
CLOSED 3 weeks Nov
MANAGER Maurizio Pozielli

L e Anfore is a useful base for exploring the Val d'Orcia, and prices are reasonable. It's an old farmhouse, restored without particular flair or style, and, it must be said, the odd lapse of taste: there is a gnome near the front door, and hideous lighting in the downstairs public rooms. However, the atmosphere is pleasantly rustic and relaxed, with a huge fireplace in the brick-arched living room. The bedrooms are mostly spacious and a little more stylish than the public rooms, with dark, polished parquet floors and oriental rugs; several have sitting areas. Bathrooms are smartly tiled and well lit. Outdoors, there is plenty to do, with a big pool in the garden and tennis and riding nearby.

TUSCANY

SESTO FIORENTINO

VILLA VILLORESI
TOWN VILLA

Via Ciampi 2, 50019 Colonnata di Sesto Fiorentino, Firenze

TEL 055 443212 **FAX** 055 442063
E-MAIL cvillor@tin.it **WEBSITE**
www.villoresi@abitarefastoria.it
FOOD breakfast, lunch, dinner
PRICE €€ €€€€
CLOSED never
Contessa Cristina Villoresi

THE ARISTOCRATIC VILLA VILLORESI looks rather out of place in what is now an industrial suburb of Florence, but once in the house and gardens you suddenly feel a million miles away from modern, bustling Florence. Contessa Cristina Villoresi is a warm hostess who has captured the hearts of many transatlantic and other guests. It is thanks to her that the villa still has the feel of a private home – all rather grand, if a little faded. Bedrooms are remarkably varied – from the small and quite plain to grand apartments with frescoes and Venetian chandeliers. courtyard, others look look out on to the pool and garden. We are assured that the food is now better than it was.

SOVICILLE

BORGO DI TOIANO
COUNTRY HOTEL

Loc. Toiano, 53018 Sovicille, Siena

TEL 0577 314639
FAX 0577 314641
FOOD breakfast
PRICE €€ -€€€€
CLOSED Nov-Mar
MANAGER Pierluigi Pagni

MOST OF THE ABANDONED rural hamlets (*borgo*) that once housed small farming communities and have since been converted into distinctive hotels were located on steep hills or jumbled together behind secure walls. Borgo di Toiano, by contrast, has a pleasant open aspect: a few old stone houses, superbly restored, are spread out across acres of stone and terracotta terraces. The main public rooms also have a spacious, uncluttered feel. Bedrooms have the same mixture of rustic and modern. Swimming pool.

UMBRIA AND MARCHE

HOTELS IN UMBRIA AND MARCHE

VISITORS ARE DISCOVERING that there is more to Umbria than Assisi; but it nonetheless remains the main tourist highlight of the region. Choices of hotel here are strictly limited: there are many that are mediocre, and some of the more comfortable are too big for a full entry here; of these, the Subasio (tel 075 812206) is a 70-room, polished, rather formal place, but notable for the views from its better bedrooms and beautiful flowery terraces. We continue to recommend the Umbra (page 243) in town, and Le Silve (page 242) in the countryside, and we have added two new finds, the Sant' Andrea in Bettona, just 11 km away (page 246), and L' Orto degli Angeli in Bevagna, 24 km away (page 247).

Perugia is not nearly so well known as Assisi, but well worth a visit if you can penetrate the infuriating defences of its traffic system. Since its massive expansion to over 90 bedrooms, we have dropped our entry for the Brufani (tel 075 5732541), though it's worth knowing about, if expensive. Just along from the Brufani is La Rosetta (tel 075 5720841); though also large, it is not worryingly impersonal, and better value. Another possibility as a base for exploring the area is the Da Sauro (tel 075 826168), a family hotel on the peaceful island of Maggiore in Lake Trasemino. We have a new recommendation for the centre of Orvieto, and there's plenty of choice for relaxing hotels in the Umbrian countryside.

Marche's coast, like the rest of the Adriatic, offers large resorts with plenty of hotels, but not many suitable for this guide. Pesaro, though a big town, is a more interesting mixture of old town and beach resort than many along this coastline; along with the Villa Serena (page 262) we have added a new entry, Villa La Torraccia (page 263), and we might also mention the Vittoria, a stylish, well-equipped hotel on the seafront (tel 0721 34343). Ancona, regional capital of the Marche and a big seaport, is definitely not the place to stay but 12 km down the coast, at the popular resort of Portonovo, we have the Emilia and, as a back-up address can also suggest the Fortino Napoleonico (tel 071 801450). This is an extremely unusual hotel, built within a single-storey seaside fortress. Simple, clean and roomy, it particularly suits families, as many of its 30 rooms can accommodate three or four people. Further south at Numana, the Eden Gigli (tel 071 933 0652) is a smart, modern hotel in a beautiful setting overlooking the sea.

Inland from Pesaro, the Renaissance art city of Urbino is an essential place to visit, but there is no hotel here which we can wholeheartedly recommend. Our best suggestion is the Raffaello (tel 0722 4896), a straightforward 19-room place; it has no restaurant but this is not a problem since it is right in the middle of the town.

Gubbio is an equally compelling place to visit; try the Bosone (tel 075 9220688), or alternatively the Torre dei Calzolari Palace (tel 075 925 6327). Slightly out of town are the Villa Montegranelli (tel 075 9220185), a severe stone-built villa in hillside grounds, or the extravagant Park Hotel ai Cappuccini (tel 075 9234).

UMBRIA AND MARCHE

AMELIA

PICCOLO HOTEL CARLENI

∼ TOWN HOTEL ∼

Via Pellegrino Carleni 21, 05022 Amelia, Terni
TEL 0744 983925 **FAX** 0744 978143
E-MAIL carleni@tin.it **WEBSITE** www.giubileoitalia.com/carleni

IT IS THOUGHT THAT THE LITTLE hill town of Amelia was founded as early as the 12thC B.C., making it amongst the oldest settlements in Italy. It has a beautiful setting on the ridge that divides the Nera and Tiber valleys.

The Carleni started life as a restaurant run by an Italian-French couple and this is still very much the heart of the place. Two cosily rustic rooms with warm yellow walls and an inviting fireplace make a civilized setting for Marie France's excellent regional dishes with a French twist. The accommodation was added a couple of years ago in the form of delightful rooms and suites in the adjacent building, reached via an external stairway. Comfortably rustic in style with beamed ceilings, they are tastefully and carefully furnished with a mix of country antiques and pine or wicker pieces; country fabrics contrast with colourful oriental designs; the white-tiled bathrooms are impeccable. Walls, here too, are warm yellow, and duvets on the beds add a touch of luxury. The suites, one of which has a private terrace, are equipped with kitchenettes, and views are spectacular. In warm weather, breakfast is served in a charming walled garden among wisteria and olive trees.

∼

NEARBY Orvieto (32 km); Spoleto (40 km); Viterbo (30 km).
LOCATION 20 km SW of Terni, in centre of town; public car parking 100 m from hotel
FOOD breakfast, lunch, dinner
PRICE €-€€
ROOMS 7; 4 double and 3 suites, 6 with bath, 1 with shower; all rooms have phone, TV, minibar, hairdrier
FACILITIES restaurant, breakfast room, garden
CREDIT CARDS AE, DC, MC, V
DISABLED 4 specially adapted rooms **PETS** not accepted
CLOSED 3-4 weeks around Jan, Feb
PROPRIETORS Massimo Ralli and Marie France de Boiscuillé

UMBRIA AND MARCHE

ASSISI

LE SILVE

~ COUNTRY HOTEL ~

Loc. Armenzano, 06081 Assisi, Perugia
TEL 075 8019000 **FAX** 075 8019005
E-MAIL hotellesilve@tin.it **WEBSITE** www.lesilve.it

EVEN IF YOU ARE NOT PLANNING to stay at this sophisticated gem, the road up to Le Silve is worth exploring for its own rewards – or perhaps avoiding if you are the nervous sort. It winds up over a series of hills and passes until you reach the house, set on its own private hill-ridge, 700 m above sea level. The views are wonderful.

Le Silve is an old farmhouse (parts of it very old indeed – 10th century) converted to its new purpose with great sympathy and charm. There is a delightfully rambling feel to the place, with rooms on a variety of levels. The rustic nature of the building is preserved perfectly – all polished tile floors, stone or white walls, beamed ceilings, the occasional rug – and it is furnished with country antiques. Public rooms are large and airy, bedrooms stylishly simple. The self-contained suites are in villas about 1.5 km from the main house.

We have had two conflicting reports of the food, using oil, cheese and meat from the associated farm. 'Regional dishes presented with great flair and imagination,' says one; 'pretentious *cuisine minceur* at astronomical prices', says another. What do you think? Le Silve is close enough to Assisi for sightseeing expeditions but remote enough for complete seclusion – and with good sports facilities immediately on hand (fair-sized pool). But it's not for vertigo sufferers.

~

NEARBY sights of Assisi.
LOCATION in countryside 12 km E of Assisi, between S444 and S3; ask hotel for directions; ample car parking
FOOD breakfast, lunch, dinner; room service
PRICE €€€€ **ROOMS** 18; 11 double, 3 single, 4 self-contained suites, all with bath; all rooms have phone, TV, minibar, safe **FACILITIES** 2 sitting rooms, dining room, bar, terrace, swimming pool, tennis, sauna, riding, archery, mini-golf, motorbike **CREDIT CARDS** AE, DC, V **DISABLED** no special facilities **PETS** not accepted **CLOSED** mid-Nov to mid-Jan **MANAGER** Daniela Taddia

UMBRIA AND MARCHE

ASSISI

UMBRA

~ TOWN VILLA ~

Via degli Archi 6, 06081 Assisi, Perugia
TEL 075 812240 **FAX** 075 813653
E-MAIL humbra@mail.caribusiness.it **www**.caribusiness.it/carifo/iz/hotelumbra

Tucked away down a little alley off the main square of Assisi is this delightful little family-run hotel.

The Umbra consists of several small houses – parts date back to the 13th century – with a small gravelled courtyard garden shaded by a pergola. The interior is comfortable and in parts more like a private home than a hotel; there is a bright little sitting room with Mediterranean-style tiles and brocaded wing armchairs, and a series of bedrooms, mostly quite simply furnished but each with its own character and some with lovely views over the Umbrian plain. When we returned to reconsider the hotel for this new edition, we enjoyed eating in the elegant dining room (meals are served outside in fine weather) but agreed with past reports that the food was only 'all right'. Happily, there is no shortage of nearby alternative eating places in this popular tourist town.

The Umbra offers all the peace which you might hope to find in Assisi, and nothing is too much trouble for Alberto Laudenzi, whose family has run the hotel for more than 50 years. In our opinion, one of the best middle-range hotels in the region. However: one reader reports that some of the bedrooms are in need of redecoration, and another that parking can be a problem.

~

NEARBY basilica of St Francis, church of Santa Chiara, cathedral; medieval castle.
LOCATION in centre of town, off Piazza del Comune, with small garden; nearest car park some distance away
FOOD breakfast, lunch, dinner
PRICE €€
ROOMS 25; 16 double, 5 single, 4 suites, all with bath; all rooms have phone, TV
FACILITIES 3 sitting rooms, dining room, bar, garden
CREDIT CARDS AE, DC, MC, V **DISABLED** access difficult **PETS** not accepted
CLOSED mid-Nov to mid-Dec, mid-Jan to mid-Mar
PROPRIETOR Alberto Laudenzi

UMBRIA AND MARCHE

BETTONA

SANT' ANDREA

~ TOWN VILLA ~

Via Santa Caterina 2, 06084 Bettona, Perugia
TEL 075 987114 **FAX** 075 9869130
E-MAIL hsandrea@tin.it **WEBSITE** www.hotelsantandrea.it

BETTONA, SURROUNDED BY OLIVE GROVES with an interesting Etruscan history, is almost in the shape of an ellipse. It is a pretty, sleepy little place centred around an attractive *piazza* and only a few miles from the area's main attraction, Assisi.

Our inspector was surprised and delighted to stumble on the stylish Sant' Andrea in such an unlikely setting. Situated just off the main square, it occupies a medieval building which has undergone various identities in its time, from hospital to oratory (for the adjacent church) to – most recently – an oil press. It has been carefully renovated with respect for its many original features such as brick vaulting, heavy roof beams and brick arches, but it is decorated in contemporary style. Modern art works adorn the bright reception/sitting area where you will be greeted by one of the helpful young staff. The bedrooms have dark hardwood floors, stylish cherrywood furniture and dark blue bedcovers and upholstery; kilims provide a touch of colour and each room has its own set of black-and-white flower photographs. The smart bathrooms are in muted grey with shiny chrome fittings. The brick-vaulted basement restaurant serves local specialities.

NEARBY Assisi (11 km); Perugia (22 km).
LOCATION 11 km SW of Assisi, in centre of town; with car parking
FOOD breakfast, lunch, dinner
PRICE €€
ROOMS 19; 18 double, 1 single. 4 with bath, 15 with shower; all rooms have phone, TV, minibar, hairdrier **FACILITIES** sitting room, bar, restaurant, lift
CREDIT CARDS AE, MC, V
DISABLED 1 adapted room
PETS not accepted
CLOSED never
MANAGER Marco Bolatti

UMBRIA AND MARCHE

BEVAGNA

L'ORTO DEGLI ANGELI

~ TOWN HOTEL ~

Via Dante Alighieri, 06031 Bevagna, Perugia
TEL 0742 360130 **FAX** 0742 361756
E-MAIL ortoangeli@ortoangeli.it **WEBSITE** www.ortoangeli.it

BEVAGNA IS ANOTHER OF THOSE SLEEPY little Umbrian places full of artistic gems, this time on the old Via Flaminia. Situated in the centre of town, l'Orto degli Angeli is a 17thC property which is remarkable for two features. The delightful hanging garden occupies the site of a Roman amphitheatre, and one rough stone wall of the pretty, lemon-painted restaurant is a remnant of a first century temple to Minerva.

The grandly-named Antonini Angeli Nieri Mongalli family have restored their fascinating home with much care. Its dimensions are grand, too, complete with frescoes, aged terracotta floors and vast stone fireplaces are still there, but it manges to be homely and comfortable too – anything but overwhelming. The bedrooms are imaginatively decorated with great style; smart fabrics blend with the original terracotta floor tiles, gorgeous family antiques and painted woodwork. Modern equipment is carefully hidden from view. The menu in the restaurant changes every week, and Tiziana Antonini oversees the cooking. She bakes fresh bread daily, and even grinds her own flour. The jams and cakes served at breakfast are home made.

~

NEARBY Assisi (24 km); Perugia (45 km); Spello (13 km).
LOCATION 8 km SW of Foligno, in centre of town; public car parking 100 m
FOOD breafast, lunch, dinner
PRICE €€€
ROOMS 9; 6 double and 3 suites, 2 with bath, 7 with shower; all rooms have phone, TV, air conditioning, minibar, hairdrier
FACILITIES breakfast room, restaurant, sitting room, reading room, garden
CREDIT CARDS AE, DC, MC, V
DISABLED not suitable **PETS** accepted
CLOSED mid-Jan to mid-Feb
PROPRIETORS Tiziana and Francesco Antonini Angeli Nieri Mongalli

UMBRIA AND MARCHE

CAMPELLO SUL CLITUNNO

IL VECCHIO MOLINO
∼CONVERTED MILL ∼

Loc.Pissignano, Via del Tempio 34, 06042 Campello sul Clitunno, Perugia
TEL 0743 521122 **FAX** 0743 275097 **WEBSITE** www.perugiaonline.com

IT IS A MYSTERY HOW THIS INN, so close to the busy Perugia-Spoleto road, remains so peaceful. Almost the only sound is of gurgling brooks winding through the leafy gardens. As befits an old mill, all the buildings live in close harmony with the river: the drive sweeps around the mill pond to a creeper-covered building against which old grinding-stones rest. The gardens are a spit of land, with weeping willows dipping into streams on both sides. Water even runs through some of the old working parts, where the mill machinery has been built into the decorative scheme.

There seems to be no end to the number of public rooms, all furnished in a highly individual manner: elegant white sofas in front of a big brick fireplace, surmounted by carved wooden lamps; tables with lecterns bearing early editions of Dante's *Purgatorio*; mill wheels used as doors. The bedrooms were, we were relieved to note, pleasingly dry and decorated in a restrained manner with fine antiques, the white walls lit up by parchment-shaded lamps.

It's worth remembering that the hotel is popular in the wedding season and during the Spoleto festival.

NEARBY Spoleto (11 km); Perugia (50 km).
LOCATION 50 km SE of Perugia between Trevi and Spoleto; in own grounds by the Clitunno river; ample car parking
FOOD breakfast
PRICE €€
ROOMS 13; 6 double, 2 single, 5 suites, all with bath or shower; all rooms have phone, minibar, some have air conditioning **FACILITIES** sitting rooms, bar, gardens
CREDIT CARDS AE, DC, MC, V
DISABLED access difficult
PETS accepted **CLOSED** Nov-Mar
PROPRIETOR Paolo Rapanelli

UMBRIA AND MARCHE

CANALICCHIO

RELAIS IL CANALICCHIO

~ HILLTOP HOTEL ~

Via della Piazza 13, 06050 Canalicchio, Perugia
TEL 075 8707325 **FAX** 075 8707296
E-MAIL relais@ntt.it **WEBSITE** www.wel.it/Rcanalicchio.html

One of the paradoxes of modern Italy is that what were once the modest homes of farmers and artisans have become, with careful restoration, exemplars of modern taste and comfort. What makes this possible is the Italian genius for combining everyday materials of quality – brick, wood, plaster, terracotta – with style and flair.

The owners of Relais Il Canalicchio have taken over most of the semi-fortified, hilltop town of the same name and created a hotel that not only respects the native Umbrian qualities but imaginatively enhances them with contemporary Italian panache. Public rooms are in the old working areas of the mill: brick arches and the massive grinding stones set off the comfortable, elegant furniture. The plain plaster walls are decorated with English prints, oil portraits and brilliant local ceramics. An old wine-press remains.

Each bedroom has been individually furnished; some have terrace gardens and many have superb views. The restaurant serves exquisitely prepared produce from its own farm (please note: we have had one dissenting report on the food). If you feel guilty about such hedonism, there is a gym, a pool and a sauna. Even if you are a prince, this is one hamlet certainly good enough for you.u

~

Nearby Perugia, Assisi, Gubbio, Todi (all within 40 km).
Location quiet hilltop village 40 km SE of Perugia; car parking
Food breakfast, lunch, dinner
Price €€-€€€
Rooms 27; 18 double; 5 single; 4 suites, all with bath or shower; all rooms have phone, TV, air-conditioning, minibar, safe
Facilities sitting rooms, restaurant, billiard room, gym, sauna, terraces, gardens, swimming pool, mountain bikes **Credit cards** AE, DC, MC, V
Disabled some rooms suitable **Pets** accepted **Closed** never
Proprietor Antonio Setter

UMBRIA AND MARCHE

CASTEL RIGONE

RELAIS LA FATTORIA
~ TOWN HOTEL ~

Via Rigone 1, 06060 Castel Rigone, Lago Trasimeno, Perugia
TEL 075 845322 **FAX** 075 845197
E-MAIL pammelati@edisons.it **WEBSITE** www.relaislafattoria.com

ON THE HILLS BEHIND LAKE TRASIMENO lies the small medieval town of Castel Rigone, a mere handful of houses grouped about a handsome *piazza*. Right at its centre is this pleasant, family-run hotel occupying what was once a manor house.

You feel a sense of welcome the moment you step inside the reception area, which has a wooden ceiling, stone walls and comfortable Knole sofas. Keen young staff are on hand to make you feel at home. The public rooms are tastefully decorated, with Persian rugs on the polished cork floors and bright modern paintings on the white walls. The only addition to the building that has been allowed by the Italian Fine Arts Ministry is a restaurant perfectly in keeping with the original style. Dishes include fresh fish from the lake.

Bedrooms have been designed with an eye more to modern comfort than to individual style and some have lake views. The bathrooms are bright and new.

Along the front of the house is a terrace with sitting areas and a small swimming pool. An excellent, extensive buffet breakfast (home-made bread and jams, cheeses and cured meats) is served here in fine weather.

~

NEARBY Perugia (27 km); Assisi (35 km); Gubbio (50 km).
LOCATION 27 km NW of Perugia, in centre of town; car parking nearby
FOOD breakfast, lunch, dinner
PRICE €€
ROOMS 29; 23 double, 3 single, 3 junior suites, all with bath or shower (suites with Jacuzzis); all rooms have phone, TV, minibar **FACILITIES** sitting room, restaurant, terrace/garden, swimming pool
CREDIT CARDS AE, DC, MC, V
DISABLED no special facilities **PETS** accepted
CLOSED hotel never; restaurant only, Jan **PROPRIETORS** Pammelati family

UMBRIA AND MARCHE

CENERENTE

CASTELLO DELL'OSCANO
∽ CASTLE VILLA ∽

06134 Loc. Cenerente, Perugia
TEL 075 690125 **FAX** 075 690666
E-MAIL info@oscano.com **WEBSITE** www.oscano.it

A T FIRST SIGHT CASTELLO DELL'OSCANO appears like a fairytale medieval castle: ivy-clad turrets, battlements and crenellated towers rise above a steep, hillside pine forest. In fact, this is an 18thC re-creation, and the inside reveals that century's genius for civilized living.

The interiors are finely proportioned, spacious and light. The hall rises the entire height of the castle, with an imposing carved stairway, polished wood floors and neo-Gothic windows. One public room leads into another, all filled with the castle's original furniture: a library which will entrance any bibliophile with its carved classical bookcases and 18thC volumes; sitting rooms with wooden panelling, tapestries and sculpted fireplaces; a dining room with old display cases full of Deruta pottery.

Upstairs, the floors are of geometrically patterned, black-and-white marble. There are only ten bedrooms in the castle, each with its own antique furnishing. The remainder, in the Villa Ada next door, are less exciting and cheaper. The most spectacular (but strictly for the agile) is in the turret, with a four-poster bed and a door to the ramparts which look over the romantic gardens below.

∽

NEARBY Perugia (5 km); Assisi (28 km); Gubbio (40 km).
LOCATION on a hillside in its own grounds; ample car parking
FOOD breakfast, dinner
PRICE €€-€€€€
ROOMS 11 double (Castello), 8 double, 2 single (Villa Ada), all with bath or shower; all rooms have phone, TV, air conditioning, minibar, hairdrier
FACILITIES sitting rooms, dining room, library, bar, gardens, swimming pool
CREDIT CARDS AE, DC, MC, V
DISABLED 1 suitable bedroom
PETS accepted
CLOSED never; restaurant only, mid-Jan to mid-Feb
MANAGER Maurizio Bussolati

UMBRIA AND MARCHE

FOLIGNO

VILLA RONCALLI

~ TOWN VILLA ~

Via Roma 25, 06034 Foligno, Perugia
TEL 0742 391091 **FAX** 0742 391001

DON'T BE PUT OFF BY the depressing light-industrial surroundings in which this splendid 18thC villa now finds itself. The tall chestnut trees which line the drive and encircle this former hunting lodge screen off the outside world almost entirely.

Although the present owners acquired the villa only relatively recently, they have succeeded in creating within it the atmosphere of a family home. The public rooms are furnished with magnificent pieces of antique furniture and paintings.

The ground floor is dominated by the elegant dining room, formerly the villa's entrance hall, with its long sideboard and massive glass-fronted wine cabinet. Angelo's wife Alessandra runs the kitchen, which has become one of the gastronomic temples of central Umbria, while their daughter Maria Luisa oversees the front-of-house with amiable efficiency.

Upstairs, on the *piano nobile*, four airy bedrooms with large shuttered windows lead off the cool, frescoed sitting room, while the remainder are in the second floor mansard. Each is furnished opulently in a timeless modern style.

~

NEARBY Spello (7 km); Montefalco (12 km); Assisi (15 km).
LOCATION 1.5 km S of Foligno; ample car parking
FOOD breakfast, lunch, dinner
PRICE €€
ROOMS 10; 8 double, 2 single, all with shower; all rooms have TV, air-conditioning, minibar
FACILITIES sitting room, breakfast room, restaurant, bar
CREDIT CARDS AE, DC, MC, V
DISABLED no special facilities
PETS not accepted
CLOSED hotel never; restaurant only, 2 week in Mar
PROPRIETORS Angelo and Alessandra Scolastra

UMBRIA AND MARCHE

MONTECASTELLO VIBIO

FATTORIA DI VIBIO
∽ FARM GUESTHOUSE ∽

Loc. Buchella 1a, 9-Doglio, 05010 Montecastello Vibio, Perugia
TEL 075 8749607 **FAX** 075 8780014
E-MAIL info@fattoriadivibio.com **WEBSITE** www.fattoriadivibio.com

OCCASIONALLY, THE WHOLE ATMOSPHERE of a place is captured by a small detail: here it is the hand-painted pottery used to serve Signora Saladini's delicious food which sums up the relaxed elegance of this renovated 18thC farmhouse. The style is modern rustic Italian, with pleasing open spaces, defined by white walls that contrast with the colourful fabrics and ceramics. Light, airy and well proportioned, there is an feeling of effortless simplicity which, you quickly realize, required a great deal of taste and effort. Most of the bedrooms, of similar style, are in the house next door.

The Saladini family are serious about their visitors' comforts and wellbeing, starting in the kitchen. Much of what goes into the guests comes out of the farm or the market garden and the preparation is a spectacle in itself, open to all. The mandatory half board should not prove a penance. If you need to lose calories, you can swim, play table tennis, ride or walk in the magnificent countryside around; tennis is also available nearby. Or you may prefer to relax in the quiet of the garden. Otherwise, there is not much to do – but then that is the whole point of this soothing guesthouse.

∽

NEARBY Todi (20 km); Orvieto (30 km).
LOCATION on quiet hillside off S448 road between Todi and Orvieto; ample car parking
FOOD breakfast, lunch, dinner
PRICE €€; half board obligatory; 1-week minimum stay in Aug
ROOMS 10 double and twin, all with bath or shower; some rooms have TV
FACILITIES sitting room, dining room, terrace, garden, swimming pool, bicycles, riding, fishing
CREDIT CARDS AE, DC, MC, V
DISABLED 1 suitable room
PETS accepted **CLOSED** Jan and Feb, Nov to Dec
PROPRIETORS Gabriella, Giuseppe & Filippo Saladini

UMBRIA AND MARCHE

MONTEFALCO

VILLA PAMBUFFETTI

~ VILLA HOTEL ~

Via della Vittoria 20, 06036 Montefalco, Perugia
TEL 0742 379417 **FAX** 0742 379245
E-MAIL villabianca@interbusiness.it **WEBSITE** www.umbria.org

LIKE HEMINGWAY IN SPAIN, the poet D'Annunzio seems to have stayed everywhere in Italy; however, in the case of Villa Pambuffetti the claim is better justified than most. Not only did he dedicate a poem to the near-by walled town of Montefalco (known as 'Umbria's balcony' for its unrivalled views of the region), but the villa itself has a turn-of-the-century elegance that fits the poet's legend.

Ten thousand square metres of shady garden surround the main building. Inside, furniture and decoration have been kept almost as they were at the start of the 1900s when the Pambuffetti family began taking 'paying guests': floors and panelling of seasoned oak, bamboo armchairs (which took D'Annunzio's fancy), Tiffany lampshades and old family photographs in art nouveau frames pay tribute to a century that started optimistically. Many of the bedrooms are furnished with the family's older and finer antiques and all have bathrooms which, though recent, are stylistically nearly perfect. If you like a room with a view, try the tower, which has one of the six-windowed, all-round variety. The dining room's view is more modest, but then the food deserves attention, too.

~

NEARBY Montefalco; Assisi (30 km); Perugia (46 km).
LOCATION just outside Montefalco, in its own grounds; with ample car parking
FOOD breakfast, dinner
ROOMS 15; 11 double and twin, 1 single; 3 suites, 2 with bath, 13 with shower; all rooms have phone, TV, air conditioning, minibar, hairdrier
PRICE €€-€€€
FACILITIES sitting room, bar, restaurant, *loggia*, garden, swimming pool
CREDIT CARDS AE, DC, MC, V
DISABLED 2 rooms on ground floor
PETS not accepted **CLOSED** never
MANAGERS Alessandra and Mauro Angelucci

UMBRIA AND MARCHE

ORVIETO

LA BADIA

~ CONVERTED ABBEY ~

Loc. La Badia, 05019 Orvieto, Terni
TEL 0763 301959 **FAX** 0763 305396

ARRIVING AT TWILIGHT AT LA BADIA is like landing in a scene from a Gothic novel: ruined arches, rooks cawing from a crenellated bell tower, dark cypresses silhouetted against the sky and, across the valley, the evening profile of Orvieto's cathedral, secure on its fortress crag. But the golden stone monastery on the hill, surrounded by Umbria's intense green countryside, soon reveals itself as an outstanding hotel that would have delighted any Renaissance cardinal.

Restraint is the hallmark of this fine building's conversion into a distinctive hotel. The robust architecture of the old abbey is always allowed to speak for itself, and modern embellishments have been kept to a minimum. The heavy wooden period furniture goes well with the massive stone walls; wrought-iron lights illuminate vaulted ceilings; floors are either of plain or geometrically-patterned terracotta. Here and there, an unexpectedly-placed church pew reminds the guest of what once was.

On the hill behind is a pool fit for a pope. In front of the abbey, beside the famous 12-sided tower, is a peaceful garden where the meditative visitor can contemplate the view of Orvieto.

~

NEARBY Orvieto (5 km); Todi (40 km); Viterbo (45 km).
LOCATION on quiet hillside, 5 km S of Orvieto; own car parking
FOOD breakfast, lunch, dinner
PRICE €€€
ROOMS 26; 16 double, 3 single, 7 suites, all with bath or shower; all rooms have phone, air-conditioning
FACILITIES sitting room, breakfast room, bar, restaurant, tennis, swimming pool
CREDIT CARDS AE, V
DISABLED access difficult
PETS not allowed **CLOSED** Jan, Feb
PROPRIETOR Luisa Fiume

UMBRIA AND MARCHE

ORVIETO

PALAZZO PICCOLOMINI

~ TOWN HOTEL ~

Piazza Ranieri 36, 05018 Orvieto, Terni
TEL 0763 341743 **FAX** 0763 391046
E-MAIL piccolomini.hotel@orvieto.it **WEBSITE** www.argoweb.it/hotel_piccolomini/

AT LAST A DECENT HOTEL has been created in the centre of this remarkable town which sits on a pedestal of tufa some 300 m above sea level. Orvieto is a charming place with a fabulous, candy-striped cathedral, an atmospheric *centro storico*, a choice of restaurants serving fine, regional food and last, but not least, an excellent local white wine.

Pale pink Palazzo Piccolomini (so-named after the family who built it at the end of the 16th century) is situated at the heart of the old city and was beautifully restored as a hotel in 1998. Inside, there is a wonderful sense of calm throughout the cool, vaulted rooms, which have been furnished with what some might call Spartan good taste. In the spacious salon, wrought-iron candelabras and white covers on sofas and chairs are stylish against white walls and polished terracotta floors; filmy white curtains ripple in the breeze and filter the sunlight. The bedrooms, although varying in shape and size, are similar, with modern, dark wooden furniture and the odd splash of deep blue. Some have rooftop views. You eat breakfast in a vaulted basement room which has Etruscan origins.

~

NEARBY cathedral; underground caves.
LOCATION on the S side of town near Porta Romana; public car parking 200 m away
FOOD breakfast
PRICE €€
ROOMS 31; 22 double and twin, 6 single, 3 suites, all with shower; all rooms have phone, TV, air conditioning, minibar, hairdrier
FACILITIES breakfast room, sitting room, bar, lift
CREDIT CARDS AE, DC, MC, V
DISABLED some adapted rooms
PETS accepted **CLOSED** 1 week Jan
MANAGER Roberto Mazzolai

UMBRIA AND MARCHE

PANICALE

LE GROTTE DE BOLDRINO

~ TOWN HOTEL ~

Via Virgilio Cappari 30, 06064 Panicale, Perugia
TEL 075 837161 **FAX** 075 837166

THE FORMER PALAZZO BELLESCHI-GRIFONI, hewn into the walls of the medieval brick-built hill town of Panicale, was converted only in 1990 to its present use. In contrast to its stern front, the interior is small and intimate, designed in the finest contemporary manner, with particularly imaginative use of iron and wood.

The hotel can be entered through a doorway from one of the narrow passageways of the old *borgo* or, more conveniently, via the lower restaurant entrance on the road which encircles the town. A warren-like corridor takes you to the parquet-floored bedrooms. In surprising contrast to their modern finish, they are furnished with imperious late-19thC furniture – towering walnut bedheads, and so on. Noteworthy also is the gentle use of lighting.

The reputation of the downstairs restaurant is increasing by leaps and bounds. Again, you find a pleasing mix of old and new, with the unplastered medieval wall and traditional oak and brick-tile ceiling against the modern plastered walls and iron railings of the restaurant's upper gallery. The short, mainly Umbrian, menu offers a variety of local specialities.

NEARBY Castiglione del Lago (15 km); Città della Pieve (25 km).
LOCATION built into the town walls; car parking nearby
FOOD breakfast, lunch, dinner
PRICE €
ROOMS 11; 9 double and twin, 2 single, all with bath or shower; all rooms have phone, TV
FACILITIES sitting room, breakfast room, restaurant
CREDIT CARDS AE, DC, MC, V
DISABLED access difficult **PETS** small pets accepted
CLOSED never
PROPRIETOR Attilio Spadoni

UMBRIA AND MARCHE

PANICALE

VILLA DI MONTESOLARE
~ COUNTRY VILLA ~

Loc. Colle San Paolo, 06070 Panicale, Perugia
TEL 075 832376 **FAX** 075 8355462
E-MAIL info@villamontesolare.it **WEBSITE** www.villamontesolare.it

HIGH WALLS KEEP OUT the arid scenery around, enclosing the stuccoed villa in a green oasis. The present building dates back to 1780, although the 16thC chapel in the garden suggests a much earlier house was on the site. When the present owners bought it, they set about restoring the 19thC garden (and the secret garden behind it), building the swimming pool a discreet distance away, and converting the villa without interfering with its patrician character.

The result is one of the most comfortable country retreats of the Trasimeno area. The bedrooms of the villa retain their original character – beamed ceilings, quarry tile floors and whitewashed walls, furnished in squirely fashion with turn-of-the-century high- backed beds, cabinets and wardrobes. The cool blue sitting-room on the *piano nobile* certainly is noble, while the dining rooms and the bar are situated more humbly, downstairs. In 1995, Mrs Strunk and her husband Filippo converted a *casa colonica* which stands outside the walls. They divided it into five suites, building by it the villa's second swimming pool. Another annexe has been added more recently. Rooms are simply furnished in country style.

~

NEARBY Panicale (12 km); Città della Pieve (25 km).
LOCATION 2 km N of the SS220, direction Colle S. Paolo; ample car parking
FOOD breakfast, lunch, dinner
PRICE ©©; minimum stay three days
ROOMS 8 double with bathroom, 2 suites in the villa; 10 suites in 2 annexes, all with bath or shower **FACILITIES** 2 dining rooms, sitting room, bar, 2 swimming pools, tennis court, bowls, riding
CREDIT CARDS DC, MC, V
DISABLED 1 suitable apartment
PETS accepted
CLOSED mid-Dec to mid-Jan
PROPRIETOR Rosemarie Strunk

UMBRIA AND MARCHE

PESARO

VILLA SERENA
~ COUNTRY VILLA ~

Via San Nicola 6/3, 61100 Pesaro
TEL 0721 55211 **FAX** 0721 55927

THE ADRIATIC COAST south of Rimini is not short of hotels, but it is very short of our kind of hotel, which makes this one a real find – a handsome 17thC mansion with some token castellations, standing in a wooded park high above the hubbub of the coast.

The villa has always belonged to one family – the counts Pinto de Franca y Vergaes, who used it as a summer residence until, in 1950, they turned it into a small hotel to be run like a family home. Renato Pinto does the cooking and serves up some better-than-average dishes (order in advance out of high season); Stefano and Filippo see to guests and reception; while their mother, Signora Silvana busies herself in the house and garden, with its terracotta pots and orange trees; all the family are reassuringly down-to-earth. The emphasis is on character, simplicity and peace, not luxury. There are salons of baronial splendour, and corridors delightfully cluttered with bric-à-brac and potted plants. A few faded corners reinforce the villa's appealing air of impoverished aristocracy. No two bedrooms are alike, but antiques and fireplaces feature in most. A couple could do with painting and some trees could well be lopped to let in light.

NEARBY municipal museum, at Pesaro; Ducal Palace at Urbino.
LOCATION 4 km SE of Pesaro and beach, in a large wooded park on hillside, with private car parking
FOOD breakfast, lunch, dinner
PRICE €€
ROOMS 10 double and twin, all with bath or shower; all rooms have phone
FACILITIES sitting rooms, dining room, bar, terrace, swimming pool
CREDIT CARDS AE, DC, V
DISABLED access difficult
PETS accepted
CLOSED 2 weeks early Jan
PROPRIETOR Renato Pinto

UMBRIA AND MARCHE

PORTONOVO

EMILIA

~ SEASIDE HOTEL ~

Via Poggio, 149/A Portonovo, 60020 Ancona
TEL 071 801145 **FAX** 071 801330
E-MAIL info@hotelemilia.com

ALTHOUGH THE EMILIA IS a seaside hotel, it stands aloof from the beaches south of Ancona, on the flanks of Monte Conero above the little resort of Portonovo (which is a car-journey away for all but the most energetic). It is a modern building of no great architectural merit. But its proprietors some years ago hit on a clever way of giving the hotel a distinctive appeal: they invited artists to come and stay, and to pay their way in kind. The results continue to accumulate on the walls: score upon score of paintings (none, we are assured, has ever been sold). Among the Italian signatures, our inspector spotted Graham Sutherland's.

Even without the extraordinary wall-covering, the hotel would have an attractive atmosphere. A long, low sitting room with clusters of chunky modern armchairs links reception to the large, light, simply furnished dining-room, which has big windows looking on to a passable imitation of a *prato inglese* (a lawn). Food is taken seriously, although it no longer earns a Michelin star. Fish dominates the menu, and is competently cooked, though expensive. Bedrooms are thoroughly modern and snazzy. Most are in the older part of the hotel, arranged at an angle to give each room a sea-view and a balcony. Recently two 'wonderful' suites were created.

NEARBY church of Santa Maria (at Portonovo); Monte Conero; Ancona (12 km).
LOCATION 2 km W of Portonovo on cliffs; ample car parking
FOOD breakfast, lunch, dinner
PRICE €€€-€€€€
ROOMS 33; 28 double and twin, 2 with bath, 26 with shower; 2 single with shower; 3 suites, 2 with bath, 1 with shower; all rooms have phone, TV, air conditioning, minibar
FACILITIES dining room, TV room, bar, gazebo bar, swimming pool, tennis
CREDIT CARDS AE, DC, MC, V **DISABLED** some rooms on ground floor **PETS** accepted
CLOSED Nov to Mar
PROPRIETOR Maurizio Fiorini

UMBRIA AND MARCHE

SPOLETO

GATTAPONE

~ TOWN VILLA ~

Via del Ponte 6, 06049 Spoleto, Perugia
TEL 0743 223447 **FAX** 0743 223448
E-MAIL gattapone@mail.caribusiness.it **WEBSITE** www.caribusiness.it/gattapone

THERE ARE TWO THINGS you can do in this hotel just outside Spoleto's centre. The most obvious is to gape at the unparalleled views of the 13thC Bridge of Towers spanning the Tessino Valley. The other is to enjoy the quaintness of its Sixties jet-set decoration, all wood, glass, chrome and leather. If you tire, as some do, of the oh-so-prevalent rustic antique look, then you will enjoy the now dated, but meticulously maintained 'modern' style of the much-loved Gattapone.

The hotel is a favourite of the Spoleto Festival crowd, and the walls of the American Bar are festooned with pictures of the famous and would-be famous who throng its salons late into the evening. Even if you do not stay at the Gattapone, you will notice it. From the outside it looks like a solid, two-storey villa with classic ochre walls and green shutters. Inside, one becomes aware how the original building and its more modern extension have been constructed downwards to exploit the hillside position. Many of the bedrooms have large picture windows to capture the panorama.

We have visited the hotel in low season and enjoyed the peace and quiet. During the Festival (June-July), rooms are hard to get.

~

NEARBY Assisi (48 km); Todi (42 km); Perugia (63 km).
LOCATION on hillside, just outside historic centre of Spoleto; no private car parking facilities
FOOD breakfast
PRICE €€
ROOMS 14; 7 double and twin, 7 junior suites, all with bath or shower; all rooms have phone, TV, air conditioning, minibar
FACILITIES sitting room, breakfast room, bar, terrace
CREDIT CARDS AE, DC, MC, V
DISABLED no special facilities **PETS** accepted **CLOSED** never
PROPRIETOR Pier Giulio Hanke

UMBRIA AND MARCHE

TORGIANO

LE TRE VASELLE

~ VILLAGE HOTEL ~

Via Garibaldi 48, 06089 Torgiano, Perugia
TEL 075 9880447 **FAX** 075 9880214
E-MAIL 3vaselle@3vaselle.it **WEBSITE** www.3vaselle.it

THREE MONASTIC WINE JUGS discovered during the restoration of the original 17thC *palazzo* are what give this exceptional hotel its name and its theme: wine. Owned by the Lungarotti family, makers of Umbria's finest vintages, the *palazzo* is packed with still lifes of grapes, prints of the gods carousing and statues of Bacchus. However, nothing but sober professionalism characterizes the day-to-day management.

Bedrooms, some in a more modern building behind the main one and others in a luxury annexe a short walk away, are all furnished to the highest standards: comfortable striped sofas, antique chests, individually chosen prints and lamps give an air of unrushed elegance. Public rooms are open and spacious, spanned by sweeping white arches and softly lit. Breakfast, an extensive buffet, is served on a secluded back terrace. The restaurant is outstanding, with a wine list the size of a telephone directory.

A recent visitor to Le Tre Vaselle could report only improvements. It could not be more professional; you could not feel more at home.

~

NEARBY Deruta (5 km); Perugia (8 km); Assisi (16 km).
LOCATION in quiet street in village of Torgiano, 13 km SE of Perugia; car parking in nearby *piazza*
FOOD breakfast, lunch, dinner; room service
PRICE €€€-€€€€
ROOMS 61; 52 double and twin, 2 singles, 7 suites, most with bath, some with shower; all rooms have phone, TV, air conditioning, hairdrier
FACILITIES sitting rooms, dining rooms, breakfast room, bar, lift, terrace, swimming pool, sauna **CREDIT CARDS** AE, DC, MC, V
DISABLED access possible
PETS not accepted **CLOSED** never
MANAGER Giovanni Margheritini

UMBRIA AND MARCHE

ASPROLI

POGGIO D'ASPROLI

COUNTRY GUESTHOUSE

Loc. Asproli 7, 06059 Todi, Perugia

TEL and **Fax** 075 8853385
E-MAIL aovalp@tin.it
WEBSITE www.emmeti.it/asproli
FOOD breakfast; dinner on request
PRICE €-€€€
CLOSED mid-Jan to mid-Mar
Bruno Pagliari

IF YOU ARE TIRED OF NAPLES, you may not be tired of life – just in need of peace and quiet. Such was the case with Bruno Pagliari, so he sold his large southern hotel to continue his career as an artist in the peace of Umbria. But the tradition of hospitality remained, and he has opened up his farmhouse to guests. The rambling building of local stone is packed with an arresting mixture of antiques and Bruno's own modern art. The main sitting room, with its great fireplace and white sofas, is flanked by a long terrace where one can eat or just relax. The bedrooms will inspire many a pleasant dream.

BASCHI

POMURLO VECCHIO/LE CASETTE

COUNTRY GUESTHOUSE

Loc. Pomurlo Vecchio, 05023 Baschi, Terni

TEL 0744 950190/950475 **FAX** 0744 950500 **FOOD** lunch, dinner
PRICE €; minimum stay 1 week in Aug **CLOSED** never
Lazzaro and Daniela Minghelli

LAZZARO MINGHELLI'S 350-ACRE FARM estate stretches from the shores of Lago di Corbara almost to Baschi. His romantic family home, Pomurlo Vecchio, is an eccentric 12thC tower, jutting out of a wooded hillock. It also has four small apartments: they are homely, though when we last visited we felt they were rather frayed at the edges. The principal guest accommodation, Le Casette, stands on the other side of the estate. Three stone cottages have been rebuilt around a swimming pool. Though lacking the patina of age, they provide a summer oasis particularly suitable for families. Rooms are simply decorated. The restaurant, overseen by daughter Daniela, is noteworthy.

UMBRIA AND MARCHE

BASCHI

VILLA BELLAGO
COUNTRY HOTEL

*Strada per Todi (SS 448), 05023
Baschi, Terni*

TEL 0744 950521 **FAX** 0744 950524
FOOD breakfast, lunch, dinner
PRICE €·€€
CLOSED never; restaurant only,
Tue
MANAGER Massimiliano Benedetti

UNDENIABLY MODERN, but stylish in its own way, Villa Bellago will appeal to travellers who enjoy contemporary comforts and the full range of facilities. Magnificently situated on the shores of Lago di Corbara, a man-made lake, the 'villa' was originally a set of 19thC farm buildings, but is now rigorously updated. The hotel certainly makes full use of its lakeside location: large picture windows carry your eyes over its rippling surface to green hills beyond. The gardens are meticulously cared for, with acres of rolling lawns and brightly coloured flowers in terracotta urns, and there is an outdoor pergola next to the restaurant where you can enjoy not just your food and the view, but perhaps a cool evening breeze from the lake.

NARNI

DEI PRIORI
TOWN HOTEL

*Vicolo del Comune 4,Narni, 05035
Narni, Terni*

TEL and **FAX** 0744 726843
FOOD breakfast, lunch, dinner
PRICE €
CLOSED never
Maurizio Bravi

TUCKED AWAY IN A QUIET ALLEY in the medieval heart of one of southern Umbria's unsung towns, this friendly small hotel provides an ideal staging post for travellers who prefer the 'backroads' route along the via Flaminia to Rome. As well as the magnificent Piazza dei Priori, the town's Romanesque *duomo* and the 14thC Palazzo del Podestà provide ample reason for an overnight detour. A lift, or a grandiose black oval staircase, takes you up to the comfortable modern bedrooms which look out into the central courtyard or over the pantiled roofs of the medieval *borgo*. A few have small balconies. Downstairs, the restaurant spills out into the court-yard in the summer months. Its menu is mainly Umbrian.

UMBRIA AND MARCHE

ORVIETO

VILLA CICONIA

COUNTRY VILLA

Loc. Ciconia, Via dei Tigli 69,
05018 Orvieto, Terni

TEL 0763 305582/3 **FAX** 0763
302077
FOOD breakfast, lunch, dinner
PRICE €€-€€€€
CLOSED mid-Jan to mid-Feb;
restaurant only, Mon
Valentino Petrangeli

PROTECTED FROM THE NEARBY busy road and the encroachments of
Orvieto's new suburbs by its tree-filled gardens, La Ciconia is a small,
attractive 16thC grey stone villa. Spacious ground-floor public rooms with
massive stone fireplaces and frescoed friezes contrast with simpler, more
restful sitting rooms on the upper floor. The bedrooms are in a more rustic
style, with wrought-iron or four-poster beds and antique chests that combine well with the exposed roof-beams and warm, terracotta floors.
Bathrooms are gleaming new. The gardens are a delight, bounded by two
streams, but there is some noise from the road. The restaurant serves
Umbrian specialities. A pleasant alternative to La Badia (page 231).

OSPEDALICCHIO DE BASTIA

LO SPEDALICCHIO

MEDIEVAL MANOR

Piazza Bruno Buozzi 3, 06080
Ospedalicchio de Bastia, Perugia

TEL and **FAX** 075 801 0323
FOOD breakfast, lunch, dinner
PRICE €€
CLOSED never
MANAGER Signor Costarelli

DESPITE THE ATTRACTIONS OF ASSISI, for the touring motorist there is much
to be said for staying out of town. This one is the best around: a four-
square manor house on the road to Perugia. The ground-floor rooms have
high, vaulted brick ceilings and tiled floors with the occasional rug. The
restaurant (which enjoys a high local reputation) is on one side – stylishly
set out; in contrast, the sitting room-bar area is traditionally sparse with
exposed stone walls. Bedrooms vary widely – some high-ceilinged, some
two-level affairs with sitting space. The staff are courteous and helpful;
their French is better than their English. We are pleased to hear that the
noisy church bells are now stopped during the night.

UMBRIA AND MARCHE

VILLA LA TORRACCIA
COUNTRY VILLA

Strada Torraccia 3, 61100 Pesaro

TEL and **FAX** 0721 21852
WEBSITE www.dimorestoriche.com
FOOD breakfast
PRICE €€
CLOSED never
Antonio Galeazzi

V ILLA LA TORRACCIA is an unusual structure: a solid, rectangular house with a tower which seems to grow out of its middle. The 13thC building was constructed as a watchtower and later used as an of inland lighthouse which lit the way to Pesaro. This spot could make an ideal base for anyone who wants a bit of culture (Urbino and other art sights are within easy reach) combined with a bit of beach (coast, 4 km). Extensive restoration work was done in 1994 using traditional building materials. The rather intimidating dimensions of the house are softened by comfortable furnishings and some clever duplex arrangements in the spacious bedroom suites. These are all different, furnished with antiques and rustic pieces.

SAN LUCA
TOWN HOTEL

Via Interna delle Mura 21, 06049 Spoleto, Perugia

TEL 0743 223399
FAX 0743 223800
E-MAIL sanluca@hotelsanluca.com
WEBSITE www.hotelsanluca.com
FOOD breakfast
PRICE €€-€€€
CLOSED never
Daniela Zuccari

W HEN POPE INNOCENT II came to this spot in 1198, his presence is reputed to have caused a fountain to begin spouting, giving renewed strength to himself and his retinue. Today the site is occupied by an impressive 19thC building, with soft yellow painted exterior walls, which was transformed into an elegant hotel in 1995. The yellow colour scheme continues inside in the light, sunny hallway and sitting areas. Several of the pastel-toned bedrooms have a balcony or terrace; all of them are soundproofed and have a large bathroom. Right in the centre of Spoleto, but peacefully set in lush gardens, the San Luca also has a roof garden and a spacious courtyard, where you can try the 'therapeutic' waters.

LAZIO AND ABRUZZO

HOTELS IN LAZIO AND ABRUZZO

ALTHOUGH ROME IS A CITY of grand hotels rather than small and charming ones, we have managed to make a few interesting discoveries for this new edition. They include the delightful Due Torri and its stylish sister hotel, the Fontanella Borghese, and, on the outskirts of the city centre, the peaceful Villa del Parco in a leafy garden. Other small hotels that we have upgraded from short to long entries are the Teatro di Pompeo, Pensione Parlamento, Portoghesi and Gregoriana. We have not included the luxurious 37-room Lord Byron (tel. 06 3220404), at the top end of the market (and of the Spanish Steps) – certainly less impersonal than most smart Rome hotels, but still impressively ritzy – and not really right for this guide.

Within easy driving distance of Rome to the north just outside Poggio Mirteto Scalo is the country-club-style Borgo Paraelios, and on the coast outside Palo Laziale, is Posta Vecchia, the 17thC mansion that once belonged to Jean Paul Getty. A stay here surrounded by the fabulous art-works and faded grandeur is an expensive but unique experience. Also within day-trip range of the capital to the east are Palestrina (birthplace of the 16thC composer) and Tivoli (villas of Emperor Hadrian and the 16thC Cardinal d'Este). If you want to stay overnight in Palestrina, go for the Stella – an excellent, modern restaurant with clean spacious bed-rooms (tel 06 9538172).

North of Rome is the pretty wooded countryside around Viterbo and Lago di Vico, the homeland of the Etruscans. An average town hotel in the heart of Viterbo is the Leon d'Oro (tel 0761 344444). Further north-west, we have a new find near Farnese, Il Voltone, an appealing hotel in glori-ously unspoiled country.

In an area to the east of Rome, where previous editions of the guide featured nothing, we have found Antico Borgo, a simple bed-and-breakfast in the medieval village of Fumone. To the south, on Lazio's coast at San Felice Circeo, Punta Rossa is a pleasant holiday hotel, and on the nearby island of Ponza, Gennarino a Mare is a delight.

Abruzzo is a wild and wooded mountainous region, forming part of the Apennine mountains. Charming small hotels are hard to find here and you might do best to explore the area from a base nearer Rome. One of our favourite hotels, however, is the tiny Villa Vignola on the coast at Vasto. You could try the tiny Villa Vignola on the coast at Vasto (tel 0873 310050), the medieval Castello di Balsorano at Balsorano (tel. 0863 951236), and in Scanno, the friendly chalet, Mille Pini (tel. 0864 74387), or Del Lago (tel 0864 74343), in a lakeside setting 3 km outside the town.

L'Aquila, the capital of the region, is a big town further north but still in the heart of the mountains. Though mainly a business centre today, the surrounding mountains and the imposing historical buildings within the town itself still make it an interesting place to stay. Try the Grand Hotel del Parco (tel 0862 413248), which with 36 rooms is smaller and less busi-ness-oriented than most of the hotels in the town.

LAZIO AND ABRUZZO

FARNESE

IL VOLTONE

~ COUNTRY HOTEL ~

Il Voltone, 01010 Farnese, Viterbo
TEL and **FAX** 0761 422540
E-MAIL info@voltone.it **WEBSITE** www.voltone.it

HARDLY ANYONE ARRIVES at Il Voltone without getting lost (make sure you have precise directions and don't give up on a road that seems never-ending); or without falling in love at first sight with this charming, individual hotel. A clutch of beautifully restored 17thC buildings – including a small church – colour-washed in pinks, yellows and creams, it stands high in the middle of a 465-hectare estate. Rolling hills, vineyards, woods and fields stretch out on three sides – scenery you can admire from reception rooms, bedrooms and even the swimming pool.

The unfussy decoration is more Tuscan than Roman with warm, fresh colours that echo the exterior. Floors are terracotta-tiled, scattered with the occasional Persian carpet. Almost everywhere table lamps cast a warm, flattering light. Bedrooms are graced with a few handsome pieces of furniture, and some have lovely old beams.

In the dining room, choose from a range of local dishes, made from the freshest ingredients, and drink wine from the estate's own vineyards. For relaxing outside, there is a terrace with tables and chairs, shaded by horse chestnuts and parasols. There is so much to see locally that the thoughtful Parenti sisters have planned itineraries for guests who want to explore.

~

NEARBY Farnese (12 km); Lake Bolsena.
LOCATION N of Farnese off the Ischia di Castro-Latera road; car parking
FOOD breakfast, lunch, dinner
PRICE €€
ROOMS 30 double and twin, triple and family, all with bath or shower; all rooms have phone, TV, hairdrier **FACILITIES** sitting room, breakfast room, terrace, garden, swimming pool
CREDIT CARDS MC, V
DISABLED ground-floor room with special facilities
PETS accepted by arrangement **CLOSED** early Nov to early Apr
PROPRIETORS Daniela and Donatella Parenti

LAZIO AND ABRUZZO

FUMONE

ANTICO BORGO

∽ VILLAGE BED-AND-BREAKFAST ∽

Via del Fico 5, 3010 Fumone , Frosinone
TEL and **FAX** 0775 49791
E-MAIL lisaeagles@infinito.it **WEBSITE** www.italiaabc.it/az/anticoborgo

LITTLE SEEMS TO HAVE CHANGED over the centuries in the charming medieval fortress village of Fumone (the name means 'big smoke', after the smoke signals sent up from here to warn Rome of imminent invasion from Naples). No cars are permitted inside the old walls, still intact and with only two entrances: one facing Rome, the other, Naples. So if you arrive by car, you must park outside and walk through the labyrinthine streets until you reach this simple, friendly B&B in one of the ancient village houses. Once inside, all is airy and bright. Upstairs and down, the plain white-walled rooms are lifted by warm terracotta floors and attractive timberwork. There are wooden panels on the bar, wooden stairs, doors and even ceilings.

Don't worry about the lack of a dining room. There is a choice of restaurants and pizzerias in the village, two of them only a couple of minutes' walk away. Guests will be helped and advised by their delightful English host, Lisa Eagles, who, with her Italian husband Giampaolo, provides a very personal service. They will even pick up and drop off at Rome airport or local stations. In an area where this guide has no other hotels, we feel that Antico Borgo is a real find.

∽

NEARBY Frosinone (21 km); Lake Canterno.
LOCATION in centre of Fumone, 12 km N of Ferentino; public car park outside fortress walls.
FOOD breakfast
PRICE ⓔ
ROOMS 8; 7 double and twin, 1 with bath, 6 with shower, 1 single with shower; all rooms have TV
FACILITIES sitting/breakfast room, bar
CREDIT CARDS AE, DC, MC, V
DISABLED access difficult **PETS** not accepted **CLOSED** never
PROPRIETOR Lisa Eagles

LAZIO AND ABRUZZO

POGGIO MIRTETO SCALO

BORGO PARAELIOS

~ COUNTRY VILLA ~

Valle Collicchia, 02040 Poggio Mirteto Scalo, Rieti
TEL 0765 26267 **FAX** 0765 26268
E-MAIL borgo@fabaris.it

A 19THC VILLA IS AT THE HEART of this attractive country club-style development in the hills halfway between Rome and Rieti, with most of the immaculately furnished rooms and suites spread around the beautiful gardens and courtyards, ensuring peace and seclusion for their occupants. Each room also has its own terrace. Decoration varies from room to room, but the predominant style is Italian 'rustic chic' – a blend of warm colours, chintzes and period furniture. Some also have exposed rafters and brass beds. The numerous public rooms are grander: don't be surprised to spot a Canaletto or an Attardi among the fine paintings on their walls. This show of wealth is not off-putting, however, and the place exudes warmth and hospitality, thanks in great measure to the friendly staff.

One of the most relaxing places to sit is the huge covered terrace with splendid views of the hills and masses of padded wicker chairs. Whenever possible, food is served outside, and consists largely of simple but tasty local specialities.

An excellent range of facilities includes indoor and outdoor pools, sauna, Turkish bath and a minibus service to Rome.

~

NEARBY Rome (40 km); Marmore Falls; Lake Piediluco.
LOCATION 4 km N of Poggio Mirteto off SS313; car parking
FOOD breakfast, lunch, dinner
PRICE €€€
ROOMS 15; 13 double and twin, 2 suites, all with bath or shower; all rooms have phone, TV, air conditioning, hairdrier
FACILITIES sitting rooms, restaurant, games rooms, meeting room, spa, garden, indoor and outdoor swimming pool, tennis, golf
CREDIT CARDS AE, DC, MC, V **DISABLED** access difficult
PETS small dogs accepted **CLOSED** never; restaurant Tues
PROPRIETORS Salabe family

LAZIO AND ABRUZZO

PONZA

GENNARINO A MARE

~ WATERFRONT RESTAURANT-WITH-ROOMS ~

Via Dante 64, 04027 Ponza , Latina
TEL 0771 80071/80593 **FAX** 0771 80140
E-MAIL pagreca@tin.it **WEBSITE** www.wel.it/gennarino

THE *RAISON D'ETRE* OF THE Gennarino a Mare is its popular, buzzing restaurant, spread out over a covered timber deck, perched on piles, jutting into the sea. There are no prizes for guessing what the cuisine is based on – seafood, including fish and shellfish of all descriptions. The Gennarino provides moorings so, in the holiday season, hotel guests rub shoulders with yachties who come ashore to sample the daily catch.

A small blue-painted box-shaped building, with a backdrop of Ponza's colourful houses climbing the cliffside, the hotel is modest but full of sunlight. White-walled rooms are simply furnished with ceiling fans, brightly co-ordinating curtains and bedspreads, and balconies overlooking the sea; the best have large terraces with table and deckchairs.

The hotel had its genesis in the tiny *pensione* run by the parents of the present owner Francesco Silvestri, who has lived here all his life. A charming man, for whom nothing is too much trouble, he will direct you to the island's many natural treasures: beaches, cliffs, caves and grottoes. There are other hotels on Ponza but this one has the edge, combining a terrific restaurant, character and unbeatable prices.

NEARBY Chiaia di Luna beach; Pilatus caves.
LOCATION on waterfront opposite harbour; garage for 30 cars
FOOD breakfast, lunch, dinner
PRICE €€
ROOMS 12 double and twin with bath; all rooms have phone, TV, minibar
FACILITIES sitting room, restaurant, bar
CREDIT CARDS AE, DC, MC, V
DISABLED access difficult
PETS not accepted
CLOSED never
PROPRIETOR Francesco Silvestri

LAZIO AND ABRUZZO

ROME

CARRIAGE

~ TOWN HOTEL ~

Via della Carrozze 36, 00187 Roma
TEL 06 699 0124 **Fax** 06 678 8279
E-MAIL hotel.carriage@alfanet.it **WEBSITE** www.hotelcarriage.net

This smart little hotel stands in one of the narrow streets near the Piazza di Spagna, renowned for their elegant boutiques dealing in impossibly-priced clothes. The Carriage matches the designer style of its surroundings, though its prices for this part of Rome are not at all unreasonable. 'It is a perfect size,' comments a recent visitor, 'one feels like one is the only one there.'

The reception area of fat-cushioned, expensive-looking sofas and chairs in gold and blue stripes, the pretty breakfast room of black bentwood and rattan and twirly gilt, the cool flower arrangements – all seem to await only the photographer and slinky models. Upstairs, the small, but comfortable bedrooms are less florid in blue and white, with fine, solid reproduction French-look furnishings. Bathrooms are clean and streamlined, with spotlit mirrors, heated floors and all the usual trimmings. At the top of the hotel there is a small roof terrace, slightly less orderly than the rest of the hotel, but allowing a breath of air along with your summer breakfast. This meal is of above-average standard, with a wide choice of pastries and espresso or capuccino. One satisfied visitor found the staff 'most courteous'. 'Nothing was too much trouble.'

NEARBY Piazza di Spagna; Via del Corso.
LOCATION between Via del Corso and Piazza di Spagna
FOOD breakfast
PRICE €€€
ROOMS 17 double and twin with bath, 3 single with shower, 2 suites with bath; all rooms have phone, TV, air-conditioning, minibar, hairdrier
FACILITIES breakfast room, reception/sitting room
CREDIT CARDS AE, DC, MC, V
DISABLED no special facilities
PETS not accepted
CLOSED never
MANAGER Signor Cau

LAZIO AND ABRUZZO

ROME

CELIO
~ TOWN HOTEL ~

Via SS Quattro 35/C, 00184 Roma
TEL *06 70495333* **FAX** *7096377*
E-MAIL *info@hotelcelio.com* **WEBSITE** *www.hotelcelio.com*

THE MASSIVE BULK of the Colisseum stands guard at the end of the quiet, largely residential street where stands the Hotel Celio. Those two reasons – the quiet, and the proximity of the amazing ancient arena (plus important nearby remains of the ancient city), make the Celio a prime base in central Rome. Ease of parking (own small drive, and a garage nearby), is a bonus, too, and driving in from Ciampino airport is no big deal – as quick as half an hour on the Via Appia. The rooms aren't large, but they are rather fun if you don't mind deep red brocade on the walls, and paintings and mirrors created by an artist from Brescia to look at least 200 years older than they actually are. The floors are wonderful: high-quality imitation ancient mosaic, designed by the owner, Roberto Quattrino, who (with his brother) also runs the Santo Stefano in Venice. There is no lift to the bedrooms, and it is a moderate climb to the roof where guests can sunbathe and where there is a penthouse suite, complete with own roof terrace and views across Rome to St Peter's. Breakfast is served in fine weather in a courtyard imaginatively roofed in with a tent.

NEARBY Coliseum, Roman forums.
LOCATION central Rome, near Coliseum
FOOD breakfast
PRICE EE-EEE
ROOMS 19 doubles and suites, all with en suite bath, shower; all rooms have phone, TV, hairdryer, air-conditioning
FACILITIES roof terrace, breakfast area, sitting area
CREDIT CARDS AE, DC, MC, V
DISABLED no lift
PETS small ones by arrangement
CLOSED never
PROPRIETOR Roberto Quattrini

LAZIO AND ABRUZZO

ROME

CONDOTTI

~ TOWN HOTEL ~

Via Mario De' Fiori 37, 00187 Roma
TEL 06 6794661 **FAX** 06 6790457
E-MAIL hotelcondotti@italyhotel.com **WEBSITE** www.hotelcondotti.com

THE OWNERS CONTINUE to make improvements to this appealing little hotel located in an attractive street in the heart of Rome's chicest shopping zone. The warmly-lit reception hall looks inviting from the street side of the double glass doors; guests are greeted from an antique table, often by a professional and helpful Canadian. The reception incorporates a smart sitting area where low, deep sofas in yellow and blue stacked with cushions are made for lounging. Down a marble staircase is the attractive, newly-decorated breakfast room where cream-coloured walls, touches of blue and soft lighting make the very best of a windowless basement.

Refurbishment of the bedrooms (now divided into two categories – standard and superior) was halfway complete when our inspector visited. She found them much improved; blue and gold predominate (it seems to be *the* colour scheme in Roman hotels this year) on fabrics and carpets while furniture and bedheads are in rich cherry wood. Several rooms have spacious terraces. Five new rooms in an annexe round the corner will help satisfy demand for this rightfully popular hotel.

~

NEARBY Spanish Steps; Via del Corso; Villa Borghese.
LOCATION between Via del Corso and Piazza di Spagna; public car park nearby
FOOD breakfast
PRICE ⓔⓔⓔ
ROOMS 17 double and twin, 12 with bath, 5 with shower; all rooms have phone, TV, air conditioning, minibar, hairdrier
FACILITIES reception, breakfast room, lift
CREDIT CARDS AE, DC, MC, V
DISABLED access difficult
PETS not accepted
CLOSED never
PROPRIETOR Massimo Funaro

LAZIO AND ABRUZZO

ROME

DUE TORRI
~ TOWN GUESTHOUSE ~

Vicolo del Leonetto 23, 00186 Roma
TEL 06 68806956 **FAX** 06 68805531
E-MAIL hotelduetorri@interfree.it **WEBSITE** www.hotelduetorriroma.com

THIS STYLISH LITTLE HOTEL in a quiet, cobbled lane just north of Piazza Navona is a real discovery. The newly painted façade offers a foretaste of the neat interior where the spacious reception area leads into a series of comfortable public rooms. Marble floors gleam and provide a suitable setting for some lovely antiques while chairs and sofas are upholstered in red velvet or smart red and beige, a colour scheme which is continued throughout the house. There are some fine antique mirrors (including a huge one on each landing), old lamps and attractive prints, all of which are offset by cool, cream walls.

The bedrooms (each with its own brass doorknocker) are arranged on five floors and reached by an elegant marble staircase with *fin-de-siècle* iron banister (or there's a lift). None of them are very large (one or two are, in fact, quite small), but all are pretty and comfortable. Bedheads, valances, curtains and bedcovers are all in co-ordinated red and beige; attractive but never fussy. Some rooms have great views over rooftops and terraces, excellent for an inside glimpse of Roman domestic life. Four – including a single – have terraces equipped with tables and chairs.

~

NEARBY Piazza Navona; Piazza di Spagna; Via del Corso.
LOCATION in quiet side street just N of Piazza Navona; public car park nearby
FOOD breakfast
PRICE €€
ROOMS 26; 15 double and twin, 7 single, 4 family, all with shower; all rooms have phone, TV, air conditioning, minibar, hairdrier
FACILITIES sitting rooms, breakfast room, lift
CREDIT CARDS AE, DC, MC, V
DISABLED no special facilities
PETS not accepted **CLOSED** never
PROPRIETOR Cinzia Giordani Pighini

LAZIO AND ABRUZZO

ROME

FONTANELLA BORGHESE

∽ TOWN GUESTHOUSE ∽

Largo Fontanella Borghese 84, 00186 Roma
TEL 06 68809504 **FAX** 06 6861295
E-MAIL fontanellaborghese@interfree.it **WEBSITE** www.fontanellaborghese.com

OCCUPYING THE TOP TWO FLOORS of an elegant 16thC building which once belonged to the Borghese princes, this new hotel is under the same ownership as the more modest Due Torri (see page 277). A neoclassical courtyard separates it from the bustle of the busy road and a discreet lift whisks you up to the hotel.

The open-plan reception area gives a taste of the style of the establishment: smart marble floors, cool cream walls, leafy pot plants, some fine antiques and plenty of light. The space is dominated by a sweeping, open staircase in wrought iron, brass and marble, and behind this are several comfortable sofas which make a sunny spot for relaxing with a magazine. The owner has kept the decoration of the stylish bedrooms simple; co-ordinating fabrics (in green and cream on the lower floor, blue and cream upstairs), dark parquet floors, neutral cream walls, brass light fittings, some antique furniture and prints on the walls. Bathrooms (off-white with the appropriate-coloured trim) needless to say, are smart and well equipped and the whole place is spotless. This is a classy place, offering reasonable prices for the standard of accommodation provided.

∽

NEARBY Augustus Mausoleum; Piazza di Spagna; Pantheon.
LOCATION N of the Pantheon between Via del Corso and Via di Ripeta; public car park nearby
FOOD breakfast
PRICE €€-€€€
ROOMS 29; 21 double and twin, 5 single, 3 suites, all with bath or shower; all rooms have phone, TV, air conditioning, minibar, hairdrier
FACILITIES sitting room, breakfast room, lift
CREDIT CARDS AE, DC, MC, V
DISABLED access possible **PETS** accepted
CLOSED never
PROPRIETOR Maria Pighini Giordani

LAZIO AND ABRUZZO

ROME

GREGORIANA
~ TOWN GUESTHOUSE ~

Via Gregoriana 18, 00187 Roma
TEL 06 6797988 **FAX** 06 6784258

THE DISTINCTIVE DECORATION in this little hotel will certainly not be to everybody's taste, and prices are quite high for the facilities on offer, but the location (in a street leading up to the Trinita dei Monti at the top of the Spanish Steps) and – above all – the warmest of welcomes should help to make amends.

The pleasant, shuttered house has virtually no public space at all; indeed, breakfast is served in the bedrooms although room service is available round the clock. The decoration is an extraordinary mix of rather dated Chinoiserie and art deco. A woven bamboo effect covers walls and ceiling in the tiny reception area while carpets are deep, Siamese pink. Upstairs, one landing is covered in leopard print, and another in William Morris; Erté alphabet figures grace each black-painted door. Inside the simple rooms, walls are light pink and Chinese-red lacquer furniture is mixed with rather dated seventies-style pieces. The best are at the back of the building where three have small private terraces and others enjoy peaceful rooftop views. Bathrooms are refreshingly normal with pretty floral wallpapers and white tiles.

~

NEARBY Spanish Steps; Via del Corso; Trevi Fountain.
LOCATION just SE of the top of the Spanish Steps; public car park nearby
FOOD breakfast; room service
PRICE €€€
ROOMS 19 double and twin with bath or shower; all rooms have phone, TV, air conditioning, hairdrier
FACILITIES lift
CREDIT CARDS not accepted
DISABLED no special facilities
PETS accepted
CLOSED never
PROPRIETOR Maria Novella Panier Bagat

LAZIO AND ABRUZZO

ROME

LOCARNO
~ TOWN HOTEL ~

Via della Penna 22, 00186 Roma
TEL 06 3610841 **FAX** 06 321 5249
E-MAIL info@hotellocarno.com **WEBSITE** www.hotellocarno.com

To STEP INSIDE THE FINE, *fin-de-siècle* doors of this stylish, wisteria-clad hotel just north of the Piazza del Popolo is to enter a time warp. The ground-floor public rooms house an impressive collection of original art nouveau and art deco pieces; fabulous lamps, Thonet bentwood furniture, old posters and a grandfather clock in reception with a resonant chime. The bar leads into a spacious sitting room where a fire is lit in winter.

A birdcage lift creaks up to the bedrooms, each one different from the next, but all furnished with antiques, original lamps and rich fabrics. Bathrooms are mostly in marble; one is huge and has the original tub and basin. New rooms and suites in the recently-acquired 1905 villa next door are more luxurious with opulent fabrics and more marble.

There is plenty of outside space, too; in warm weather, breakfast is served until 11.30 am in either the roof garden which runs around three sides of the original building or on the ground-floor terrace. A fleet of bicycles is available for guests' use. The laid-back feel to this hotel and its understated glamour make it a favourite with musicians, artists and the cinema crowd.

~

NEARBY Piazza del Popolo; Villa Borghese; Via del Corso.
LOCATION in side street just N of Piazza del Popolo; public car parking nearby
FOOD breakfast
PRICE €€€
ROOMS 59; 44 double and twin, 15 single, all with bath or shower; all rooms have phone, TV, air conditioning, minibar, hairdrier; de luxe rooms have video and stereo
FACILITIES sitting room, breakfast room, bar, lift, roof garden, terrace, free bicycles
CREDIT CARDS AE, DC, MC, V
DISABLED some adapted rooms
PETS accepted **CLOSED** never
PROPRIETOR Maria-Teresa Celli

LAZIO AND ABRUZZO

ROME

MOZART

～ TOWN HOTEL ～

Via dei Greci 23b, 00187 Roma
TEL 06 36001915 **FAX** 06 36001735
E-MAIL info@hotelmozart.com **WEBSITE** www.hotelmozart.com

IDEALLY PLACED FOR SHOPAHOLICS on one of the narrow, cobbled streets that run between Via del Corso and Via del Babuino, the Mozart is one of the pleasantest of the numerous hotels in the area. It has recently expanded into the adjacent building, so there is an 'old' part and a 'new' part. Our inspector only saw the latter, which was impressively elegant for a three-star hotel, although possibly a little lacking in character.

The lobby is a calm expanse of cool, creamy archways, marble floors and stylish parlour palms. On the first floor, a long, comfortable sitting room has pale yellow walls, dark hardwood floor broken by oriental rugs and invitingly squashy sofas. An open fire cheers up chilly evenings. The smart and well-equipped bedrooms, off light corridors, have pale terracotta floors and dark cherry wood furniture with the odd antique piece. In the bathrooms, chrome fittings gleam; one even opens on to a little terrace. From the delightful roof garden, which is on two levels and equipped with stylish garden furniture and white umbrellas, you can see most of Rome. There is a little bar up there, too – a superb spot for an *aperitivo*.

～

NEARBY Piazza di Spagna; Piazza del Popolo; Villa Borghese.
LOCATION in side street between Via del Corso and Via del Babuino; public car parking nearby
FOOD breakfast
PRICE €€€
ROOMS 56; 45 double and twin, 9 single, 2 suites, all with bath or shower; all rooms have phone, TV, air conditioning, minibar, hairdrier
FACILITIES sitting room, breakfast room, bar, roof garden
CREDIT CARDS AE, DC, MC, V
DISABLED some adapted rooms
PETS not accepted **CLOSED** never
PROPRIETOR Mario Pinna

LAZIO AND ABRUZZO

ROME

PENSIONE PARLAMENTO
～ TOWN GUESTHOUSE ～

Via delle Convertite, Roma 00187
TEL 06 6792082 **FAX** 06 69921000
E-MAIL hotelparlamento@libero.it

ONE OF ONLY A HANDFUL of two-star establishments that we feature in Rome, the friendly Parlamento enjoys an excellent central location for those on a budget; and anyone interested in the contortions of Italian politics can wander over to the Quirinale in nearby Piazza del Parlamento to watch the comings and goings of politicians and officials.

The *pensione* occupies the third and fourth floors of a 17thC *palazzo*. The front door opens on to the tiled reception area, where one of the young helpful staff sits at a desk in front of a modern fresco of Roman rooftops. Another fresco brightens up the pleasant breakfast room where the odd elegant touch (such as a glinting chandelier) softens the modern decoration. Bedrooms – where pale, dusty pink predominates – vary in size from quite spacious to tiny. They are simply furnished but not completely devoid of comfort and style, typically in the form of painted friezes round the walls, antique bedheads, green marble in the bathrooms and heated towel rails. One room (much in demand) has a private terrace. The roof garden, where breakfast is served in warm weather, is a bonus.

～

NEARBY Via del Corso; Spanish Steps; Pantheon.
LOCATION between Via del Corso and Piazza San Silvestro; public car parking nearby
FOOD breakfast
PRICE €€
ROOMS 23; 13 double and twin, 4 single, 6 family, all with bath or shower; all rooms have phone, TV, hairdrier; some have air-conditioning
FACILITIES breakfast room, roof garden
CREDIT CARDS AE, DC, MC
DISABLED not suitable **PETS** accepted
CLOSED never
PROPRIETOR Plinio Chini

LAZIO AND ABRUZZO

ROME

PORTOGHESI

~ TOWN HOTEL ~

Via dei Portoghesi 1, 00186 Roma
TEL 06 6864231 **FAX** 06 6876976

JUST NORTH OF LOVELY PIAZZA Navona and situated in the heart of what was the Portuguese quarter of 17thC Rome, the Portoghesi has an attractively old-fashioned look to it from the outside. Until recently, it was pretty old-fashioned on the inside too, but major refurbishment has brought increased comfort although possibly at the expense of character.

Bedrooms (a few are large enough to be called suites) have been thoroughly modernized with quality reproduction furniture mixed with some antiques, padded bedheads, pleasant wallpapers and co-ordinated fabrics in rich colours. The brand new bathrooms sparkle. Depending on which floor you are on, views may include the neighbour's washing hanging out to dry or little terraces tucked away among the rooftops. The pretty glassed-in breakfast room, decked out in sunny, modern fabrics, and adjoining flower-filled terrace are at the top of the building, and look on to the ancient 'Torre della Scimmia' or 'Tower of the Monkey', so named from a legend which claims that a baby was rescued and carried to the top by a monkey in the 17th century.

~

NEARBY Piazza Navona; Pantheon; Castel Sant' Angelo.
LOCATION in a side street just N of Piazza Navona; public car parking nearby
FOOD breakfast
PRICE €€
ROOMS 28 double and twin, single and suites, 5 with bath, 23 with shower; all rooms have phone, TV, air conditioning, hairdrier
FACILITIES breakfast room, roof garden, lift
CREDIT CARDS MC, V
DISABLED access difficult
PETS small ones accepted
CLOSED never
PROPRIETORS Claudio and Marco Trivellone

LAZIO AND ABRUZZO

ROME

RAPHAEL

~ TOWN HOTEL ~

Largo Febo 2, 00186 Roma
TEL 06 682831 **FAX** 06 6878993
E-MAIL info@raphaelhotel.com **WEBSITE** www.raphaelhotel.com

CLOAKED IN STALACTITES OF IVY, the Hotel Raphaël stands back from the bustle of Piazza Navona and belongs, instead, to the quiet refinement of the antiques and antiquarian bookshops and local *trattorias* of Via dei Coronari which runs beside it. The discreet façade conceals one of the most evocative and theatrical lobbies in the city. A pair of marble musical muses inside the entrance door announces an eclectic mix of Byzantine icons, Old Master paintings, prints by the Italian Futurists and ceramics by Picasso displayed in baroque furniture. The aroma of white lilies in large vases pervades the atmosphere. It is hardly surprising that the acting profession has embraced this establishment.

The lobby is punctuated by the only disappointing feature – a functional marble and glass staircase connecting the five floors of the hotel. Other modernist features have been softened by sweeping redecoration. New panelled doors and stone architraves offer a more pleasing character and bedrooms drip in rich paisley fabrics, but are perhaps smaller than prices would suggest. A visit here will be as memorable as the splendid terrace view of Bramante's magnificent cupola of Santa Maria della Pace.

~

NEARBY Piazza Navona; Palazzo Altemps; Santa Maria della Pace.
LOCATION at the N end of Via dell' Anima behind Piazza Navona; public car park nearby
FOOD breakfast, lunch, dinner
PRICE €€€€
ROOMS 72; 65 double and twin, 7 suites, all with bath; all rooms have phone, TV, air conditioning, minibar
FACILITIES breakfast room, dining room, bar, conference room, fitness centre, roof dining terrace **CREDIT CARDS** AE, DC, MC, V
DISABLED no special facilities **PETS** accepted
CLOSED never
PROPRIETOR Roberto Vannoni

LAZIO AND ABRUZZO

ROME

LA RESIDENZA
~ TOWN HOTEL ~

Via Emilia 22, 00187 Roma
TEL 06 4880789 **FAX** 06 485721
E-MAIL hotel.la.residenza@venere.it **WEBSITE** www.venere.it/roma/la.residenza

FASHIONABLE VIA VENETO is home to some of Rome's grandest hotels. La Residenza is not one of these, but its position, just a block away from the sweeping, tree-lined avenue, is only one of its advantages. The hotel has undergone a transformation since its last entry in this guide. For a start, it has been upgraded from three to four stars but has managed, so far, to maintain very reasonable prices. The refurbishment that was begun several years ago is now complete with the result that both public areas and bedrooms are much more stylish and personalized. A bar and sitting rooms lead off the front hall on the elevated ground floor. These are now smartly kitted out in a deep-pink striped fabric, with cream on the walls, a mixture of modern and antique furniture, attractive paintings and leafy pot plants. The windowless breakfast room at the back has also been prettified and better-than average fare is prepared here in the morning by a cook who will make hot food to order on his grill.

Bedrooms are comfortable and well equipped; those at the back are quieter. Some have fair-sized terraces and there is also a rooftop terrace with excellent views.

~

NEARBY Spanish Steps; Villa Borghese; Via del Corso.
LOCATION in side street off Via Veneto; limited car parking
FOOD breakfast
PRICE ©©-©©©
ROOMS 29; 17 double and twin, 5 single, 7 suites, all with bath; all rooms have phone, TV, air conditioning, minibar, hairdrier
FACILITIES sitting rooms, breakfast room, bar, lift, patio, terrace
CREDIT CARDS MC, V
DISABLED access difficult
PETS small ones accepted **CLOSED** never
MANAGER Vincenzo Casaburo

LAZIO AND ABRUZZO

ROME

SCALINATA DI SPAGNA
~ TOWN GUESTHOUSE ~

Piazza Trinità dei Monti 17, 00187 Roma
TEL 06 6793006 **FAX** 06 69940598
E-MAIL info@hotelscalinata.com **WEBSITE** www.hotelscalinata.com

FOR MANY VISITORS TO ROME, the Spanish Steps represent the heart of the city, a popular, lively rendezvous. At their summit stand two hotels which represent the epitomes of their respective markets: the Hassler, one of the city's grandest establishments, and this individual little *pensione* which, now more than ever, wins our accolade for genuine charm.

In previous editions of our guide, we acknowledged the hotel's attractions but expressed reservations about the old-fashioned bedrooms and unremarkable bathrooms. Now, a major programme of redecoration, by the proprietor's daughter, Claudia, has brought about some very pleasing changes. Rooms are now coated in pretty blue and gold floral fabrics and illuminated by Murano chandeliers. Neoclassical scroll sofas and small tables enhance a mood of comfort and intimacy. Bathrooms have been re-equipped. The tiny entrance hall and corridors have been redesigned, too, with a new reception desk and polished stucco walls. Inevitably, prices have risen and are now among the highest of hotels in this category, and with this in mind a reader reports that breakfast was disappointing. There are just 16 rooms, so book well ahead.

NEARBY Piazza di Spagna; Villa Medici; Villa Borghese.
LOCATION at top of Spanish Steps; public car parking nearby
FOOD breakfast
PRICE €€€
ROOMS 16 double and twin with bath; all rooms have phone, TV, air conditioning, minibar, hairdrier
FACILITIES sitting room, breakfast room, roof terrace
CREDIT CARDS AE, DC, MC, V
DISABLED no special facilities
PETS accepted
CLOSED never
PROPRIETOR Renato Bellia

Lazio and Abruzzo

Rome

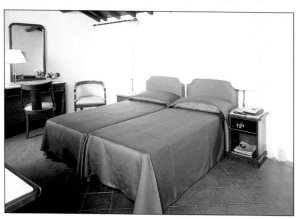

Teatro di Pompeo

~ Town guesthouse ~

Largo del Pellaro 8, 00186 Roma
Tel 06 6872812 **Fax** 06 68805531

A RECENT VISITOR BEGGED US not to include this modest hotel (tucked away in a little-frequented corner off the rather shabby but nonetheless picturesque Campo di Fiori); he wanted to keep it to himself. However, we liked what we saw on our visit, and here it is ... with apologies to the anonymous reader. The hotel has a unique and extraordinary feature: it is built on the site of the Teatro di Pompeo which dates from 55 B.C., and the breakfast room is hewn from the ancient tufa walls. The adjoining sitting room shares the same setting but is rather spoiled by hideous lighting; however, a table is thoughtfully laden with guidebooks and magazines.

Upstairs, the bedrooms are fairly simple, but padded bedheads and bedspreads in attractive fabrics, the odd antique combined with good reproduction furniture and filmy white curtains add a touch of style to white walls and standard terracotta flagstones. Rooms on the top floor are cosier, with beamed, attic ceilings and those at the front of the building have a bird's-eye view of the sometimes noisy comings-and-goings in the *piazza* below.

~

Nearby Campo dei Fiori; Piazza Navona; the Vatican.
Location just E of Campo dei Fiori; car parking nearby
Food breakfast
Price €€-€€€€
Rooms 13 double and twin with bath or shower; all rooms have phone, TV, air conditioning, minibar, hairdrier
Facilities sitting rooms, breakfast room, bar, lift
Credit cards AE, DC, MC, V
Disabled no special facilities
Pets not accepted
Closed never
Proprietor Lorenzo Mignoni

LAZIO AND ABRUZZO

ROME

VILLA FLORENCE

~ TOWN VILLA ~

Via Nomentana 28, 00161 Roma
TEL 06 4403036 **FAX** 06 4402709
E-MAIL villa.florence@flashnet.it **WEBSITE** www.venere.it/roma/villa_florence

WHEN OUR INSPECTOR VISITED this hotel, located on the busy Via Nomentana just beyond Porta Pia to the north-east of the centre of Rome, it was in the final stages of major refurbishment, so it was difficult to form a complete impression. But judging from what had already been completed, the final result will be very pleasing.

The work began on the outside: the newly-pointed façade is now an elegant pale yellow. The builders were still working on the downstairs public areas during our visit, but the bedrooms were complete. Here, the step up in terms of elegance and comfort is considerable. Once merely functional, the rooms are now decked in richly-coloured, elegant fabrics (on walls, beds and curtains) with the colour schemes changing depending on the floor. The furniture is mostly good quality neoclassical-style reproduction which blends well with original features such as fine walnut bedroom doors. The smart bathrooms are also new.

There is a small, secluded terrace behind the house, on to which some of the bedrooms (in outbuildings) have direct access. The private car parking – albeit limited – is a big plus in this city.

~

NEARBY Villa Borghese; Via Veneto; Piazza di Spagna.
LOCATION about 1 km NE of Via Veneto, NE of Porta Pia; private car parking in garden
FOOD breakfast
PRICE €€€
ROOMS 32; 27 doubles, 2 singles, 3 family, all with bath or shower; all rooms have phone, TV, minibar, hairdrier
FACILITIES sitting room, breakfast room, bar, lift, roof terrace, garden
CREDIT CARDS AE, DC, MC, V
DISABLED ground-floor rooms available
CLOSED never
PROPRIETORS Tullio and Fabio Capelli

LAZIO AND ABRUZZO

ROME

VILLA DEL PARCO

~ TOWN VILLA ~

Via Nomentana 110, 00161 Roma
TEL 06 44237773 **FAX** 06 44237572
E-MAIL villaparco@mclink.it **WEBSITE** www.venere.it/roma/villaparco

OUR INSPECTOR WAS FULL of enthusiasm after her visit to this mellow, 1910 villa situated in a little oasis of calm off the busy Via Nomentana and a 20-minute bus ride from the centre of Rome. It was worth the journey: she had found a delightful hotel with a truly warm welcome and very reasonable prices.

The pretty walled gardens to either side (where breakfast is served in summer) only partially protect against traffic noise, but once inside, all is peaceful and elegant. The reception lobby emanates a cosy glow with deep yellow sofas and armchairs grouped around a coffee table laden with magazines. An old grandfather clock, some fine oil portraits and a collection of covetable antiques add to the feeling of well-being. From here, steps lead down to a series of sunny rooms: a bar, two breakfast rooms and a sitting area. The ambience, here too, is both restful and tasteful; more antiques, green fabrics, plants and a mass of nicely-framed pictures. Bedrooms vary in size: some are quite small, others larger but all have touches of elegance. Six new attic rooms have been added recently and they are charmingly decorated in fresh greens and cream. Excellent value.

~

NEARBY Villa Torlonia; Villa Borghese; Catacombe of S. Agnese.
LOCATION in residential area, NE of city centre (Porta Pia); public car parking nearby
FOOD breakfast
PRICE €€
ROOMS 29; 15 double and twin, 14 single, all with bath or shower; all rooms have phone, TV, air conditioning, minibar, hairdrier
FACILITIES 2 sitting rooms, breakfast rooms, bar, lift, garden
CREDIT CARDS AE, DC, MC, V
DISABLED ground-floor room available
PETS accepted **CLOSED** never
PROPRIETOR Elisabetta Bernardini

LAZIO AND ABRUZZO

ROME

VILLA DELLE ROSE

~ TOWN VILLA ~

Via Vicenza 5,00185 Roma
TEL 06 4451788 **FAX** 06 4451639
E-MAIL villadellerose@flashnet.it

THE AREA ROUND TERMINI TRAIN STATION is scruffy, but Via Vicenza is a once-elegant street lined with mellow old villas set in attractive gardens. Shady-looking characters lurch around, but the location of Villa delle Rose is convenient for those who arrive in Rome by train. What it lacks in comfort and style is made up for by the warmth and enthusiasm of the Filippo family, and the very reasonable prices. The façade could do with painting, but the bar-sitting room is surprisingly grand, with marbled columns, elaborate plasterwork and a frescoed ceiling. The basement breakfast room is somewhat stark, but the buffet is well above average. There's equipment for boiling your own eggs and making toast.

The bedrooms are adequately furnished – though more practical than elegant – and decorated in soft colours and pale wallpapers. Some are split-level, ideal for families. The owner is gradually redecorating: some of the bathrooms are new and there are plans for upgrading the bedrooms, which should smooth over the rough edges. The pretty garden is an unusual feature so close to the station.

~

NEARBY Termini station; Villa Borghese; Roman Forum.
LOCATION in a residential street just N of Termini station; limited free car parking
FOOD breakfast
PRICE €€
ROOMS 38; 23 double and twin, 7 single, 8 family, all with bath or shower; all rooms have phone, TV, air-conditioning
FACILITIES sitting room, breakfast room, bar, lift, garden
CREDIT CARDS AE, DC, MC, V
DISABLED ground-floor rooms available
PETS accepted **CLOSED** never
PROPRIETORS Frank and Claude Filippo

LAZIO AND ABRUZZO

SAN FELICE CIRCEO

PUNTA ROSSA

～ SEASIDE HOTEL ～

Latina, 04017 San Felice Circeo
TEL 0773 548085 **FAX** 0773 548075
E-MAIL punta_rossa@iol.it **WEBSITE** www.venere.it/lazio/punta_rossa

SAN FELICE IS AN AMIABLE VILLAGE at the foot of the 550-metre Monte Circeo, which is an isolated lump of rock at the seaward point of a flat area, once marshland but now drained, except for zones which have been declared a national park. The Punta Rossa curves around the mountain in a secluded setting above an exposed and rocky shore, laid out like a miniature village. Reception is in a lodge just inside an arched gateway, and beyond that is a little *piazza* enclosed by white-walled buildings in rough Mediterranean style. Public rooms are light and beautifully decorated. Bedrooms are spread around in low buildings at or near the top of a flowery garden which drops steeply to the sea. All of them are pleasant, with balconies and sea views; but sizes vary, and some of the colour schemes look dated. The main attraction of the suites is their generous size. The restaurant (food is 'exceptional' according to a recent report) is some-way down the garden towards the sea and glorious sea-water pool. In another rave report, a guest says his only regret was 'not to stay longer.'

～

NEARBY Terracina (20 km); Circeo national park.
LOCATION 4 km W of San Felice, isolated on rocky shore; private car parking
FOOD breakfast, lunch, dinner
PRICE €€€
ROOMS 34; 27 double, 7 suites, all with bath or shower; all rooms have phone, TV, air-conditioning, minibar
FACILITIES bar, dining room, spa, terrace, garden, swimming pool
CREDIT CARDS AE, DC, MC, V
DISABLED access difficult
PETS small dogs accepted by arrangement
CLOSED Nov
MANAGER Maria Fiorella Battaglia

LAZIO AND ABRUZZO

PALO LAZIALE

POSTA VECCHIA
COUNTRY VILLA

Palo Laziale, 00055 Ladispoli
Roma

TEL 06 9949501 **FAX** 06 9949507
E-MAIL postavec@caerenet.it
WEBSITE www.lapostavecchia.com
FOOD breakfast, lunch, dinner
PRICE €€€€ **CLOSED** Nov-Mar **MANAGER** Harry Charles Mills Sciò

THE TYRRHENIAN SEAFRONT mansion that belonged to John Paul Getty and which he filled with fabulous artworks and antiques makes one of Italy's most remarkable hotels. Staying here, surrounded by priceless *objets* but with none of the formality that you might expect from a grand hotel, is a unique experience. While excavating the indoor pool, the remains of a Roman villa were discovered, which are now on display in a mini museum, visible through glass panels in the floor. The setting is spectacular, with six hectares of parkland and a formal garden on one side and the water lapping the dining terrace on the other – a wonderfully romantic place to dine on a warm summer's evening.

ROME

HOTEL DEI BORGOGNONI
TOWN HOTEL

Via del Bufalo 126, 00187 Roma

TEL 06 69941505 **FAX** 06 6780041
E-MAIL
hotel.borgognoni@flashnet.it
WEBSITE www.hotelborgognoni.it
FOOD breakfast, snacks
PRICE €€€
CLOSED never
MANAGER Claudio Marca

IN THE HEART OF WHAT WAS the Burgundian quarter of 17thC Rome and what is today a very convenient location for both shopping and sightseeing, the Borgognoni occupies an ex-convent. Don't expect, however, an ecclesiastical feel to the place: this is a modern hotel equipped to host small conferences which, in recent years, has turned its sights to the discerning tourist as well. Extensive refurbishment is planned in 2001, when the smallish bedrooms and bathrooms will be smartened up. The spacious open sitting area on the ground floor has a glassed-in flower bed planted with palm trees and a feeling of seclusion. There is no restaurant, but the barman will prepare a range of snacks and light meals.

LAZIO AND ABRUZZO

ROME

SOLE AL PANTHEON
TOWN HOTEL

Piazza della Rotonda 63, 00F Roma

TEL 06 6780441
FAX 06 69940689
E-MAIL hotsole@flashnet.it
FOOD breakfast
PRICE €€€€
CLOSED never
MANAGER G. Piraino

A DELIGHTFUL SMALL HOTEL with a privileged position – to one side of the square in front of the famous Pantheon, one of Rome's few perfectly preserved ancient Roman buildings – the Sole is now one of the city's most expensive hotels. In fact, a recent reporter felt that she did not get value for money here: 'the hotel had a great setting but was not worth the price.' Bedrooms feature fascinating coffered and painted ceilings, and are gorgeously furnished in imaginative styles. However, the overall refurbishment of 1988 is now looking a little tired in places. Public areas are pleasant: a salon of white leather seating straight from the pages of some glossy magazine, and a small, cosy bar downstairs.

ROME

VALADIER
TOWN HOTEL

Via della Fontanella 15, 00187 Roma

TEL 06 3610559 **FAX** 06 3201558
E-MAIL info@hotelvaladier.com
WEBSITE www.hotelvaladier.com
FOOD breakfast, lunch, dinner
PRICES €€€€
CLOSED never
Rinaldo Lasalandra

T HE VALADIER BEGAN ITS METAMORPHOSIS from gracious decay into its present slick form – something like the interior of a millionaire's yacht (or our idea of one) – some years back. The refit is now complete, with the most recent construction, an elegantly intimate restaurant, adding to an already generous assortment of smallish but very smart public rooms. The cabin-like bedrooms are what mostly remind us of a yacht, or rather, a gin palace. Not only are they very cleverly fitted out to make the most of their compact dimensions, but also they bristle with electronic gadgetry. Charming? Well, not in the strictest sense. But distinctive and exceptionally comfortable – and well run by a pleasant staff. A good location, too.

CAMPANIA

HOTELS IN CAMPANIA

CAMPANIA HAS FOUR DISTINCT parts: the frantic, magnificent, decaying city of Naples; the fabulous coastline between Sorrento and Ravello; the islands of Capri and Ischia; and the coast and countryside north of Naples.

Don't fight shy of Naples. Plunge down its central artery, Spaccanapoli, if you do nothing else. An authentic pizza for lunch, and a more refined dinner at La Cantinella, next door to the Miramare (page 307) and owned by the same family, makes a good combination. We have found one more recommendable hotel in Naples for this edition: the Soggiorno Sansevero (page 308).

Unless you are there for its thermal baths, crowded Ischia is less appealing than Capri, whose natural beauty is liberally doused in glitz. Ischia is harder work for the seeker of small hotels than Capri, but we have found three. Capri has a good selection, and we can also recommend the Luna (tel 081 8370433/fax 081 8377035) and, as a budget option, Villa Helios (tel/fax 081 8370240). All our recommendations are in or just outside car-free Capri town (you walk to your hotel and your luggage is transported from the ferry by porter); we don't have any recommendations for Anacapri.

Hotels on the Sorrento and Amalfi coasts are well represented in the pages that follow. Sadly, the famous Cappuccini Convento in Amalfi has deteriorated to the point where we have had to drop it, with several outraged readers' letters to prove the point; and the Caruso Belvedere in Ravello has new owners and is closed for major renovation. Positano, the famously pretty fomer fishing village has dozens hotels; we believe that our selection is the best of the bunch. We haven't included the famous San Pietro, too plush for our purposes, but nonetheless a memorable place.

Along the coast and in the countryside north of Naples we have just two recommendations, one on the coast at Baia Domizia, and one in the medieval village of Dragoni.

CAMPANIA

AMALFI

LIDOMARE

~ SEASIDE BED-AND-BREAKFAST ~

84011 Amalfi , Salerno
TEL 089 871332 **FAX** 089 871394
E-MAIL lidomare@amalficoast.it **WEBSITE** www.amalficoast.it/hotel/lidomare

LOCKED IN A TIME WARP, you might suspect this modest two star of being fusty; in fact, it has its share of charm. Floor tiles are burnished to such a gleam you can see your reflection; huge bookcases are bursting with battered leather-bound volumes; miniature figures are displayed in a glass-fronted cabinet; and the large high-ceilinged rooms are full of family antiques and traditional hand-painted furniture. From the entrance you can glimpse, through the family's own parlour, the charming old tiled kitchen where breakfast is prepared. It is served in the only reception room, where guests sit at little wooden tables between a grand piano and potted plants. With the exception of the minibar and satellite TV in every bedroom – grating additions to our mind – little seems to have changed at the Lidomare for the last 100 or so years.

Though the entrance to the 15thC house is off a little square, the front faces the sea and the best rooms, with small balconies, are on this side. The others have no view to speak of save the peace of the *piazzetta*. All are simple and spotless. From the moment you step inside, you know that this is not only a family hotel but a home, and the warmth of the owners resonates through the quirky old-fashioned rooms and corridors.

~

NEARBY cathedral and Paradise cloisters; Ravello (6 km).
LOCATION in *piazzetta* off Piazza del Duomo; public car parking nearby
FOOD breakfast
PRICE €
ROOMS 15 double and twin with bath or shower; all rooms have phone, TV, air-conditioning, minibar
FACILITIES sitting/breakfast room **CREDIT CARDS** AE, DC, MC, V
DISABLED not suitable **PETS** accepted **CLOSED** never
PROPRIETORS Camera family

CAMPANIA

AMALFI

LUNA CONVENTO
~ CONVERTED MONASTERY ~

Via P. Comite 33, 84011 Amalfi, Salerno
TEL 089 871002 **FAX** 089 871333
WEBSITE www.amalficoast.it/hotel/luna

SINCE THE DEMISE OF the famous Cappuccini Convento (still open but no longer recommendable after a stream of dire reports from readers), the Luna Convento has become the most appealing Amalfi hotel. A five-minute walk uphill from the bustling town centre, it occupies two separate buildings, divided by the winding coast road – one of them an old Saracen tower perched right on the sea.

The hotel opened in 1825 (it is the oldest in Amalfi), and has been in the same family for five generations. But you only have to step inside to see that the building's history goes back much further than the 19th century. The unique feature is the Byzantine cloister enclosing a garden and ancient well. The arcade serves as a quiet and civilized sitting area and breakfasts are served within the actual cloister – a delightful spot to start the day. You have the choice of modern or traditional bedrooms, and for a premium you can have your own private sitting room. Lunch and dinner are taken either in the vaulted restaurant in the main building, where large arched windows give beautiful views of the bay, or better still across the road where the terrace and parasols of the tower restaurant extend to the water's edge. The swimming pool forms part of the same complex – as does the somewhat incongruous disco. The hotel is well known for its week-long cooking courses.

~

NEARBY cathedral and Paradise cloisters; Ravello (6 km).
LOCATION 5 minutes walk uphill from town centre, overlooking sea; car parking
FOOD breakfast, lunch, dinner; room service
PRICE €€€
ROOMS 45; 40 double and twin, 2 single, 3 suites, all with bath; all rooms have phone, TV, hairdrier **FACILITIES** sitting room, 2 dining rooms, 2 bars, cloister, swimming pool, disco **CREDIT CARDS** AE, DC, MC, V
DISABLED not suitable **PETS** not accepted
CLOSED never **MANAGER** Signor Milone

CAMPANIA

BAIA DOMIZIA

HOTEL DELLA BAIA

~ SEASIDE HOTEL ~

81030 Baia Domizia, Caserta
TEL 0823 721344 **FAX** 0823 721566

BAIA DOMIZIA IS A MODERN and quite sophisticated seaside resort, stretching along a splendid, broad, sandy beach north of Naples. But at the Hotel della Baia you are unaware of being in a resort at all. It is a low-lying white building, standing well away from the main development, and its lush gardens lead straight past the tennis court to the beach.

The hotel was opened about 35 years ago by the three Sello sisters from Venice, who have successfully reproduced the peaceful atmosphere of a stylish, if rather large, private villa. Spotless white stucco walls, cool tiled floors and white sofas are offset by bowls of fresh flowers and potted plants, and the antique and modern furnishings blend well together. The house feels lived-in, with books and magazines around, and an interesting range of pictures on the walls.

Bedrooms are no less attractive; many have balconies. A smartly furnished veranda links the house to the garden, and deckchairs and extravagant white parasols are set out on the lawn.

The hotel has traditionally aimed high with its food, but we lack recent reports on the accuracy of that aim.

~

NEARBY Gaeta (29 km); Naples within reach.
LOCATION in S part of resort, with gardens leading down to long sandy beach; ample car parking
FOOD breakfast, lunch, dinner; room service
PRICE €€€
ROOMS 56; 54 double, 18 with bath, 36 with shower, 2 single, 1 with bath, 1 with shower; all rooms have phone, air conditioning; TV on request
FACILITIES 2 sitting rooms, TV room, dining room, bar, terrace, garden, tennis, beach
CREDIT CARDS AE, DC, MC, V
DISABLED no special facilities **PETS** accepted **CLOSED** Oct to mid-May
PROPRIETORS Elsa, Velia and Imelde Sello

CAMPANIA

CAPRI

LA PAZZIELLA

~ TOWN VILLA ~

Via P. R. Giuliani 4, 80073 Capri, Napoli
TEL 081 8370044 **FAX** 081 8370085

THE SCENT OF EXOTIC flowers greets you on the path leading up to this low white bougainvillea-draped villa set in a romantic garden of lawns, lemon trees and classical statues. Despite being so close to Capri town, birdsong is the only sound likely to disturb you here. Our inspectors liked La Pazziella: a smart yet well-priced hotel (at the lower end of its price bracket) that has successfully side-stepped Capri's glitter and gloss and strikes all the right chords.

The decoration is fresh and bright. Plain white walls and blue-and-white-tiled floors set off attractive polished wood furniture. Moorish arches, a recurring theme both inside and out, link one area to another, form niches and alcoves and announce flights of steps. Plants and flowers add colour to the ground-floor sitting area and arched picture windows frame the garden. Breakfast is served on a glorious covered terrace.

Decorated in the same vein, the bedrooms are stylish and comfortable. Even the standard doubles have dainty writing tables and large antique chests. The superior rooms have their own balcony or terrace. The icing on the cake is the large pool with plenty of sunbathing space – quite a rarity on this island.

~

NEARBY Capri town; monastery of San Giacomo.
LOCATION off Le Botteghe Fuoriovado, 5 minutes' walk E of Capri town
FOOD breakfast
PRICE €€€
ROOMS 19; 17 double and twin and suites, 2 single, all with bath; all rooms have phone, TV, air conditioning, minibar, hairdrier, safe
FACILITIES sitting area, terrace, garden, shared swimming pool
CREDIT CARDS AE, DC, MC, V
DISABLED not suitable **PETS** not accepted **CLOSED** Oct to Mar
MANAGER Silvio del Pizzo

CAMPANIA

CAPRI

VILLA BRUNELLA
~ TOWN HOTEL ~

Via Tragara 24a, 80073 Capri, Napoli
TEL 081 8370122 **FAX** 081 8370430
E-MAIL villabrunella@capri.it **WEBSITE** www.caprionline.com/villabrunella

THE VILLA BRUNELLA IS a great find on Capri because it perfectly combines the warmth and friendliness of a small, family-run hotel with Capri-style glamour and all the services of a much larger establishment. The drawback is the very long flight of steps to and from the bedrooms; if you can face those, you are on to a winner.

The hotel consists of a series of tumbling terraces, ending in a garden, with fabulous views of sea and coast across to Marina Piccolo. It begins with its restaurant, whose entrance is on narrow Via Tragara. With picture windows and a romantic atmosphere, it is staffed by friendly waiters and a characterful *maitre d'*, and the food is good. The hotel then continues down the hillside, accessed by the steps. Next comes the cosy, cluttered reception area, presided over by the charming and welcoming Ruggiero family, with the kitchen open to view next door. Then the glamour begins: first at the pool, with its spacious sun terrace where poolside lunches are served, and then, further down, in the bedrooms. These are a great surprise: very Capri, with silk materials, marble bathrooms, terraces, Jacuzzis, fancy bedheads and gladioli by the vaseful.

Here is a small, personal hotel, with all the advantages of the nearby Grand Hotel Quisisana, but much less formal; we loved it, steps and all.

~

NEARBY monastery of San Giacomo; Punta Tragara.
LOCATION on lane leading to Punta Tragara, 10 minutes walk from Capri town
FOOD breakfast, lunch, dinner
PRICE €€€
ROOMS 20; 8 double, 12 suites, all with bath; all rooms have phone, TV, air conditioning, minibar, hairdrier, safe
FACILITIES sitting area, bar, restaurant, terrace, garden, swimming pool
CREDIT CARDS AE, DC, MC, V **DISABLED** not suitable **PETS** not accepted
CLOSED Nov to Easter **PROPRIETORS** Vincenzo and Brunella Ruggiero

CAMPANIA

CAPRI

VILLA SARAH

~ TOWN VILLA ~

Via Tiberio 3a, 80073 Capri, Napoli
TEL 081 8370122 **FAX** 081 8370430
E-MAIL info@villasarah.it **WEBSITE** www.villasarah.it

IT'S A STIFF UPHILL WALK out of town (on the road to Emperor Tiberius's palace, (Villa Jovis) to Villa Sarah, surrounded by a large, abundant kitchen garden. (As with all Capri town hotels, you can arrange to have your luggage carried by porter from the ferry.) The reward is peace and simplicity in a calm family-run hotel far removed from the bustle and vulgarity of the town.

Villa Sarah, set back from the road, is a spacious whitewashed villa whose bedrooms have old pictures and prints on white walls, plain curtains on wooden poles, dark wood furniture, tiled floors and simple bathrooms. The best have balconies and sea views. Breakfast is served in a no-frills dining room or on the terrace, with a good selection of rolls and croissants, home-made jam, yoghurts, cold meats and cereals. Afterwards, you can lounge on the terrace, and then take a turn around the garden. This is the pride and joy of Signor de Martino: vine-covered paths skirt trees laden with fruit, including oranges and lemons, as well as beds stuffed with aubergines, peppers, tomatoes and much more. The de Martino's love to treat their guests, allowing them to pick what they want themselves.

~

NEARBY Villa Jovis, Capri town.
LOCATION on lane leading to Villa Jovis, 15 minutes' walk from Capri town
FOOD breakfast
PRICE €€
ROOMS 19; 14 double, 5 single; all single rooms with shower, all double rooms with bath; all rooms have phone, TV, minibar, hairdrier
FACILITIES sitting area, bar, breakfast room, terrace, garden
CREDIT CARDS AE, DC, MC, V
DISABLED not suitable
PETS not accepted **CLOSED** Nov to Easter
PROPRIETORS de Martino family

CAMPANIA

DRAGONI

VILLA DE PERTIS
~COUNTRY VILLA~

Via Ponti 30, 81010 Dragoni , Caserta
TEL and FAX 0823 866619
E-MAIL info@villadepertis.it **WEBSITE** www.villadepertis.it

ORIGINALLY A NOBLEMAN's country residence dating back to the 17th century, Villa de Pertis has been restored to provide plain but comfortable and very reasonably priced accommodation in the form of five bedrooms and two suites. Its owner, Nicola de Pertis, is a charming host and very knowledgeable about the area. This is a place in which to wind down: there is little to do other than to walk or bicycle (bikes provided) in the Matese mountains, or to wander around the medieval village of Dragoni with its fine church, and the nearby village of Baia e Latina. On your return you might be diverted by a game of billiards or table tennis. Dinner, featuring regional dishes in a firelit room, was 'special' according to one reader's report; another wrote that 'an excellent dinner was arranged, at short notice, almost exactly in line with our requests'.

The same correspondent reports that her room was clean, cool and large, with a comfortable bed, a good bathroom and a wonderful view on to a small square in the centre of Dragoni where 'it seems time has stood still'. There is a charming terrace overlooking the Matese hills where you can take breakfast, with home-made jams, in the morning.

~

NEARBY Matese lake (30 km); Naples (55 km).
LOCATION in small town of Dragoni, overlooking countryside; car parking
FOOD breakfast, dinner
PRICE €
ROOMS 7; 5 double and 2 suites, all with bath; all rooms have phone; suites have TV and hairdrier
FACILITIES sitting room, dining room, billiard room, terrace, garden
CREDIT CARDS AE, V
DISABLED access difficult
PETS accepted
CLOSED Jan to Mar
PROPRIETOR Nicola de Pertis

CAMPANIA

ISCHIA

IL MONASTERO

~ CONVERTED MONASTERY ~

Castello Aragonese 3, Ischia Ponte, 80070 Ischia , Napoli
TEL 081 992435
WEBSITE www.castelloaragonese.it

ISCHIA PONTE GETS ITS NAME from the low bridge giving access to the precipitous islet on top of which stands the island of Ischia's original settlement, known collectively as the Castello, although it consists of several buildings. One of these is an old monastery which is run as a simple but captivating *pensione.*

A lift reached by a tunnel in the rock of the island takes you up to the Castello (there are steps too). Discreet signs bring you to the locked door of the *pensione*, and a ring on the bell summons the amiable *padrone*. Up a final flight of stairs and at last you are there. Paintings hang on the plain walls of the hallway and the neat little sitting room. Bedrooms, white with blue tiles, are the former monks' cells and correspondingly simple; some are reached from the spacious terrace, which gives a breathtaking view of the town and the island.

On a recent visit, we were hoping to sample the food (half board is inescapable) but by force of circumstance arrived too late (dinner is served promptly at 8 pm) and were offered no further sustenance. Doubtless dinner is plain, like the breakfast and the rooms, but that is entirely in keeping with the monastic theme of the place, and it remains extremely popular. A new manager took over in 2001. He was making some minor improvements as we went to press and reassured us that the place will remain essentially unchanged.

~

NEARBY Ischia Ponte, Ischia Porto.
LOCATION on island E of Ischia town, linked by causeway
FOOD breakfast, dinner
PRICE €€
ROOMS 21 double, 1 single, most with bath or shower
FACILITIES sitting room, dining room, bar, terrace **CREDIT CARDS** not accepted
DISABLED not suitable **PETS** not accepted **CLOSED** mid-Oct to Easter
PROPRIETOR Nicola Matera

CAMPANIA

ISCHIA

LA VILLAROSA
~ TOWN VILLA ~

Via Giacinto Gigante 5. Porto d'Ischia, 80077 Ischia , Napoli
TEL 081 991316 **FAX** 081 992425

THIS IS A SHARP CONTRAST to the Monastero (page 304) in every way: it is immersed in a jungle of a garden right in the heart of the little town of Ischia, and its great attraction – apart from the garden and pleasant thermal pool – is its series of delectable sitting rooms, which are beautifully furnished with comfortable armchairs and ornate antiques. The bedrooms are furnished with 19thC pieces of Neopolitan, Sicilian and French origin.

The light, welcoming restaurant upstairs leads out on to a terrace overlooking the garden and the rooftops of Ischia, and meals are served there in summer. At one time only full board terms were offered, but we are pleased to report that Signor Amalfitano now offers 'room only' and half-pension terms as we have no evidence about the standard of cooking: whenever we have tried to send someone to stay, the hotel has been fully booked. Readers' reports would therefore be especially welcome.

Like many hotels on the island, the Villarosa offers thermal treatments of various sorts – with a private 'thermalist physician' on hand to supervise – but the atmosphere is far removed from that of the traditional spa hotel, and those not seeking a *kur* will feel quite at home.

~

NEARBY Port of Ischia (500 m); Castello d'Ischia (2 km).
LOCATION 200 m from lido; with limited car parking
FOOD breakfast, lunch, dinner
PRICE €€
ROOMS 40; 34 double and twin, 20 with bath, 14 with shower; 6 single, all with shower; all rooms have phone
FACILITIES sitting room, dining room, TV room, bar, lift, terrace, swimming pool, sauna **CREDIT CARDS** AE, DC, MC, V
DISABLED access difficult
PETS not accepted
CLOSED Nov to Mar
PROPRIETOR Paolo Amalfitano

CAMPANIA

NAPLES

MIRAMARE

~ WATERFRONT HOTEL ~

Via Nazario Sauro 24, 80132 Napoli
TEL 081 7647589 **FAX** 081 7640755
E-MAIL info@hotelmiramare.com **WEBSITE** www.hotelmiramare.com

THERE ARE TWO COMPELLING REASONS for choosing the Miramare as your Naples base. The first is its owner, Enzo Rosolino (attended by his comic-serious Skye terrier, Gavroche), whose warmth and charm filters through to his loyal and attentive staff. The second is the rooftop terrace, with sunloungers, capacious hammock and terrific views across the Bay of Naples to the Sorrento coast, Vesuvius and Capri. You will have to ignore the roar of traffic on the *lungomare* below; this is Naples after all. In summer a varied breakfast is served here; you could also have a romantic *dinner à deux*, with dishes brought in from Cantinella, the excellent Michelin-starred restaurant belonging to Enzo's brother next door (discount for hotel guests).

The building, dating from 1914, is a gracious Liberty-style villa which served as the American Consulate before becoming a hotel, well known for its piano bar, The Shaker Club, in 1944. Nowadays the lobby and breakfast room, in high romantic Neopolitan style, are resplendent in green, gold and red Venetian and Florentine silks. Bedrooms, which are gradually being redecorated in the same mood, are compact, but they have high ceilings and tall windows, as well as effective air-conditioning and thoughtful extras such as kettles for tea and coffee and a supply of videos. The best have sea views.

~

NEARBY Piazza dei Plebiscito; Castel dell' Ovo; ferry ports.
LOCATION on waterfront road, 10 minutes' walk from city centre, close to ferry ports; adjacent garage parking
FOOD breakfast; lunch and dinner available on request; room service
PRICE €€€€ **ROOMS** 30; 27 double and twin, 3 single, all with bath or shower; all rooms have phone, TV, video, air-conditioning, minibar, hairdrier
FACILITIES sitting room, breakfast room, bar, lift, roof terrace **CREDIT CARDS** AE, DC, MC, V **DISABLED** access difficult **PETS** not accepted **CLOSED** never
PROPRIETOR Enzo Rosolino

CAMPANIA

NAPLES

SOGGIORNO SANSEVERO

~ TOWN GUESTHOUSE ~

Piazza San Domenico Maggiore 9, 80134 Napoli
TEL 081 5515949 **FAX** 081 211698
E-MAIL albergo.sansevero@libero.it

PEACE REIGNS IN THIS no-frills guesthouse circling the internal courtyard of an old *palazzo*, but it hasn't always been so. In 1590, here in the home of the Princes of Sansevero, the troubled madrigal composer Carlo Gesualdo murdered his wife and her lover in a frenzied attack. But we didn't feel the presence of any ghosts in the newly painted cream bedrooms or their modern grey bathrooms. The decoration is modest – mosaic floors, functional furniture – but the rooms are spacious and prices rockbottom. Our favourite is No. 6, 'Marechiaro', vast with a vaulted ceiling and more character than the others, and it only costs L10,000 more. The owner, Armida Auriemma, a kindly Italian woman who speaks no English, is an unlikely property magnate, but she owns two other guesthouses in Naples: Albergo Sansevero, similar in style, and Albergo Sansevero (Degas), aimed at students.

Breakfast is not provided at the Soggiorno Sansevero, but you'll find Scaturchio, one of the best known cafés in the city, in the colourful *piazza* below. Don't miss the Sansevero chapel next door to (and once part of) the *palazzo*, which contains an extraordinary, spooky sculpture, *Shrouded Christ* by Sanmartino.

~

NEARBY Capella Sansevero; Santa Chiara.
LOCATION in heart of city at Spaccanapoli; car parking at Albergo Sansevero
FOOD none
PRICE ⓔ
ROOMS 6; 4 double and twin and triple, all with showe, 2 single with shared shower; all rooms have phone, TV, air conditioning, hairdrier
FACILITIES none
CREDIT CARDS AE, DC, MC, V
DISABLED not suitable
PETS small dogs accepted
CLOSED never
PROPRIETOR Armida Auriemma

CAMPANIA

POSITANO

CALIFORNIA

~ TOWN BED-AND-BREAKFAST ~

Via C. Columbo 141, 84017 Positano, Salerno
TEL 089 875382 **FAX** 089 812154
E-MAIL albergo.california@hpe.it **WEBSITE** www.hpe.it/california

DIRECTLY OPPOSITE THE SIRENUSE (see page 314), this is another
Neapolitan nobleman's *palazzo*, built in 1677, but in all other respects
completely different. Come here if you want atmosphere, a warm welcome
and (for Positano) budget prices. The *châtelaine* is Mary Cinque (English
first name, but 100 per cent Italian *mamma*) who now runs the hotel
opened by her father-in-law in 1968 and named after his much-missed sister who had emigrated to California. "I want my guests to be happy," she
says, and she means it. Mary tries hard to keep up with modern requirements and a programme of renovation is slowly in progress. Luckily most
of the rooms, though plain, still retain an old-fashioned charm. No. 54 is
large, with green tiled floor and high painted ceiling. No. 55 is even bigger,
with a terrace. No. 61 is one of the rooms in which Mary has proudly
installed a Jacuzzi, and benefits from windows on two sides.

The hotel's star feature, notwithstanding Mary herself, is the upper-
floor terrace which stretches along the front of the building. It has a pure
turn-of-the-century feel, leafy, elegant, dotted with wrought-iron and wicker furniture. There are no other public spaces; breakfast is served here or
in your room. The California is new to this edition of the guide and we
would welcome comments, especially as we were unable to stay the night.
As the Eagles sang of another *Hotel California*, we thought it was 'a lovely
place' - but we'd be reassured by some positive readers' letters .

~

NEARBY Amalfi (17 km); Ravello (23 km).
LOCATION on road leading into/out of town, overlooking town and sea, 10 minutes'
walk from waterfront; car parking
FOOD breakfast **PRICE** €-€€ **ROOMS** 18 double and twin, all with bath; all rooms
have phone, hairdrier; some rooms have TV, air conditioning, minibar
FACILITIES terrace **CREDIT CARDS** AE, DC, MC, V
DISABLED not suitable **PETS** not accepted **CLOSED** mid-Nov to Mar
PROPRIETOR Mary Cinque

CAMPANIA

POSITANO

LA FENICE

~ SEASIDE BED-AND-BREAKFAST ~

Via G. Marconi 8, 84017 Positano , Salerno
TEL 089 875513 **FAX** 089 811309

G UESTS SHOULD BE ISSUED with a health warning before arriving at this unusual B&B. Some 400 steps (and a main road) separate the beach from the breakfast terrace, reception-sitting area and main bedrooms. Only the fit should attempt the climb (though a section can be done by stair lift). The rest of the bedrooms are in cottages that cascade down the steep cliff, reached by little staircases and narrow paths, ending with a glorious salt water swimming pool and waterfall, hewn out of the rock face. The pool was built by Costantino Mandara, the enterprising owner, who gave up being a vet in 1982 to turn his family home into a hotel. But Solomon the myna bird, Asuaro the dog, Tiberius the cat and a flock of geese – mementoes of his earlier life – are still in residence.

Handsome antique beds, huge *armoires* and family heirlooms fill the modest bedrooms, whose white walls and vaulted ceilings keep them beautifully cool with no need for air conditioning. Some of the cottages have private patios (we liked the one belonging to No 2). The trek from here up to the flowery terrace for breakfast is well rewarded by Signora Mandara's delicious home-made jams and Solomon's cheery *'buon giorno'*.

~

NEARBY Amalfi (17 km); Ravello (23 km).
LOCATION on Amalfi road, 15 minutes' walk E of centre of town; car parking
FOOD breakfast
PRICE ©©
ROOMS 12 double and twin, 6 with bath, 6 with shower; 1 apartment for 4; all rooms have phone
FACILITIES sitting area, terraces, swimming pool, private beach, fishing
CREDIT CARDS not accepted
DISABLED not suitable **PETS** not accepted
CLOSED Christmas
PROPRIETOR Costantino Mandara

CAMPANIA

POSITANO

MARINCANTO

～ TOWN HOTEL ～

Via Cristoforo Colombo 56, 84017 Positano, Salerno
TEL 089 875130 **FAX** 089 875595
E-MAIL marincanto@starnet.it **WEBSITE** www.webspace.it/marincanto

THE ENTRANCE THROUGH the car park is unprepossessing, but once the lift had whisked our inspector down to the main floor, a huge tiled room overlooking the sea across a flowery terrace, she had fallen for this unpretentious B&B. Coming out of the lift is like stepping back into the 1950s, with decoration and furnishings endearingly outmoded. Busy orange tiles cover the floor and velvet armchairs cluster around perspex coffee tables. The charming Vespoli family have owned and run the hotel for several generations, and they and their friendly staff take great trouble to look after their guests, with small services such as turning down their beds at night – a rare luxury even in much grander establishments.

Pretty painted wood details lift the bedrooms in the main building, the best of which have balconies with sea views. While the annexe rooms are not so well furnished, most are larger and several have lovely secluded terraces. Steps lead down to the beach past a succession of terraces, some with sunloungers for everyone's use.

Breakfast – outside in fine weather, inside if it's cold or wet – is an impressive buffet of cereals, juices, rolls, cake, cold meat and yoghurt.

～

NEARBY Amalfi (17 km); Ravello (23 km).
LOCATION on road leading into/out of town, overlooking town and sea, 10 minutes' walk from waterfront; car parking
FOOD breakfast
PRICE €€€
ROOMS 25 double and twin, triple and family, one suite, all with bath or shower; all rooms have phone, TV, air conditioning, minibar, hairdrier
FACILITIES sitting area, lift, terraces
CREDIT CARDS AE, DC, MC, V
DISABLED access possible **PETS** accepted
CLOSED Nov to week before Easter
PROPRIETOR Celeste Vespoli

CAMPANIA

POSITANO

MIRAMARE

∿ TOWN BED-AND-BREAKFAST ∿

Via Trara Genoino 25-27, 84017 Positano Salerno
TEL 089 875002 **FAX** 089 875219
E-MAIL miramare@starnet.it **WEBSITE** www.starnet.it/miramare

WHATEVER BEDROOM YOU ARE GIVEN at the Miramare, baby sister of the San Pietro and Palazzo Murat (see opposite), it will have a private sea-facing terrace, shaded by vine or bougainvillea and furnished with table and deckchairs. The rooms were revamped in 2000 and look stunning with white walls, terracotta floors, elegant fabrics and antiques; minibar and safe kept well out of sight. Bathrooms (some with sea views themselves) are spacious, and decorated with hand-painted tiles.

The sitting room is an attractive area with a vaulted ceiling, more terra-cotta tiles, antique and pale upholstered furniture and plenty of plants and flowers. The breakfast room is a delight: a glassed-in terrace with bougainvillea hanging from the ceiling in great swathes, and views to the beach far below.

Set on the steep hill to the west of the beach, down seven or eight flights of steps (more steps lead to the seafront), the Miramare is a series of old fishermen's houses joined to make what recent visitors call a 'posi-tively gorgeous' hotel but they also warn that, 'It's not for people who can't negotiate lots of stairs two or three times a day.' This was less of a problem a few years ago when it had its own restaurant, and there's talk that this might reopen.

∿

NEARBY Amalfi (17 km); Ravello (23 km).
LOCATION 3 minutes' walk W of main beach; car parking
FOOD breakfast
PRICE €€€
ROOMS 15 double and twin with bath; all rooms have phone, TV, air conditioning, minibar, hairdrier, safe
FACILITIES sitting room, dining room, bar
CREDIT CARDS AE, DC, MC, V
DISABLED not suitable **PETS** accepted
CLOSED Nov to week before Easter **PROPRIETORS** Attanasio family

CAMPANIA

POSITANO

PALAZZO MURAT

~ TOWN HOTEL ~

Via dei Mulini 23, 84017 Positano, Salerno
TEL 089 875177 **FAX** 089 811419
E-MAIL hpm@starnet.it **WEBSITE** www.starnet.it/murat

MOST HOTELS IN POSITANO are ranged up the steep hills on either side of the ravine leading down to the sea. The Palazzo Murat, in contrast, is right in the heart of things – just inland of the *duomo*, and on a pedestrian alley lined with trendy boutiques.

The main building is a grand L-shaped 18thC *palazzo*. Within the L is a charming courtyard – a well in the middle, bougainvillea trained up the surrounding walls, palms and other exotic vegetation dotted around – occupied by the independent Al Palazzo restaurant. Breakfast is served here (though in spring early risers will find it sunless) and it makes a romantic spot for dinner. Along one side of this courtyard run the interconnecting sitting rooms, beautifully furnished with antiques.

Bedrooms in the *palazzo* itself are attractively traditional in style – some painted furniture, some polished hardwood – and have doors opening on to token balconies (standing room only). Rooms in the more modern extension on the seaward side of the main building have the attraction of bigger balconies.

Positano's many restaurants are mainly congregated behind the beach, a short stroll away. 'Excellent value, stunning location', was one visitor's verdict.

~

NEARBY Amalfi (17 km); Ravello (23 km).
LOCATION in heart of resort; public car park nearby
FOOD breakfast
PRICE €€€
ROOMS 30 double and twin with bath; all rooms have phone, TV, air conditioning, minibar, hairdrier, safe **FACILITIES** sitting rooms, bar, terrace
CREDIT CARDS AE, DC, MC, V
DISABLED access difficult **PETS** small ones accepted **CLOSED** early Jan to first week Mar
PROPRIETORS Attanasio family

CAMPANIA

POSITANO

SIRENUSE

~ TOWN HOTEL ~

Via C. Colombo 30, 84017 Positano Salerno
TEL 089 875066 **FAX** 089 811798
E-MAIL info@sirenuse.it **WEBSITE** www.sirenuse.it

We HAVE NOT PREVIOUSLY included the famous Sirenuse in these pages,
believing it too grand, and with too many bedrooms for our purposes;
but a recent visit has made us think again. It is, simply, too beautiful to
ignore, filled with so many lovely things that it feels like a mix between a
living museum of decorative arts and the private home of an aristocratic
family – which is exactly what it was. Though until recent times Positano
was a simple fishing village, it was always a popular summer destination
for Neapolitan nobility, and this 18thC *palazzo* was the residence of
Marchese Sersale. At the end of the Second World War, it was used as a
rest house for a British guards regiment, some of whose members later
wanted to return with their families. It became a hotel, still to this day
owned and run by the Sersale family. Over the years, the *palazzo* has
expanded to include more rooms (not all with views), a web of public and
private terraces, a delightfully pretty swimming pool (which can become
crowded in summer), and a glamorous restaurant with top-flight food.

The cool, white-walled bedrooms are heavenly, especially those in the
old house. They are liberally endowed with family heirlooms – including
fine paintings and delightful Venetian and Neapolitan furniture – which
complement the original ceramics.

~

NEARBY Amalfi (17 km); Ravello (23 km).
LOCATION on road leading into/out of town, overlooking town and sea, 10 minutes'
walk from waterfront; car parking
FOOD breakfast, lunch, dinner; room service
PRICE €€€€
ROOMS 63 standard and de luxe double and twin bedrooms and suites, with or
without view; all rooms have phone, TV, air-conditioning, minibar, hairdrier, safe
FACILITIES sitting room, dining room, bar, lift, terraces, swimming pool
CREDIT CARDS AE, DC, MC, V **DISABLED** access possible **PETS** accepted **CLOSED** never
PROPRIETORS Sersale family

CAMPANIA

POSITANO

VILLA FRANCA

~ TOWN HOTEL ~

Via Pasitea 318, 84017 Positano, Salerno
TEL 089 875655 **FAX** 089 875735
E-MAIL hvf@starnet.it **WEBSITE** www.villafrancahotel.it

PROVIDED YOU ARE NOT WORRIED by heights, or by remoteness from the centre of things, this smartly traditional hotel has much to commend it. The position, high on the western side of the Positano ravine, gives an excellent view of the resort and the coast beyond from the windows and terraces – but does mean that the walk down to the resort centre and beach takes a few minutes and that the walk back up is exhausting. Happily, there is a private bus to and from the beach at certain times.

If the hotel's panoramic position is its first attraction, the second is its smart, cool sitting area – a series of interconnecting spaces with white-tiled floors and white-painted walls, linked by arched doorways. Comfortable armchairs with vivid blue covers are grouped around low tables, punctuated by enormous potted plants. The dining room has the same decorative style, and the food is reported to be satisfying and freshly-prepared.

The newly decorated bedrooms are spacious and comfortable, and the best have their own sea-view terraces. The small pool also shares the view. A basement gymnasium, steam bath, sunbed and massage room are recent additions.

Our inspector found the proprietor and staff warm and welcoming. More reports please.

~

NEARBY Amalfi (17 km); Sorrento (17 km); Ravello (23 km).
LOCATION on main road above town; car parking
FOOD breakfast, snacks, dinner; room service
PRICE €€
ROOMS 26 double and twin with bath or shower, 10 rooms in annexe; all rooms have phone, TV, air conditioning, minibar, hairdrier, safe
FACILITIES sitting room/bar, dining room, fitness centre, lift, swimming pool
CREDIT CARDS AE, DC, MC, V **DISABLED** access difficult **PETS** small ones accepted
CLOSED Nov to Mar
PROPRIETOR Mario Russo

CAMPANIA

POSITANO

VILLA ROSA

～ TOWN BED-AND-BREAKFAST ～

Via C. Colombo 127, 84017 Positano, Salerno
TEL 089 811955 **FAX** 089 812112

VILLA ROSA IS THE PARENT of the chirpy young Villa La Tartana (see opposite), by dint of the fact that its owners, the Caldieros, are the parents of Beniamino, the chirpy young owner of La Tartana. Although it lacks the freshness and zest of La Tartana, Villa Rosa has plenty to impress, and makes an excellent choice for a very reasonably priced stay in Positano. Its greatest assets are undoubtedly its spacious private terraces, all with fabulous views over the town and the Mediterranean. Its drawbacks are the many thousands of steps (well it seems that way) that lead from the road up to the reception lobby. However, as long as you are averagely fit you will cope, and luggage is taken for you.

Apart from the reception lobby with comfortable sitting area, there are no other public rooms, but the terraces more than compensate. The bedrooms are arranged on three tiers looking out to sea. Nos 8-11 have particularly huge terraces, which feel like a second room. Our favourite, however, is No. 14, with a charming lime tree plum in the middle, shading the patio table and chairs. No. 13 is good for families, with two extra beds and a large outside table.

Villa La Rosa has the feel of a comfortable old house. Bedrooms are simply but pleasantly decorated, some with original tiled floors and large French windows. Breakfast is served in your room or on the terrace. ～

NEARBY Amalfi (17 km); Ravello (23 km).
LOCATION on road leading into/out of town, overlooking town and sea, 10 minutes' walk from waterfront; public car parking nearby
FOOD breakfast **PRICE** €€ **ROOMS** 12 double all with terrace, 11 with shower, one with bath; all rooms have phone, TV, air conditioning, fridge, hairdrier
FACILITIES sitting area, garden **CREDIT CARDS** AE, DC, MC, V
DISABLED not suitable **PETS** not accepted
CLOSED Nov to Easter
PROPRIETORS Franco and Virginia Caldiero

CAMPANIA

POSITANO

VILLA LA TARTANA

~ TOWN BED-AND-BREAKFAST ~

Via Vicolo Vito Savino 6/8, 84017 Positano , Salerno
TEL 089 812193 **FAX** 089 8122012
E-MAIL info@villalatartana.it **WEBSITE** www.villalatartana.it

A TERRIFIC NEW ADDITION to the hotel scene in Positano, opened in summer
2000. The owner, Beniamino Caldiero, may be young, but he has the
touch. His modern *pensione* is deliciously fresh and clean, with simple
bedrooms that feel good to wake up in and are a joy to come home to.

Villa La Tartana is pristine as well as admirably simple, and its good
vibrations emanate from the fact that all the decorative elements have
been chosen with attention to detail and an eye for quality, and all locally
made, from the charming ceramic wall lights to the carved and painted
bedheads and hand-painted bathroom tiles. Gaily tiled floors, white walls,
floaty white curtains, a vase of flowers, a little terrace with pretty table
and chairs overlooking the sea where breakfast is served ...delightful.

Villa La Tartana (*tartana* means fishing boat) can be found right at the
base of Positano, near the main square and the beach. The sherbet lemon
tiled reception lobby, reached via a flight of stairs next to the Caldiero's
clothing and ceramics shop, sets the tone. The same zingy yellow tiles are
continued throughout the corridors, which, teamed with plain white walls,
account for much of the place's feel-good factor. Along with charming
staff, and a good breakfast, well presented, we could hardly find a fault.

~

NEARBY Amalfi (17 km); Ravello (23 km).
LOCATION beside the church of Santa Maria Assunta, overlooking the beach and
sea; public car parking nearby
FOOD breakfast
PRICE €€
ROOMS 12 double all with shower, 9 with sea view; all rooms have phone, TV, air
conditioning, fridge, hairdrier **FACILITIES** sitting area **CREDIT CARDS** AE, DC, MC, V
DISABLED not suitable **PETS** not accepted **CLOSED** Nov to Easter
PROPRIETOR Beniamino Caldiero

CAMPANIA

RAVELLO

PALUMBO

~ CONVERTED *PALAZZO* ~

Via S. Giovanni del Toro 16,84010 Ravello , Salerno
TEL 089 857244 **FAX** 089 858133
E-MAIL reception@hotelpalumbo.it **WEBSITE** www.hotelpalumbo.it

ALTHOUGH IT HAS LONG been in our guide, we have not perhaps done jus-
tice to this lovely hotel, very much our kind of place in the luxury
bracket. It stands next to the much-vaunted Palazzo Sasso, but is in every
way different: while the international-style Sasso could be anywhere, the
Palumbo oozes individuality, panache and understated elegance. It feels
like a private house – or rather a private Moorish-style 12thC *palazzo* –
which is what it was until converted by its Swiss-Italian owners, the
Vuilleumier family.

Public rooms focus on the core of the *palazzo*, an inner courtyard
where Corinthian-topped columns, a dazzling deep blue-and-white tiled
floor, imaginative modern wall ceramics in the bar area, and comfortable
sofas and chairs create a strong first impression. The first floor-restaurant
is equally elegant, graced by lovely antiques and paintings including a
(school of) Caravaggio. Or you can eat on the terrace, with views over
vineyards to the dazzling blue sea below. Half board is compulsory in high
season, but this is no hardship. Bedrooms, accentuated by antiques and
rugs, are elegant and unpretentious, as are the bathrooms, some with
quite elderly fittings. We don't mind: if you want state-of-the-art, go to
Palazzo Sasso. Bedrooms in the annexe are much less appealing, and
much cheaper.

~

NEARBY Villa Rufolo; Villa Cimbrone; Amalfi (7 km).
LOCATION perched on cliffs, close to town centre, 200 m from the main square;
garage parking
FOOD breakfast, lunch, dinner; room service **PRICE** €€€€ **ROOMS** 11 in main
house; 8 double and twin, 3 suites, all with bath; 7 double and twin in annexe, all
with bath; all rooms have phone, TV, air conditioning, minibar, hairdrier, safe
FACILITIES sitting room, dining room, bar, terrace, garden, swimming pool (by
arrangement at nearby hotel) **CREDIT CARDS** AE, DC, MC, V **DISABLED** access difficult
PETS accepted **CLOSED** never **PROPRIETOR** Marco Vuilleumier

CAMPANIA

PARSIFAL
~ CONVERTED MONASTERY ~

Viale G. d'Anna 5, 84010 Ravello , Salerno
TEL 089 857144 **FAX** 089 857972
E-MAIL hparsifal@tin.it **WEBSITE** www.italyone.com/Hparsifal

THE PARSIFAL (WHICH WAGNER composed in Ravello) retains a certain monastic simplicity along with its 13thC cloister. The former convent is still owned by nuns, but for many years now has been a family-run hotel. On a recent visit we discovered that the place has changed hands, and is now run by Antonio Mansi and his young family. Signor Mansi comes from Ravello, and worked at the Parsifal as a teenager. He went on to become general manager of the famous Danieli in Venice, before returning home to pursue his dream of owning his own small-scale hotel. It couldn't be more different than the Danieli: though professional, the family are particularly friendly and willing to please.

While gradually upgrading the Parsifal (the hotel had become very tired), Signor Mansi wants to retain its simple feel. Certainly the panoramic but dowdy dining room could do with his attention, but it bhas heart-stopping views. Here, and on the creeper-clad terrace, honest food with creative touches is served (half-board is compulsory for three nights or less). Bedrooms are plainly furnished, and some are smallish: ask for the one with the terrace and sea view.

~

NEARBY Villa Rufolo; Villa Cimbrone; Amalfi (7 km).
LOCATION overlooking the town and sea, 5 minutes' walk from main square; parking in street or public garage nearby
FOOD breakfast, lunch, dinner
PRICE ©©
ROOMS 19; 18 double and twin, 1 single, 10 with bath, 9 with shower, 8 with sea view; all rooms have phone, TV
FACILITIES sitting room, dining room, bar, terrace, garden
CREDIT CARDS AE, DC, MC, V
DISABLED not suitable
PETS accepted
CLOSED never
PROPRIETOR Antonio Mansi

CAMPANIA

RAVELLO

VILLA CIMBRONE

~~ TOWN VILLA ~~

Via Santa Chiara 26, 84010 Ravello Salerno
TEL 089 857459/858072 **FAX** 089 857777
E-MAIL info@villacimbrone.it **WEBSITE** www.villacimbrone.it

IT'S HARD TO IMAGINE a more romantic setting than the Villa Cimbrone's, in the fabulous gardens laid out by English aristocrat Lord Grimthorpe in the early 19th century. A formal network of paths and beds with wilder landscaped areas, they boast a belvedere, from where you can admire 'the most beautiful view in the world', according to Ravello *habitué* Gore Vidal. The villa is equally enchanting. A 12thC building, revived by Grimthorpe and recently restored again, it has kept all its period features including splendid stone fireplaces and tiled floors, and is crammed with knick-knacks, books, oil paintings and antiques. Through white Gothic doors, the comfortable bedrooms are all individually and exquisitely decorated. It feels exactly like a private house, and it's easy to see why the famous, from D.H. Lawrence to Greta Garbo and her lover Leopold Stokowsky, have taken refuge here.

Although we were enchanted by the Villa Cimbrone, a recent guest expressed a caveat: 'Prices are steep for just bed-and-breakfast, and it's a 10-minute hike into town for other meals. The pleasure of having the gardens all to yourselves once the trippers have left is marred by the fact that by then it's getting dark.'

~~

NEARBY Monastero di Santa Chiara; Convento di San Francesco.
LOCATION in Villa Cimbrone gardens, 10 minutes' walk from town centre; public car park in town (luggage service)
FOOD breakfast
PRICE €€€
ROOMS 13 double and twin with bath or shower; all rooms have phone, hairdrier
FACILITIES sitting room, breakfast room, terrace, garden
CREDIT CARDS AE, MC, V
DISABLED access difficult **PETS** not accepted **CLOSED** Nov to Apr
MANAGER Giorgio Vuilleumier

CAMPANIA

VILLA MARIA
~ TOWN VILLA ~

Via Santa Chiara 2, 84010 Ravello , Salerno
TEL 089 857255 **FAX** 089 857071
E-MAIL villamaria@villamaria.it

SIT IN THE SUNSHINE AT one of the tables in the Villa Maria's lovely garden restaurant, sip chilled white wine, eat perfectly cooked pasta and enjoy the glorious vista of mountains sweeping down to a glittering sea. This is an understandably popular place. Inside, a charming medley of potted palms, busts, piano, inlaid furniture and silver arranged on wooden shelves lends the old villa a distinctly Edwardian feel. Up the marble staircase and through heavy wooden doors, the bedrooms strike the same note, with vaulted ceilings and solid furniture. Though almost double the price of a standard room, No. 3 is a cut above the rest, with its huge terrace, five sets of French windows and handsome *secretaire*. In a modern annexe there are six rooms with picture windows but little character.

Never far behind the scenes is the kindly Vincenzo Palumbo, who keeps a book of comments from his guests ('The food was superb – the best in all of Europe'), masterminds cookery courses and walking tours, and enjoys rubbing shoulders with the stars. Guests may use nearby Villa Eva's lawn (useful for kids) and of the pool belonging to sister hotel, the Giordano.

NEARBY Convento di San Francesco; Villa Cimbrone.
LOCATION on path leading to Villa Cimbrone, 5 minutes' walk from town centre; car parking
FOOD breakfast, lunch, dinner
PRICE €€€
ROOMS 24 double and twin with bath or shower; all rooms have phone, TV, air-conditioning, minibar, hairdrier, safe
FACILITIES sitting room, breakfast room, dining room, dining terrace, garden, swimming pool
CREDIT CARDS AE, DC, MC, V
DISABLED access difficult **PETS** accepted **CLOSED** never
PROPRIETOR Vincenzo Palumbo

CAMPANIA

SORRENTO

LA BADIA

~ OUT-OF-TOWN VILLA ~

Via Nastro Verde 8, 80067 Sorrento, Napoli
TEL 081 878 1154 **FAX** 081 8074159

ON FIRST ACQUAINTANCE La Badia, simple and old-fashioned, seemed a great new find, almost too good to be true, until we discovered at dinner that it was a base for package tours and not a find at all. Nevertheless, if you can overlook the mainly British babble at mealtimes, you will find other compensations, not least the lovely hilly setting on the outskirts of town, set amid groves of olives and oranges, with stunning views across the Bay of Sorrento. Then there is the pretty circular swimming pool, surrounded by greenery, and the several terraces, both on the roof and at ground level.

Run by the Picco family for decades (mother oversees, daughter serves, granddaughter toddles about), this handsome stone-built former 16thC monastery, has changed little. There are lace curtains and doilies, bamboo blinds, Edwardian family antiques, potted plants, dark stained doors and wooden shutters. Rooms, many with lovely views, are plain and elderly but spacious, with simple bathrooms. A plant-filled courtyard separates the reception area from the bedrooms, and a door at the end of the first-floor corridor leads to a charming, little-used *loggia* overlooking the olive groves. The dinner menu is limited and the food as old-fashioned as the house (tinned fruit salad for dessert), but all in all we felt we had value for money.

~

NEARBY Sorrento; Amalfi coast.
LOCATION in hills, 2 km by road outside Sorrento, 10 minutes' walk by path from town centre; ample car parking
FOOD breakfast, lunch, dinner
PRICE €
ROOMS 14 double and twin, all with shower; all rooms have phone, TV, hairdrier
FACILITIES sitting room, dining room, bar, lift, terraces, garden, swimming pool
CREDIT CARDS MC, V **DISABLED** access possible **PETS** accepted **CLOSED** Nov to mid-Mar **PROPRIETOR** Marisa Picco

CAMPANIA

SORRENTO

BELLEVUE SYRENE

~ SEAFRONT HOTEL ~

Piazza della Vittoria 5,80067 Sorrento, Napoli
Tel 081 87810241604 **Fax** 081 8783963
E-MAIL info@bellevue.it **WEBSITE** www.bellevue.it

AFTER A STYLISH MAKEOVER, this *grande dame* hotel appeals to us as much as it clearly did to its distinguished 19thC guests, among them Eugenie, Empress of France. Built as a count's summer retreat in 1750 in a magnificent clifftop position, it opened as a hotel in 1820, and over the years no expense has been spared in its restoration. Well-proportioned reception rooms, corridors and bedrooms, painted in restful shades of yellow, are brought to life with stunning frescoes and *trompe l'oeil*. Fabrics range from elegant brocades and smart Regency stripes to bold zebra prints; furniture comprises a fine collection of European antiques, mixed with wrought iron and marble in the smart majolica-tiled bedrooms.

The airy dining room is staffed by an army of impeccable waiters and features a menu of robust, mainly local specialities. Decorated with panels depicting enormous tiered confections, this room looks ordinary in comparison with the Villa Pompeiana restaurant, a fabulous replica of the Vetti brothers' house in Pompei created by Lord Astor in 1905-7. Though rarely used (except for private parties), you can peep through the door to see the wonderful mosaics, frescoes, stucco and columned terrace beyond.

~

NEARBY Piazza Tasso; *duomo*; Piazza San Antonio.
LOCATION on cliff overlooking bay, 5 minutes' walk from town centre; garage parking
FOOD breakfast, light or packed lunch, dinner
PRICE €€€
ROOMS 76 double and twin and suites with bath or shower; all rooms have phone, TV, air conditioning, minibar, hairdrier, safe
FACILITIES sitting rooms, meeting room, 2 dining rooms, 2 bars, gym, lift, terraces, garden, private beach
CREDIT CARDS AE, DC, MC, V
DISABLED access possible
PETS small pets accepted **CLOSED** never
PROPRIETOR Giovanni Russo

CAMPANIA

CAPRI

SCALINATELLA
TOWN HOTEL

Via Tragara 10, 80073 Capri
Napoli

TEL 081 8370633
FAX 081 8378291
FOOD breakfast, buffet poolside
lunch
PRICE €€€€
CLOSED Nov to mid-Mar
Morgano family

L ittle expense has been spared in the creation of this exclusive small hotel. A spotless white building with a profusion of arches and oriental ornamentation, it feels distinctly Moorish. Inside, a world of cool luxury awaits you. Every corner is air conditioned and the rooms have all the trimmings that you might expect for the very high price you will be paying — telephones in the bathroom, private terraces and some beds that disappear into alcoves, converting your rooms into a sitting room by day. The location, with views to the Carthusian monastery of San Giacomo, leaves little to be desired; the garden and pool (where buffet lunches are served) are immaculate.

CONCA DEI MARINI

BELVEDERE
SEASIDE HOTEL

Strada Statale 163, 84010 Conca
dei Marimi, Salerno

TEL 089 831282
FAX 089 831439
FOOD breakfast, lunch, dinner
PRICE €€
CLOSED mid-Oct to Mar
Lucibello family

O NCE A STOPOVER on the Grand Tour, the Belvedere still radiates grandeur from the outside, but is disappointing within. Though fresh, the decoration – particularly in the bedrooms – looks old-fashioned and run-of-the-mill. But our inspectors were prepared to overlook any imperfections because of its spectacular situation, perched on the edge of a cliff with breathtaking views along the Amalfi coast. Although the bedrooms are uninspired, they all turn their backs on the busy coast road and have balconies and sea views. A lift takes you down to a sea-water pool and steps to a private rocky beach. If you have a car, Conca dei Marini makes a useful base for local exploration and the hotel has a covered garage.

CAMPANIA

ISCHIA

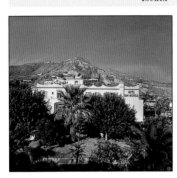

HOTEL TERME SAN MICHELE
SEASIDE HOTEL

Sant' Angelo, 80070 Ischia, Napoli

TEL 081 999276 **FAX** 081 999149
E-MAIL sanmich@metis.it
WEBSITE www.ischiaonline.it/
hotels/hsanmich **FOOD** breakfast,
lunch, dinner (half board only in
high season) **PRICE** ⓔⓔ **CLOSED**
mid-Oct to late Apr or May
Claudio Iacono

Although the San Michele has recently doubled the number of its bedrooms – and normally we would consider 85 too many for this guide – it still feels like a small hotel. We like its traditional qualities: old-style service and old-fashioned decoration. Immaculate waiters serve wholesome food and dance attendance in the brightly-lit white and wood-furnished dining room. The simple, rough-plastered bedrooms have no TV, hairdrier or safe, but do have starched mats on the tiled floors beside the beds. The charm of this place is also in the setting: it nestles serenely on the hillside above the little car-free village of Sant' Angelo. The pool, kept at 35ºC, and 'thermal facilities', are a big draw for many guests.

SORRENTO

LORELEY ET LONDRES
TOWN HOTEL

Via Califano 2, 80067 Sorrento, Napoli

TEL 081 8073187
FAX 081 5329001
FOOD breakfast, lunch, dinner
PRICE ⓔ
CLOSED mid-Nov to Easter
Giuseppina Ercolano

A complete dump. Tatty, scruffy and seedy are just some of the adjectives that come to mind to describe the present-day condition of this once-dignified hotel. Why include it? If rock-bottom budget is what you require, and if you are a connoisseur of quirky time warps, then you may well forgive the shortcomings, at least for a night. The splendidly atmospheric façade and old sepia photographs in the lobby attest to its former status as a favoured stop-off on the Grand Tour, and it still has a few attractive old pieces of furniture, a (very) faded charm and an air of lingering regret. Bedrooms and service are absolutely basic, with prices to match. Ask for a 'room with a view'; some have a tiny balcony giving on to the sea.

THE HEEL AND TOE

HOTELS IN THE HEEL AND TOE

To SAY THAT CHARMING SMALL HOTELS in the heel and toe of Italy are difficult to find is a wild understatement. It would be nearer the truth to
say that they don't exist. Much of the landscape is stony and barren, with
imposing mountains, and a rugged, inhospitable western coastline. The
exception is the area around the little resort of Maratea, where you will
find two of our hotels. Most of our other recommendations are on the
Strait of Otranto coast along the outside of Italy's heel. Here you will find
almost deserted beaches, punctuated by small communities, and an interi-
or that becomes more mountainous the further you go. The hotels which
appear in the following pages are the best there are, but some alternative
recommendations may be helpful, particularly in the heel.

The San Nicola (tel 080 8705199), a smart, 30-roomed hotel in the heart
of Altamura, is one possibility, as is the Villa Cenci in Cisternino (tel. 080
718208), with some accommodation in *trulli (* ancien t stone dwellings*)*, a
stylish restaurant and pleasant gardens and pool. If you want to make it
right to the southern tip of the heel, you could aim for the Terminal (tel
0833 758242), a well-run seaside holiday hotel at Marina di Léuca.

For travellers in the 'toe' heading south with time to spare, the SS18
makes a slow-paced alternative to the A3 motorway, sticking to the eastern coast south of Lagonegro where the motorway takes a long detour
inland. There are a few places further south than Maratea that are worth
bearing in mind. At Diamante is the Mediterranean-style Ferretti (tel
0985 81428), with terraces overlooking the sea and a highly reputed
restaurant. The 65-room Grand Hotel San Michele (tel 0982 91012) at
Cetraro is rather more swish – a well-restored old house in an attractive
informal garden on cliffs above the beach.

The main tourist attraction of the toe, however, is on the other side of
the A3 – the magnificently wild landscape of the Sila mountains east of
Cosenza and north of Catanzaro. Each of these towns has a handful of
acceptable hotels. South of Catanzaro at Stilo is the charming San Giorgio
(tel 0964 775047), a 17thC village house, once a cardinal's palace, whose
terrace garden affords splendid views.

THE HEEL AND TOE

MASSERIA MARZALOSSA

~ FARMHOUSE HOTEL ~

Calle da Pezze Vicine 65, 72015 Fasano Brindisi
TEL and **FAX** 080 4413780
E-MAIL masseriamarzalossa@puglianet.it **WEBSITE** www.marzalossa.puglianet.it

THE SCENT OF LEMONS lingers in the air around this fortified 17thC farmhouse just inland from the Adriatic coast north-west of Brindisi. Basking in a landscape of olive and citrus groves, the house is arranged around a series of shady courtyards and sunny terraces, with an interior that has been sympathetically restored. Typically, rooms have flagstone floors, beamed ceilings and white walls. Some of the simple bedrooms still have meat hooks in the beams, dating back to a time when pork or beef was hung here to cure. Beds have pretty wrought-iron heads and colourful printed covers. Period furniture, pictures and ornaments have been carefully chosen to suit each room.

The same style is evident in the small, cosy reception rooms. As you might expect, the food is unpretentious – like the decoration – and based on the rich supply of ingredients grown on the estate. Although lunch is not served, dinner is always deliciously filling, and don't miss the mouthwatering home-made jams which appear on the breakfast table.

The *pièce de résistance* is a beautiful swimming pool, encircled by columns, which occupies one of the terraces.

~

NEARBY Castellana Caves; Martina Franca (17 km).
LOCATION Ostoni exit off SS16, 61 km NW of Brindisi; car parking
FOOD breakfast, dinner
PRICE €€€
ROOMS 7; 6 double and twin, 1 suite, all with bath or shower; all rooms have hairdrier, minibar; TV on request; safe and phone at reception
FACILITIES sitting room, dining room, garden, swimming pool
CREDIT CARDS MC, V
DISABLED access difficult
PETS not accepted **CLOSED** Oct-Mar
PROPRIETORS Guarini family

The heel and toe

MARATEA

Locanda delle Donne Monache

~ VILLAGE HOTEL ~

Via Carlo Mazzei 4, 85046 Maratea, Potenza
Tel 0973 877487 **Fax** 0973 877687

F OR YEARS, MARATEA WAS one of the most unspoiled seaside villages on Italy's west coast, its pink and white houses clustered on low cliffs above the harbour and its old quarter crammed with interesting buildings, including two medieval churches. In the last decade or so new hotels have been built and restaurants opened, but its essential character remains intact, and this *locanda* is an example of how past and present can be successfully combined. Originally an old monastery, it has received an elegant contemporary facelift.

The flamboyance of the entrance hall gives way to cool modern *chic* in the bedrooms, each slightly different, but all comfortable with tiled floors and smart Italian-designed furniture and lighting. White drapes hang at the windows, while patterned or coloured drapes encircle canopy beds.

Jasmine, bougainvillea and lemon trees grow in the lovely peaceful garden at the front which contains a fair-sized swimming pool with a terrace and plenty of sunbeds. Not only does the hotel have a private beach, but it also has its own boat, so guests can venture out into the Gulf of Policastro and explore its coast.

~

NEARBY Monte San Biagio; Lagonegro (20 km).
LOCATION in village; car parking
FOOD breakfast, lunch, dinner
PRICE €€€
ROOMS 30 double and twin, suites, all with bath; all rooms have phone, TV, air conditioning, minibar, hairdrier
FACILITIES sitting room, piano bar, restaurant, garden, swimming pool, private beach
CREDIT CARDS AE, DC, MC, V
DISABLED access difficult **PETS** not accepted
CLOSED Nov-Mar
PROPRIETOR Raffaele Bruno

THE HEEL AND TOE

MARATEA

VILLA CHETA ELITE

~ LAKESIDE HOTEL ~

Via Nazionale, 85041 Acquafredda di Maratea, Potenza
TEL 0973 878134 **FAX** 0973 878135
E-MAIL villacheta@labnet.it **WEBSITE** www.costadimaratea.com/villacheta

THE REMOTE AND MOUNTAINOUS region of Basilicata does not possess much coastline. But the tiny stretch of shore on the west side, where a corniche cuts through wild and beautiful cliffs, is one of the most spectacular parts of Italy's deep south. Villa Cheta Elite is set high up on this precipitous coastline, with splendid views. If the villa enjoyed no other distinction, its position would be enough to attract many travellers to the south. But this gracious art nouveau building has other attractions.

The villa is a pleasure to behold: a confection of ochre and cream stucco, decorated with ornate mouldings that would look at home in a grand Edwardian living room. It lies among lush, flowery terraces, one of which is set out with café-style chairs and smartly-laid dining tables. Inside, lace tablecloths, chintz sofas, carefully-chosen period pieces and abundant pictures create the feel of a private house.

The beaches in the area are small, but the waters are clear, and reached in only a few minutes from the villa. The Aquadros are relaxed and charming hosts, who take great care over every aspect of their hotel, including the food.

~

NEARBY Maratea (8 km); Lagonegro (20 km).
LOCATION 1.5 km S of Acquafredda; car parking
FOOD breakfast, lunch, dinner
PRICE ©©
ROOMS 18; 16 double and twin, one with bath, 15 with shower; 2 family with shower; all have phone
FACILITIES dining room, TV/reading room, bar, terrace, garden
CREDIT CARDS AE, DC, MC, V
DISABLED access difficult
PETS small ones accepted
CLOSED never
PROPRIETOR Lamberto Aqadro

THE HEEL AND TOE

IL MELOGRANO
~ COUNTRY VILLA ~

Contrada Torricella 345, 70043 Monópoli Bari
TEL 080 6909030 **FAX** 080 747908
E-MAIL melograno@melograno.com **WEBSITE** www.melograno.com

SOPHISTICATED ROOMS, filled with fine antiques, paintings, fabrics and oriental carpets, give us a clue to the profession of the man who masterminded the transformation of this 16thC fortified farmhouse, used by the Guerra family as a holiday home, to a luxurious small hotel. Until the mid-1980s Camillo Guerra was an antiques dealer, and his special, personal touch is evident everywhere. The elegant reception rooms are housed in the main building. But for the individually-furnished bedrooms, he built a clutch of white Moorish houses around a *piazza*, overlooking orange and olive groves, lemon and pomegranate trees (the name 'melograno' means 'pomegranate').

Dinner, a Mediterranean feast, is usually *al fresco* on a canopy-covered veranda beside a wonderfully gnarled old olive tree. Breakfast is served beside the outdoor pool, bordered by prickly pear, almond and citrus trees, whose fruit is the basis for the juice and jams on the table.

If relaxing by the pool or on the private beach begins to pall, there is plenty to see in the area, including Frederick II's Swabian castles and the mysterious *trulli* of Alberobello.

~

NEARBY ruins of Egnazia; Castellana caves; Alberobello (19 km).
LOCATION 3 km from Monópoli towards Alberobello; car parking
FOOD breakfast, lunch, dinner
PRICE €€€
ROOMS 37; 33 double and twin, 4 suites, all with bath; all rooms have phone, TV, air conditioning, minibar, hairdrier, safe
FACILITIES sitting rooms, dining room, bar, health centre, indoor and outdoor swimming pools, garden, tennis, private beach, helipad
CREDIT CARDS AE, DC, MC, V
DISABLED access possible
PETS not accepted **CLOSED** Dec-Apr
PROPRIETORS Guerra family

THE HEEL AND TOE

MASSERIA SAN DOMENICO

~ FARMHOUSE HOTEL ~

Litoranea 379, 72010 Savelletri di Fasano, Brindisi
TEL 080 4827990 **FAX** 080 4827978
E-MAIL masseriasandomenico@puglianet.it **WEBSITE** www.imasseria.com

O N ONE OF THE SPRAWLING agricultural estates with a fortified farmhouse
at its centre that crop up all over Puglia, this *masseria* has its origins
in the 14th century when the knights of Malta used it as a watchtower
against the Turks. Set in 60 acres of orchards and olive groves, its metamorphosis into an impressive hotel was completed in 1996. The architecture is typically Moorish – pristine white walls, turrets and arched windows and doorways – with fitting decoration inside, where details like
curvy wrought-iron bedheads and fabrics in vibrant colours or floral
designs bring the rooms to life. The marble-floored bedrooms are attractively and individually furnished and equipped with large modern bathrooms.

Although the hotel is only 200 m from the sea, the huge salt-water
swimming pool might have even greater appeal. Skilfully built, with no
straight lines, so that it looks like a huge natural rock pool, it is surrounded by gnarled old olive trees. Drinks and meals are served here at the pool
bar and barbecue grill, while in the dining room seafood is one of the specialities in a range of delicious regional dishes.

~

NEARBY Castellana Caves; Fasano (7 km).
LOCATION 2 km S of Savelletri on SS379 to Torrecane; car parking
FOOD breakfast, lunch, dinner; room service
PRICE €€€
ROOMS 35 double and twin with bath; all rooms have phone, TV, air conditioning,
minibar, hairdrier
FACILITIES sitting room, dining room, terrace, garden, swimming pool, pool bar,
tennis
CREDIT CARDS AE, DC, MC, V
DISABLED access difficult
PETS accepted **CLOSED** Jan
MANAGER Luigi Anfosso

THE HEEL AND TOE

ALTOMONTE

BARBIERI
VILLAGE HOTEL

*Via San Nicola 30, 87042
Altomonte Cosenza*

TEL 0981 948072 **FAX** 0981 948073
E-MAIL barbieri@esperia.it
WEBSITE
www.esperia.it/barbieri.htm
FOOD breakfast, lunch, dinner
PRICE €
CLOSED never
PROPRIETORS Patrizia and
Vincenzo Barbieri

YOU MAY WONDER WHAT this hotel is doing in the guide – it's not much to look at from the outside and inside, though the rooms are comfortable and well equipped, the decoration tends to be bland and unexciting. There are however four good reasons for choosing it. First, the setting is wonderful, at the top of a natural amphitheatre above a valley with sweeping views over the Pollino and Sila massifs and down to the lovely medieval village of Altomonte. The second and perhaps most seductive reason is its distinguished restaurant, one of the – if not *the* – best in Calabria and renowned even further afield. The third reason will be clear when you get your bill. Prices are unbelievably low.

PARGHELIA

BAIA PARAELIOS
RESORT VILLAGE

*Fornaci, 88035 Parghelia ,
Catanzaro*

TEL 0963 600300 **FAX** 0963 600074
FOOD breakfast, lunch, dinner
PRICE € € €
CLOSED Oct to Apr
Adolfo Salabe

OVERLOOKING A PICTURE-POSTCARD BAY of white sand washed by a turquoise sea, Baia Paraelios is not so much a hotel as an upmarket holiday camp with accommodation in 83 small bungalows sprawled across a wooded hillside. Each has a private terrace, a view of its own, one or two bedrooms and a sitting room in mellow colours. Communal areas are equally stylish. Prints add colour to plain walls; tiled floors and a scattering of plants bask in a cosy glow from artful lighting. There is a relaxing sitting room, open-air bar and terrace dining room beside the sea. Three swimming pools (one salt-water), flood-lit tennis courts, mini-golf, bowling, windsurfing, canoeing and child-minding make this a choice for families.

THE ISLANDS

HOTELS IN THE ISLANDS

SICILY, THE LARGEST AND MOST POPULOUS island in the Mediterranean, has an extraordinary mix of sightseeing interest – spectacular scenery, ancient Greek ruins, medieval towns, splendid cathedrals, busy street markets, not to mention an active volcano – and therefore attracts many visitors in the summer months. Taormina is the main resort and is well represented by hotels on the following pages. Another possibility is the elegant Villa Riis (tel 0942 24874) which has its own swimming pool. Of the large cities, we have yet to find a recommendable hotel in Palermo, but we do have three recommendations for Siracusa. To see the sights of Palermo, you could stay in Cefalu, a pretty fishing port 60 km to the east. The Riva del Sole (tel 0921 21230) is a comfortable hotel close to the beach and the port, or the Baia del Capitano (tel 0921 20003) is a 39-room hotel 5 km out of town.

If you plan a more peaceful holiday, you might do best to choose one of the Aeolian (or Lipari) Islands, seven beautiful volcanic islands to the north of Sicily. We have a new entry on Panarea, the Raya. As possibilities on Lipari we suggest Villa Diana (tel 090 9811403); Villa Meligunis (tel 090 9812426), Giardino sul Mare (tel 090 9811004) and the Oriente (tel 090 9811493). On the neighbouring island of Salina, try a clifftop hotel, Punta Scario (tel 090 9844139), or a restaurant-with-rooms, L'Ariana (tel 090 9809075).

Although about the same size as Sicily, Sardinia is completely different: its population is sparse; there are few major sightseeing attractions and no very large towns or resorts; and there are no crowds, even in the most developed area for tourists, the Costa Smeralda – which is where most of our recommendations are located. Development is gradually spreading along the coastline from there in both directions. On the north coast, the Shardana (tel 0789 75403) and the Li Nibbari (tel 0789 754453), both at Santa Teresa Gallura, are possibilities.

On the east coast, the Pensione l'Oasi (tel 0784 93111) at Dorgali is a well-equipped hotel set on a hill overlooking the sea, amidst gardens and pinewoods. But if you really want to get away from it all, two small islands just off the south-west coast of Sardinia may appeal: Sant' Antioco – try the Club Ibisco Farm (tel 0781 809003) – and the Isola San Pietro – try the Hieracon (tel 0781 854028) on the waterfront at Carloforte.

PANAREA

SAN PIETRO

RAYA

~ SEASIDE HOTEL ~

Isole Eolie o Lipari, San Pietro, 98050 Isola Panarea, Messina
TEL 090 983013 **FAX** 090 983103
E-MAIL informations@hotelraya.it **WEBSITE** www.hotelraya.com

THIS UNIQUE, STYLISH HOTEL was the creation of Myriam Beltrami and Paolo Tilche, who came to the alluring, car-less little island of Panarea in the 1960s, were enthralled and never left. The Raya consists of a cascade of pink and white bungalows, linked by arches and whitewashed steps, tumbling down the hillside through a Mediterranean garden to the sea. At every level bougainvillea-shaded terraces – for dining, sunbathing or attached to bedrooms – look out to the uninhabited Lipari islands with the threatening vision of the volcano, Strómboli, in the distance.

Inside all is cool and white – from the tiled floors to the sofas and chairs – a fitting background for the dramatic pieces of ethnic art from Polynesia, Africa and Asia that Myriam collects and loves to display. She sells similar pieces in her boutique (next door). Also predominately white, some of the bedrooms have a slightly dated feel, with Indian bedspreads and rush ceilings.

Choose between a continental breakfast in the small bar or on your terrace; or brunch in the airy dining room. In the evening, this room is lit by oil lamps on tables, which in summer are set out on the panoramic terrace. No young children.

~

NEARBY Strómboli; Salina; Sicily
LOCATION 400 m from port on hillside; hydrofoil from Naples, Milazzo, Reggio Calabria, Palermo, Messina
FOOD breakfast, brunch, dinner
PRICE €€€€
ROOMS 36 double and twin, duplex, all with shower; all rooms have phone, air conditioning, minibar, hairdrier
FACILITIES sitting areas, bar/breakfast room, dining room, disco, terraces, garden
CREDIT CARDS AE, DC, MC, V
DISABLED access difficult **PETS** accepted **CLOSED** mid-Oct to mid-Apr
PROPRIETOR Myriam Beltrami

SARDINIA

ALGHERO

VILLA LAS TRONAS
~ SEASIDE HOTEL ~

Lungomare Valencia 1, 07041 Alghero, Sassari
Tel 079 981818 **Fax** 079 981044

THIS CASTELLATED, 19THC FOLLY lords it over its own bare, rocky promontory, and it stands aloof from the blocks of flats that otherwise characterize this unattractive part of modern Alghero. The interior – all marble floors and ornate chandeliers – is as grand as you might expect of somewhere that was a holiday retreat for Italian royalty until the 1940s. Yet the unstuffy and businesslike staff ensure it is not intimidatingly formal.

Antiques abound, including in the luxurious bedrooms, which feature brass or sleigh beds and grand canopies, along with swanky marble bathrooms. Those billed as having garden views in reality overlook Alghero's apartment blocks. You pay extra to open the shutters on a view across the bay to the awesome cliff of Capo Caccia; priciest sea-facing rooms come with balconies.

There are no beaches in this part of Alghero, but the hotel has a pool, and many guests swim off the rocks and from an old dockyard.

When we inspected, breakfast was dire. For food, you may be better off making the five-minute stroll along the seaside promenade into the magical backstreets of old Alghero, where you'll find a wide choice of cafés and restaurants. Bicycles are provided free.

~

Nearby Maria Pia, the best nearby beach, is 4 km north.
Location in modern Alghero, 800 m S of old Alghero; with car parking
Food breakfast, lunch, dinner
Price €€€
Rooms 29; 22 double and 1 suite with bath, 6 single with shower; all rooms have phone, TV, air-conditioning, minibar, hairdrier
Facilities sitting room, dining room, bar, sea-water swimming pool, gym, bicycles
Credit cards AE, DC, MC, V
Disabled not suitable
Pets accepted **Closed** never
Manager Maria Teresa Masia

SARDINIA

OLIENA

SU GOLOGONE

～ COUNTRY HOTEL ～

08025 Oliena, Nuoro
TEL 0784 287512 **FAX** 0784 287668
E-MAIL gologone@tin.it

THE BARBAGIA IS A MOUNTAINOUS inland region where the land-scape is wild, the villages remote and bandits still thrive – though tourists are unlikely to encounter them. The hotel is a low-lying white villa, covered in creepers, surrounded by flowing shrubs and set in a land-scape of rural splendour: wooded ravines, fields of olives, pinewoods and the craggy peaks of the Supramonte mountains. It feels isolated, and it is; but the Su Gologone is far from undiscovered. Once, only a few adventur-ous foreign travellers found their way here; now, they come for the peace, or indeed for the food alone, which is typically Sard: cuts of local meats, roast lamb and the speciality of roast suckling pig – you can watch it being cooked on a spit in front of a huge fireplace. The wines are produced in the local vineyards. The dining room spreads in all directions – into the vine-clad courtyard, the terrace and other rooms, all in suitably rustic style. The bedrooms are light and simple, again in rustic style, in keeping with the surroundings. Walls are whitewashed, floors are tiled and there are lovely views. Despite its size, the Su Gologone still feels small and friendly, and, in most respects, still typically Sard

～

NEARBY Gennargentu mountains; Monte Ortobene (21 km).
LOCATION 8 km NE of Oliena, in remote mountain setting, with private car parking
FOOD breakfast, lunch, dinner
PRICE €€€-€€€€
ROOMS 65; 53 double and twin, 8 suites, 4 family rooms, all with bath; all rooms have phone, TV, air conditioning, minibar, hairdrier
FACILITIES 5 dining rooms, 2 bars, swimming pool, tennis, bowls, mini-golf, bicycles, Land Rover and horses for excursions
CREDIT CARDS AE, MC, V
DISABLED no special facilities
PETS accepted
CLOSED Nov to Feb, except Christmas
PROPRIETOR Giuseppe Palimodde

SARDINIA

PALAU

CAPO D'ORSO

~ SEASIDE HOTEL ~

Loc. Cala Capra, 07020 Palau
TEL 0789 702000 **FAX** 0789 702009

THIS CIVILIZED YET UNPRETENTIOUS waterside hotel stands in marked contrast to the flashy establishments on the nearby Costa Smeralda. It's a place for slow-paced, laid-back, water and beach-oriented holidays. Basking in mesmerising views of the verdant yet rocky coastline and offshore islands, its secluded setting – the nearest centre, the humdrum port of Palau, is a 10-minute drive away – could hardly be prettier. For chilling out, choose between two picturesque, sheltered slips of sand, a lovely amoeba-shaped pool and, in what amount to the focus of the hotel, thoroughly romantic drinks and dining terraces shaded by olive trees and tamarisks. The food is praised; breakfasts come in the form of buffets, and there is also a lunchtime pizzeria.

The simple bedrooms, in low-rise blocks, are lifted by cheerful paintings and the fact that all face the sea and have a balcony or terrace. Suites suit families: the sitting room, connected to a bedroom by a sliding door, has a sofa bed.

If boredom sets in, the hotel can arrange diving and riding. Boat trips from its jetty visit Maddalena and Caprera, and the fleshpots of the Costa Smeralda's Porto Cervo.

~

NEARBY Maddalena and Caprera islands; Costa Smeralda.
LOCATION 6 km E of Palau, car parking
FOOD breakfast, lunch, dinner
PRICE €€€
ROOMS 60; 33 double, 9 family, 18 suites, all with shower; all rooms have phone, TV, air conditioning, minibar, hairdrier, balcony or terrace
FACILITIES sitting room, 2 restaurants, bar, swimming pool, tennis, boat trips, watersports **CREDIT CARDS** AE, DC, MC, V
DISABLED no special facilities **PETS** accepted
CLOSED Oct to May
MANAGER Alessandro Fumagalli

SARDINIA

PORTO CERVO

CALA DI VOLPE

~ SEASIDE HOTEL ~

07020 Porto Cervo, Costa Smeralda, Sassari
TEL 0789 976111 **FAX** 0789 976617 **E-MAIL** res059_caladivolpe@sheraton.com
WEBSITE www.luxurycollection.com/caladivolpe

APPROACHED FROM THE FRONT, Cala di Volpe has the slightly forbidding exterior of a Moorish fortification, with towers, crenellations and turrets. Viewed from the sea, however, the hotel resembles a simple fishing village, where clusters of little houses painted in shades of ochre and amber are softened by arches and porticoes – an magical sight when lit up at night. Simplicity of style is carried through into the interior: niches, painted stairways and modern stained glass insets in the hallways; plain bedrooms, (some with *trompe l'oeil* embellishments), with terraces or gardens overlooking the sea. Overall, the effect of wooden beams, bamboo, terracotta floors, and orange, yellow and brown colours, offset by cool white, creates an air of Sardinian rustic chic.

The super-rich turn up by boat and moor their vessels in the small marina. If you don't have a boat, don't worry: a free hotel launch leaves half hourly for a private beach – a little paradise, complete with sunloungers, towels and crystal clear water. Or it's just a short stroll away along a wooded track.

Beware the veneer of simplicity at Cala di Volpe: it belies discreet, understated luxury. Your credit card needs to be in good working order.

~

NEARBY Porto Cervo (8 km); Olbia (25 km).
LOCATION S of Porto Cervo, Costa Smeralda; car parking
FOOD breakfast, lunch, dinner; room service
PRICE €€€€
ROOMS 121; 100 double, 9 single, 12 suites, all with bath; Presidential suite has private pool; all rooms have phone, TV, air conditioning, minibar, hairdrier
FACILITIES restaurant, bar, swimming pool, terrace, garden, beach, private harbour, jetty, water-skiing, 9-hole putting green, tennis, bike hire, boat hire, fitness centre
CREDIT CARDS AE, DC, MC, V
DISABLED not suitable **PETS** not accepted **CLOSED** Nov-Feb
MANAGER Robert Koren

SARDINIA

PORTO CERVO

CERVO
~ SEASIDE HOTEL ~

07020 Porto Cervo, Costa Smeralda, Sassari
TEL 0789 931111 **FAX** 0789 931613
E-MAIL res064_cervo@sheraton.com **WEBSITE** www.sheraton.com/cervo

A STONE'S THROW from the old quay, this Mediterranean-style hotel over-looks the *piazzetta* right in the heart of Porto Cervo – an almost too perfect resort village, crammed with designer shops and smart restaurants. It is part of the Costa Smeralda development, started in the late fifties by a consortium led by the Aga Khan.

Within the hotel it is refreshingly airy and simple. There are textured white walls, terracotta floors, plain, bright fabrics and wooden furniture. Ceilings are low and windows are arched. Despite the fact that the Cervo has a purpose-built conference centre a short distance away and some-times hosts large groups, the terraces and shaded dining areas are small in scale and intimate. There are several restaurants to choose from: the Grill specializes in Italian cuisine and has splendid views over the marina; Il Pescatore serves fish and seafood; Il Pomodoro is informal and rustic.

For sports enthusiasts, a short walk over a little wooden bridge leads to the sports complex where tennis, squash, a fully-equipped gym and jogging track are available. Sun worshippers and sea bathers will appreciate the free boat service (between May and September) that whisks them away to a secluded beach.

~

NEARBY Olbia (30 km); Costa Smeralda coastline; boat trips
LOCATION in middle of Porto Cervo; car parking
FOOD breakfast, lunch, dinner
PRICE ©©©©
ROOMS 108 all with bath and shower; 6 suites with private pool; all with air conditioning, minibar, satellite TV
FACILITIES 5 restaurants, bars, 3 swimming pools, sports centre and golf nearby
CREDIT CARDS AE, DC, MC, V **DISABLED** not suitable
PETS not accepted **CLOSED** never
MANAGER Marco Battistotti

SARDINIA

PORTO CERVO

PITRIZZA
～ RESORT VILLAGE ～

07020 Porto Cervo, Costa Smeralda, Sassari
TEL 0789 930111 **FAX** 0789 930611

THE SMART PLAYGROUND of the Costa Smeralda is liberally endowed with luxury hotels, but there is one that stands out from the rest: the Pitrizza. What distinguishes it (apart from its small size) is its exclusive, intimate, club-like atmosphere. No shops, disco or ritzy touches here. Small private villas are scattered discreetly among the rocks and flowering gardens, overlooking a private beach. Rooms are furnished throughout with immaculate taste, some of them amazingly simple. The style is predominantly rustic, with white stucco walls, beams and locally crafted furniture and fabrics. Each villa has four to six rooms, and most have a private terrace, garden or patio. The core of the hotel is the club house, with a small sitting room, bar, restaurant and spacious terrace where you can sit, enjoying the company of other guests or simply watching the sunset. A path leads down to the golden sands of a small beach and a private jetty where you can moor your yacht. Equally desirable is the sea-water pool, which has been carved out of the rocky shoreline.

There is of course a hitch to the Pitrizza. The rooms here are among the most expensive on the entire Italian coastline.

～

NEARBY beaches of the Costa Smeralda; Maddalena archipelago.
LOCATION 4 km from Porto Cervo, at Liscia di Vacca; ample car parking
FOOD breakfast, lunch, dinner; room service
PRICE €€€€
ROOMS 51; 38 double and twin, 13 suites, all with bath; all rooms have phone, TV, air conditioning, minibar, hairdrier
FACILITIES dining room, bar, terrace, fitness centre, sea-water swimming pool, beach, water-skiing, boat hire, windsurfing, private mooring
CREDIT CARDS AE, DC, MC, V
DISABLED no special facilities
PETS not accepted
CLOSED mid-Oct to Apr
MANAGER Pierangelo Tondina

SARDINIA

PORTO CERVO

ROMAZZINO

~ SEASIDE HOTEL ~

07020 Porto Cervo, Costa Smeralda, Sassari
TEL 0789 977111 **FAX** 0789 96258

THOUGH FABULOUSLY STYLISH and punitively expensive, the Romazzino is a little less exclusive and pricey than its smaller sister, the Pitrizza (see page 000). It's a better choice if a beach is important in your plans, since the whitewashed, terracotta-roofed complex presides over one of the biggest on the Costa Smeralda (as well as an enormous pool). Families in particular should be more at home here.

Make no mistake, however: this is still one of Europe's most luxurious beach hotels. The interior has the airiness and understated elegance of a giant Moorish-cum-Mediterranean mansion. For example, whimsical, painted ceramics adorn the walls of the sitting room, while gay colour schemes complement soothing Sardinian fabrics in the tasteful bedrooms.

A veritable army of staff panders to your every need. At dinner, it's hard to know whether to be more impressed by the creative Franco-Italian cuisine, or the zealously attentive, multilingual service. Although the Romazzino exceeds our normal room limit by a considerable margin, we continue to include it because it has the feel of a much smaller place.

~

NEARBY Hotel Cala di Volpe, a jaw-dropping faux-Medieval castle.
LOCATION 11 km from Porto Cervo; car parking
FOOD breakfast, lunch, dinner; room service
PRICE ©©©©
ROOMS 91; 77 double and twin, 14 suites, all with bath; all rooms have phone, TV, air conditioning, minibar, hairdrier
FACILITIES sitting room, 2 restaurants, bar, terrace, swimming pool, tennis, watersports
CREDIT CARDS AE, DC, MC, V
DISABLED access difficult
PETS not accepted
CLOSED mid-Oct to late Apr
MANAGER Carlo Ferraris

SARDINIA

SANTA MARGHERITA DI PULA

IS MORUS

∽ SEASIDE HOTEL ∽

09010 Santa Margherita di Pula, Pula
TEL 070 921171 **FAX** 070 921596

IS MORUS IS ONE OF SEVERAL upmarket and isolated hotels along a strip of flat coastline dotted with holiday homes and greenhouses, and backed by parched, rocky hills.

Secluded within an oleander-rich garden, and a pine and eucalyptus wood, pantiled and whitewashed Is Morus is a Mediterranean rendition of a smart country-house hotel. In keeping with the fairly formal service, an understated elegance pervades the place, both in the cool, light sitting rooms that are interconnected by arches and furnished with squashy modern soft furnishings, and in bedrooms that are almost minimalist in style. Some of these are in the main building (avoid those without a sea view or balcony), others in villas sprinkled through the wood, with two or three bedrooms per villa.

The sandy beach isn't one of Sardinia's best (it can be weedy), but it is yards from the main building, private and immaculately maintained, and the swimming pool is large and inviting.

This is a civilized and peaceful corner of Sardinia, bereft of bright lights or of even anything amounting to a resort.

∽

NEARBY the sand-dune beaches at Chia; the Punic and Roman ruins at Nora.
LOCATION on the coast S of Pula; car parking
FOOD breakfast, lunch, dinner; room service
PRICE €€€€
ROOMS 85 double and twin, single and suites, all with bath or shower; all rooms have phone, TV, air conditioning, minibar, hairdrier
FACILITIES sitting room, restaurant; bar, terrace, swimming pool, tennis, watersports **CREDIT CARDS** AE, DC, MC, V
DISABLED no special facilities
PETS accepted
CLOSED Jan to Apr
MANAGER Martina Ketzer

SICILY

AGRIGENTO

FORESTERIA BAGLIO DELLA LUNA

~ COUNTRY VILLA ~

Contrada Maddalusa, 92100 Agrigento
TEL 0922 511061 **FAX** 0922 598802

SITUATED IN AGRIGENTO'S VALLEY of the Temples, this is a useful hotel owned by a family with deep roots in the area. The Baglio (motto: *Parva Domus Magna Quies*), is dominated by its sturdy square tower, constructed in the 13th century and rebuilt in 1555. In the 18th century it became a private country residence. Recent restoration has rendered the interior somewhat characterless but has maintained the original structure, with high walls enclosing the gardens, in which you can stroll along pretty paths. The courtyard now makes a shaded terrace, where the mellow stone and terracotta downpipes can be seen to best advantage. Public rooms, contained in the tower (with a mezzanine floor above the bar area) are furnished (mostly reproduction) in traditional Sicilian style, as are the bedrooms; suites (hardly) have Jacuzzi baths.

The restaurant at Baglio della Luna serves both classic Italian and traditional Sicilian dishes, and wine from the owner's private vineyard is on offer. Here, in the dining room, is the hotel's best and most eye-catching feature: full-length windows (which are opened in warm weather) through which there is a panoramic view of the Valley of the Temples.

~

NEARBY Valley of the Temples, Agrigento.
LOCATION 3 km S of Agrigento; at Porto Empedone take left fork at Agip petrol station, and in 3 km, after bridge, turn right down track; ample car parking
FOOD breakfast, lunch, dinner
PRICE €€€
ROOMS 24; 21 double and twin, 3 suites, all with bath or shower; all rooms have phone, TV, air conditioning, minibar, hairdrier
FACILITIES sitting room, dining room, bar, terrace, garden
CREDIT CARDS AE, MC, V
DISABLED no special facilities
PETS accepted
CLOSED never
PROPRIETOR Ignazio Altieri

SICILY

ERICE

MODERNO
~ TOWN HOTEL ~

Via Vittorio Emanuele 63, 91016 Erice, Trapani
TEL 0923 869300 **FAX** 0923 869139

DESPITE THE TOURISTS, Erice is an enchanting medieval town, encircled by walls, and makes an excellent base for a night or two, as does the Moderno, situated toward the top of the narrow main street (it's best to park in the public parking area near Porta Trapani, then walk through the arch and up the narrow main street to the hotel). As the name suggests, the hotel, in a 19thC building, is decorated in contemporary style – mixed with traditional Sicilian elements – which shows flair, with pictures, ornaments and plants everywhere. Public rooms are simply but effectively furnished, with several groups of sofas, chairs and tables at which to sit and relax, including a mezzanine floor. Bedrooms are generally spacious, some furnished in traditional style, some with modern pine furniture. Bathrooms are small, but spotless.

The restaurant, according to a recent reporter, offers 'a well-prepared, wide-ranging menu', and the roof terrace provides a wonderful view of the tiled roofs of Erice, and (for those who are prepared to look down) of the silver-grey stone-paved roads below.

~

NEARBY Greek temple and theatre at Segesta; Trapani (15 km); Egadi islands; Pantelleria island.
LOCATION in town centre; public car parking nearby
FOOD breakfast, lunch, dinner
PRICE €€
ROOMS 41 double and single, all with bath or shower; all rooms have phone, TV, minibar
FACILITIES sitting areas, dining room, bar, roof terrace, lift
CREDIT CARDS AE, DC, MC, V
DISABLED no special facilities
PETS accepted
CLOSED never
PROPRIETOR Giuseppe Catalano

SICILY

GANGI

TENUTA GANGIVECCHIO
∼ COUNTRY GUESTHOUSE ∼

Contrada di Gangivecchio, 90024 Gangi, Palermo
TEL and **FAX** 0921 689191

IF YOU WANT PEACE AND SECLUSION, then look no further than this converted 13thC monastery, reached after a long drive through the beautiful Madonie region. The home of the Tornabene family, the monastery lies at the bottom of a steep valley, hidden behind tall wooden doors that open to reveal a magnificent courtyard and magical buildings. First came a restaurant, whose reputation for marvellous Sunday lunches soon spread far and wide. Later, the family converted the stables into guest accommodation. This building, separate from the monastery (which you must not fail to see) lacks character, but bedrooms are 'large and light, with good beds, country antiques, and adequate bathrooms', reports a recent guest. In colder months there is a roaring fire in the reception area. The guest wing has its own dining room, with views on to the garden; here variations on typical Sicilian dishes invented by the family are prepared with care and imagination, mainly using home-grown ingredients. Dinner is a four-course set menu, so warn the 'laconic' Signor Tornabene in advance of any individual requirements. 'You will find his sister Giovanna (who speaks English) much more welcoming,' says our reporter, who found excellent value for money and would happily return. 'In many ways it's a very special place.'

∼

NEARBY Gangi (6 km); Madonie region.
LOCATION 130 km SE of Palermo. Go through Gangi, turn right to Gangivecchio; after 1 km, turn left at yellow sign indicating Tenuta Gangivecchio; after 5 km, the Tenuta is on right; car parking
FOOD breakfast, lunch, dinner **PRICE** €
ROOMS 9 double and triple, all with shower; all rooms have phone
FACILITIES dining room, restaurant, sitting rooms, swimming pool, table tennis, mountain bikes, horse riding **CREDIT CARDS** MC, V
DISABLED not suitable **PETS** not accepted **CLOSED** mid-July to Aug
PROPRIETOR Paolo Tornabene

SICILY

GIARDINI-NAXOS

ARATHENA ROCKS

~ SEASIDE HOTEL ~

Via Calcide Eubea 55, 98035 Giardini-Naxos, Messina
TEL 0942 51349 **FAX** 0942 51690
E-MAIL arathena@taormina-ol.it

An attractive and well-priced alternative to staying in a hotel on the busy sands of Giardini-Naxos (not a peaceful resort), where you can swim in the sea from the rocks, as well as in the pool.

The Arathena Rocks is run by a friendly family (who speak English), and reception staff on hand in the airy lobby are welcoming. The sitting room, which has a distinctly baroque feel, is full of brightly coloured sofas. There is a blue-tiled bar and salon, and tiles also feature in the dining room (where simple dishes are served). There are other ceramics too, such as the Chinese dragons at the entrance, and the green shrubs which decorate the top-floor balconies. All in all, the white-walled Mediterranean building, with its balconies and terraces, and its shady gardens with statues and palms, is a delight. Hewn from the rocks is a large (unheated) swimming pool, where, in season, you can enjoy snacks at the poolside bar.

Bedrooms are cool, spacious and cheerfully decorated, each one different, but often containing painted furniture, many with views over the sea and Mount Etna. Try, if you can, for one of the top-floor balcony rooms.

~

NEARBY Taormina; Mount Etna.
LOCATION at the end of the bay, down a private road; car parking
FOOD breakfast, lunch, dinner
PRICE €€
ROOMS 45, all with bath or shower; all rooms have phone
FACILITIES sitting room, dining room, 2 bars, lift, terrace, garden, swimming pool, tennis, minibus to Taormina
CREDIT CARDS MC, V
DISABLED no special facilities
PETS accepted
CLOSED Nov to Mar
PROPRIETOR Natale Arcidiacono

SICILY

EREMO DELLA GIUBLIANA
~ COUNTRY HOTEL ~

Contrada Giubiliana, S.P. per Marina di Ragusa, 97100 Ragusa
TEL 0932 669119 **FAX** 0932 623891

IF YOU ARE COMING BY CAR, this small, elegant hotel is well worth the journey. Alternatively, you can fly to the hotel's private airfield, from where you can also take sightseeing trips as far away as Malta or Tunisia.

Situated far away from major roads in a pastoral landscape of rolling farmland cut by white lanes, the hotel has been the home of the Nifosì family since the 18th century. It was built as a fortified convent in the 15th century, and was later used by the Knights of the Order of St John on their way to Malta. In converting the central core of the convent, Signor Nifosì, an architect, has spared no effort to ensure that it is displayed to its best advantage, retaining the original structure and the pitch and limestone floors, and transforming the monks' cells into comfortable bedrooms, with elegant, modern bathrooms.

Food is important at the Eremo, and the owners personally supervise the cooking, using local produce, of traditional Sicilian highland dishes. It was unfortunate, therefore, to hear recently from a German reader disappointed by the food. The best Sicilian wines – some of them full of character – are available from the well-stocked medieval cellar.

~

NEARBY Ragusa (7 km).
LOCATION signposted off the road from Ragusa to Marina di Ragusa; ample car parking
FOOD breakfast, lunch, dinner
PRICE €€
ROOMS 10 double, 2 suites, all with bath; all rooms have phone, TV, hairdrier
FACILITIES sitting room, dining room, terrace, swimming pool, meeting room
CREDIT CARDS AE, MC, V
DISABLED 3 rooms on ground floor
PETS accepted
CLOSED never
MANAGER Elena Restuccia

SICILY

LIMONETO
~ COUNTRY GUESTHOUSE ~

Via del Platano 3, 96100 Siracusa
TEL and **FAX** 0931 717352
E-MAIL limoneto@tin.it

A S A VERY DIFFERENT ALTERNATIVE to our other suggestions for staying in the fascinating city of Siracusa, we include for the first time this family guesthouse some nine kilometres outside the city. We must be honest: we have been urged by a reader to recommend it, but we have not yet visited it ourselves. However, the owners sound charming, and the place feels 'right'; we would welcome any more first-hand reports, because our information is sketchy.

Limoneto is set among the owners' lemon, orange and olive groves, and that the place is run by husband and wife Alceste and Adelina Norcia, and their son Francesco. Guests are treated very much as part of the family, and the welcome is warm and genuine. Some of the guest rooms are in the main house, others in a renovated barn; some are large, sleeping up to four, perfect for a family. Though they are 'modern' rather than characterful, they are 'comfortably fresh and spotlessly clean'.

The main focus of a stay at Limoneto, however, is definitely the food. Adelina's kitchen is open to everyone, and here she prepares local Sicilian dishes using home-grown ingredients. A glass (or more) of the family's own *limoncello* makers a great digestive. ~

NEARBY Siracusa (9 km).
LOCATION signposted off route 14 to Palazzolo, in own grounds; with car parking
FOOD breakfast, lunch, dinner
PRICE €-€€€
ROOMS 6 double, all with shower or bath; all rooms have phone
FACILITIES sitting room, dining room, terrace, garden
CREDIT CARDS not accepted
DISABLED no special facilities
PETS accepted
CLOSED never
PROPRIETORS Norcia family

SICILY

TAORMINA

VILLA BELVEDERE

~ SEASIDE VILLA ~

Via Bagnoli Croce 79, 98039 Taormina, Messina
TEL 0942 23791 **FAX** 0942 625830
E-MAIL hotbelv@tao.it

THE BELVEDERE IS A REFRESHINGLY unpretentious, discreet and welcoming hotel, one of the first to be built in Taormina (in 1902). It has been in the same family ever since, and subsequent generations have managed to make their changes without altering the inherent charm of the place, Currently in charge is Frenchman Claude Pécaut and his Italian wife, both of them friendly and helpful.

As you would expect from its name, the Belvedere's greatest asset is its position. Close to the centre of town, near the public garden, it commands a spectacular panorama of the bay and the slopes of Etna to the south. Flowery gardens lead down to a small, delightful swimming pool where the setting and the poolside bar (serving light meals and Sicilian regional dishes) tempt guests to linger all day and postpone the more serious business of sightseeing. Arrangements can also be made to take guests to and from local beaches.

There is no proper dining room, but plenty of choice amongst restaurants in Taormina. And the hotel does have two prettily furnished sitting rooms, and a sunny breakfast room. All in all a sound choice for a reasonably priced family hotel, warmly endorsed by a recent reporter who also mentioned the 'slick valet parking (parking is at a premium in the town)' and the 'clean bright bedrooms with stunning views from the balconies'.

~

NEARBY Greek theatre; Corso Umberto, public gardens
LOCATION next to the Belvedere of the Via Roma, close to public gardens and old town; with car parking
FOOD breakfast, light meals **PRICE** €€ **ROOMS** 50, all with bath or shower; all rooms have phone; 26 have air conditioning **FACILITIES** 2 sitting areas, 2 bars, breakfast room, TV room, terrace, garden, swimming pool, poolside snack bar
CREDIT CARDS MC, V **DISABLED** no special facilities **PETS** accepted
CLOSED mid-Nov to mid-Dec, mid-Jan to Mar **PROPRIETORS** Claude and Silvia Pécaut

SICILY

TAORMINA

VILLA DUCALE

~ HILLTOP VILLA ~

Via Leonardo da Vinci 60, 98039 Taormina , Messina
TEL 0942 28153 FAX 0942 28710
E-MAIL villaducale@tao.it

IT'S HARD TO FAULT VILLA DUCALE. Originally a coaching inn, it was converted into a patrician home at the turn of the century by the great-grandfa-
ther of the present owner, Andrea Quartucci. In 1993, he and his wife
opened the house to guests and their new venture was an instant success.
Why? Because of the wonderful terrace, the feel of a family home, the
unexpected, special touches and the friendliness of the staff.

No two rooms are alike (try for one with a private terrace), but they all
have fine linen on the beds, billowing curtains and terrazzo floors, painted
furniture and pretty bedheads; in one junior suite is the painted bed,
inlaid with mother-of-pearl, of Andrea's grandparents. Many walls are decorated with *trompe l'oeil* or with fruit, a symbol of richness in Sicily.

Perhaps the real quality of Villa Ducale comes through best at breakfast, served until 11.30 am. You won't easily forget sitting on the broad balcony, the table before you laden with fruit, local cheeses, specially baked
bread and Sicilian iced cakes, with its amazing view across the town, the
bay and Mount Etna. Sipping a drink there at sunset is pretty romantic,
too. A recent ecstatic report from a reader only confirms our enthusiasm.

~

NEARBY Greek theatr; Corso Umberto; excursions to Etna.
LOCATION above Taormina, on road to Castelmola; limited car parking
FOOD breakfast, light snacks
PRICE €€€-€€€€
ROOMS 13; 10 double and twin, 1 single, 2 junior suites, all with bath; all rooms
have phone, TV, air conditioning, minibar, hairdrier
FACILITIES sitting room, library, bar, breakfast room, terrace, free shuttle to
beaches CREDIT CARDS AE, DC, MC, V
DISABLED access difficult
PETS accepted
CLOSED mid-Nov to mid-Dec
PROPRIETORS Dr Andrea and Rosaria Quartucci

SICILY

TAORMINA

VILLA PARADISO

~ SEASIDE HOTEL ~

Via Roma 2, 98039 Taormina, Messina
TEL 0942 23921 **FAX** 0942 625800

NEXT TO THE PUBLIC GARDENS and close to the heart of historic Taormina, the Villa Paradiso also has the advantage of a glorious panorama along the coast and across to the hazy cone of Etna. The only drawback to the location is that it is on a main road, which means some noise for back rooms and major problems with parking in high season.

The hotel is a well-maintained white building, and the public rooms have all the style and atmosphere of a private villa: white arches, patterned carpets on tiled floors, stylish sofas and an imaginative collection of prints, paintings and watercolours. The restaurant makes the most of the views, and the food is distinctly above average. Every bedroom has a balcony, and inevitably the most sought-after are those at the front with sea views. The majority are larger than you would expect from a *pensione;* some have attractive painted furniture. You can reach the beaches by cable car or – more conveniently – the hotel minibus, which takes you to the Paradise Beach Club in Letojanni (free facilities for guests from the beginning of June).

~

NEARBY Greek theatre, Corso Umberto and public gardens; excursions to Etna.
LOCATION on SE edge of town; small public car park next door, paying garage nearby
FOOD breakfast, dinner
PRICE €€
ROOMS 38; 25 double and twin, 13 junior suites, all with bath; all rooms have phone, TV, air conditioning, hairdrier
FACILITIES 2 sitting rooms, dining room, bar, terrace
CREDIT CARDS AE, DC, MC, V
DISABLED access possible
PETS accepted
CLOSED never
PROPRIETOR Salvatore Martorana

SICILY

TAORMINA

VILLA SIRINA

~ COUNTRY VILLA ~

Contrada Sirina, 98039 Taormina, Messina
TEL 0942 51776 **FAX** 0942 51671
E-MAIL villasirina@tao.it **WEBSITE** www.villasirina.tao.it

JUST A KILOMETRE BELOW the town centre, in a valley in the Taormina foothills, Villa Sirina sits in its own grounds filled with citrus and olean- der. Rooms in the pink-washed house have views either to the sea (500 m away), or the mountains.

First impressions of this restored old country house are favourable. The entrance hall, with its antique Sicilian furniture mixed with modern, and unframed montage of bright splashy paintings on the walls, has great style, and there is a warm welcome from the kind host, Salvatore Cacopar- do. Bedrooms are simply furnished, white walled, clear and bright, enlivened by the jolly views through the French windows. These lead, in every case, to a terrace or a balcony. Bathrooms are neat and white.

The same lime-green paint which decorates some of the bedheads and mirrors in the bedrooms has found its way into the informal dining room, covering the rush-seated chairs and creating a colourful contrast with the bright yellow tablecloths. Here breakfast is served, and, in the evening, traditional Sicilian dishes. A large picture window overlooks the pool and terrace with its bar and seaward views.

~

NEARBY Greek theatre; Corso Umberto and public gardens.
LOCATION 1.5 km S of town centre, in own garden; car parking
FOOD breakfast, dinner
PRICE €€
ROOMS 15 double, all with bath or shower; all rooms have phone, TV, hairdrier
FACILITIES dining room, 2 sitting rooms, reading room, terraces, sun room, swimming pool
CREDIT CARDS AE, DC, MC, V
DISABLED no special facilities
PETS not accepted
CLOSED Nov to Mar
PROPRIETOR Salvatore Cacopardo

SARDINIA/SICILY

COSTA DORATA

DON DIEGO
RESORT HOTEL

Porto San Paolo, Costa Dorata,
07020 Vaccileddi, Sassari

TEL 0789 40007
FAX 0789 40026
Food breakfast, lunch, dinner
PRICE €€€
CLOSED never
Luigi Mennella

DESPITE A READER'S REPORT criticizing the pool and beach for being dirty, the Don Diego keeps its place in these pages on account of its sheer charm. It stands in a secluded position south of Olbia on the Costa Dorata, a quieter stretch of coastline than the Costa Smeralda, with many coves and beaches. The hotel, of typical Sardinian design, consists of airy, comfortable and stylish single-storey cottages scattered amongst the *macchia* and pine trees. Double bedrooms are located further away from the main building than the junior suites, which enjoy sea views (though they may be obscured by vegetation). From the lovely curving sea-water swimming pool there are views across to the islands of Molara and, close by, Tavolara.

ERICE

ELIMO
TOWN HOTEL

Via Vittorio Emanuele 75, 91016
Erice, Trapani

TEL and **FAX** 0923 869377
Food breakfast, lunch, dinner
PRICE €€
CLOSED never
Tilotta family

SITUATED IN THE SAME STREET as the Moderno (see page 000) the Elimo makes an excellent alternative. One of our reporters described it as 'a happy mixture of traditional and modern, with attractive public rooms, individual bedrooms, a rooftop terrace and a pretty courtyard'. A more recent visitor endorses this view. The Elimo is a simple, straightforward hotel with no pretensions – but well run. Public rooms consist of a combined lobby, bar and small sitting area with a homely feel, and a dining room where fairly plain dishes are served (breakfast is basic). Bedrooms are clean, modern and simple, not too small, with functional but acceptable bathrooms. Some have views over the roof to the sea beyond.

SICILY

SIRACUSA

GRAND HOTEL
LUXURY TOWN HOTEL

Viale Mazzini 12, 96100 Siracusa

TEL 0931 464600 **FAX** 0931 464611
FOOD breakfast, lunch, dinner;
room service
PRICE €€€
CLOSED never
MANAGER Signor Caladrucceo

SITUATED IN THE OLD PART of Siracusa on the island of Ortigia, the Grand Hotel is a splendid example of a luxurious, but not exorbitant, Mediterranean hotel. You are greeted by a cool and elegant reception area with circular marble stairs and bronze sculpture. Other public rooms are clad in marble, stained glass, and crystal, mixing modern art and furnishings with antiques. Bedrooms, are luxurious and thoughtfully equipped. There is a bar in the old pale stone-walled cistern and a sophisticated roof garden restaurant, with magnificent views of the Grand Harbour and seafront. It may not be charming and small, but the Grand makes a good base in the centre of Siracusa.

VALDERICE

BAGLIO SANTACROCE
COUNTRY HOTEL

91019 Valderice, Trapani

TEL 0923 891111
FAX 0923 891192
FOOD breakfast, lunch, dinner
PRICE €€
CLOSED never
Cusenza family

LOCATED IN THE ERICE FOOTHILLS, on the outskirts of Valderice, this is a family-owned and run hotel set in a predominantly stone farmhouse dating back to 1636. With its central courtyard, thick bare stone walls (in both bedrooms and bathrooms), terracotta tiled floors and beamed ceilings, the hotel has a rustic, countrified feel – except for the annexe bar and dining room. Our original inspector liked this hotel, at least the old part, but recent guests have been disappointed by the plumbing. Breakfast is standard hotel fare, but the dinners, especially the fish, are above average. There is a small swimming pool, with superb views to the Gulf of Cornino and Mount Cofano, and the gardens are very peaceful.

HOTEL NAMES

In this index, hotels are arranged in order of the first distinctive part of their names. Very common prefixes such as 'Hotel', 'Albergo', 'Il', 'La', 'Dei' and 'Delle' are omitted. More descriptive words such as 'Casa', 'Castello', 'Locanda' and 'Villa' are included.

HOTEL NAMES

HOTEL NAMES

HOTEL NAMES

HOTEL LOCATIONS

In this index, hotels are arranged in order of the names of the cities, towns or villages they are in or near. Hotels located in a very small village may be indexed under a larger place nearby. An index by hotel name precedes this one.

Hotel Locations

HOTEL LOCATIONS

Hotel Locations

SPECIAL OFFERS

Buy your *Charming Small Hotel Guide* by post directly from the publisher and you'll get a worthwhile discount. *

Titles available:	Retail price	Discount price
Austria	£10.99	£9.50
Britain	£11.99	£10.50
France	£11.99	£10.50
France: Bed & Breakfast	£10.99	£9.50
Germany	£9.99	£8.50
Greece	£10.99	£9.50
Ireland	£9.99	£8.50
Paris	£10.99	£9.50
Southern France	£10.99	£9.50
Spain	£10.99	£9.50
Switzerland	£9.99	£8.50
Tuscany & Umbria	£10.99	£9.50
USA: New England	£10.99	£9.50
Venice and North-East Italy	£10.99	£9.50

Please send your order to:

Book Sales,

Duncan Petersen Publishing Ltd,

31 Ceylon Road, London W14 OPY

enclosing: 1) the title you require and number of copies

2) your name and address

3) your cheque made out to:

Duncan Petersen Publishing Ltd

*Offer applies to this edition and to UK only.

VISIT DUNCAN PETERSEN'S TRAVEL WEBSITE AT
www.charmingsmallhotels.com
• Research interesting places to stay • Online book ordering –special discounts • Room booking service

Visit charmingsmallhotels.co.uk
Our website has expanded enormously since
its launch and continues to grow. It's the
best research tool on the web for our kind of
hotel.

Exchange rates
As we went to press, $1 bought 1.02 euros
and £1 bought 1.58 euros